Managing Internetworks with SNMP

The Definitive Guide to The Simple Network
Management Protocol (SNMP) and SNMP version 2

D0861890

THE NETWORK TROUBLESHOOTING LIBRARY

Managing Internetworks with SNMP

The Definitive Guide to The Simple Network
Management Protocol (SNMP) and SNMP version 2

Mark A. Miller, P.E.

M&T BOOKS

M&T Books
A Division of MIS:Press
A Subsidiary of Henry Holt and Company, Inc.
115 West 18th Street
New York, New York 10011

Limits of Liability and Disclaimer of Warranty
The Author and Publisher of this book have used their best efforts in preparing the book and the programs contained in it. These efforts include the development, research, and testing of the theories and programs to determine their effectiveness.

The Author and Publisher make no warranty of any kind, expressed or implied, with regard to these programs or the documentation contained in this book. The Author and Publisher shall not be liable in any event for incidental or consequential damages in connection with, or arising out of, the furnishing, performance, or use of these programs.

Library of Congress Cataloging-in-Publication Data

Miller, Mark, 1955–
    Managing Internetworks With SNMP: the definitive guide to the Simple Network
    Management Protocol (SNMP) and SNMP version 2 / by Mark A. Miller.
       p. cm. — (Network troubleshooting library)
    Includes bibliographical references and index.
    ISBN 1-55851-304-3 : $44.95
    1. Simple Network Management Protocol (Computer network protocol) 2. Computer
    networks — Management. 3. Internet (Computer network)
    I. Title. II. Series.
TK5105.55.M55   1993   93-25669
004.6'2--dc20   CIP

96 95 94 93   4 3 2 1

Trademarks
All products, names and services are trademarks or registered trademarks of their respective companies. See "Trademarks" section beginning on page 497.

Permissions
This book contains material that is reproduced with permission from American National Standard ANSI X3.139-1987, copyright 1987 by the American National Standards Institute. Copies of this standard may be purchased from the American National Standards Institute at 11 West 42nd St., New York, NY 10036.

The information contained herein in italics is copyrighted information of the IEEE, extracted from IEEE Std 802.1B-1992, IEEE Network Magazine, March 1988 and July 1990, copyright 1988, 1990, and 1992 by the Institute of Electrical and Electronics Engineers, Inc. This information was written within the context of IEEE Std 802.1B-1992. The IEEE takes no responsibility or liability for and will assume no liability for the damages resulting from the reader's misinterpretation of said information resulting from the placement and context in this publication. Information is reproduced with the permission of IEEE.

Development Editor: Cheryl Goldberg   **Cover Design:** Lauren Smith Design
Technical Editor: John Thompson   **Production Editor:** Eileen Mullin
Copy Editor: Laura Moorehead

To Holly, for her steadfast support

Contents

Table of Illustrations

Preface

When I began writing this, the sixth volume of the *Network Troubleshooting Library*, network management appeared to be a technical utopia that we were striving for but never quite achieving. After studying the subject for about a year, I am convinced that this is true. (If you doubt this, spend a few days reading the messages on the Internet's SNMP mailing list and you will become a believer.)

Therefore, it's nice to have a few friends whom I consider experts in network management. The following individuals added their expertise by reviewing individual sections of the text. In alphabetical order, they are Dan Callahan, Paul Franchois, Robert Graham, Dan Hansen, David Perkins, Carl Shinn, Jr., Rodney Thayer, and Steve Wong.

My editors, Brenda McLaughlin, John Thompson, and Cheryl Goldberg, did an excellent job of balancing the technical with the literary. Merideth Ittner, Laura Moorehead, Eileen Mullin, and Peggy Watt provided the production support that kept the project on schedule. Carol Goodwin did much of the research for the appendices, Krystal Valdez provided word processing support, and David Hertzke turned my rough sketches into legible figures. Thanks to all of you for the excellent work.

Several members of the vendor community assisted with information on their network management architectures. These individuals were Jack Dwyer, Susan Kaufman, Stan Kimer, Jim McQuaid, Jeff Thiemann, and Sally Swift.

All of the case studies in this book were captured using a Network General Sniffer protocol analyzer. I thank Bob Berger of Network General Corporation for this contribution. I also appreciate the generous time given by the following network managers who provided their networks for the purpose of researching this book: Eural Authement, John Case, John Cornell, Paul Franchois, Jude George, John Hardin, James Davidson, David Heck, Mark Ryding, and Rodney Thayer.

As always, I owe a great deal to my family. Holly, Nathan, and Nicholas provide a support system that accommodates the long hours and teaching trips. Boomer and Brutus take responsibility for household security in my absence. Their companionship makes the journey easier.

mark@diginet.com
June 1993

Why This Book is for You

Managing Internetworks with SNMP, the sixth volume in *The Network Troubleshooting Library*, is a comprehensive guide and reference for network managers and administrators responsible for maintaining a complex internetwork. This book will give you a clear understanding of SNMP and SNMP version 2, the protocols developed by the Internet community to simplify the management of internetworks. It is packed with illustrations, case studies, and helpful examples that give you the techniques and know-how you'll need to maintain a productive LAN or WAN using the SNMP.

Some of the topics covered in *Managing Internetworks with SNMP* are network-management concepts, plus standards from ISO, IEEE, OSF, and the Internet. There is also an analysis of network management architectures from DEC, Hewlett-Packard, IBM, and SunConnect. Additionally, the book provides you with a tutorial on the Structure of Management Information (SMI), including ASN.1 encoding examples. Management Information Bases (MIBs), including MIB-I and MIB-II, the Remote Monitoring (RMON) MIBs, and private enterprise MIBs defined by vendors are also covered in detail.

Other areas discussed are SNMP operation, including the Protocol Data Unit (PDU) formats and application examples, and lower-layer protocol support for SNMP, including UDP, IP, ICMP, ARP, and RARP. Real-world experience is provided in case studies taken from live internetworks demonstrating SNMP in use. Find out about SNMP version 2 and the enhancements it provides in areas of bulk data retrieval, manager-to-manager communications, multi-protocol-transport support and security. Use the appendices, which are packed with vendor information and Internet network-management parameters, as a handy reference.

If you are responsible for a complex internetwork, put this book next to your network management console.

Introduction

Since it was developed in 1988, the Simple Network Management Protocol (SNMP) has become the de facto standard for internetwork management. SNMP has a number of advantages that contribute to its popularity. Because it is a simple solution, requiring relatively little code to implement, vendors can easily build SNMP agents to their products. SNMP is extensible, allowing vendors to easily add network management functions. And SNMP separates the management architecture from the architecture of the hardware devices, which broadens the base of multivendor support. Perhaps most important, unlike other so-called standards, SNMP is not a mere paper specification, but an implementation that is widely available today.

This book, the sixth volume in the *Network Troubleshooting Library*, discusses network management in general, and SNMP in particular.

In a nutshell, a network management system contains two primary elements: a manager and agents. The manager is the console through which the (human) network administrator performs network management functions. Agents are the entities that interface to the actual device being managed. Bridges, routers, or network servers are examples of managed devices that contain managed objects. These managed objects might be hardware, configuration parameters, performance statistics, and so on, that directly relate to the current operation of the device in question. These objects are arranged in what is known as a virtual information database, called a management information base (MIB). SNMP allows managers and agents to communicate for the purpose of accessing these objects.

In order to fully understand the depth of network management, I will discuss these concepts one chapter at a time.

Chapter 1 provides an overview of the concepts of network management. Individual sections discuss the OSI, IEEE, and Internet network management standards. Other sections consider architectures from four vendors that support these standards: Digital Equipment Corp, Hewlett-Packard, IBM, and SunConnect.

SNMP is only part of what is known as the Internet Network Management Framework. Chapters 2, 3, and 4 discuss individual sections of that framework. In order, these topics are the structure of management information (SMI), management information bases (MIBs), and SNMP itself.

The SMI provides a mechanism for describing and naming the objects being managed. This structure allows the values of these objects to be retrieved and manipulated, that is, managed. It accomplishes this by using a message description language, defined by ISO 8824, known as the Abstract Syntax Notation One (ASN.1). ASN.1 is used to define the syntax, or form, of a management message. Once this syntax has been specified with ASN.1, the Basic Encoding Rules (BER)—from ISO 8825—encode that message into a format that can be transmitted on a LAN or WAN.

The MIBs more precisely delineate the managed objects and organize these objects for ease of use. Different types of MIBs are available, including the Internet-standard MIB, defined in Request for Comments (RFC) documents 1212 and 1213; the remote monitoring MIB, defined in RFC 1271; and numerous private enterprise MIBs that vendors define specifically for their products.

SNMP completes the story by providing a mechanism for the manager to communicate with the agents. This communication involves reading the values of the objects within a MIB, and altering the values as appropriate—in other words, managing the objects.

Since SNMP is an Application layer protocol, it must rely upon other protocols at the lower OSI layers for other communication functions. Chapter 5 studies these protocols. For example, the User Datagram Protocol (UDP) transports the SNMP message through the internetwork. The Internet Protocol (IP) provides Network Layer functions, such as addressing, for the datagram. A third protocol, such as Ethernet or token-ring, then delivers the information to the local network.

Once we have studied the protocols, we can look at examples of their use. Chapter 6 offers ten case studies that detail the use of SNMP in managing actual networks.

Enhancements, known as SNMP version 2 (SNMPv2), extend the capabilities of this popular protocol. Chapter 7 provides an overview of the management and security improvements found in SNMPv2.

With this information, you'll have a full understanding of the real-world, practical applications of this popular network management standard.

1 Network Management Architectures

This chapter gives an overview of the currently available network management technologies, and explains how the subject of this book, the Simple Network Management Protocol (SNMP), fits into the big picture.

1.1. Three Decades of Network Evolution

The 1970s was the decade of the centralized network. In a decade dominated by mainframe processing, data communication allowed terminals to talk to the mainframe (see Figure 1-1). Low speed, asynchronous transmission was the norm. Mainframe providers such as IBM and communication circuit providers such as AT&T or the local telephone company managed the network for those systems.

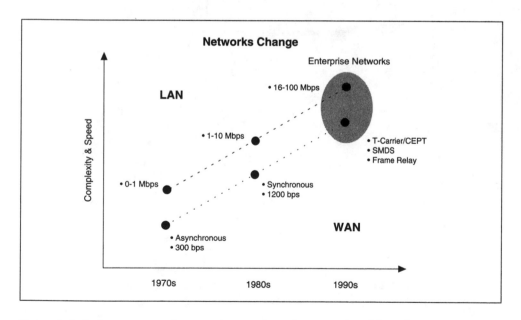

Figure 1-1. Evolution in networking complexity and speed *(courtesy Wandel & Goltermann)*

The 1980s saw three significant changes in data communications. Micro-processors came onto the scene, offering significant price and performance advantages over mainframes. The number of microcomputer-based LANs increased. And high-speed wide area transmission facilities, such as T-carrier circuits, emerged to connect microcomputer-based LANs. The proliferation of LANs gave rise to distributed processing—and moved applications off the mainframe and onto the desktop. And as data communication shifted to distributed networks, network management became distributed as well (see Figure 1-2).

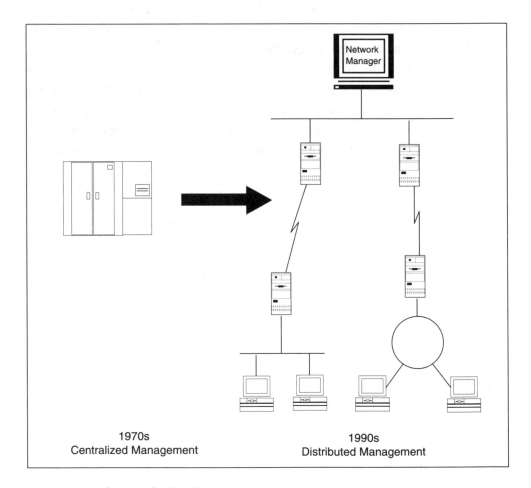

Figure 1-2. Evolution in distributed systems

Today, LANs and distributed computing have matured. *Wide area network* (WAN) technologies such as *Asynchronous Transfer Mode* (ATM), *Switched Multimegabit Data Service* (SMDS), and *Frame Relay* are meeting the needs of high-speed applications. Network management capabilities have matured as well.

1.2. The Challenge of Distributed Network Management

Sometimes people forget that network management has two parts, the network and the management. To manage a network properly, all of the people involved must agree on the meaning of network management and on its objectives.

Network management can mean different things to the different individuals in an organization, such as the chief executive officer (CEO), the chief information officer (CIO), and the end users. The CEO tends to view the network (and its manager) as a line item on the expense budget. CEOs consider computing and data communications as a way to manage orders, inventory, accounting information, and so on. As long as overall corporate revenues hit their target, these budget items are likely to remain intact. Therefore, the CEO would define network management as the financial management of the corporate communications network.

The CIO must look at network management from the theoretical perspective of the CEO and the corporate budget, and from the practical perspective of the end users. The goal is to keep the corporate network running 99.99 percent of the time and to schedule periods of downtime on weekends and holidays when few are around to notice. The CIO would, therefore, define network management as the ability to balance increasing end-user requirements with decreasing resources—that is, the ability to provide more service with less money.

End users spend their days in the network trenches, designing airplanes, writing dissertations, and attending boring meetings. Their job depends on the network's remaining operational. Thus, end users would define network management as something that keeps the data communication infrastructure on which they depend working at all times. A network failure could threaten their livelihood.

From the standpoint of the financial health of the corporation, its customers, and its employees, an all-encompassing definition of network management would be something like this: the communications network is the vital link between customers and products. Our objective is to keep that link operating at all times, because when it fails our financial health suffers.

1.3. The System Being Managed

Now, I'll shift to a systems-engineering perspective on network management. Figure 1-3 shows the big picture. On the left side of the diagram are centralized applications such as an inventory control system or the corporate financial database. The right side illustrates distributed applications, such as those that run on client-server LANs. In the middle is the glue that connects the different types of systems—the wide area transport. This transport may consist of public and private networks and *software defined networks* (SDN).

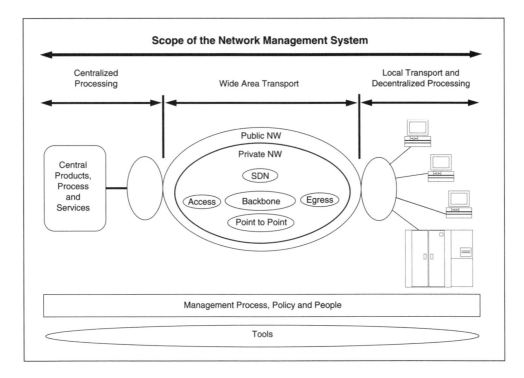

Figure 1-3. The scope of network management systems *(courtesy EDS)*

1.4. Elements of a Network Management Architecture

How does a network manager know what he or she is responsible for and manage such a network? To answer these questions, you need to understand the architecture of a network management system and how it accomplishes its tasks.

The network management system, called the manager/agent model, consists of a manager, a managed system, a database of management information, and the network protocol (see Figure 1-4).

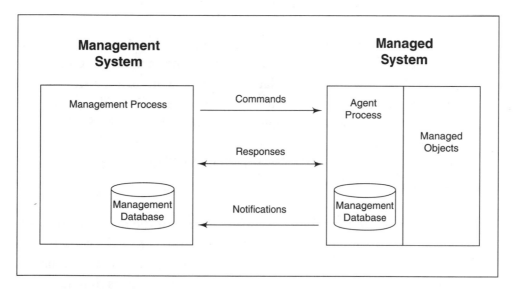

Figure 1-4. Network manager/agent relationships

The manager provides the interface between the human network manager and the devices being managed. It also provides the network management process. The management process performs tasks such as measuring traffic on a remote LAN segment or recording the transmission speed and physical address of a router's LAN interface. The manager also includes some type of output, usually graphical, to display management data, historical statistics, and so on. A common example of a graphical display is a map of the internetwork topology showing the locations of the LAN segments; selecting a particular segment might display its current operational status.

As Figure 1-4 shows, the managed system consists of the *agent process* and the *managed objects*. The agent process performs network management operations such as setting configuration parameters and current operational statistics for a router on a given segment. The managed objects include workstations, servers, wiring hubs, communication circuits, and so on. Associated with the managed objects are *attributes*, which may be statically defined (such as the speed of the interface), dynamic (such as entries in a routing table), or require ongoing measurement (such as the number of packets transmitted without errors in a given time period).

A database of network management information, called the *management information base* (MIB), is associated with both the manager and the managed system. Just as a numerical database has a structure for storing and retrieving data, a MIB has a defined organization. This logical organization is called the *structure of management information* (SMI). The SMI is organized in a tree structure, beginning at the root, with branches that organize the managed objects by logical categories. The MIB represents the managed objects as leaves on the branches.

The network management protocol provides a way for the manager, the managed objects, and their agents to communicate. To structure the communication process, the protocol defines specific messages, referred to as commands, responses, and notifications. The manager uses these messages to request specific management information, and the agent uses them to respond. The building blocks of the messages are called *protocol data units* (PDUs). For example, a manager sends a GetRequest PDU to retrieve information, and the agent responds with a GetResponse PDU.

How does the manager/agent model relate to the network you need to manage? As you can see in Figure 1-5, the console, such as a SPARC station from Sun Microsystems, Inc., performs the network manager functions. The devices on the internetwork, such as routers and host computers, contain network management agents. MIBs are associated with both the manager and agents, but the router's MIB and the host's MIB are unlikely to be the same for two reasons. First, these devices usually come from different manufacturers who have implemented network management functions in different, but complementary, ways. Second, routers and hosts perform different internetworking functions, and may not need to store the same information. For example, the host may not require routing tables, and thus won't need to store routing table-related parameters such as the next hop to a particular destination in its MIB. Conversely, a router's MIB wouldn't contain a statistic such as CPU utilization that may be significant to a host.

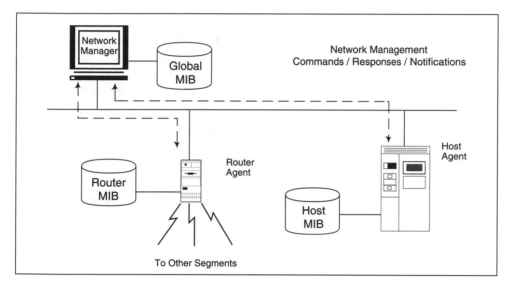

Figure 1-5. Network manager/agent realization

A protocol such as SNMP allows the manager and the agents to communicate. This protocol provides the structure for commands from the manager, notifies the manager of significant events from the agent, and responds to either the manager or agent.

Before examining systems from specific vendors, it is useful to look at the various network management implementations. These include the network management system for the International Standards Organization's (ISO) *Open Systems Interconnection* (OSI) model (examined in Section 1.5), the IEEE network management architecture (Section 1.6), the Open Software Foundation's *Distributed Management Environment* (Section 1.7), the *Internet Network Management Framework* (Section 1.8), and SNMP (Section 1.9).

1.5. The OSI Network Management Architecture

The ISO/OSI model (see Reference [1-1]) has been a benchmark for computer networking since it was first published in 1978. Figure 1-6 shows the familiar seven-layer structure. Following is a summary of the seven layers:

Layer	Description
Physical	Provides the physical transmission medium for carrying the raw data, such as electrical or optical impulses, from one network node to the next.
Data Link	Provides reliable communications on the link; that is, it creates the channel between adjacent nodes on a LAN, MAN, or WAN. Functions include addressing, framing, and error control on the link.
Network	Provides communications functions for an internetwork. These include tasks such as the global addressing, routing, and switching that take data from its source to its destination via an internetwork of LANs, MANs, and WANs.
Transport	Assures the reliable end-to-end delivery of data. Its functions include error control and sequence control.
Session	Establishes the logical connection between end-user applications. These functions include mechanisms that synchronize the data transfer once a connection is established.
Presentation	Represents the application data so that it can be properly interpreted at the distant location. Examples of these functions include data compression/decompression, encryption, or ASCII to EBCDIC code conversion.
Application	Includes the functions responsible for end-user applications, such as file transfer, electronic mail, or remote terminal access. SNMP is an Application layer protocol.

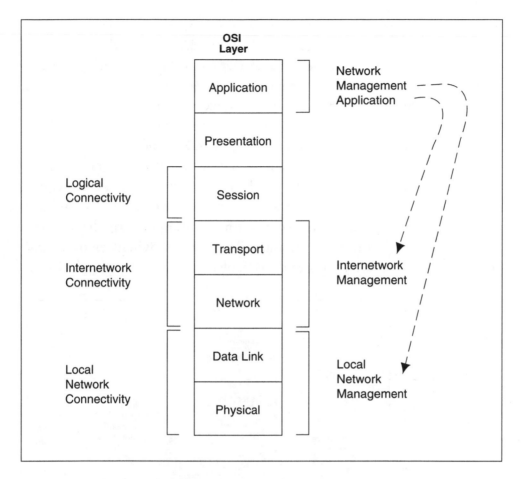

Figure 1-6. Network Management within the OSI framework

While the entire OSI model has yet to be widely implemented, elements of its architecture are finding their way into multivendor systems such as electronic mail, directory services, and network management applications. History may prove, however, that the real value of the OSI model is in the organizational structure it provides for multivendor networks rather than specific protocol implementations.

Reviewing Figure 1-6, note that the network management application manages internetwork and local network functions.

What do these seven layers have to do with managing a real network? Consider the network shown in Figure 1-7. Suppose that a network management console (called the manager) needs to retrieve entries from a routing table. To do so, the manager generates a request message and passes it down through the layers of the protocol stack. The Data Link layer inserts the message (or fragments of a long message) into a frame for transmission on the local network. (Figure 1-7 shows an Ethernet LAN, so an Ethernet frame would contain the request message.) The Data Link layer would then convert the frame into a bit stream and transmit it over the physical network to the intended receiver. At the distant end, the network management command would trigger another network management process (the agent) to perform the requested function, and build a response message. The response would follow a similar, but opposite, journey back to the console.

Figure 1-7.
Network management protocol stack operation

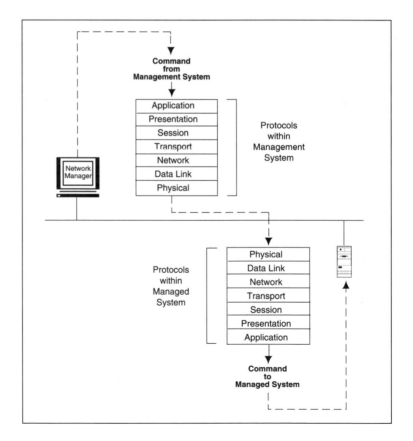

From this example, I can make several observations. First, the manager's network management application must be compatible with that of the agent. Since this example used an OSI-based network management scheme, the *Common Management Information Protocol* (CMIP) could provide compatible communication. Second, the other layers of the two computing architectures must also be compatible. For example, if the Network layer of the console uses the ISO *Connectionless Network Protocol* (CLNP), defined by ISO 8473, the router must also understand that protocol. (For example, if the console used the CLNP network addressing scheme to insert the 20-octet CLNP address in its Network layer process, the router's Network layer process would have to recognize that address in order to respond.) Finally, the same physical path must connect the manager and agent, although that path doesn't have to be on the same LAN or even in the same country.

The ISO/OSI model extends beyond the seven layers, however, for the management of open systems. OSI standards include a model of network management and a network management protocol.

1.5.1. The OSI management model

The manager/agent model includes a number of interactive components. The OSI network management framework defines the roles of those components. ISO/IEC 7498-4 [1-2] defines the OSI network management framework. ISO/IEC 9595, or CCITT X.710, defines the Common Management Information Service, or CMIS [1-3]; ISO/IEC 9596-1, or CCITT X.711, defines the Common Management Information Protocol, or CMIP [1-4].

Mark Klerer's paper "The OSI Management Architecture: an Overview" divides the OSI management environment into several models: organizational, informational, and functional [1-5]. Another resource, Yemini's "The OSI Network Management Model" [1-6] discusses the relationships between OSI management systems and agents.

The organizational model uses a management domain (see Figure 1-8a). The domain may contain one or more management systems, managed systems, and subdomains. The managed system may, in turn, contain one or more managed objects. Each object is a network resource that one of the management systems may monitor and/or control.

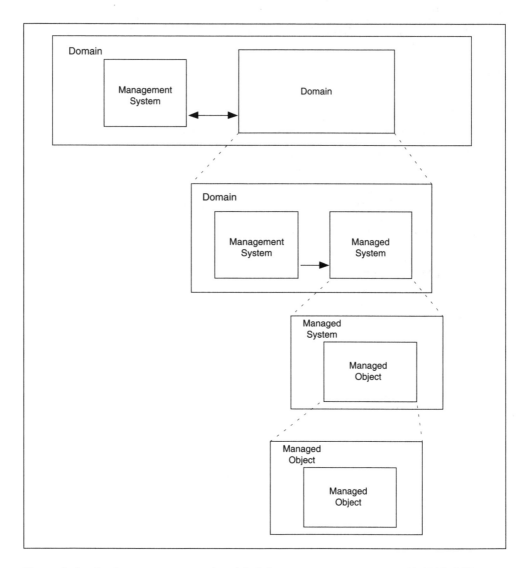

Figure 1-8a. An abstract organizational model of the management environment (©1988, IEEE)

An information model associated with the organizational model defines the structure of the management information and the management information base (MIB). As you can see in Figure 1-8b, a tree structure groups objects sharing similar characteristics into classes. These objects are represented as an entry in the management information tree; each entry has defined attributes and values.

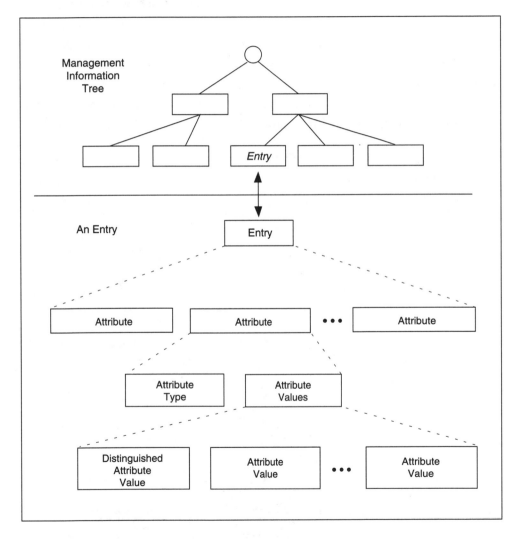

Figure 1-8b. Management information tree *(©1988, IEEE)*

The functional model defines five areas of network management used for specific purposes. The next section (Section 1.5.2) explores these five areas in detail.

Figure 1-8c demonstrates how the various elements work together. This model relates the *system management application process* (SMAP) to the management information base (MIB) and the seven layers of the network management system. It defines interfaces for system management (the *system management interface*, or SMI) and layer management (the *layer management interface*, or LMI). The layer management functions are specific to a particular OSI layer entity. Examples of these functions would include layer specific parameters, tests, or services which would reside in a *layer management entity* (LME). The model also specifies a protocol for manager/agent communication, known as the Common Management Information Protocol, or CMIP.

Figure 1-8c. The architectural model of OSI management (©1988, IEEE)

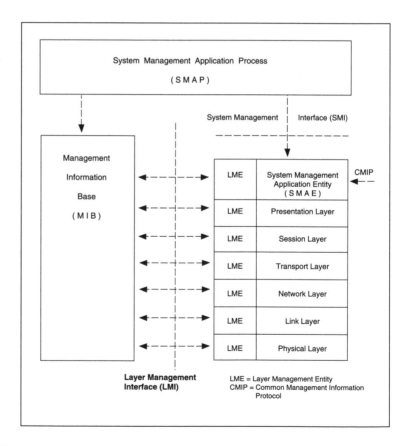

1.5.2. OSI Specific Management Functional Areas (SMFAs)

The OSI management environment includes five areas of network management, which are called the *OSI specific management functional areas* (SMFAs) (see Figure 1-9). These are fault management, accounting management, configuration management, performance management, and security management. ISO 7498-4 discusses these functional areas using academic—and often incomprehensible—language, so I'll explain how these functional areas relate to the management of real networks.

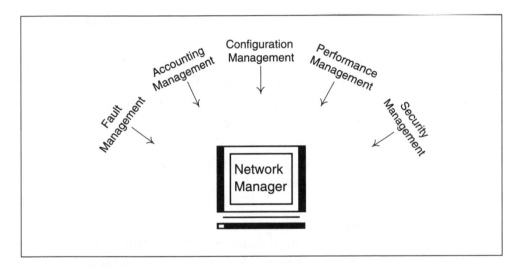

Figure 1-9. OSI network management functional areas

1.5.2.1. Fault management

The standard says that fault management "encompasses fault detection, isolation, and the correction of the abnormal operation of the OSI environment." The standard goes on to consider error logs, fault identification, and diagnostic testing.

In plain English, fault management means that you need to first identify, then repair, network faults. There are two ways to manage faults, reactivity or proactively. A reactive manager waits for a problem and then troubleshoots it. A proactive manager examines the manager and agents to determine whether they are exceeding critical operational thresholds, such as network utilization. If excesses occur, the proactive administrator determines their source and reduces them accordingly.

1.5.2.2. Accounting management

The standard says that accounting management "enables charges to be established for the use of resources in the OSI environment, and for cost to be identified for the use of those resources." Other considerations include informing the users of the costs and resources consumed, setting accounting limits, and incorporating tariff information in to the overall accounting process.

In the real world, accounting means dealing with real people using real network resources with real operating expenses. Examples of these costs include disk usage and data archiving, telecommunication expenses for access to remote data, and charges for sending electronic mail messages. You can also use accounting management to determine whether network resource utilization is increasing because of growth, which might indicate the need for additions or rearrangements in the near future.

1.5.2.3. Configuration management

The standard says that configuration management "identifies, exercises control over, collects data from and provides data to open systems for the purpose of preparing for, initializing, starting, providing for the continuous operation of, and terminating interconnection services." These services might include the collection of information regarding the system, alerts regarding system changes, and changes to the configuration of the system.

In the real world, the acronym MAC, which stands for *moves, adds and changes,* typifies the management work. Networks are dynamic systems, and network administrators need to move personnel and rearrange their processing needs. This aspect of network management may be as simple as rearranging modular connectors at a wiring hub, or as complex as installing a

LAN and its associated servers, communication circuits, and so on, at a remote location. Therefore, a significant aspect of the network management function involves keeping track of all these changes by using some type of database.

1.5.2.4. Performance management

In the standard, performance management "enables the behavior of resources in the OSI environment and the effectiveness of communication activities to be evaluated." These functions include gathering statistical and historical information, and evaluating the system's performance under a variety of real and hypothetical conditions.

Practically, performance management assures that the administrator satisfies the end users' needs at all times. To do this, the administrator must select hardware and software systems according to the needs of the internetwork, then exercise these systems to their maximum potential. Performance and fault management are closely related, since you need to eliminate, or at least minimize, faults to obtain optimum performance. Many tools are available to measure performance. These include protocol analyzers, network monitoring software, and various utilities that come with the console programs of network operating systems.

1.5.2.5. Security management

Academically, "the purpose of security management is to support the application of security policies by means of functions which include the creation, deletion, and control of security services and mechanisms; the distribution of security-relevant information; and the reporting of security related events."

In other words, security protects the network. It defends against viruses, assures that remote and local users are authenticated, and includes installing encryption systems on any communication circuits that connect to a remote site.

1.6. The IEEE Network Management Architecture

The Institute of Electrical and Electronics Engineers (IEEE) is perhaps best known for developing the 802 series of LAN standards. These include specifications for *Carrier Sense Multiple Access with Collision Detection* (CSMA/CD) LANs such as 802.3 10BASE-T and 802.5 token-ring LANs. But the IEEE 802.1B [1-7] LAN/MAN management standards are another key element of the IEEE work.

The IEEE Project 802 addresses the Physical and Data Link layers and extends into the higher layers of the architecture where appropriate. The IEEE LAN/MAN management standard uses ISO's CMIP, which was discussed in Section 1.5, to extend into the higher layer. This architecture includes three elements (see Figure 1-10a): the *LAN/MAN Management Service* (LMMS), the *LAN/MAN Management Protocol Entity* (LMMPE), and the *Convergence Protocol Entity* (CPE). The LMMS defines the management service available to the *LAN/MAN Management User* (LMMU). The LMMPE communicates management information via protocol exchanges. LMMS and LMMPE use the ISO CMIS and CMIP standards, and enable two LMMUs to exchange management information. The CPE allows LAN/MAN environments to provide LMMS. The CPE adds functions of reliable and sequential data delivery on top of the unacknowledged connectionless service provided by the IEEE 802.2 Logical Link Control (LLC) layer. The unacknowledged connectionless service is known as LLC Type 1.

Figure 1-10b illustrates the interaction between these network management operations. Several cooperative processes make up the request from a manager (a LMMU) to an agent (another LMMU). The manager's LMMS communicates a request (REQ) using the *LAN/MAN Management Protocol* (LMMP). The agent receives this request as an *indication* (IND). The agent performs operations on the managed objects, and then returns the results as a response (RSP). Finally, the LMMPE conveys the *confirmation* (CONF) to the manager.

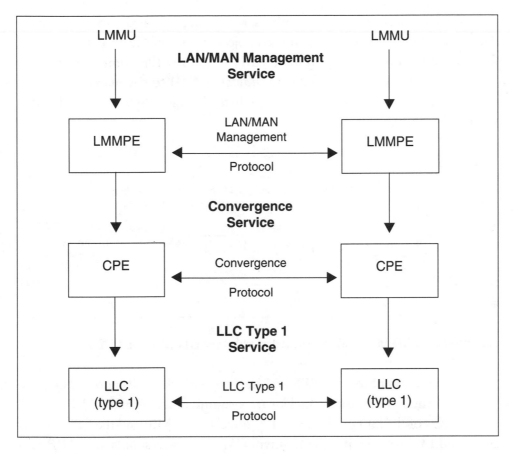

Figure 1-10a. LAN/MAN management communication architecture *(©1992, IEEE)*

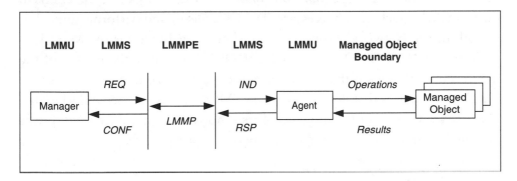

Figure 1-10b. LAN/MAN management information exchanges: operations *(©1992, IEEE)*

A managed object performs a similar series of steps to notify the manager of events (see Figure 1-10c). The managed object sends a notification to the agent, generating a request (REQ) at the LMMS. The LMMPE communicates that request across the LAN, yielding an *indicate* (IND) to the manager. Finally, the manager issues a response (RSP), which the agent receives as a Confirmation (CONF).

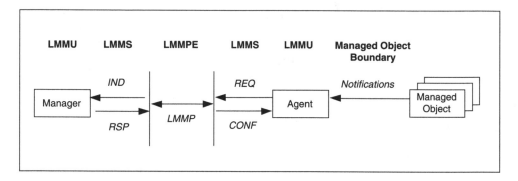

Figure 1-10c. LAN/MAN management information exchanges: notifications (©1992, IEEE)

Figure 1-10d compares the IEEE architecture with the OSI model. The complexity of the two protocol stacks varies significantly. While CMIP uses all seven layers of the ISO model, the IEEE model runs CMIP and the CPE directly over the LLC layer—hence the acronym *CMOL*, which stands for *CMIP over LLC*. Because LLC provides connectionless service to the management application, some of the *Association Control Service Element* (ACSE) functions in the full CMIP stack are unnecessary. The CPE fills in and performs some, but not all, of the Network through Presentation layer functions. As Mary Jander's article "Can CMOL Challenge SNMP" [1-8] notes, the benefit of the reduced CMOL stack is that it minimizes the memory requirements for agents. The disadvantage is that you cannot route CMOL across internetworks because it lacks Network layer functionality. This is not surprising, since CMOL was designed from a LAN and not an internetwork perspective.

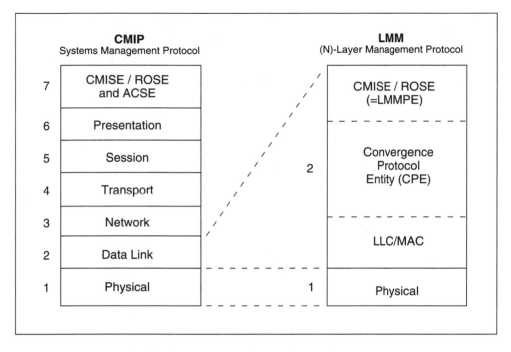

Figure 1-10d. Comparing CMIP and LMMP protocol stacks *(©1992, IEEE)*

1.7. The Open Software Foundation Distributed Management Environment

The last decade has seen a dramatic move from proprietary systems toward open systems and interfaces. The *Distributed Computing Environment* (DCE) [1-9] from the Open Software Foundation (OSF) of Cambridge, Mass., provides enabling technologies designed to ease the development, use, portability, and management of software in heterogeneous computing environments. Within the DCE, the Distributed Management Environment (DME) manages distributed multivendor networks and systems.

The OSF recognizes that heterogeneous networks typically include PCs, workstations, and mainframes, each of which runs different operating systems and management applications [1-10]. To effectively manage this type of environment, you need to be able to scale the process from a single system to an enterprise-wide network.

The DME architecture addresses the needs of distributed systems (see Figure 1-11a and reference [1-11]) via the following protocols and services. The management user interface and management protocols provide building blocks that allow for access to other heterogeneous systems. Distribution services include license management, software management, printing, and event services. Management services allow you to customize the management model. Object services provide functions required by the network's managed objects. Finally, the development tools simplify application development.

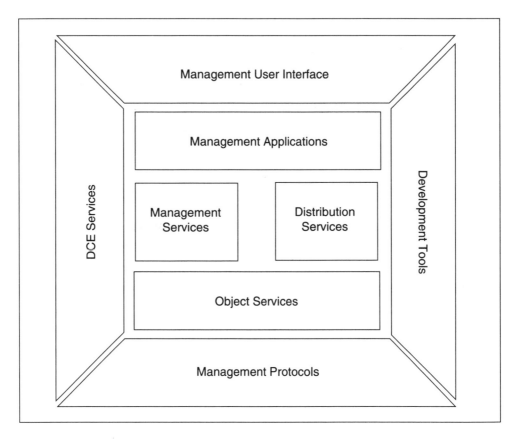

Figure 1-11a. The DME architecture *(courtesy the Open Software Foundation)*

The OSF issued a Request for Technologies in July of 1990 seeking vendors to supply technologies for incorporation into the DME architecture, and announced the selected technologies in September, 1991. DME is now composed of building blocks from multiple vendors (see Figure 1-11b). The application programming interfaces include the ANSI-C API from Tivoli Systems, Inc. (Austin, Texas), and the CM-API, now called XMP, from Groupe Bull. The *management request broker* (MRB) functions, which handle routing, address resolution, and authentication, are performed by Hewlett-Packard's Postmaster for CMIP and SNMP applications and Tivoli's Object Dispatcher for applications that use the DME *remote procedure call* (RPC). Transport protocols, such as TCP/IP or OSI, are implemented as appropriate, based on the higher layer management protocol.

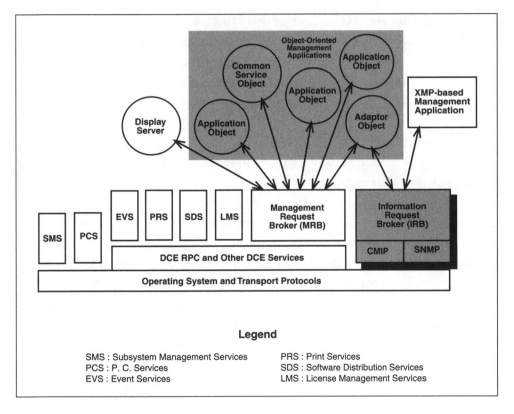

Figure 1-11b. OSF DME architecture *(courtesy the Open Software Foundation)*

What are the implications of the DME technology for network managers? In theory, an open platform with open interfaces for network management sounds like a wonderful solution. In practice, the jury is still out. The final product is not due for release until late 1993.

In summary, neither the OSI nor IEEE network management architectures have received widespread industry support, and DME is still under development. Network managers need a solution for today's networks. That solution is the Simple Network Management Protocol (SNMP), which is part of the Internet Network Management Framework.

1.8. The Internet Network Management Framework

The three network management architectures discussed so far have one common denominator: their design was a formal process, involving participants worldwide. More importantly, the network management architecture was in place first, and vendors were then encouraged to implement it.

The Internet, however, was an operational world-wide internetwork, so its administrators couldn't study network management for years before coming up with an implementation.

The Internet was derived from U.S. Government research that began in 1969. The objective was to develop communication technologies and protocols so that government organizations, defense contractors, and academic researchers using dissimilar computer systems could collaborate on projects. The result of the government's research project was the Advanced Research Projects Agency network (ARPANET), which used packet switching technology to connect dissimilar systems. ARPANET came on-line in 1969 with nodes in four locations in the United States. From that humble beginning, the Internet now connects more than one million host computers worldwide.

By the late 1980s, the Internet Activities Board (IAB) realized that it needed a method to manage the growing Internet and the other attached networks. The board considered three proposals: the *high-level entity management sys-*

tem (HEMS) [1-12]; an OSI-based system, utilizing CMIS and CMIP; and extensions to the existing *Simple Gateway Monitoring Protocol* (SGMP) [1-13] that the regional networks that made up the Internet were using.

The IAB decided to take a two-step approach to Internet management. Enhancements to the SGMP, which became known as the *Simple Network Management Protocol* (SNMP), would provide a short-term solution. The long-term solution would be based on the CMIS/CMIP architecture, and was called *CMOT* (CMIP over TCP/IP). RFC 1052 [1-14] summarized these directives.

(Documentation for the Internet and its protocols is based on the Request for Comments (RFC) documents. Upon publication, these documents are given a number, such as 1052, that is used for identification. This text will make numerous references to RFCs. You can obtain RFCs from the Network Information Center (NIC) for a small fee, or via the Internet (on-line) without charge. Appendix D gives complete details on how to obtain the RFCs and other pertinent Internet documentation.)

The long-term CMOT solution, however, has never received the widespread acceptance of SNMP, though it is still discussed with some network management architectures. CMOT is currently designated "historic," meaning that more recent standards have superseded it or it is considered obsolete for some other reason. Nevertheless, Section 1.8.2 will discuss CMOT briefly.

1.8.1. SNMP, the Simple Network Management Protocol

SNMP is based on the manager/agent model (see Figure 1-4). SNMP is referred to as "simple" because the agent requires minimal software. Most of the processing power and data storage resides on the management system, while a complementary subset of those functions resides in the managed system.

To achieve its goal of being simple, SNMP includes a limited set of management commands and responses (see Figure 1-12a). The management system issues Get, GetNext, and Set messages to retrieve single or multiple object variables or to establish the value of a single variable. The managed system sends a Response message to complete the Get, GetNext, or Set. The managed system sends an event notification, called a *trap*, to the management system to identify the occurrence of conditions such as a threshold that exceeds a predetermined value.

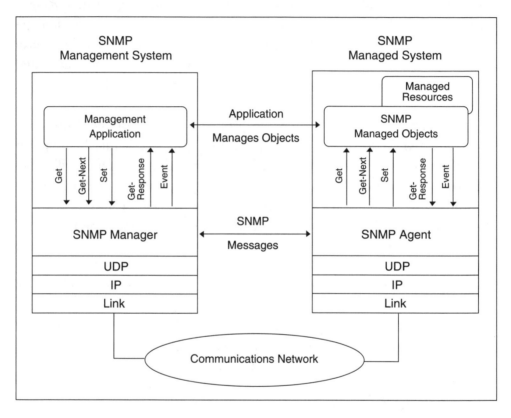

Figure 1-12a. SNMP architecture (©1990, IEEE)

SNMP assumes that the communication path is a connectionless communication subnetwork. In other words, no prearranged communication path is established prior to the transmission of data. As a result, SNMP makes no guarantees about the reliable delivery of the data; although in practice most messages get through, and those that don't can be retransmitted. Reviewing Figure 1-12a, the primary protocols that SNMP implements are the *User Data-*

gram Protocol (UDP) and the *Internet Protocol* (IP). SNMP also requires Data Link layer protocols, such as Ethernet or token-ring, to implement the communication channel from the management to the managed system.

SNMP's simplicity and connectionless communication also produce a degree of robustness. Neither the manager nor the agent relies on the other for its operation. Thus, a manager may continue to function even if a remote agent fails. When the agent resumes functioning, it can send a trap to the manager, notifying it of its change in operational status.

SNMP is defined in RFC 1157 [1-15]. For more information, refer to Reference [1-16] and [1-17].

1.8.2. CMIP over TCP/IP (CMOT)

As a result of its study of various Internetwork management strategies, in 1990 the IAB developed a strategy to implement CMOT [1-18]. Although the Internet Engineering Task Force (IETF, the standards setting body of the Internet) has designated this work as "historic," a number of vendors have included CMOT into their architecture plans. Therefore, a brief discussion is in order.

Architecturally, CMOT fits the manager/agent paradigm (see Figure 1-12b). Unlike SNMP, which provides connectionless service using UDP/IP, however, CMOT uses an association-oriented communication mechanism and the TCP/IP protocol to assure reliable transport of data. To guarantee reliable transport, CMOT systems establish Application layer connections prior to transmitting management information. CMOT's application layer services are built on three OSI services, the *Common Management Information Service Element* (CMISE), the *Remote Operation Service Element* (ROSE) and the *Association Control Service Element* (ACSE). A *Lightweight Presentation Protocol* (LPP) provides Presentation layer services.

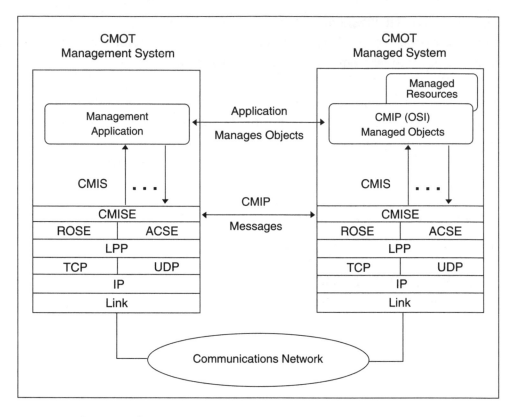

Figure 1-12b. *CMOT architecture (©1990, IEEE)*

The CMOT model is also more rigorous than SNMP. Ben-Artzi's paper [1-17] notes that the CMIP object definitions are more comprehensive and include attributes, events emitted, and imperative actions. As I will discuss, SNMP primarily defines objects by functional groups.

Nonetheless, SNMP is here today, and many vendors of both agent and management systems implement SNMP.

1.9. Supporting SNMP: Agents

The use of SNMP agents within internetworking devices has increased dramatically in the last few years. There are five general categories of devices in which you'll find agents: wiring hubs; network servers and their associated operating systems; network interface cards and the associated hosts; internetworking devices, such as bridges and routers; and test equipment, such as network monitors and analyzers. Other devices, such as uninterruptible power supplies, have also become SNMP-compatible.

Each of these categories makes a significant contribution to the overall network management scheme. Thus, network administrators who practice proactive network management should seriously consider using network devices that have these imbedded agents. References [1-19] through [1-21] list recent journal articles that detail the widespread acceptance of SNMP.

Edwin Mier of Mier Communications (Princeton Junction, NJ) has made significant contributions to the network management industry by testing SNMP-compatible devices. Mier uses five criteria for evaluating SNMP agents [1-22]. Phase One includes device setup, documentation, ease of configuration, cabling, user interface, support for community name passwords, and support for multiple management systems. Phase Two deals with support for SNMP standards, including the various object groups, the Trap function, and the Set function. Phase Three considers configuration reporting, which encompasses both standard and vendor-specific MIB information. Phase Four considers the accuracy of network traffic statistics that the agent reports to the manager. Phase Five considers the ability of a remote manager to control agents. This capability includes port configurations and remote diagnostics.

In conclusion, you can find SNMP agents in almost every internetworking device. Some vendor implementations are better than others. As a result—as the case studies in Chapter 6 demonstrate—not all of these agents are interoperable. You should therefore become as knowledgeable as possible about the details of SNMP. The rest of this book will help with that assignment.

1.10. Supporting SNMP: Managers

Now that I've discussed the elements of a network management system, I can describe management architectures from prominent vendors that support SNMP-based network management. This section discusses, in alphabetical order, offerings from Digital Equipment Corp. (DEC), Hewlett-Packard, IBM, and SunConnect. References [1-23] through [1-25] provide general information and product evaluations.

1.10.1. DEC POLYCENTER Network Manager

DEC has built its business on distributed peer-to-peer architectures, and this philosophy is evident in its network management product line, called Enterprise Management Architecture, or EMA (see References [1-26] and [1-27]).

The DEC POLYCENTER Network Manager 200 and 400 implements the EMA. This network management software runs on a variety of operating systems, including VAX VMS, RISC ULTRIX, and UNIX System V Release 4 (available from Olivetti Systems and Networks for their 486 PCs). A future release is also planned for DEC OSF/1.

EMA consists of two components, the *entity* and the *director* (see Figure 1-13a). The entity is any device being managed. The director is the system that does the managing.

Figure 1-13a. EMA entity agent-director interaction *(courtesy Digital Equipment Corp.)*

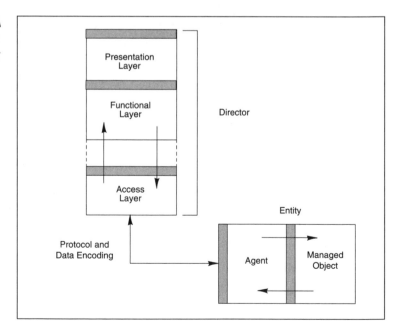

The entity consists of a managed object and its agent. The managed object provides some service or function within an internetwork, and maintains state variables or attributes. The agent is the entity's management software. In the EMA documentation [1-26], DEC describes the entity agent as the control panel that you use to observe and control the managed object's internal state.

The director contains three layers called Presentation, Functional, and Access. The Presentation layer supports the end-user interface, the Function layer provides management application services, and the Access layer accesses the entities. A network management protocol, such as SNMP, and the associated data encodings connect the director and entity.

Function modules support the five OSI functional areas of network management and other capabilities. Figure 1-13b shows a number of these functions. For example, the Domains functional module allows you to place the managed entities in user-defined groups for more focused management. The Alarms functional module allows you to define critical conditions. The Autoconfig-

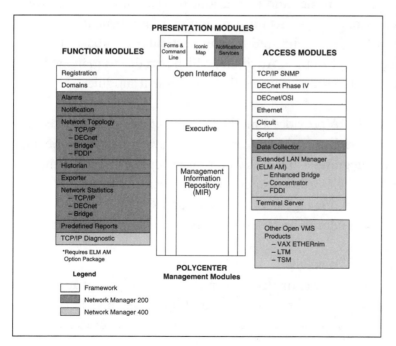

Figure 1-13b. POLYCENTER network manager, an EMA director implementation *(courtesy Digital Equipment Corp.)*

uration functional module provides node discovery, registration, and mapping. The Historian functional module collects and stores management data over a selected time period.

The Access modules access entities and provide information about them. Note from Figure 1-13b that Access modules are available to connect with entities based upon protocols such as DECnet Phase IV, OSI, SNMP, and Ethernet. DEC considers these modules a key element in the management of multivendor, heterogeneous networks because they allow the director to be independent of the protocol of the entity being managed.

The director includes three additional elements: the Executive, the Presentation modules, and the Management Information Repository. The EMA Executive provides the operating environment for the management modules and various director components. The Presentation modules provide the user interfaces for both input and graphical output of the management information. The Management Information Repository specifies and stores the information about the managed entities and the various services of the management modules. The repository stores this information in an implementation-independent manner, which is not limited by any particular database. It stores four types of data: Class; Instance; Attribute, which pertains to managed entities; and Private, which pertains to specific management modules.

In conclusion, DEC's EMA provides a modular architecture for distributed network management. Based upon the concepts of open systems, POLYCENTER Network Manager integrates a smorgasbord of user functions with numerous access interfaces to make a protocol-independent system. Support for SNMP, as well as other network management protocols and systems, places DEC in a strong position as a vendor of multivendor, networked systems management.

1.10.2. Hewlett-Packard OpenView

Hewlett-Packard, prominent for decades in the test equipment market, is steeped in a culture committed to standards and open systems. This culture is evident in HP's multivendor network management architecture, which is appropriately named OpenView. Originally built upon the OSI network management model and CMIP, OpenView currently supports SNMP, and provides a migration path to DME. OpenView is based on the UNIX operating system, and operates on HP 9000 series workstations and servers and Sun Microsystems, Inc. workstations (see references [1-28] and [1-29]).

Hewlett-Packard believes that network management should be distributed and that elements of the network management system may be derived from many vendors. Therefore, the OpenView architecture incorporates several interfaces to facilitate multivendor interoperability. One application programming interface (API) separates the end user from the network management application. This allows a single management console to display multiple management applications or a single application to be distributed across multiple consoles. Another API isolates the management application from the underlying services, such as the protocols that communicate with managed objects. Thus, HP allows you to display one vendor's management application alongside another's; and each may operate over different lower-layer communication protocols.

The OpenView Distributed Management Platform services shown in Figure 1-14a provide examples of these interfaces. This architecture is based on the HP OpenView Windows (OVw) graphical user interface (GUI) which, in turn, is based on the industry standard OSF/Motif GUI. This interface provides a consistent end-user environment for the graphical maps used to display the network management and topological information. Management applications communicate with managed agents using the X/Open Management Protocol (XMP) API, which provides access to the communication services, such as SNMP or CMIP.

The SNMP Platform services supply the functions for SNMP-based network management. These services support MIB, event monitoring, and information retrieval functions. You can load standard or enterprise-specific MIBs into the platform to manage multiple vendors' objects. The SNMP MIB browser allows users to query, display, or graph MIB values from selected objects. The

IP discovery and mapping function monitors the network for any changes in topology, configuration, or status, and then records results in a database. SNMP events, or traps, are recorded and displayed in several categories, including threshold, network topology, error, status, node configuration, and application alert traps.

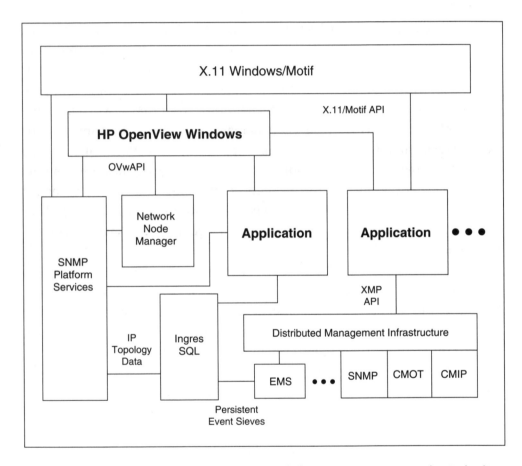

Figure 1-14a. HP OpenView distributed management platform services *(courtesy Hewlett-Packard)*

At the heart of OpenView is the distributed management infrastructure shown in Figure 1-14b. This infrastructure links managers, agents, and management services. The Postmaster manages communication between network objects, such as requests and responses between managers and agents. The Object

Registration Services (ORS) creates a global directory of the agents, their locations, and the protocol they use. These services then map object names to the appropriate network address, so that information requests from the Postmaster can be sent to the correct destination. In Figure 1-14b, note the modularity that the XMP API provides to the management application, and the underlying communication protocols, SNMP, CMOT, and CMIP.

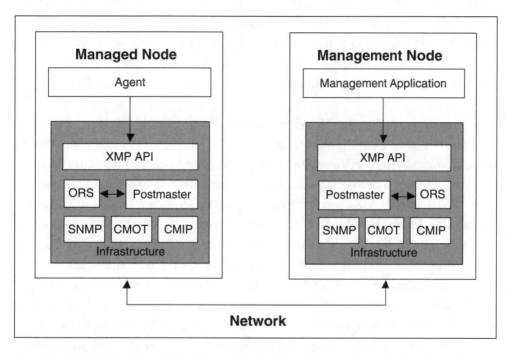

Figure 1-14b. HP OpenView distributed management infrastructure *(courtesy Hewlett-Packard)*

Another aspect of HP's OpenView concept is the OpenView Solution Partners program. This program tests third-party applications and certifies that they operate with OpenView. Currently, applications are available to manage NetWare, SNA, and DECnet networks.

In summary, OpenView's strength is its ability to integrate multiple management applications and protocols into the same system.

1.10.3. IBM AIX NetView/6000

Announced in 1986, IBM NetView was the textbook example of a centralized network management system based on the IBM mainframe. Therefore, NetView incorporates three types of interfaces: focal points, entry points, and service points. The focal point supports centralized network management including data collection and analysis, and the user interface. *Systems Network Architecture* (SNA) devices connect via entry points, which also extend the network management functions to attached peripherals. Service points allow NetView to manage non-SNA by allowing incompatible systems to support the NetView protocols. The protocol for network management applications is called the *network management vector transport* (NMVT).

One way to integrate the NetView system on the mainframe with information from non-SNA systems is to use the AIX NetView Service Point option, which comes with NetView/6000 (see reference [1-30] and Figure 1-15a). NetView/6000 is a network management solution for heterogeneous networks. This UNIX-based (AIX) software runs on a RISC System/6000, and can manage all IP-addressable SNMP and CMOT devices. The NetView Service Point option is one of NetView's strong points, since it allows NetView to manage a distributed network. It works by converting SNMP trap messages to SNA alerts, then sends them to NetView. Conversely, it can use NetView management facilities to generate SNMP commands. Other strengths of the system include the dynamic device discovery and mapping, a MIB compiler for integrating Internet-standard and vendor-specific MIBs, and network monitoring for fault and performance measurement.

AIX NetView/6000's architecture contains several cooperative processes (see reference [1-31] and Figure 1-15b), three of which comprise the core of the software. The trapd process receives SNMP traps from the managed nodes, and significant events from other processes. The netmon process provides node discovery and node status information, and polls those nodes with SNMP agents to determine MIB information. It enters the information it discovers into a topological database. The xnm process generates the graphical end-user display. Other processes include the xnmevents, which records pending but unacknowledged events; xnmappmon, which initiates and displays results of diagnostic tests; and a Data Collector that polls nodes on a periodic basis for MIB values.

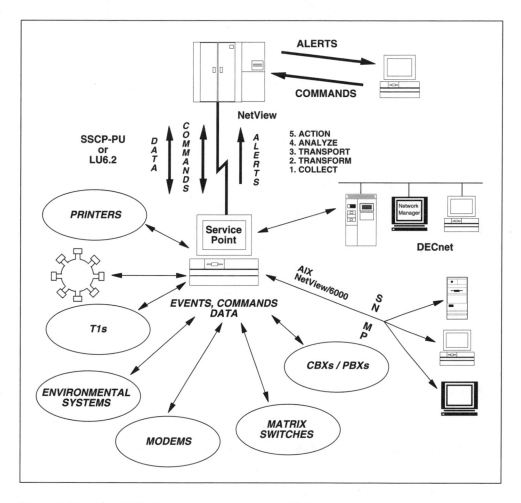

Figure 1-15a. The AIX NetView service point *(courtesy IBM Corporation)*

In summary, AIX NetView/6000 can operate as a stand-alone system or in conjunction with NetView. In its latter role, it creates a powerful distributed network management system that opens the SNA world to the broader world of SNMP-based internetworking.

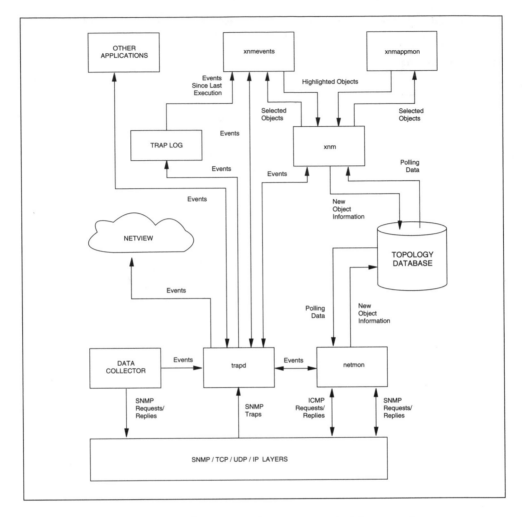

Figure 1-15b. Internal structure of AIX NetView/6000 *(courtesy IBM Corporation)*

1.10.4. SunConnect SunNet Manager

Unlike the network management systems from DEC, Hewlett-Packard, and IBM that offer manager and agent devices, the SunNet Manager from Sun-Connect (a unit of Sun Microsystems, Inc.) is a network management system for heterogeneous (SNMP, CMIP, and RPC proxy) agent-based internetworks. The SunNet Manager accomplishes this through its architectural design and by adhering to the Internet standards.

Sun's network management strategy has three objectives. First, users should be empowered to manage even the most complex networks. Second, diverse environments, ranging from small to large systems, must be integrated into the network management schema. Third, it should be able to solve even problems unique to a particular configuration.

The SunNet Manager runs on a Sun SPARC or compatible workstation. The architecture is designed in layers (see reference [1-32] and Figure 1-16). The Sun network management features include: configuration management, problem solving, capacity planning, security, and resource accounting. It offers heterogeneous management links to other network types, such as DECnet, FDDI, and AppleTalk, as well as interfaces to other management systems, such as IBM NetView. It can manage an array of local and wide area networks, including Ethernet, FDDI, and token-ring.

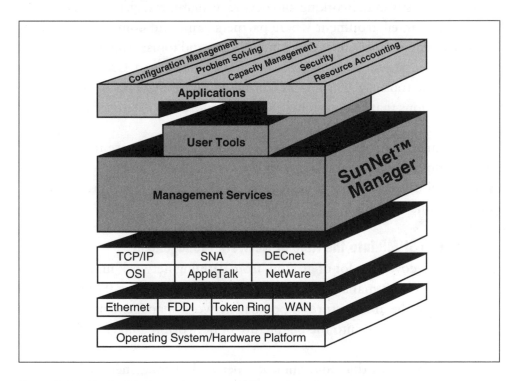

Figure 1-16. The SunNet Manager environment *(courtesy SunConnect)*

The core management services come with a user-friendly, object-oriented, graphical user interface. They provide information on network configuration, fault identification and analysis, network monitoring, and capacity planning. The system also provides tools that allow the user to define macros, called "requests," that monitor and control network resources. A Browser tool facilitates data retrieval and organization, and a Grapher tool presents this data in two- or three-dimensional graphs.

The architecture also supports two types of agents, those that directly access managed devices, and proxy agents that provide indirect access. The benefit of the proxy agents is that they can manage multiprotocol network objects. SunNet also offers the Agent Services API, which allows SunNet Manager capabilities to extend to other protocol environments.

With the diversity in networking and devices available today, the SunNet Manager creates an environment where partners can build compatible applications. This environment includes standard APIs and tools; graphical and viewing facilities; standard protocols, such as SNMP and CMIP; and data manipulation tools, such as logs and browsers. With these tools, you can create applications that manage environments tailored to customer needs.

To summarize, SunNet Manager is straightforward software for managing multivendor internetworks. Not only does it support SNMP, it also provides APIs for third-party applications. References [1-33] and [1-34]) provide recent reviews of the system.

1.11. Fitting SNMP into the Role of Network Management

This chapter covered a lot of ground, from defining network management to exploring network management concepts, from the familiar ISO/OSI model to examining the architecture of popular network management systems. So where does SNMP fit into the big picture of network management?

SNMP is a protocol that communicates network management information. Therefore, SNMP fits into the Application layer of the OSI model. But if you only look at SNMP in this context, you're ignoring the structure that supports it—and that fills out the remaining layers of the OSI model. In order to study SNMP in detail, you need to thoroughly understand the supporting structures.

This book takes several chapters to explain these structures. Chapter 2 discusses the structure of management information (or the SMI), which provides the organization and communication structures for the management information. Chapter 3 discusses management information bases (MIBs) that formally define the managed objects and their attributes. Chapter 4 examines the SNMP protocol in detail. Chapter 5 discusses the underlying protocols, such as the User Datagram Protocol (UDP), the Internet Protocol (IP), and the local network protocols, such as Ethernet or token-ring, upon which SNMP operates. Chapter 6 provides case studies of live networks that demonstrate these protocols in action. Chapter 7 examines the second-generation protocol, SNMP Version 2.

So put that network management console in monitor mode, get yourself a strong cup of coffee, and fasten your seat belt. The work for the real network manager is about to begin!

1.12. References

[1-1]   International Organization for Standardization, Information Processing Systems: Open Systems Interconnection, Basic Reference Model, ISO 7498-1984.

[1-2]   International Organization for Standardization, Information Processing Systems: Open Systems Interconnection, Basic Reference Model, Part 4: Management Framework, ISO 7498-4-1989.

[1-3]   International Organization for Standardization, Information Processing Systems: Open Systems Interconnection, Common management information service definition, ISO/ICE 9595, CCITT Recommendation X.710, IEEE 802.1-91/20, November 1990.

[1-4]   International Organization for Standardization, Information Processing
         Systems: Open Systems Interconnection, Common management infor-
         mation protocol specification, ISO/IEC 9596-1, CCITT Recommen-
         dation X.711, IEEE 802.1-91/21, November 1990.

[1-5]   Klerer, S. Mark. "The OSI Management Architecture: an Overview."
         IEEE Network (March 1988): 20-29.

[1-6]   Yemini, Yechiam. "The OSI Network Management Model." *IEEE
         Communications Magazine* (May 1993): 20-29.

[1-7]   Institute of Electrical and Electronics Engineers. LAN/MAN Man-
         agement. IEEE Std 802.1b–1992.

[1-8]   Jander, Mary. "Can CMOL Challenge SNMP?" *Data Communica-
         tions* (May 21, 1992): 53–57.

[1-9]   Millikin, Michael. "Taking a Closer Look at the DCE." *Network
         World* (March 30, 1992): 26-30.

[1-10]   Open Software Foundation. *Distributed Management Environment
         Rationale*, 1991.

[1-11]   Herman, James. "OSF DME: The Final Selections." *Patricia Seybold's
         Network Monitor* (October 1991): 1-19.

[1-12]   Partridge, Craig and Glenn Trewitt. "The High-Level Entity Man-
         agement System (HEMS)." *IEEE Network* (March 1988): 37-42.

[1-13]   Case, Jeffrey D., et. al. "Introduction to the Simple Gateway Moni-
         toring Protocol." *IEEE Network* (March 1988): 43-49.

[1-14]   Cerf, V. "IAB Recommendations for the Development of Internet Net-
         work Management Standards." RFC 1052, April 1988.

[1-15] Case, J.D., M. Fedor, M.L. Schoffstall, C. Davin. "Simple Network Management Protocol (SNMP)." RFC 1157, May 1990.

[1-16] Rose, Marshall T. "A Brief History of Network Management of TCP/IP Internets." *ConneXions, the Interoperability Report* (August 1990): 18-27.

[1-17] Ben-Artzi, Amatzia, et. al. "Network Management of TCP/IP Networks: Present and Future." *IEEE Network* (July 1990): 35-43.

[1-18] Warrier, U.S., et. al. "Common Management Information Services and Protocols for the Internet (CMOT and CMIP)." RFC 1189, October 1990.

[1-19] Axner, David H. "Wiring hubs: keys to the network infrastructure." *Networking Management* (November 1992): 48-56.

[1-20] Jander, Mary. "Extending SNMP to the Desktop." *Data Communications* (November 21, 1992): 49-52.

[1-21] Mier, Edwin. "SNMP's Best & Brightest for 1992." *Communications Week* (November 16, 1992): 81-86.

[1-22] Mier, Edwin. "How SNMP Was Tested—Methodology Evaluates Agents in Five Key Phases." *Communications Week* (June 22, 1992): 53-62.

[1-23] Herman, James G. "Enterprise Network and System Management, Architectures, Strategies and Issues." *Patricia Seybold's Office Computing Group* (Boston, MA), 1991.

[1-24] Treece, Terry. "Control From the Console." *LAN Technology* (October 1992): 67-78.

[1-25]   Mier, Edwin. "SNMP Stations Pull It All Together." *Communications Week* (April 6, 1992): 45-56.

[1-26]   Digital Equipment Corporation. Enterprise Management Architecture General Description. Document number EK-DEMAR-GD-001, 1989.

[1-27]   Sylvester, Tim. "DECmcc puts your network on the map." *Digital News and Review* (November 23, 1992): 37-39.

[1-28]   Hewlett-Packard Company. *HP OpenView Technical Evaluation Guide*. Document 5091-5134E, 1992.

[1-29]   Klemba, Keith S., et. al. "HP OpenView Network Management Architecture." *Hewlett-Packard Journal* (April 1990): 54-59.

[1-30]   IBM Corporation. *AIX NetView/6000 at a Glance*. Document GC31-6175, 1992.

[1-31]   Chou, J.H., et. al. "AIX NetView/6000." *IBM Systems Journal* (1992): 270-285.

[1-32]   Sun Microsystems, Inc. SunConnect Network Management Strategy Presentation, 1993.

[1-33]   Huntington-Lee, Jill. "SunNet Manager Focuses on Unix Networks." *LAN Times* (February 8, 1993): 27-30.

[1-34]   Wittman, Art. "SunNet Manager v2.0: A New Generation of Network Management." *Network Computing* (September 1992): 28-30.

2 The Structure of Management Information

This and the next three chapters explore the theory of network management and the components of the Internet Network Management Framework. In this chapter, you'll learn about the *structure of management information* (SMI), which defines the rules for identifying managed objects. SMI is described in RFC 1155 [Reference 2-1], and refined in RFC 1212 and RFC 1215.

Chapter 3 discusses the management information bases (MIBs), examined in RFC 1213 [2-2], that describe the managed objects themselves. Chapter 4 discusses SNMP, which defines the mechanism by which managers and agents communicate, and is described in RFC 1157 [2-3]. Finally, Chapter 5 studies the underlying communication protocols, such as the User Datagram Protocol (UDP) and the Internet Protocol (IP), that transport SNMP messages between the manager and agents. Chapter 6 offers case studies demonstrating real-world use of SNMP. I will revisit the SMI, MIB, and SNMP in Chapter 7 to compare and contrast SNMP with its intended successor, SNMP Version 2.

2.1. Managing Management Information

In the Manager/Agent paradigm for network management, managed network objects must be physically and logically accessible. By "physically accessible" I mean that some entity must physically check the address, count the packets, or otherwise quantify the network management information. Logical accessibility means that management information must be stored somewhere, and, therefore, that the information must be retrievable and modifiable. (SNMP actually performs the retrieval and modification.) The structure of management information (SMI) (RFC 1155 [2-1]) organizes, names, and describes information so that logical access can occur.

The SMI states that each managed object must have a name, a syntax, and an encoding. The name, an *object identifier* (OID), uniquely identifies the object. The syntax defines the data type, such as an integer or a string of octets. The encoding describes how the information associated with the managed objects is serialized for transmission between machines.

This chapter discusses how the SMI applies to SNMP. It begins by looking at the syntax (the Abstract Syntax Notation One, ASN.1, in Section 2.1), the encoding (the Basic Encoding Rules, examined in Section 2.5), and finally the names (the object identifier, discussed in Section 2.6). In this way, the discussion moves from the abstract to the practical. Chapter 3 discusses how the MIBs use these names.

2.2. Presenting Management Information

In terms of the ISO/OSI model [2-4], the ASN.1 syntax is a Presentation layer (layer 6) function. Recall that the Presentation layer defines the format of the data stored within a host computer system.

In order for managers and agents to exchange data, both must understand it, regardless of the way either machine represents data internally. For this to occur, two items must be standardized, the abstract syntax and the transfer syntax. The *abstract syntax* defines specifications for data notation. The *transfer syntax* defines (transmittable) encodings for the elements in the abstract syntax.

The Internet SMI specifies that ASN.1 define the abstract syntax for messages; that is, ASN.1 defines the basic language elements and provides rules for combining elements into messages. The Basic Encoding Rules (BER) provide the transfer syntax. The BER are associated with the abstract syntax and provide bit-level communication between machines. Thus, the SMI and SNMP use the ASN.1 formalizations (ISO 8824 [2-5]) and BER (ISO 8825 [2-6]) to define various aspects of the Internet network management framework. The specifics of ASN.1 are discussed in the next section.

2.3. ASN.1 Elements

Network administrators often criticize ASN.1 for its complexity. Some of their criticisms are fair: it is quite difficult to interpret the standard. However, ASN.1 has a straightforward objective. It is designed to define structured information (messages) in a machine-independent (or host-independent) fashion. To do this, ASN.1 defines basic data types, such as integers and strings, and new data types that are based on combinations of the basic ones. The BER then define the way the data is serialized for transmission.

ASN.1 defines data as a pattern of bits in computer memory, just as any high-level computer programming language defines data that the language manipulates as variables. The BER define a standard way to convert ASN.1 definitions into bit patterns for transmission, and then they actually transfer the data between computers. The BER are necessary because the ASN.1 description is "human-readable" and must be translated differently for each type of computer. The BER representation, however, is always the same for any ASN.1 description, regardless of the computers that send or receive that information. This assures communication between machines, regardless of their internal architecture.

My objective here is to describe ASN.1 to the level of detail necessary to apply it to network management and SNMP. (SNMP uses a subset of ASN.1 for the sake of simplicity.) For additional information, refer to Douglas Steedman's *Abstract Syntax Notation One, the Tutorial and Reference* [2-7] or Motteler and Sidhu's "Components of OSI: Abstract Syntax Notation One (ASN.1)" [2-8].

ASN.1 uses some unique terms to define its procedures, including type definitions, value assignments, macro definitions and evocations, and module definitions. You need to understand these terms before the discussion can proceed. Moreover, ASN.1 specifies some words as keywords, or reserved character sequences. Keywords, such as INTEGER, OBJECT, and NULL, have special meanings and appear in uppercase letters.

2.3.1. Types and values

A *type* is a class of data. It defines the data structure that the machine needs in order to understand and process information. The SMI defines three types: Primitive, Constructor, and Defined. ASN.1 defines several *Primitive types* (also known as Simple types), including INTEGER, OCTET STRING, OBJECT IDENTIFIER, and NULL. By convention, types begin with an uppercase letter. (ASN.1 also defines the four types listed here as reserved character sequences, and therefore represents them entirely in uppercase.) *Constructor types* (also known as Aggregate types) generate lists and tables. *Defined types* are alternate names for either simple or complex ASN.1 types and are usually more descriptive. Examples of SNMP-defined types include IpAddress, which represents a 32-bit Internet address, and TimeTicks, which is a time-stamp.

The *value* quantifies the type. In other words, once you know the *type*, such as INTEGER or OCTET-STRING, the *value* provides a specific instance for that type. For example, a value could be an entry in a routing table. By convention, values begin with a lowercase letter.

Some applications allow only a subset of the possible type values. A *subtype specification* indicates such a constraint. The subtype specification appears after the type and shows the permissible value or values, called the *subtype values,* in parentheses. For example, if an application uses an INTEGER type and the permissible values must fit within an 8-bit field, the possible range of values must be between 0 and 255. You would express this as

INTEGER (0..255)

The two periods (..) are the range separator and indicate the validity of any integer value between 0 and 255.

2.3.2. Macros

Annex A of ISO 8824 defines a macro notation that allows you to extend the ASN.1 language. By convention, a macro reference (or macro name) appears entirely in uppercase letters.

For example, MIB definitions make extensive use of the ASN.1 macro, OBJECT-TYPE (originally defined in RFC 1155 and now replaced by the definition in RFC 1212 [2-9]). The first object in MIB-II is a system description (sysDescr). RFC 1213 uses the OBJECT-TYPE macro in RFC 1213 to define sysDescr, as follows:

```
sysDescr OBJECT-TYPE
        SYNTAX   DisplayString (SIZE (0..255))
        ACCESS   read-only
        STATUS   mandatory
        DESCRIPTION
                "A textual description of the entity. This value should include the
                full name and version identification of the system's hardware
                type, software operating-system, and networking software. This
                must contain only printable ASCII characters."
        ::= { system 1 }
```

Thus, one concise package defines the object sysDescr. Section 2.4.1 explores the details of the OBJECT-TYPE macro (SYNTAX, ACCESS, and so on). Note that the range notation (0..255) specifies the permissible size of the DisplayString type, which in this case is between 0 and 255.

2.3.3. Modules

ASN.1 also collects descriptions into convenient groups, called modules. For example, the remote monitoring (RMON) MIB is a discrete unit that is also part of MIB-II.

The module starts with a module name, such as RFC1271-MIB. Module names must begin with an uppercase letter. The BEGIN and END statements enclose the body of the module. The body may contain IMPORTS, which are the names of types, values, and macros, and the modules in which they are declared. Following is the header section of the RMON MIB (from RFC 1271), representing a MIB module. Comment lines within ASN.1 syntax begin with a double hyphen (--).

```
RFC1271-MIB DEFINITIONS ::= BEGIN
    IMPORTS
        Counter                 FROM RFC1155-SMI
        DisplayString  FROM RFC1158-MIB
        mib-2                   FROM RFC1213-MIB
        OBJECT-TYPE  FROM RFC-1212;
        -- This MIB module uses the extended OBJECT-TYPE macro as
        -- defined in RFC 1212.


        -- Remote Network Monitoring MIB
        rmon    OBJECT IDENTIFIER ::= { mib-2 16 }


        -- textual conventions
        .
        .
        .
        END
```

In the previous example, you can see the OBJECT IDENTIFIER value notation for rmon. Section 2.6 discusses this notation in detail, but for now simply note that the value of rmon is the sixteenth defined object under the mib-2 object tree. The curly brackets ({}) indicate the beginning and end of a list—in this case a list of the OBJECT IDENTIFIER values defining rmon.

2.3.4. Summary of ASN.1 conventions

In summary, ASN.1 makes distinctions between upper- and lowercase letters, as follows:

Item	Convention
Types	Initial uppercase letter
Values	Initial lowercase letter
Macros	All uppercase letters
Modules	Initial uppercase letter
ASN.1 keywords	All uppercase letters

The ASN.1 keywords that are frequently used within SNMP are BEGIN, CHOICE, DEFINED, DEFINITIONS, END, EXPORTS, IDENTIFIER, IMPORTS, INTEGER, NULL, OBJECT, OCTET, OF, SEQUENCE, and STRING.

ASN.1 also gives special meanings to certain characters:

Item	Name
-	Signed number
--	Comment
::=	Assignment (defined as)
|	Alternation (options of a list)
{ }	Starts and ends a list
[ ]	Starts and ends a tag
( )	Starts and ends a subtype expression
..	Indicates a range

The sections that follow emphasize some of these special characters. Philip Gaudett's paper, "A Tutorial on ASN.1" [2-10] provides a good summary of this notation.

2.4. Details of ASN.1—Objects and Types

The previous discussion provided an overview of ASN.1. This section focuses on the ASN.1 objects and data types used within the Internet Network Management framework. Where possible, I will provide examples derived from the SMI (RFC 1155), the Concise MIB Definitions (RFC 1212), and MIB-II (RFC 1213) documents.

2.4.1. Defining objects in the MIBs

A MIB contains the objects to be managed. The OBJECT-TYPE macro defines these objects in a standard format that is consistent across various public and

private MIBs. (Chapter 3 will discuss MIBs in greater detail.) The MIB-II
ASN.1 definitions (RFC 1213, page 48) appear as follows:

```
tcpInSegs OBJECT-TYPE
        SYNTAX  Counter
        ACCESS  read-only
        STATUS  mandatory
        ::= { tcp 10 }
```

In English, this ASN.1 definition means: This defines an object named tcpIn-
Segs that contains Counter information. The Counter type is a non-negative
number that increases monotonically. (Section 2.4.4 discusses counters, which
is a defined type.) This object is read-only and is mandatory for all managed
devices that support its parent, mib.tcp. When a management protocol accesses
this object, it uses the name { tcp 10 }, which identifies the tenth defined object
within the tcp group. (Section 2.6 provides more detail on how the SMI names
manage objects.)

2.4.2. Primitive (Simple) types

To maintain SNMP's simplicity, the Internet SMI uses a subset of the ASN.1
data types. These are divided into two categories, the Primitive types and Constructor types (see Section 2.4.3).

Primitive data types (also called Simple types) include INTEGER, OCTET
STRING, OBJECT IDENTIFIER, and NULL. The following examples come
from MIB-II (RFC 1213). You may also want to refer to Section 2.7, "The
Concise SMI Definition," and locate the Primitive types under the SimpleSyntax
definition.

INTEGER is a primitive type with distinguished (or unique) values that are
positive and negative whole numbers, including zero. The INTEGER type has
two special cases. The first is the *enumerated integer type,* in which the objects
have a specific, nonzero number such as 1, 2, or 3. The second, the *integer-*

bitstring type, is used for short bit strings such as (0..127) and displays the value in hexidecimal. An example of INTEGER would be:

```
ipDefaultTTL OBJECT-TYPE
     SYNTAX   INTEGER
     ACCESS   read-write
     STATUS   mandatory
     DESCRIPTION
             "The default value inserted into the Time-To-Live field of the IP header
             of datagrams originating at this entity, whenever a TTL value is not
             supplied by the transport layer protocol."
     ::= { ip 2 }
```

The OCTET STRING is a primitive type whose distinguished values are an ordered sequence of zero, one, or more octets. SNMP uses three special cases of the OCTET STRING type: the DisplayString, the octetBitstring, and the PhysAddress. In the DisplayString, all of the octets are printable ASCII characters. The octetBitstring is used for bit strings that exceed 32 bits in length. (TCP/IP frequently includes 32-bit fields. This quantity is a typical value for the internal word width of various processors—hosts and routers—within the Internet.) MIB-II defines the PhysAddress and uses it to represent media (or Physical layer) addresses.

An example of the use of a DisplayString would be:

```
sysContact  OBJECT-TYPE
     SYNTAX   DisplayString (SIZE (0..255))
     ACCESS   read-write
     STATUS   mandatory
     DESCRIPTION
             "The textual identification of the contact person for this managed
             node, and information on how to contact this person."
     ::= { system 4 }
```

Note that the subtype indicates that the permissible size of the DisplayString is between 0 and 255 octets.

The OBJECT IDENTIFIER is a type whose distinguishing values are the set of all object identifiers allocated according to the rules of ISO 8824. The ObjectName type, a special case that SNMP uses, is restricted to the object identifiers of the objects and subtrees within the MIB, as for example:

```
ipRouteInfo  OBJECT-TYPE
        SYNTAX   OBJECT IDENTIFIER
        ACCESS   read-only
        STATUS   mandatory
        DESCRIPTION
    "A reference to MIB definitions specific to the particular routing protocol responsible
    for this route, as determined by the value specified in the route's ipRouteProto value.
    If this information is not present, its value should be set to the OBJECT IDENTIFIER { 0 0 },
    which is a syntactically valid object identifier, and any conforming implementation of
    ASN.1 and BER must be able to generate and recognize this value."
        ::= { ipRouteEntry 13 }
```

NULL is a type with a single value, also called null. The null serves as a placeholder, but is not currently used for SNMP objects. (You can see NULL used as a placeholder in the variable bindings field of the SNMP GetRequest PDU. The NULL is assigned to be the value of the unknown variable; that is, the value the GetRequest PDU seeks. For more information see Section 4.3.)

Section 2.5.3 discusses the primitive types and their encodings in more detail.

2.4.3. Constructor (structured) types

The constructor types, SEQUENCE and SEQUENCE OF, define tables and rows (entries) within those tables. By convention, names for table objects end with the suffix "Table," and names for rows end with the suffix "Entry." The following discussion defines the constructor types. The example comes from MIB-II.

SEQUENCE is a constructor type defined by referencing a fixed, ordered, list of types. Some of the types may be optional, and all may be different ASN.1 types. Each value of the new type consists of an ordered list of values, one from each component type. The SEQUENCE as a whole defines a row within a table. Each entry in the SEQUENCE specifies a column within the row.

SEQUENCE OF is a constructor type that is defined by referencing a single existing type; each value in the new type is an ordered list of zero, one, or more values of that existing type. Like SEQUENCE, SEQUENCE OF defines the rows in a table; unlike SEQUENCE, SEQUENCE OF only uses elements of the same ASN.1 type.

The TCP connection table that follows illustrates both the SEQUENCE and SEQUENCE OF.

```
tcpConnTable  OBJECT-TYPE
    SYNTAX   SEQUENCE OF TcpConnEntry
    ACCESS   not-accessible
    STATUS   mandatory
    DESCRIPTION
            "A table containing TCP connection-specific information."
    ::= { tcp 13 }
tcpConnEntry  OBJECT-TYPE
    SYNTAX   TcpConnEntry
    ACCESS   not-accessible
    STATUS   mandatory
    DESCRIPTION
            "Information about a particular current TCP connection. An object
            of this type is transient; it ceases to exist when (or soon after) the
            connection makes the transition to the CLOSED state."
    INDEX   {tcpConnLocalAddress,
            tcpConnLocalPort,
            tcpConnRemAddress,
            tcpConnRemPort }
    ::= { tcpConnTable 1 }
    TcpConnEntry ::=
    SEQUENCE {
    tcpConnState
```

```
        INTEGER,
tcpConnLocalAddress
    IpAddress,
tcpConnLocalPort
    INTEGER (0..65535),
tcpConnRemAddress
    IpAddress,
tcpConnRemPort
    INTEGER (0..65535)
}
```

This example expands your ASN.1 grammar. The table name, tcpConnTable, ends with the suffix "Table." The row name, tcpConnEntry, ends with the suffix "Entry." The sequence name, TcpConnEntry, is the same as the row name, except that it begins with an uppercase letter. The INDEX clause defines the construction and order of the columns that make up the rows. Dave Perkins' excellent article "How to Read and Use an SNMP MIB" [2-11] explores table and row objects in greater detail.

2.4.4. Defined types

The Internet Network Management Framework uses the defined (or application-wide) types (described in RFC 1155). The defined types include NetworkAddress, IpAddress, Counter, Gauge, TimeTicks, and Opaque. The examples that follow come from RFC 1213. For more information, refer to Section 2.7 and locate the defined types under the ApplicationSyntax definition.

The NetworkAddress type was designed to represent an address from one of several protocol families. A CHOICE is a primitive type that provides alternatives between other types, and is found in several sections of the SMI definition given in Section 2.7. Currently, however, only one protocol family, the Internet family (called internet IpAddress in the SMI definition), has been defined for this CHOICE. Here is an example:

```
atNetAddress  OBJECT-TYPE
    SYNTAX  NetworkAddress
```

```
ACCESS   read-write
STATUS   deprecated
DESCRIPTION
        "The NetworkAddress (e.g., the IP address) corresponding to the
        media-dependent 'physical' address."
::= { atEntry 3 }
```

Because it supports only IP addresses (hence the default "choice"), the use of this type is discouraged.

IpAddress is an application-wide type that represents a 32-bit Internet address. It is represented as an OCTET STRING of length 4 (octets) in network byte-order (the order bytes are transmitted over the network).

```
tcpConnRemAddress  OBJECT-TYPE
    SYNTAX   IpAddress
    ACCESS   read-only
    STATUS   mandatory
    DESCRIPTION
            "The remote IP address for this TCP connection."
::= {tcpConnEntry 4 }
```

The Counter is an application-wide type that represents a non-negative integer that increases monotonically until it reaches a maximum value, then wraps around, and increases again from zero. The maximum counter value is $2^{32}-1$, or 4,294,967,295 decimal. In other words, the Counter is an unsigned 32-bit number. An INTEGER is a signed 32-bit value. By convention, you write the name of a COUNTER object as a plural; it ends in a lowercase *s*. Here is an example:

```
icmpInDestUnreachs  OBJECT-TYPE
    SYNTAX   Counter
    ACCESS   read-only
    STATUS   mandatory
    DESCRIPTION
            "The number of ICMP Destination Unreachable messages received."
::= { icmp 3 }
```

A Gauge is an application-wide type that represents a non-negative integer. It may increase or decrease, but it latches at a maximum value. The maximum counter value is $2^{32}-1$ (4,294,967,295 decimal). Here is an example:

```
ifSpeed  OBJECT-TYPE
    SYNTAX  Gauge
    ACCESS  read-only
    STATUS  mandatory
    DESCRIPTION
            "An estimate of the interface's current bandwidth in bits per sec-
            ond. For interfaces that do not vary in bandwidth or for those
            where no accurate estimation can be made, this object should con-
            tain the nominal bandwidth."
    ::= { ifEntry 5 }
```

TimeTicks is an application-wide type that represents a non-negative integer that counts the time in hundredths of a second since some epoch, or point in time. When the MIB defines object types that use this ASN.1 type, the description of the object type identifies the reference epoch. Here is an example:

```
sysUpTime  OBJECT-TYPE
    SYNTAX  TimeTicks
    ACCESS  read-only
    STATUS  mandatory
    DESCRIPTION
            "The time (in hundredths of a second) since the network manage-
            ment portion of the system was last re-initialized."
    ::= { system 3 }
```

Opaque is an application-wide type that permits the passing of arbitrary ASN.1 syntax. The ASN.1 basic rules encode a value into a string of octets. This string, in turn, is encoded as an OCTET STRING, in effect "double-wrap-ping" the original ASN.1 value. SNMP does not currently use Opaque, although it may be found in some private MIBs.

2.4.5. Tagged types

Tags distinguish between defined objects unequivocally. While a human reader might be able to distinguish defined objects through their names in ASN.1 notation, a machine can't without additional information. Therefore, the tagged types use a previously-defined type as a base, then add unique information. ASN.1 defines four classes of tags: universal, application, context-specific, and private. ASN.1 (ISO 8824) defines universal tags. Other standards, such as the Internet standards, assign application class tags. The SNMP definition (RFC 1157) interprets context-specific class tags according to their context. Enterprise-specific applications use private class tags.

A number within square brackets ([]) identifies tagged types. For example, the concise SMI definition (Section 2.7) shows that

```
TimeTicks ::=
    [APPLICATION 3]
        IMPLICIT INTEGER (0..4294967295)
```

Therefore, the TimeTicks type is a tagged type, designated APPLICATION 3. It is of the application class, and the tag number is 3. It may take on the range of values between 0 and 4294967295. The IMPLICIT keyword indicates that the tag associated with the INTEGER type is not transmitted, but the tag associated with TimeTicks is. This reduces the amount of data that must be encoded and transmitted.

2.5. Encoding Rules

The previous section discussed the abstract syntax that represents management information. This section discusses the encoding rules that allow that information to be transmitted on a network. The Basic Encoding Rules (BER) define this transfer syntax, and ISO 8825 specifies it [2-3].

2.5.1. Encoding management information

Recall that each machine in the management system can have its own internal representation of the management information. The ASN.1 syntax describes that information in a standard form. The transfer syntax performs the bit-level communication (the external representation) between machines. For example, assume that the host needs management information from another device. The management application would generate an SNMP request, which the BER would encode and transmit on the network media. The destination machine would receive the information from the network, decode it using the BER rules, and interpret it as an SNMP command. The SNMP response would return in a similar, but reverse, manner. The encoding structure used for the external representation is called *Type-Length-Value encoding* (see Figure 2-1).

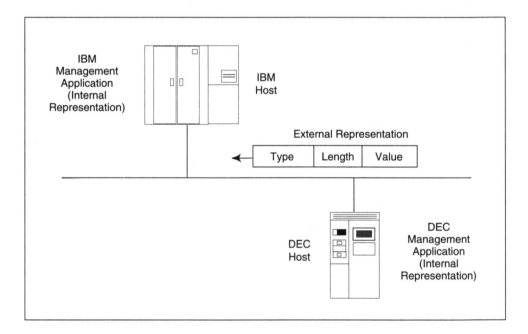

Figure 2-1. Internal and external data representations

2.5.2. Type-Length-Value encoding

To define the external data representation, the BER first specify the position of each bit within the octets being transmitted. Each octet transmits the *most significant bit* (MSB) first, and defines it as bit 8 on the left-hand side of the octet. The octet defines the *least significant bit* (LSB) as bit 1 on the right-hand side (see Figure 2-2).

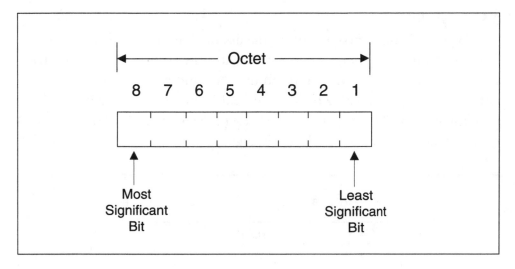

Figure 2-2. BER bit ordering, as defined in ISO 8825

The data encoding structure itself has three components: the Type, Length, and Value (TLV). Note that in the literature you will run across other names for Type-Length-Value, including Tag-Length-Value and Identifier-Length-Contents (from ISO 8825). The structure of a TLV encoding used with SNMP is shown in Figure 2-3.

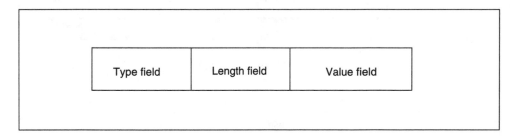

Figure 2-3. Type-Length-Value (TLV) encoding

By defining the order and structure of the bits, the BER guarantee that both ends of the communication channel interpret the bit stream consistently. The following sections examine the structure of each TLV field individually.

2.5.2.1. Type field

The Type field comes first and alerts the destination to the structure that follows. Thus, the Type field contains an identification for the encoding structure; it encodes the ASN.1 tag (both the class and number) for the type of data contained in the Value field. A subfield within the Type field contains a bit designated as P/C that indicates whether the coding is Primitive (P/C = 0) or Constructed (P/C = 1), as shown in Figure 2-4.

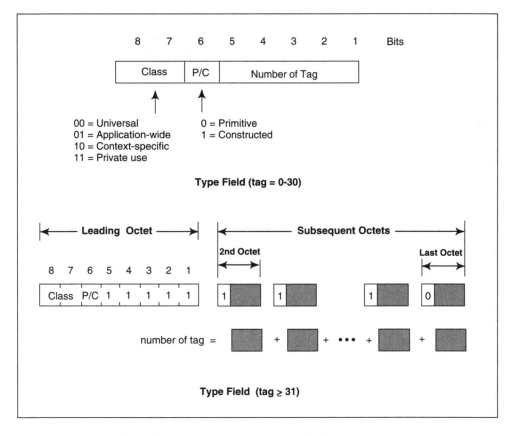

Figure 2-4. Type field encoding *(courtesy International Standards Organization)*

There are two types of Type fields; and their use depends on the magnitude of the tag number. When the tag number is between 0 and 30, the Tag field contains a single octet (see Figure 2-4). When the tag number is 31 or greater, the Type field contains multiple octets. In either case, the first octet contains three subfields: the Class, P/C bit, and tag number. The Class subfield encodes the class of tag in use:

Class	Bit 8	Bit 7
Universal	0	0
Application	0	1
Context-specific	1	0
Private	1	1

SNMP applications use the first three classes: universal, application, and context-specific. The universal class encodes the INTEGER type, OCTET STRING type, and so on. The application class encodes the defined types (IpAddress, Counter, and so on). The context-specific class encodes the five SNMP protocol data units (PDUs), GetRequest, GetResponse, and so on.

The P/C subfield (bit 6) indicates the form of the data element. Primitive encoding (P/C = 0) means that the content octets represent the value directly. A Constructor encoding (P/C = 1) means that the contents octets encode one or more additional data values, such as a SEQUENCE.

SNMP uses tag numbers between 0 and 30. The tag number appears in the third subfield and is represented in binary. Bit 5 is the tag's MSB; bit 1 is its LSB.

ISO 8824 contains tag numbers for the universal class (for example, UNIVERSAL 2 represents the INTEGER type). The SMI specification, RFC 1155, contains tag numbers for the application class (for example, IpAddress is a primitive type with tag [0]). The SNMP specification, RFC 1157, contains tag numbers for the context-specific class (for example, GetRequest PDU is a constructed type with tag [0]).

The following list summarizes the three classes of Type fields used with SNMP and the encodings for those fields: class, P/C, and tag number. These encodings appear in both binary and hexadecimal notation, where the *H* represents hexadecimal notation:

Universal Class	Type Field Value
INTEGER	00000010 = 02H
OCTET STRING	00000100 = 04H
NULL	00000101 = 05H
OBJECT IDENTIFIER	00000110 = 06H
SEQUENCE	00110000 = 30H
SEQUENCE-OF	00110000 = 30H

Application Class	Type Field Value
IpAddress	01000000 = 40H
Counter	01000001 = 41H
Gauge	01000010 = 42H
TimeTicks	01000011 = 43H
Opaque	01000100 = 44H

Context-Specific Class	Type Field Value
GetRequest	10100000 = A0H
GetNextRequest	10100001 = A1H
GetResponse	10100010 = A2H
SetRequest	10100011 = A3H
Trap	10100100 = A4H

Although the BER also provide tag numbers of 31 or greater, SNMP does not use these (see the lower portion of Figure 2-4). For SNMP tag numbers larger than 31, the Type field uses a different format. The tag number in the first octet is set to binary 11111, and subsequent octets are added to carry the tag number. Bit 8 = 1 of an octet indicates that more octets will follow; Bit 8 = 0 of an octet specifies the last octet. Bits 7 through 1 of each subsequent octet carry the unsigned binary integer of the tag number. Bit 7 of the first subsequent octet indicates the MSB of the tag number.

2.5.2.2. Length field

The Length field follows the Type field and determines the number of octets the Value field will contain. The Length field may take either the short definite or the long definite form, as shown in Figure 2-5. (Another form, called "indefinite," is not used with SNMP.) The "definite" indicates that the length of the encoding is known prior to transmission; the "indefinite" indicates otherwise.

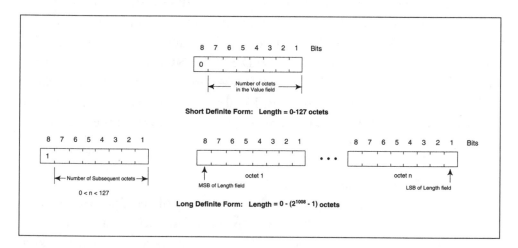

Figure 2-5. Length field encoding

The short definite form indicates a length of between 0 and 127 octets in the Contents field; the long definite form 128 or more octets in the Contents field, although it can indicate shorter lengths.

The long form uses multiple octets to represent the total length. In the long form, the first octet of the Length field has Bit 8 = 1, followed by a binary number indicating the number of octets to follow. This number must be between 1 and 126; 127 is reserved for future extensions. Bit 8 of the second octet is considered the MSB of the Length field, and the following octets make up the rest of the length. Thus, the long definite form may represent a length up to 2^{1008}-1 octets. (The 1008 is derived from the product of 126 and 8 — 126 subsequent octets times 8 bits per octet.)

2.5.2.3. Value field

The Value field contains zero or more contents octets, which convey the data values. Examples include an integer, ASCII character, or OBJECT IDENTI-FIER, such as { 1.3.6.1.2. }

2.5.3. Encoding examples

Section 2.4.2 mentioned that the Internet SMI defines a subset of the ASN.1 types. This subset includes the following universal, primitive types: INTE-GER, OCTET STRING, OBJECT IDENTIFIER, and NULL. The universal, constructor types are SEQUENCE AND SEQUENCE OF. The application, Primitive types are IpAddress, Counter, Gauge, and TimeTicks. SNMP-related applications use only these ten types. I will use this information in the case studies presented in the following chapters. For illustrations of the other types, consult ISO 8825.

2.5.3.1. INTEGER type encoding

The INTEGER type is a simple type that has values of zero, positive, or negative whole numbers. It is a Primitive type encoded with a Value field containing one or more Contents octets. The Contents octets are a two's-complement binary number equal to the integer value, and can use as many octets as necessary. For example, Boomer, my Labrador, weighs 75 pounds. The value of his weight would be encoded as: Type field = 02H, Length field = 01H, and Value field = 4BH (see Figure 2-6). Note that the value appears in quotes (Value = "75") to indicate that it represents a quantity, which can be numerical, ASCII characters, an IP address, and so on.

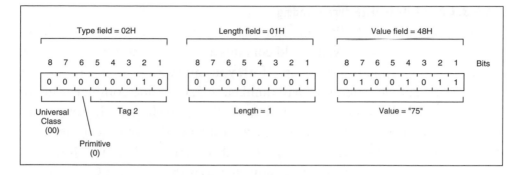

Figure 2-6. Encoding for the INTEGER type, Value = "75"

2.5.3.2. OCTET STRING type encoding

The OCTET STRING is a simple type whose distinguished values are an ordered sequence of zero, one, or more octets, each of which must be a multiple of 8 bits. Encoding for OCTET STRING values is primitive, with the Type field = 04H. The Length field and Value field depend on the encoded information.

Let's again use Boomer as an example to show the OCTET STRING type encoding. Figure 2-7 shows how I encoded the value for Boomer's initials (BBM, for Boomerang Buddy Miller). The Type field contains 04H, indicating a primitive type, OCTET STRING (tag number 4). The Length field indicates 3 octets in the Value field. The Value field encodings come from the ASCII chart.

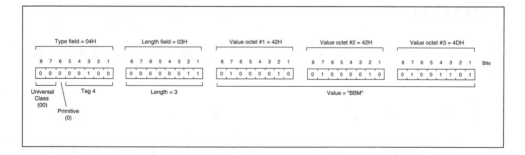

Figure 2-7. Encoding for the OCTET STRING type, Value = "BBM"

2.5.3.3. OBJECT IDENTIFIER type encoding

The OBJECT IDENTIFIER names (or identifies) items. (In SNMP, these identify managed objects.) Its Value field contains an ordered list of subidentifiers. To save encoding and transmission effort, you can take advantage of the fact that the first subidentifier is a small number, 0, 1, or 2, and combine it mathematically with the second subidentifier, which may be larger. The total number of subidentifiers is, therefore, less than the number of object identifier components in the OID value being encoded. This reduced number (one less) results from a mathematical expression that uses the first two OID components to produce another expression:

> Given X is the value of the first OID, and Y is the second:
> First subidentifier = (X * 40) + Y

The values for these subidentifiers are encoded and placed within the Value field. Bit 8 of each octet indicates whether or not that octet is the last in the series of octets required to fully describe the value. If Bit 8 = 1, at least one octet follows; Bit 8 = 0 indicates the last (or only) octet. Bits 7–1 of each octet encode subidentifiers. Using an example from the MIB-II object tree, the System group, assume that an OBJECT IDENTIFIER has a value of

> { iso org(3) dod(6) internet(1) mgmt(2) mib(1) 1 }

From the object tree (also discussed below), this is represented by

> { 1 3 6 1 2 1 1 }

Using the values of X=1 and Y=3, and the expression above for the first subidentifier value,

> (1 * 40) + 3 = 43

This results in a first subidentifier value of 43, the second subidentifier value of 6, the third subidentifier value of 1, and so on. The first value (43) needs

6 bits, or one octet, for encoding (00101011). The second value (6) needs 3 bits for encoding (110), and requires only one octet. Subsequent values also require one octet. As you can see in Figure 2-8, the encoding becomes: Type field = 06H (OBJECT IDENTIFIER, tag = 6); Length field = 06H and Value field = 2B 06 01 02 01 01 H.

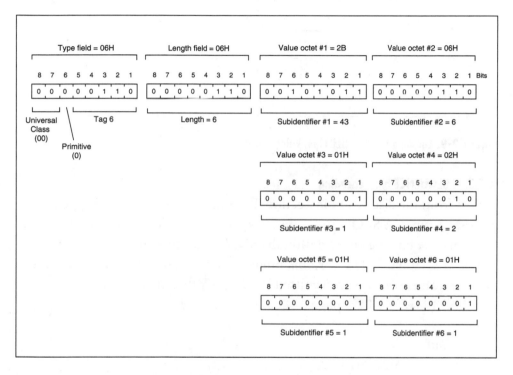

Figure 2-8. Encoding for OBJECT IDENTIFIER type, Value = { 1 3 6 1 2 1 1 }

2.5.3.4. NULL type encoding

The NULL type is a placeholder that communicates the absence of information. For example, when a Manager requests the value of a variable, it uses the NULL type as a placeholder in the position where the Agent will fill in the response.

Encoding for the NULL type is a primitive. The Type field = 05H, and the Length field = 00H. The Value field field is empty (no value octets), as shown in Figure 2-9.

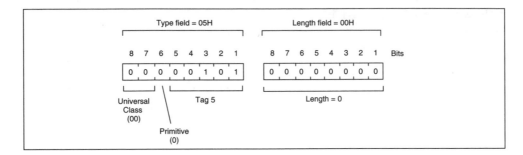

Figure 2-9. Encoding for the NULL type, Value = NULL

2.5.3.5. SEQUENCE type encoding

Recall from the discussion in Section 2.4.3 that the SEQUENCE type is a list of ASN.1 types. A SEQUENCE value is always encoded in constructed form. The variable bindings used within the SNMP messages provide a good example of SEQUENCE. The variable bindings (or VarBind) pair an object name with its value, which is transmitted inside the Value field, as shown in Figure 2-3. SNMP (RFC 1157, page 32) defines the VarBind:

```
VarBind ::=
        SEQUENCE {
            name
                    ObjectName

            value
                    ObjectSyntax
        }

VarBindList ::=
        SEQUENCE OF
            VarBind
```

As this syntax shows, the VarBind is a SEQUENCE (pairing) of a name and value, and the VarBindList is a list of names and values.

Although this is getting ahead of the sequence of our SMI, MIB, and SNMP story, I'll provide an example. Suppose you need the system description for a particular object whose name is sysDescr. To obtain the system description, the Manager transmits an SNMP GetRequest to the Agent asking for the value of object sysDescr. The Agent responds with a SNMP GetResponse message containing the value, such as "Retix Local Ethernet Bridge Model 2265M." The VarBind associates the object (sysDescr) and its value ("Retix ..."), as shown in Figure 2-10.

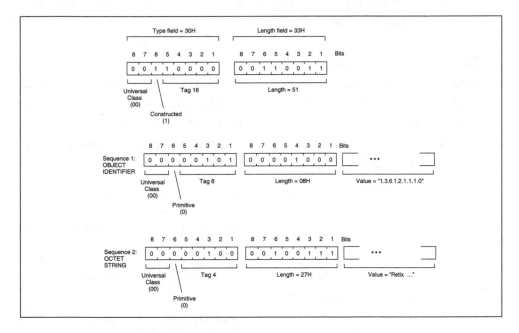

Figure 2-10. Encoding for the SEQUENCE type, a Variable Binding (VarBind)

The first Type field (30H) indicates a constructed type, with Tag = 16 (SEQUENCE). The first Length field contains 33H, indicating that 51 Value octets follow. The BER are then applied for every type in the SEQUENCE. The first sequence identifies a primitive type with Tag = 6 (OBJECT IDENTIFIER) and Length = 08H. The Value field contains the numeric representation of the sysDescr object {1.3.6.1.2.1.1.1.0}. The second sequence identifies a primitive type with Tag = 4 (OCTET STRING), and Length = 27H (39 decimal). The second Value field represents the value of the object sysDescr ("Retix Local Bridge ..."). If you've got a calculator, look at the total length of the encoding. Sequence #1 contains 10 octets (1 from the type field + 1 from the length + 8 from the value). Sequence #2 contains 41 octets (1 + 1 + 39). Sequence #1 plus Sequence #2 (10 + 41) equals the value of the first Length field (51 octets).

2.5.3.6. SEQUENCE-OF type encoding
The SEQUENCE-OF type value is encoded in Constructed form in the same way as the SEQUENCE type.

2.5.3.7. IpAddress type encoding
The discussion now moves to the application class of encodings. You can find these in Section 2.7, "The Concise SMI Definition," as tagged types. Since they are all application Class (01), primitive (P/C = 0) encodings, with tag numbers between 0 and 4, the Type fields will range from 40 to 44H (see Figures 2-11 through 2-14).

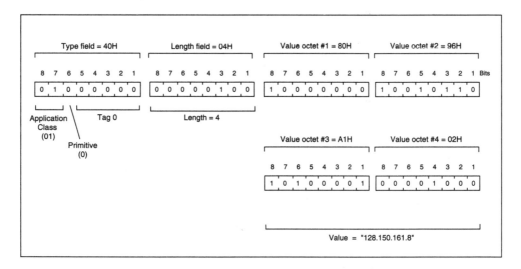

Figure 2-11. Encoding for the IpAddress type, Value = "128.150.161.8"

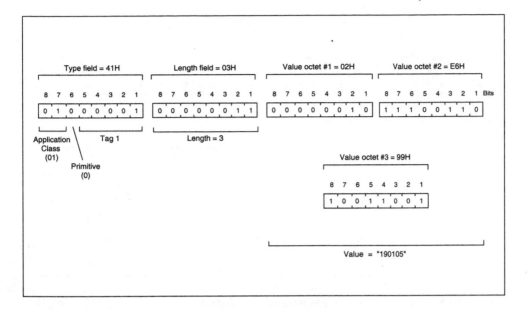

Figure 2-12. Encoding for the Counter type, Value = "190105"

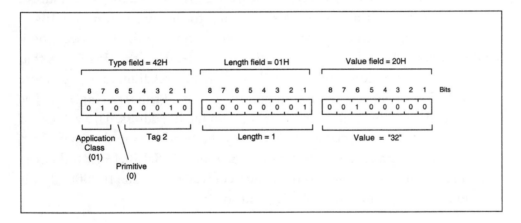

Figure 2-13. Encoding for the Gauge type, Value = "32"

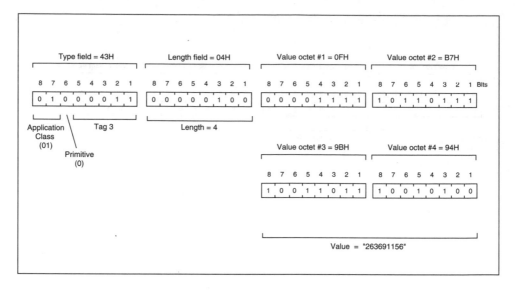

Figure 2-14. Encoding for the TimeTicks type, Value = "263691156"

The SMI defines the IpAddress type. The IpAddress carries a 32-bit IP address, which is represented in four octets. Jumping to the discussion of MIBs in Chapter 3, the IP group contains objects that relate to the IP process on a router or host. An object called IpAdEntAddr identifies the IP address that subsequent information is related to. To encode the IpAdEntAddr (see Figure 2-11), the Type field is set to 40H (application class, Primitive, Tag = 0). The Length field = 4, representing the four octets in the IP address. The Value field contains four contents octets, which convey the IP address in dotted decimal notation. For the address shown in the example [128.150.161.8], the first octet in the Value field contains the binary equivalent of 128 (10000000), the second the binary equivalent of 150, and so on.

2.5.3.8. Counter type encoding

A Counter type (also defined in the SMI) represents a non-negative integer that increases monitonically to a maximum of 4,294,967,295, and then wraps around to zero. The ICMP Group uses many counters to record message statistics. One object, icmpInMsgs, records the number of messages that the ICMP process on a router or host has received. A sample encoding (see Figure 2-12) would have a Type field = 41H, representing application class, primitive encoding, and Tag = 1. The Value (190,105) requires three octets. The Length field is, therefore, 03H, and the Value field contains 02 E6 99H, representing the 190,105 messages.

2.5.3.9. Gauge type encoding

A Gauge type (also defined in the SMI) is a non-negative integer that may increase or decrease, but latches at a maximum value of 4,294,967,295. The Gauge is not used frequently. MIB-II defines it for the ifSpeed, ifOutQLen, and tcpCurrEstab objects only. For example, Figure 2-13 assumes that the maximum output queue length of a particular interface is 32 packets. To encode this Gauge value, the Type field is set to 42H (application class, Primitive, Tag = 2). One octet encodes decimal 32, therefore, the Length field = 01H and the Value field contains 20H, the desired value of 32 decimal.

2.5.3.10. TimeTicks type encoding

The TimeTicks type (also defined in the SMI) contains a time-stamp that measures the elapsed time (in hundredths of a second) since some event. The sysUpTime object measures the time since the network management entity on a device was re-initialized. If the sysUpTime value for a particular device was 263,691,156 hundredths of a second (about 30 days), its value would be encoded as shown in Figure 2-14. The Type field would be set to 43H (application class, Primitive, Tag = 3). Four octets represent a Value equal to 263691156. Therefore, the Length field contains 04H. The four octets in the Value field contain the binary representation of the TimeTicks value.

2.5.3.11. Context-specific encodings for SNMP

The final class of encodings discussed in this chapter are the context-specific encodings, which are used within the context of SNMP. Five protocol data units (PDUs), which Chapter 4 discusses in greater detail, convey SNMP information. The PDUs are GetRequest, GetNextRequest, GetResponse, SetRequest, and Trap. These PDUs have tag numbers of 0 to 4, respectively. These encodings are all context-specific class (10) and constructed (P/C = 1). The

Type fields thus have values ranging from A0 to A4H (see Figure 2-15). The Length and Value fields depend on the information conveyed.

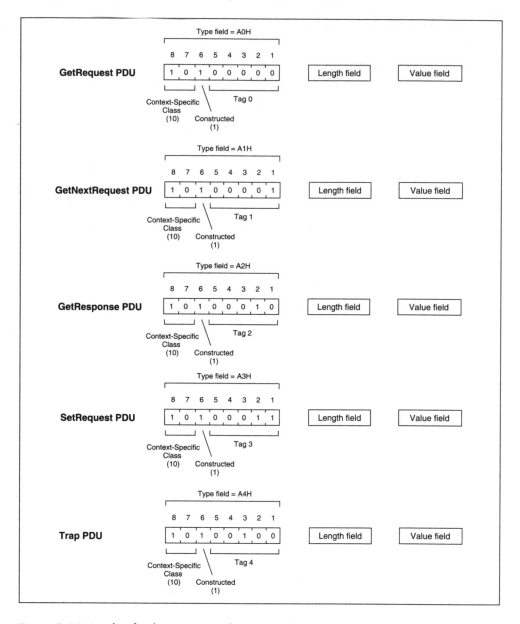

Figure 2-15. Encoding for the context-specific types used with SNMP

2.6. Object Names

Each object, whether it's a device or a characteristic of a device, must have a name by which it can be uniquely identified. That name is the *object identifier*. It is written as a sequence of integers, separated by periods. For example, the sequence {1.3.6.1.2.1.1.1.0} specifies the system description, within the system group, of the mgmt subtree.

Annexes B, C, and D of ISO 8824 define the numerical sequences, and they resemble a tree with a root and several directly attached branches, referred to as *children* (see Figure 2-16). These branches connect to other branches. You can use the structure of root, branches, sub-branches, and leaves to diagram all of the objects within a particular MIB and their relationships.

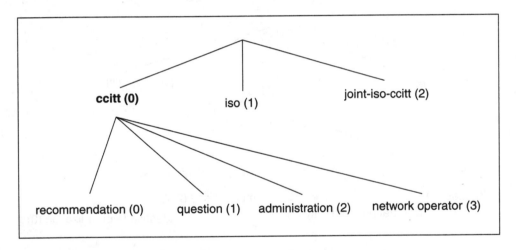

Figure 2-16. The root node and CCITT-assigned OBJECT IDENTIFIER component values

The root does not need a designation. But a specific numeric value designates the three connected branches. ISO administers the branch labeled 1, the CCITT administers the branch labeled 0, and ISO and CCITT jointly administer the third, labeled 2.

The CCITT branch has four children: recommendation (0) identifies CCITT recommendations; question (1) is used for CCITT study groups; administration (2) identifies the values of the X.121 DCCs (Data Country Codes); and network-operator (3) identifies the values of the X.121 Data Network Identification codes (DNICs).

The ISO branch (Figure 2-17) also has four children: standard (0) designates international standards; registration-authority (1) is reserved for an Addendum to ISO 8824; member-body (2) is a three-digit numeric country code that ISO 3166 assigns to each member of ISO/IEC; and identified-organizations (3) have values of an international code designator (ICD), defined in ISO 6523. The U.S. Department of Defense is assigned to one of the children under 1.3, and is designated as 6. Under this tree, the Internet community has designation 1.

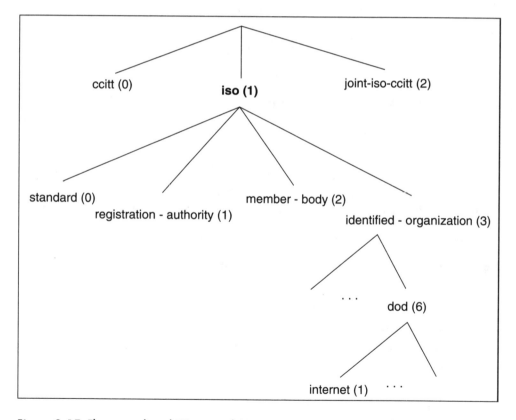

Figure 2-17. The root node and ISO assigned OBJECT IDENTIFIER component values

To identify a particular position on the tree, you list the numeric values in a string, separated by periods. For example, to identify the position of the Internet subtree, you start at the root and move down until you reach position {1.3.6.1}.

At the Internet level (Figure 2-18), you begin to see details germane to network management and SNMP. The Internet subtree has four branches:

- The directory(1) subtree, {internet 1} or {1.3.6.1.1}, is reserved for future use by the OSI directory within the Internet.

- The mgmt(2) subtree, {internet 2} or {1.3.6.1.2}, is managed by the Internet Assigned Numbers Authority, and includes the standard MIBs.

- The experimental(3) subtree, {internet 3} or {1.3.6.1.3}, is used for Internet experiments.

- The private(4) subtree, {internet 4} or {1.3.6.1.4}, allows vendors to register objects.

The Internet Assigned Numbers Authority (IANA) administers these subtrees and publishes them in the current Assigned Numbers document (currently RFC 1340). Appendix F excerpts RFC 1340 for your reference.

Chapter 3 discusses various MIBs in detail. This chapter now looks at the structure of trees applicable to the Internet Standard Network Management Framework. The Internet Standard MIB is defined by {mgmt 1} or {1.3.6.1.2.1}. Under this tree are objects defined by MIB-II (RFC 1213), such as the remote network monitoring (RMON) MIB, (RFC 1271), and others.

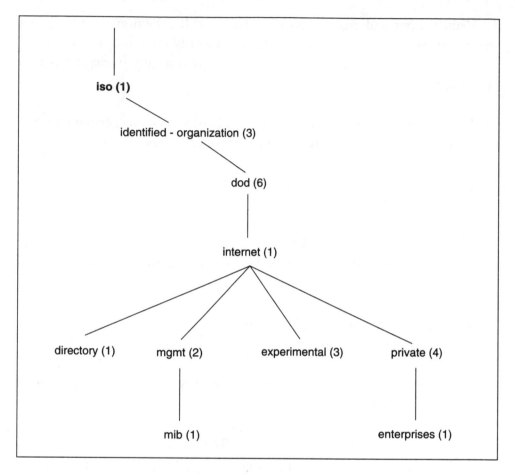

Figure 2-18. Internet assigned OBJECT IDENTIFIER component values

I now return to the example given at the beginning of this section. Now that you know the identities of the individual tree structures, I can construct the following sequence:

```
internet OBJECT IDENTIFIER ::= {iso org(3) dod(6) 1 }
mgmt OBJECT IDENTIFIER ::= { internet 2 }
mib OBJECT IDENTIFIER ::= { mgmt 1 }
system OBJECT IDENTIFIER ::= { mib 1 }
sysDescr OBJECT IDENTIFIER ::= { system 1 }
```

When the above tree structures are combined, the result becomes

sysDescr OBJECT IDENTIFIER ::= { 1.3.6.1.2.1.1.1 }

To the OID I need to add one last element—a suffix that identifies whether a particular variable occurs just once (a scalar), or whether the variable occurs multiple times (as in columnar entries).

Since sysDescr is a scalar, not columnar, object, there is only one instance of this variable. Therefore, a .0 is added to the end of the OID:

{1.3.6.1.2.1.1.1.0.}

If the object was a columnar entry, an index plus a nonzero suffix (.1, .2, an IP address, and so on) would identify the object within the table. Chapter 3 discusses tables in greater detail.

Experimental codes, with prefix {1.3.6.1.3}, have been assigned for many LAN and WAN objects and MIBs, such as ISO CLNS (Connectionless Network Service), Point to Point Protocol (PPP) objects, and the Synchronous Optical Network (SONET). As the Internet Engineering Task Force (IETF) working groups develop MIBs, they define them under a branch in the experimental tree. Once these MIBs are published and put on the standards track, they move to a branch under the Internet subtree.

Vendor-specific MIBs use private enterprise codes with prefix {1.3.6.1.4.1}. This is an area of rapid growth, since numerous vendors are developing structures to support their Internetworking devices, servers, and so on. Examples include 3Com Corporation (Santa Clara, CA) with code {1.3.6.1.4.1.43}; FTP Software Inc. (North Andover, MA) with code {1.3.6.1.4.1.121}; and US West Advanced Technologies (Denver, CO) with code {1.3.6.1.4.1.312}. Appendix F includes a complete listing of the currently assigned private enterprise codes. Readers with Internet access may find this information on host venera.isi.edu, directory mib, file snmp-vendor-contacts.

2.7. The Concise SMI Definition

Perhaps the best way to summarize this chapter is to include a module entitled RFC1155-SMI from RFC 1155, shown in Definition 2-1. This module defines all of the constructs discussed in this chapter and puts them in a form that will be useful in Chapters 3, 4, and 5. Note that a revision in RFC 1212 [2-9] makes the OBJECT-TYPE macro originally given in RFC 1155 obsolete. In the interest of timeliness, the SMI definition includes the new OBJECT-TYPE macro. Comment lines enclosed within angle brackets, <...> indicate the beginning and end of the revised section from RFC 1212.

Definition 2-1. Concise SMI definition

```
RFC1155-SMI DEFINITIONS ::= BEGIN
    EXPORTS -- EVERYTHING
    internet, directory, mgmt,
    experimental, private, enterprises,
    OBJECT-TYPE, ObjectName, ObjectSyntax,SimpleSyntax,
    ApplicationSyntax, NetworkAddress, IpAddress,
    Counter, Gauge, TimeTicks, Opaque;
    -- the path to the root (from RFC 1155)
    internet  OBJECT IDENTIFIER ::= { iso org(3) dod(6) 1 }
    directory  OBJECT IDENTIFIER ::= { internet 1 }
    mgmt  OBJECT IDENTIFIER ::= { internet 2 }
    experimental  OBJECT IDENTIFIER ::= { internet 3 }
    private      OBJECT IDENTIFIER ::= { internet 4 }
    enterprises  OBJECT IDENTIFIER ::= { private 1 }

    < definition of object types (taken from RFC 1212) >

    OBJECT-TYPE MACRO ::=
    BEGIN
        TYPE NOTATION ::=
                        -- must conform to
                        -- RFC1155's ObjectSyntax
```

```
                    "SYNTAX" type(ObjectSyntax)
                    "ACCESS" Access
                    "STATUS" Status
                    DescrPart
                    ReferPart
                    IndexPart
                    DefValPart
VALUE NOTATION ::= value (VALUE ObjectName)
Access ::= "read-only"
          | "read-write"
          | "write-only"
          | "not-accessible"
Status ::= "mandatory"
          | "optional"
          | "obsolete"
          | "deprecated"
 DescrPart ::=
      "DESCRIPTION" value (description DisplayString)
          | empty
 ReferPart ::=
      "REFERENCE" value (reference DisplayString)
          | empty
IndexPart ::=
      "INDEX" "{" IndexTypes "}"
          | empty
   IndexTypes ::=
          IndexType | IndexTypes "," IndexType
   IndexType ::=
                  -- if indexobject, use the SYNTAX
                  -- value of the correspondent
                  -- OBJECT-TYPE invocation
          value (indexobject ObjectName)
                  -- otherwise use named SMI type
                  -- must conform to IndexSyntax below
```

```
                    | type (indextype)
        DefValPart ::=
              "DEFVAL" "{" value (defvalue ObjectSyntax) "}"
                  | empty
     END
     IndexSyntax ::=
        CHOICE {
          number
             INTEGER (0..MAX),
          string
             OCTET STRING,
          object
             OBJECT IDENTIFIER,
          address
            . NetworkAddress,
          ipAddress
             IpAddress
        }
     < names of objects in the MIB (taken from RFC 1155) >
     ObjectName ::= OBJECT IDENTIFIER
     -- syntax of objects in the MIB
        ObjectSyntax ::=
            CHOICE {
                simple
                      SimpleSyntax,
     -- note that simple SEQUENCEs are not directly
     -- mentioned here to keep things simple (i.e.,
     -- prevent mis-use). However, application-wide
     -- types which are IMPLICITly encoded simple
     -- SEQUENCEs may appear in the following CHOICE
            application-wide
                      ApplicationSyntax
            }
     SimpleSyntax ::=
```

```
        CHOICE {
            number
                INTEGER,
            string
                OCTET STRING,
            object
                OBJECT IDENTIFIER,
            empty
                NULL
        }
ApplicationSyntax ::=
        CHOICE {
            address
                NetworkAddress,
            counter
                Counter,
            gauge
                Gauge,
            ticks
                TimeTicks,
            arbitrary
                Opaque
-- other application-wide types, as they are
-- defined, will be added here
        }
-- application-wide types
NetworkAddress ::=
        CHOICE {
            internet
                IpAddress
        }
IpAddress ::=
    [APPLICATION 0]         -- in network-byte order
        IMPLICIT OCTET STRING (SIZE (4))
```

```
Counter ::=
 [APPLICATION 1]
     IMPLICIT INTEGER (0..4294967295)
Gauge ::=
 [APPLICATION 2]
     IMPLICIT INTEGER (0..4294967295)
TimeTicks ::=
 [APPLICATION 3]
     IMPLICIT INTEGER (0..4294967295)
Opaque ::=
 [APPLICATION 4]        -- arbitrary ASN.1 value,
     IMPLICIT OCTET STRING  --  "double-wrapped"
END
```

This concludes the discussion of SMI. Chapter 3 will study Management Information Bases (MIBs).

2.8. References

[2-1]   Rose, M.T. and K. McCloghrie. "Structure and Identification of Management Information for TCP/IP-based Internets." RFC 1155, May 1990.

[2-2]   McCloghrie, K. and M.T. Rose, editors. "Management Information Base for Network Management of TCP/IP-based Internets: MIB-II." RFC 1213, March 1991.

[2-3]   J.D. Case, M. Fedor, M.L. Schoffstall, and C. Davin. "Simple Network Management Protocol (SNMP)." RFC 1157, May 1990.

[2-4]   International Organization for Standardization, Information Processing Systems: Open Systems Interconnection, Basic Reference Model-Part 4: Management framework, ISO 7498-4:1989.

[2-5] International Organization for Standardization, Information Technology: Open Systems Interconnection, Specification of Abstract Syntax Notation One (ASN.1), ISO/IEC 8824: 1990.

[2-6] International Organization for Standardization, Information Technology: Open Systems Interconnection, Specification of Basic Encoding Rules for Abstract Syntax Notation One (ASN.1), ISO/IEC 8825: 1990.

[2-7] Steedman, Douglas. *Abstract Syntax Notation One (ASN.1), the Tutorial and Reference.* Isleworth, Middlesex, UK: Technology Appraisals, Ltd. ISBN 1-871802-06-7, 1990.

[2-8] Motteler, Howard, and Deepinder Sidhu. "Components of OSI: Abstract Syntax Notation One (ASN.1)." *ConneXions, the Interoperability Report* (January 1992): 2–19.

[2-9] Rose, M. and K. McCloghrie. "Concise MIB Definitions." RFC 1212, March 1991.

[2-10] Gaudett, Philip. "A Tutorial on ASN.1." *NIST Technical Report* NCSL/SNA-89/12 (May 1989).

[2-11] Perkins, Dave. "How to Read and Use an SNMP MIB." *3TECH, the 3Com Technical* Journal (Spring 1991): 31–55.

3 Management Information Bases

This chapter is the second of three to discuss Internet network management standards. Chapter 2 discussed the SMI, which defines the syntax that retrieves and communicates information, the ways information is placed into logical groups, and the naming mechanisms, known as the object identifiers, that identify each managed object.

This chapter extends the discussion of naming mechanisms to include *management information bases* (MIBs), which store management information. Chapter 4 considers the protocol mechanisms, including SNMP, the User Datagram Protocol (UDP), the Internet Protocol (IP), and the Internet Control Message Protocol (ICMP), that communicate management information.

You can think of a MIB as an information warehouse. Like a warehouse with specific floors, aisles, and bins, the MIB must implement an inventory control scheme. SMI defines the scheme for the MIBs. Just as a large company can have several warehouses, there are several different types of MIBs. Some, such as Internet standards, are for public use; specific organizations have developed others for private use for their products.

Network managers must understand the concepts underlying the SMI and learn to apply them to the available MIBs.

3.1. MIBs within the Internet Object Identifier Subtree

Section 2.6 discussed the Internet network management naming structure. A tree represents the management structure, with branches and leaves representing the managed objects (Figure 3-1). This discussion focuses on the internet subtree, designated {1.3.6.1.}. In the figure, you can see four subtrees under internet: directory (1), mgmt (2), experimental (3), and private (4).

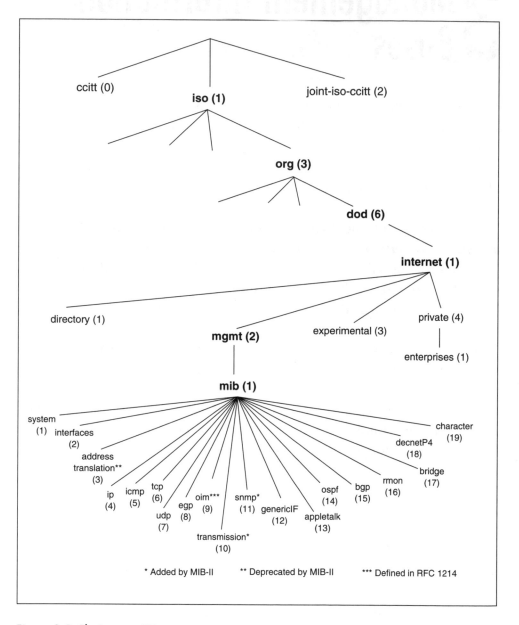

Figure 3-1. The Internet OID tree

The directory (1) subtree is reserved for future use of the OSI directory within the Internet. The mgmt (2) subtree handles Internet-approved documents, such as the Internet standard MIBs, which are MIB-I (see RFC 1156) and MIB-II (see RFC 1213). An object identifier (OID) with a prefix of {1.3.6.1.2.1} denotes managed objects within MIB-I and MIB-II.

Internet experiments use the experimental subtree (3). The Internet Assigned Numbers Authority (IANA) at the USC-Information Sciences Institute (e-mail iana@isi.edu) administers this subtree.

The private subtree (4) allows vendors to register a MIB for their equipment. The enterprise subtree, whose branches are private organizations, falls under the private subtree. The IANA assigns "enterprise codes" to branches representing private organizations and publishes them in the current assigned numbers RFC (currently RFC 1340). Enterprise OIDs begin with the prefix {1.3.6.1.4.1}. Appendix F lists the currently assigned enterprise codes.

This chapter focuses primarily on the mgmt MIBs. MIB-I was the first version of the mgmt MIBs and was defined in RFC 1156 [Reference 3-1]. MIB-II (RFC 1213) replaced the earlier version [3-2]. This chapter also discusses the *remote network monitoring* (RMON) MIBs for Ethernet and token-ring networks.

3.2. MIB Development

As noted previously, MIBs address the need for a standard network management platform by the Internet as a whole and by private enterprises. These MIBs require a consistent objective and format to realize this objective. I'll begin by discussing the history of various MIBs so you can see the basis of these developments.

3.2.1. MIB-I—RFC 1156

The first MIB, MIB-I (RFC 1156) was published in May 1990. MIB-I divided managed objects into eight groups in order to simplify OID assignment and implementation (that is, the SMI "structure"). Those groups were System,

Interfaces, Address Translation, IP, ICMP, TCP, UDP, and EGP. Elements from RFC 1212, The Concise MIB Definitions, and RFC 1213, known as MIB-II and published in March 1991, have replaced MIB-I.

3.2.2. Concise MIB Definitions—RFC 1212

With different private enterprises developing MIBs, it's necessary to develop a consistent format for MIB modules. RFC 1212, entitled "Concise MIB Definitions," addresses this issue [3-3]. Prior to the publication of RFC 1212, there were two ways to define objects, a textual definition and the ASN.1 OBJECT-TYPE macro, which is discussed in Section 2.3.5. RFC 1212 embedded the textual definition within the OBJECT-TYPE macro, reducing the amount of documentation. The Concise SMI Definition includes this macro (review Section 2.7).

3.2.3. Elements of the OBJECT-TYPE macro

Since the OBJECT-TYPE macro seems cryptic to most people, a few words of explanation are in order. Each object has a number of attributes: SYNTAX, ACCESS, STATUS, DESCRIPTION, REFERENCE, INDEX, and DEFVAL. (Dave Perkins' excellent paper "How to Read and Use an SNMP MIB" [3-4] provides all the details.)

SYNTAX defines the object's data structure. Simple data types such as INTEGER, OCTET STRING, or NULL are examples of these data structures. SYNTAX also defines special cases of the simple objects, including an enumerated integer that defines an integer value, and a DisplayString restricted to printable ASCII characters. Table objects use the SEQUENCE OF syntax.

ACCESS defines the minimum level of access to (or support of) an object. ACCESS may have values of read-only, read-write, not-accessible, or write-only. SNMP does not permit the write-only value. Table or row objects define ACCESS to be not-accessible.

STATUS defines the implementation support for the object, which may be mandatory, optional, deprecated (discouraged), or obsolete. When STATUS defines a level of support for a particular group, that level applies to all objects within the group. Objects that have been replaced by backwards-compatible objects are "deprecated." Objects that are no longer supported are "obsolete."

DESCRIPTION, which is not always present, provides a textual definition of an object type. REFERENCE, also not necessarily present, is a textual cross-reference to an object defined by another MIB module.

INDEX works only with row objects. It indexes the order in which objects appear in a row, that is, the column order.

Agents use DEFVAL, also optional, to populate values of columnar objects. For example, when an SNMP agent creates a new row, the DEFVAL clause assigns a default value to the objects within the row. For example, an OCTET STRING object may have a DEFVAL clause of 'FFFFFFFFFFFF'H.

3.2.4. Defining table structures in MIBs

To put all of the information discussed in the previous sections in perspective, Definition 3-1 (taken from RFC 1213) dissects the elements of a table. The italicized text after each section are my explanations. Double hyphens (--) indicate a comment line within the table structure. The comment defines the purpose of the table.

Definition 3-1. Defining the UDP Listener table from RFC 1213

```
-- the UDP Listener table
-- The UDP listener table contains information about this
-- entity's UDP end-points on which a local application is
-- currently accepting datagrams.

udpTable OBJECT-TYPE
    SYNTAX  SEQUENCE OF UdpEntry
    ACCESS  not-accessible
    STATUS  mandatory
```

DESCRIPTION
"A table containing UDP listener information."
::= { udp 5 }

The object name (or table name) udpTable identifies a table object. Note that this name begins with a lowercase letter. The SYNTAX defines a SEQUENCE OF UdpEntry. This refers to a type definition (listed below) that defines the objects that make up each row of the table.

udpEntry OBJECT-TYPE
SYNTAX   UdpEntry
ACCESS   not-accessible
STATUS   mandatory
DESCRIPTION
"Information about a particular current UDP listener."
INDEX   { udpLocalAddress, udpLocalPort }
::= { udpTable 1 }

The object name (or row name) udpEntry defines each row of the table. The INDEX clause specifies instances for columnar objects in the table. The instance values determine the order in which the objects are retrieved.

UdpEntry ::=
SEQUENCE {
udpLocalAddress IpAddress,
udpLocalPort INTEGER (0..65535)
}

The type definition UdpEntry identifies the objects that make up the row. Note that the type definition, often called a sequence name, is the same as the row name except that it begins with an uppercase letter. Each row has two columns, the udpLocalAddress (an IpAddress type) and the udpLocalPort (an INTEGER type).

udpLocalAddress OBJECT-TYPE
SYNTAX   IpAddress
ACCESS   read-only
STATUS   mandatory

DESCRIPTION
"The local IP address for this UDP listener. A UDP listener willing to accept datagrams for any IP interface associated with the node, uses the value 0.0.0.0."
::= { udpEntry 1 }

The notation { udpEntry 1 } indicates the first column in the table. The SYNTAX is a defined type, IpAddress. The description provides the address {0.0.0.0}.

udpLocalPort OBJECT-TYPE
SYNTAX   INTEGER (0..65535)
ACCESS   read-only
STATUS   mandatory
DESCRIPTION
"The local port number for this UDP listener."
::= { udpEntry 2 }

The notation { udpEntry 2 } indicates the second column in the table. The SYNTAX is an INTEGER type, with values ranging from 0 to 65,535.

An example of this table would be:

Local Address	Local Port
0.0.0.0	69 (TFTP)
0.0.0.0	161 (SNMP)
0.0.0.0	520 (Router)

In this example, the table contains three rows and two columns. All local addresses are [0.0.0.0], which indicates that the table is willing to accept IP datagrams from any address on this port.

Definition 3-2 is a second example of a table, the Ethernet Statistics table, which comes from the RMON MIB, RFC 1271.

Definition 3-2. The Ethernet Statistics table from RFC 1271

```
-- The Statistics Group
--
-- Implementation of the Statistics group is optional.
--
-- The Statistics group contains statistics that the probe for each
-- monitored interface on this device has measured. These
-- statistics take the form of free running counters that
-- start from zero at the creation of a valid entry.
--
-- This group currently has statistics defined only for
-- Ethernet interfaces. Each etherStatsEntry contains
-- statistics for one Ethernet interface. The probe must
-- create one etherStats entry for each monitored Ethernet
-- interface on the device.
        etherStatsTable OBJECT-TYPE
            SYNTAX   SEQUENCE OF EtherStatsEntry
            ACCESS   not-accessible
            STATUS   mandatory
            DESCRIPTION
                    "A list of Ethernet statistics entries."
            ::= { statistics 1 }
```

The object name (or table name) etherStatsTable begins with a lowercase letter, indicating a Value (see Section 2.3.4). The associated syntax definition is a sequence of the EtherStatsEntry, which begins with an uppercase letter to indicate a Type. This object is nonaccessible because it is a table. The status is mandatory, meaning all implementations must support this object. A description of the object is "A list of Ethernet statistics entries." The { statistics 1 } designation indicates that this table is the first subtree under the statistics group.

```
        etherStatsEntry OBJECT-TYPE
            SYNTAX   EtherStatsEntry
            ACCESS   not-accessible
            STATUS   mandatory
```

DESCRIPTION
"A collection of statistics kept for a particular Ethernet interface."
INDEX { etherStatsIndex }
::= { etherStatsTable 1 }

The object value (etherStatsEntry) ends with "Entry." This identifies a table row object. The index clause specifies the columns within each row that form the table. This object is the first object under the etherStatsTable subtree.

```
EtherStatsEntry ::= SEQUENCE {
etherStatsIndex                         INTEGER (1..65535),
etherStatsDataSource                    OBJECT IDENTIFIER,
etherStatsDropEvents                    Counter,
etherStatsOctets                        Counter,
etherStatsPkts                          Counter,
etherStatsBroadcastPkts                 Counter,
etherStatsMulticastPkts                 Counter,
etherStatsCRCAlignErrors                Counter,
etherStatsUndersizePkts                 Counter,
etherStatsOversizePkts                  Counter,
etherStatsFragments                     Counter,
etherStatsJabbers                       Counter,
etherStatsCollisions                    Counter,
etherStatsPkts64Octets                  Counter,
etherStatsPkts65to127Octets             Counter,
etherStatsPkts128to255Octets            Counter,
etherStatsPkts256to511Octets            Counter,
etherStatsPkts512to1023Octets           Counter,
etherStatsPkts1024to1518Octets          Counter,
etherStatsOwner                         OwnerString,
etherStatsStatus                        INTEGER
}
```

The syntax of the etherStatsTable is a sequence of EtherStatsEntry. The sequence contains 21 objects that will make up the columns of each row.

etherStatsIndex OBJECT-TYPE

```
SYNTAX  INTEGER (1..65535)
ACCESS   read-only
STATUS   mandatory
DESCRIPTION
          "The value of this object uniquely identifies
          this etherStats entry."
::= { etherStatsEntry 1 }
```

The etherStatsIndex object may take on a value between 1 and 65545. This index determines how the various objects will be retrieved.

3.3. MIB I and MIB II Groups

Managed objects are arranged into groups for two reasons. First, a logical grouping facilitates the use of the object identifiers and tree structure discussed in Section 3.1. Second, it makes the SNMP agent design more straightforward because the implementation of a group implies the implementation of all objects within the group. Thus, both the software developer and the end user can clearly understand a statement of support for, say, the TCP Group.

The next sections discuss the Internet standard MIB-I (RFC 1156) and MIB-II (RFC 1213) managed objects. MIB-I contained 114 objects. MIB-II, which is backward-compatible with MIB-I, contains these 114 objects, plus 57 more, for a total of 171 objects. Chris VandenBurg's article [3-5] discusses the MIB-II enhancements. Appendix G details the various objects.

3.3.1. The System group

The System group provides a textual description of the entity in printable ASCII characters. This description includes a system description, OID, the length of time since the reinitialization of its network management entity, and other administrative details. Implementation of the System group is mandatory. The OID tree for the System group is designated {1.3.6.1.2.1.1}, as shown in Figure 3-2.

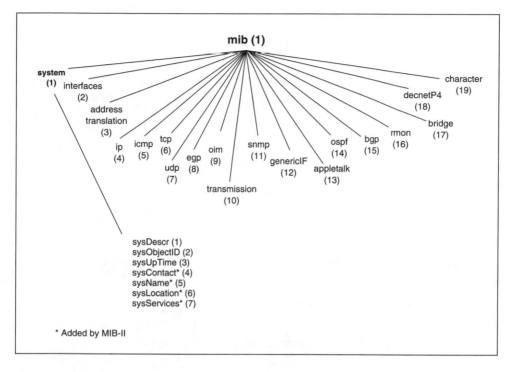

Figure 3-2. The System group

3.3.2. The Interfaces group

The Interfaces group, {1.3.6.1.2.1.2}, provides information about the hardware interfaces on a managed device, as shown in Figure 3-3. This information is presented in a table. The first object (ifNumber) indicates the number of interfaces on the device. For each interface, a row entry is made into the table, with 22 column entries per row. The column entries provide information about the interfaces, such as the interface speed, physical (hardware) address, current operational state, and packet statistics.

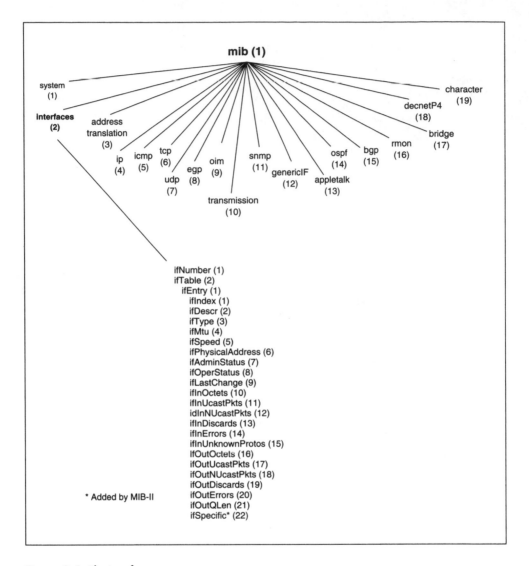

Figure 3-3. The Interfaces group

3.3.3. The Address Translation group

MIB-I included the Address Translation group, shown in Figure 3-4, but it was deprecated in MIB-II. The "deprecated" status means that MIB-II includes the Address Translation group for compatibility with MIB-I, but will probably exclude it from future MIB releases. The Address Translation group provided a table that translated between IP addresses and physical (hardware) addresses. In MIB-II and future releases, each protocol group will contain its own translation tables. The Address Translation group is designated {1.3.6.1.2.1.3}. It contains one table with three columns per row.

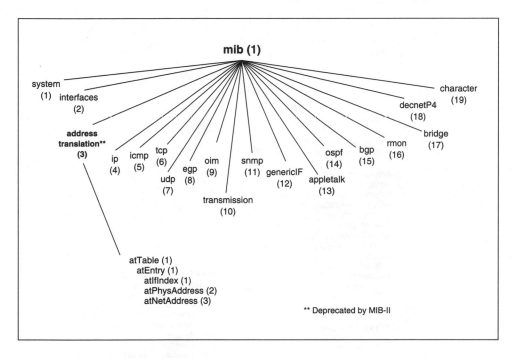

Figure 3-4. The Address Translation group

3.3.4. The IP group

The Internet Protocol (IP) group, shown in Figure 3-5, is mandatory for all managed nodes and provides information on host and router use of the IP. This group includes a number of scalar objects that provide IP-related datagram statistics and the following three tables: an address table (ipAddrTable); an IP to physical address translation table (ipNetToMediaTable); and an IP forwarding table (ipForwardTable). Note that RFC 1354 defined the ipForwardTable, which replaces and obsoletes the ipRoutingTable in MIB-II. The IP subtree is designated {1.3.6.1.2.1.4}.

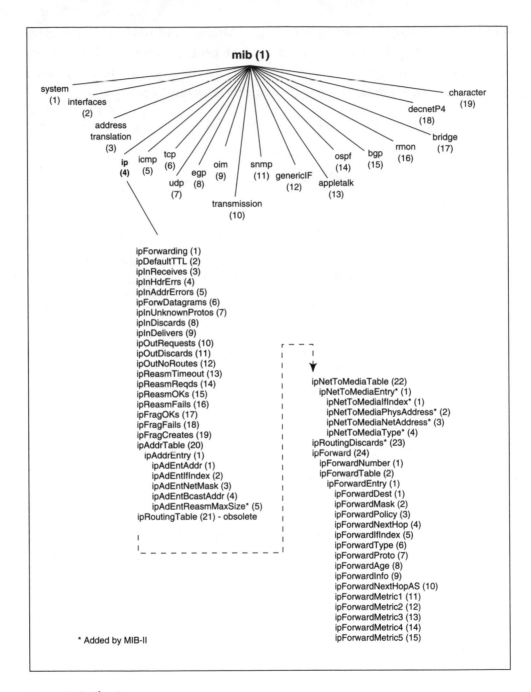

Figure 3-5. The IP group

3.3.5 The ICMP group

The Internet Control Message Protocol (ICMP) group, shown in Figure 3-6, is a mandatory component of IP, and is defined in RFC 792. The ICMP group provides intra-network control messages and represents various ICMP operations within the managed entity. The ICMP group contains 26 scalar objects that maintain statistics for various ICMP messages, such as the number of ICMP Echo Request messages received or ICMP Redirect messages sent. This group is designated {1.3.6.1.2.1.5} on the OID tree.

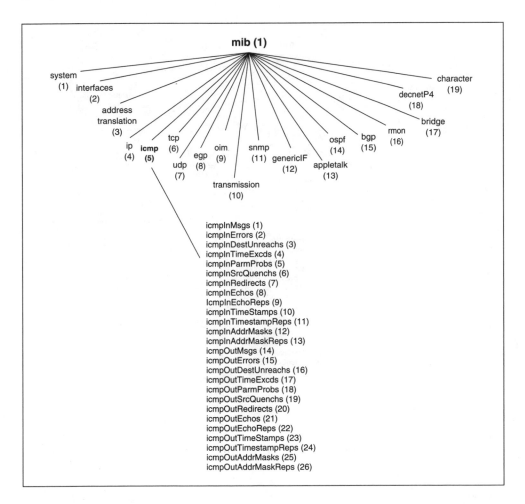

Figure 3-6. The ICMP group

3.3.6. The TCP group

The Transmission Control Protocol (TCP) group, shown in Figure 3-7, is mandatory and provides information regarding TCP operation and connections. This group contains 14 scalar objects and one table. The scalar objects record various TCP parameters and statistics, such as the number of TCP connections that the device supports, or the total number of TCP segments transmitted. The table, tcpConnTable, contains information concerning a particular TCP connection. The OID for this group is {1.3.6.1.2.1.6}.

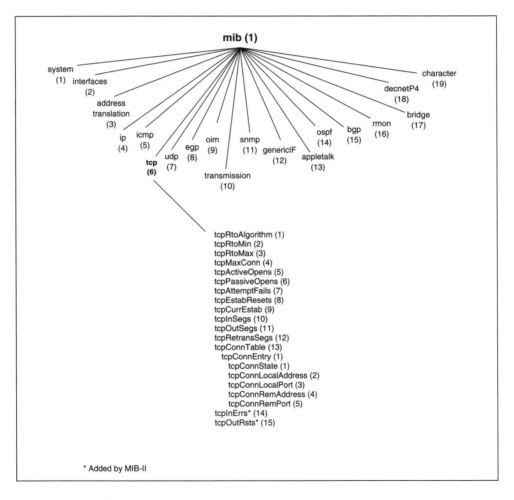

Figure 3-7. The TCP group

3.3.7. The UDP group

The User Datagram Protocol (UDP) group, shown in Figure 3-8, is mandatory and provides information regarding UDP operation. Because UDP is connectionless, this group is much smaller than the connection-oriented TCP group. It does not have to compile information on connection attempts, establishment, reset, and so on. The UDP group contains four scalars and one table. The scalar objects maintain UDP-related datagram statistics, such as the number of datagrams sent from this entity. The table, udpTable, contains address and port information. The OID for this group is {1.3.6.1.2.1.7}.

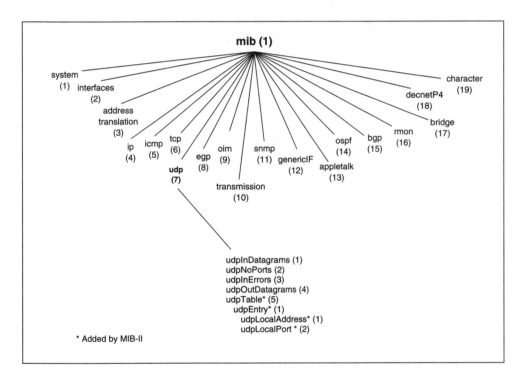

Figure 3-8. The UDP group

3.3.8. The EGP group

The Exterior Gateway Protocol (EGP) group, shown in Figure 3-9, is mandatory for all systems that implement the EGP. The EGP communicates between autonomous (self-contained) systems, and RFC 904 describes it in detail. The

EGP group includes 5 scalar objects and one table. The scalars maintain EGP-related message statistics. The table, egpNeighTable, contains EGP neighbor information. The OID for this group is {1.3.6.1.2.1.8}.

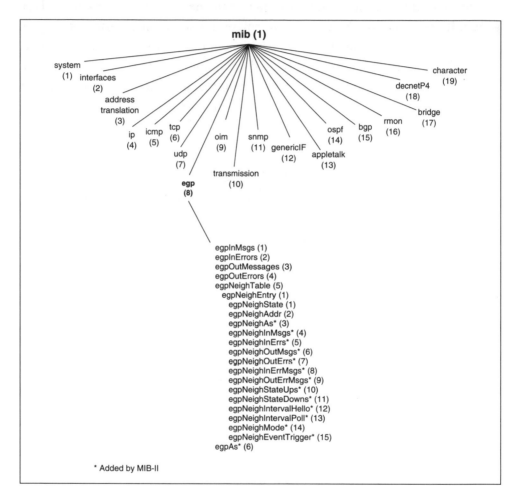

Figure 3-9. The EGP group

3.3.9. The CMOT (OIM) group

At one time, during the development of the Internet Network Management Framework, there was an effort to use SNMP as an interim step in the push for a network management standard, and to make the Common Management

Information Protocol (CMIP) over TCP/IP (CMOT) the long-term, OSI-compliant solution. As a result, the CMOT group was placed within MIB-II. Experience has shown, however, that SNMP is not an interim solution, and that the OSI-related network management protocol requires unique MIBs. Therefore, it's unlikely that you'll encounter the OIM group within any commercially available SNMP managers or agents.

Nonetheless, the CMOT group was given a placeholder of {1.3.6.1.2.1.9 } in MIB-II (review Figure 3-1). RFC 1214 details that subtree, which specifies the OSI Internet Management (OIM) MIB [3-6]. At this time, RFC 1214 is classified as a "historic" protocol.

3.3.10. The Transmission group

The Transmission group, shown in Figure 3-10, and designated {1.3.6.1.2.1.10}, contains objects that relate to the transmission of the data. RFC 1213 defines none of these objects explicitly. However, the document does say that these transmission objects will reside in the experimental subtree {1.3.6.1.3} until they are "proven."

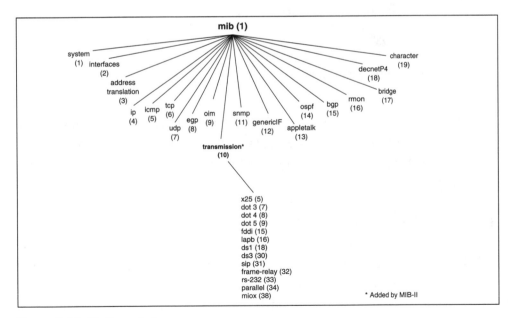

Figure 3-10. The Transmission group

The "Assigned Numbers" document (currently RFC 1340 [3-7]) lists the following objects under the Transmission group:

- X25 – X.25 Packet layer objects

- IEEE802.3 – CSMA/CD-like objects

- IEEE802.4 – Token Bus-like objects

- IEEE802.5 – Token Ring-like objects

- FDDI – FDDI objects

- LAPB – X.25 LAPB objects

- DS1/E1 – DS1 Interface objects

- DS3 – DS3 Interface objects

- SIP – SMDS Interface objects

- FRAME-RELAY – Frame Relay objects

- RS-232 – RS-232 objects

- Parallel – Parallel printer objects

RFC 1340 also lists RFC references that provide details on these transmission types. Three other object groups, x25, lapb, and miox are defined for the X.25 protocol. See RFCs 1382, 1381, and 1461 respectively, and Section 3.6 for further information.

3.3.11. The SNMP group

Since this book is about SNMP, you should be especially interested in the SNMP group, which provides information about SNMP objects (see Figure 3-11). There are a total of 30 scalar objects in this group, including SNMP message statistics, the number of MIB objects retrieved, and the number of SNMP traps sent. This group is designated {1.3.6.1.2.1.11}.

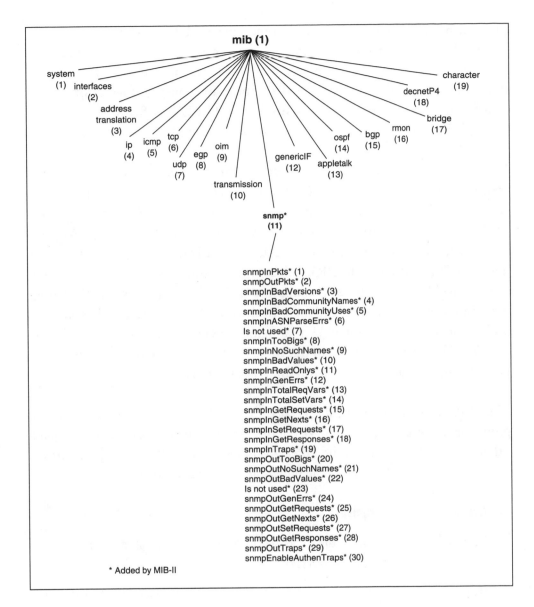

Figure 3-11. The SNMP group

3.4. The Ethernet RMON MIB

As networks have become increasingly distributed, geographically and logically, network management has become more challenging. One solution is to place remote management devices, sometimes called *probes,* on remote segments. The probes act as the eyes and ears of the network management system, providing managers with statistical information. The remote network monitoring (RMON) MIB standardizes the management information sent to and from these probes; it is presented in RFC 1271 [3-8]. References 3–9 through 3–12 discuss various applications of the RMON architecture.

Many types of hardware for distributed internetworks, such as bridges and routers from companies such as Hewlett-Packard, Novell, and Spider Systems, contain SNMP agents that support the RMON MIB. Many protocol analyzers—from companies such as Hewlett-Packard (Palo Alto, CA), Intel (Phoenix, AZ), Novell (San Jose, CA), Optical Data Systems (Richardson, TX), ProTools (Beaverton, OR), Telecommunication Techniques Corp. (Germantown, MD), and Tekelec (Calabasas, CA)—also support RMON MIB for distributed management. Analyzers capture LAN traffic, compile statistics, and report the information back to a management console. My article "Scoping Out Analyzer Purchases" in the August 31, 1992 issue of *Network World* [3-13] offers additional details on analyzer support.

The RMON MIB is assigned OID {1.3.6.1.2.1.16} and contains 9 groups. All of these groups are optional (not mandatory), but the implementation of some groups requires other groups. For example, the Filter group requires the Packet Capture group. The following is a summary of the nine Ethernet groups shown in Figure 3-12:

Group	Description
Statistics	Probe-measured statistics, such as the number and sizes of packets, broadcasts, collisions, and so on.
History	Records periodic statistical samples over time that you can use to analyze trends.
Alarms	Compares statistical samples with preset thresholds, generating alarms when a particular threshold is crossed.
Host	Maintains statistics of the hosts on the network, including the MAC addresses of the active hosts.

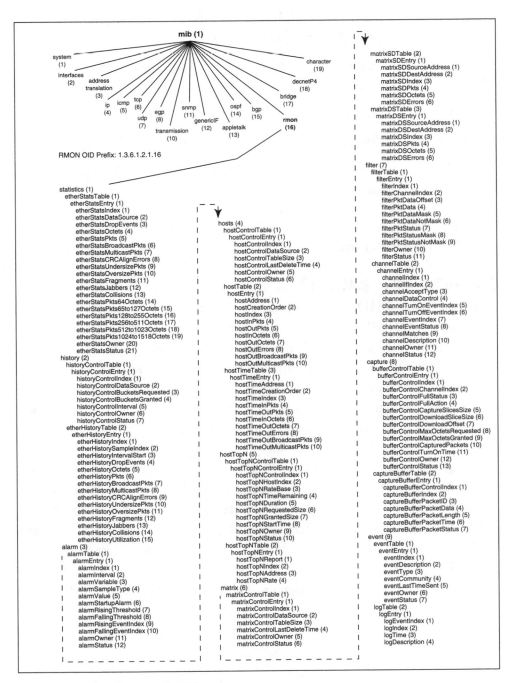

Figure 3-12. The Ethernet RMON MIB

HostTopN	Provides reports sorted by host table statistics, indicating which hosts are at the top of the list in a particular category.
Matrix	Stores statistics in a traffic matrix that tracks conversations between pairs of hosts.
Filter	Allows packets to be matched according to a filter equation.
Capture	Allows packets to be captured after they pass through a logical channel.
Event	Controls the generation and notification of events, which may include SNMP trap messages.

The current standard, RFC 1271, addresses only Ethernet network monitoring. The next section will discuss the draft for the token-ring extensions.

3.5. The Token Ring RMON MIB

The token ring RMON MIB is under development as an extension to the Ethernet RMON MIB discussed in the previous section. Because of the popularity of token-ring networks, this MIB has received a great deal of attention [3-14]. Recall that the Ethernet RMON MIB defines nine groups, Statistics through Events. The token-ring RMON MIB extends two of these groups, Statistics and History, and adds one unique group. This new group is called tokenRing, with object identifier { rmon 10 }.

The statistics extensions allow an RMON-compatible device to collect token-ring MAC-Layer errors and promiscuous errors. The MAC-Layer errors, such as token errors and frame-copied errors, are specific to the token-ring protocol; the promiscuous errors, such as counting number of broadcast packages or data packets between 512 and 1023 octets in length, are more general. Similarly, the history information (discussed in Appendix G) is divided into MAC-Layer and promiscuous details. The token-ring group records token-ring specific statistics, such as source routing information. Figure 3-13 illustrates these token-ring additions; it also shows the major Ethernet groups for clarification.

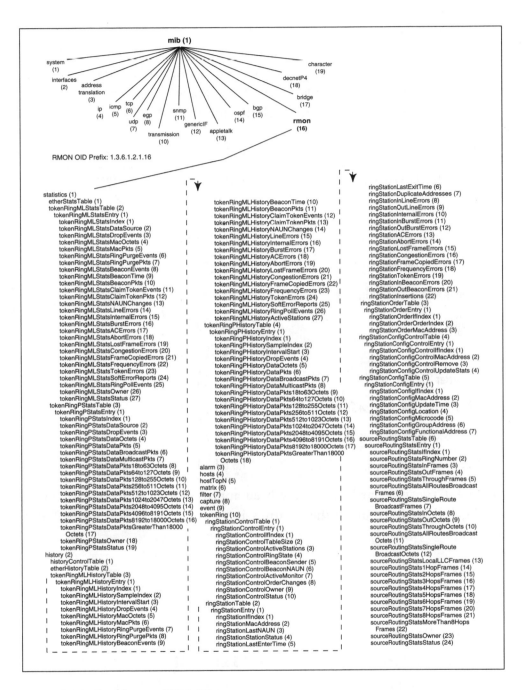

Figure 3-13. The token-ring RMON MIB

3.6. Other MIBs

The growing need for network management in general, along with SNMP's popularity, has lead to the definition of a number of MIBs that support specific network architectures or platforms. The following table lists the currently approved Internet-standard MIBs included under the MIB-II subtree.

MIB	OID	RFC
Generic Interface Extensions	1.3.6.1.2.1.12	1229
Appletalk Protocols	1.3.6.1.2.1.13	1243
Open Shortest Path First (OSPF)	1.3.6.1.2.1.14	1252
Border Gateway Protocol (BGP)	1.3.6.1.2.1.15	1269
Remote Monitoring (RMON)	1.3.6.1.2.1.16	1271
Bridges	1.3.6.1.2.1.17	1286
DECnet Phase 4	1.3.6.1.2.1.18	1289
Character Streams	1.3.6.1.2.1.19	1316
SNMP Parties *(Historic, see SNMPv2)*	1.3.6.1.2.1.20	1353
SNMP Secrets *(Historic, see SNMPv2)*	1.3.6.1.2.1.21	1353
IEEE 802.3 Repeaters	1.3.6.1.2.1.22	1368

Other Internet-standard MIBs have been approved for specific transmission media, and are listed under the transmission subtree, {1.3.6.1.2.1.10}. These include:

MIB	OID	RFC
X.25 Packet Layer objects	1.3.6.1.2.1.10.5	1382
CSMA/CD-like objects	1.3.6.1.2.1.10.7	1284
Token Bus-like objects	1.3.6.1.2.1.10.8	1230
Token Ring-like objects	1.3.6.1.2.1.10.9	1231

FDDI objects	1.3.6.1.2.1.10.15	1285
X.25 LAPB objects	1.3.6.1.2.1.10.16	1381
DS1/E1 Interface objects	1.3.6.1.2.1.10.18	1406
DS3 Interface objects	1.3.6.1.2.1.10.30	1407
SMDS Interface objects	1.3.6.1.2.1.10.31	1304
Frame Relay objects	1.3.6.1.2.1.10.32	1315
RS-232 objects	1.3.6.1.2.1.10.33	1317
Parallel Printer objects	1.3.6.1.2.1.10.34	1318
Multiprotocol Interconnect over X.25 (miox)	1.3.6.1.2.1.10.38	1461

For more up-to-date information, see the network management section of the "Assigned Numbers" document (currently RFC 1340).

3.7. Private MIBs

Many vendors have developed private MIBs that support hubs, terminal servers, and other networking systems. You can find these MIBs under the enterprises subtree, {1.3.6.1.4.1.A}. The A indicates a private enterprise code, defined in the "Assigned Numbers" RFC (currently RFC 1340) in the network management section. (Appendix F lists these enterprise numbers.)

Information on these private MIBs is available via anonymous FTP from host venera.isi.edu, directory /mib. One interesting file is snmp-vendors-contacts, which lists the currently assigned private enterprise codes. Many vendors also place their private MIBs in this subdirectory. Because of these private MIBs are vendor-specific, interoperability is not always possible. "MIB Extensions Widen SNMP's Reach" in the February 17, 1992 issue of *Communications Week* discusses some of these interoperability challenges [3-15], and a vendor-specific RMON implementation is the focus of "Continuous Monitoring of Remote Networks: The RMON MIB," in the April 1993 issue of *Hewlett-Packard Journal* [3-16].

3.8. Accessing a MIB

This section gives an example of an SNMP management console retrieving values for MIB objects from a remote SNMP agent. In this case, the manager is a Sun Microsystems' SunNet Manager, and the agent is located in a Proteon's p4100+ router. Both devices connect to an Ethernet backbone. A Network General Corp. Sniffer protocol analyzer captured the data shown in Trace 3.8.

Readers unfamiliar with the Sniffer Analyzer will find a short explanation of the functions of a protocol analyzer helpful. A protocol analyzer captures, then decodes, frames of data as they are transmitted on the LAN or WAN. These frames are numbered sequentially and stored in the same order. The analyzer can display these frames several ways; it can show all of the protocol layers, or just one. The example in this section shows only the highest layer, SNMP. The analyzer also lets you choose the amount of detail included. The minimum detail is a single summary line, and the maximum is the hexadecimal representation of the bits received on the wire. This example uses an English-language detail of the SNMP constructs. A second detail shows the ASN.1 constructs and the hexadecimal decode of the actual data. With that background, I'll summarize what we have been studying.

This exchange between the manager and the agent (see Trace 3.8a) involves two frames of information. Frame 109 contains an SNMP GetRequest PDU (protocol data unit, the core of the SNMP message) and Frame 110 contains a GetResponse PDU. (Chapter 4 examines the PDUs in depth.)

The manager sends the GetRequest to the agent asking for the values of the objects within the system subtree, OID {1.3.6.1.2.1.1}. The PDU requests information about all seven of the objects: sysDescr, sysObjectID, sysUpTime, sysContact, SysName, sysLocation, and sysServices. On the trace, you can see two coding elements for each of these objects. First, the manager requests the sysUpTime object to determine whether the agent within the router has restarted (warm or cold boot). Second, the manager asks for the values of each individual object in order (review Figure 3-2). This trace also illustrates the use of the SEQUENCE type encoding of VarBinds discussed in Section 2.5.3.5. Each object is encoded with an OBJECT IDENTIFIER type, for example {1.3.6.1.2.1.1.2.0}. The Object Value field is encoded with a NULL type because the manager does not know this information.

Frame 110 gives the agent's GetResponse. The response returns each object and its associated value in the order that Frame 109 requested. The sysDescr provides a textual description of the device (Portable I80386 C Gateway ...). The sysObjectID has a value of {1.3.6.1.4.1.1.1.1.41}. From the prefix {1.3.6.1.4.1}, you know that this is a private enterprise subtree. The next digit (.1) is the enterprise code for Proteon, Inc. (see RFC 1340, page 39, or Appendix F).

The sysUpTime object has a value of 263,621,778 hundredths of a second, which translates to roughly 30 days because the router's network management system was restarted. Two of the objects, sysContact { system 4 } and sysLocation { system 6 } appear not to have a value. In reality, they have a value of a zero-length string, but the network manager entered no values for those objects in the router's configuration file. The sysName is the domain name of the node (boulder.org). Finally, the sysServices { system 7 } is a calculated sum that indicates the services this node performs. In this case, the value is 72, indicating a host offering application services (see RFC 1213, page 15).

See Trace 3.8b for a quick review of the ASN.1-encoding discussed in Chapter 2. This data shows the details of Frame 110, but with the Sniffer's ASN.1 decoding option activated. You can trace each ASN.1 element, identifying the Type-Length-Value encodings as well as the hexidecimal display of those values. As a reference point, the first SNMP encoding (SEQUENCE [of], Length=235) appears in bold type with the characters 30 81 EB. Reviewing Chapter 2, we know that the Type field = 30H (the SEQUENCE OF type, see Figure 2-10). The Length field is the Long Definite form, with one subsequent octet (see Figure 2-5) having a value of 81 EBH. (Hexadecimal values of X are dummy characters to maintain the confidentiality of the trace.)

Trace 3.8a. Browsing the system subtree (SNMP protocol decode)

```
Sniffer Network Analyzer data 10-Nov-92 at 10:42:04 file ASAN_SYS.ENC Pg 1
---------------------------------------Frame 109 --------------------------------------
SNMP: ----- Simple Network Management Protocol -----
SNMP:
SNMP: Version = 0
SNMP: Community = boulder
SNMP: Command = Get request
SNMP: Request ID = 0
SNMP: Error status = 0 (No error)
SNMP: Error index = 0
SNMP:
SNMP: Object = {1.3.6.1.2.1.1.3.0} (sysUpTime.0)
SNMP: Value = NULL
SNMP:
SNMP: Object = {1.3.6.1.2.1.1.1.0} (sysDescr.0)
SNMP: Value = NULL
SNMP:
SNMP: Object = {1.3.6.1.2.1.1.2.0} (sysObjectID.0)
SNMP: Value = NULL
SNMP:
SNMP: Object = {1.3.6.1.2.1.1.3.0} (sysUpTime.0)
SNMP: Value = NULL
SNMP:
SNMP: Object = {1.3.6.1.2.1.1.4.0} (system.4.0)
SNMP: Value = NULL
SNMP:
SNMP: Object = {1.3.6.1.2.1.1.5.0} (system.5.0)
SNMP: Value = NULL
SNMP:
SNMP: Object = {1.3.6.1.2.1.1.6.0} (system 6.0)
SNMP: Value = NULL
SNMP:
```

SNMP: Object = {1.3.6.1.2.1.1.7.0} (system 7.0)
SNMP: Value = NULL
SNMP:

---Frame 110 -------------------------------------

SNMP: ---- Simple Network Management Protocol ----
SNMP:
SNMP: Version = 0
SNMP: Community = boulder
SNMP: Command = Get response
SNMP: Request ID = 0
SNMP: Error status = 0 (No error)
SNMP: Error index = 0
SNMP:
SNMP: Object = {1.3.6.1.2.1.1.3.0] (sysUpTime.0)
SNMP: Value = 263621778 hundredths of a second
SNMP:
SNMP: Object = {1.3.6.1.2.1.1.1.0} (sysDescr.0)
SNMP: Value = Portable I80386 C Gateway BOULDER.ORG S/N XXX V12.0
SNMP:
SNMP: Object = {1.3.6.1.2.1.1.2.0} (sysObjectID.0)
SNMP: Value = {1.3.6.1.4.1.1.1.1.41}
SNMP:
SNMP: Object = {1.3.6.1.2.1.1.3.0} (sysUpTime.0)
SNMP: Value = 263621778 hundredths of a second
SNMP:
SNMP: Object = {1.3.6.1.2.1.1.4.0} (system.4.0)
SNMP: Value =
SNMP:
SNMP: Object = {1.3.6.1.2.1.1.5.0} (system.5.0)
SNMP: Value = BOULDER.ORG
SNMP:
SNMP: Object = {1.3.6.1.2.1.1.6.0} (system.6.0)
SNMP: Value =
SNMP:

SNMP: Object = {1.3.6.1.2.1.1.7.0} (system.7.0)
SNMP: Value = 72
SNMP:

Trace 3.8b. Browsing the system subtree (ASN.1 and Hexadecimal decode)

Sniffer Network Analyzer data 10-Nov-92 at 10:42:04 file ASAN_SYS.ENC Pg 1
---Frame 110 -------------------------------------
SNMP: 1.1 SEQUENCE [of], Length=235
SNMP: 2.1 INTEGER, Length=1, Value = "0"
SNMP: 2.2 OCTET STRING, Length=7, Value = "boulder"
SNMP: 2.3 Context-Specific Constructed [2], Length=220
SNMP: 3.1 INTEGER, Length=1, Value = "0"
SNMP: 3.2 INTEGER, Length=1, Value = "0"
SNMP: 3.3 INTEGER, Length=1, Value = "0"
SNMP: 3.4 SEQUENCE [of], Length=208
SNMP: 4.1 SEQUENCE [of], Length=16
SNMP: 5.1 OBJECT IDENTIFIER, Length=8, Value = "{1.3.6.1.2.1.1.3.0}"
SNMP: 5.2 Application Primitive [3], Length=4, Data = "<0FB68C92>"
SNMP: 4.2 SEQUENCE [of], Length=74
SNMP: 5.1 OBJECT IDENTIFIER, Length=8, Value = "{1.3.6.1.2.1.1.1.0}"
SNMP: 5.2 OCTET STRING, Length=62, Value = "Portable I80386 C Gateway
                    XXX.XXX.XXXX.XXX ..."
SNMP: 4.3 SEQUENCE [of], Length=21
SNMP: 5.1 OBJECT IDENTIFIER, Length=8,Value="{1.3.6.1.2.1.1.2.0}"
SNMP: 5.2 OBJECT IDENTIFIER, Length=9,Value="{1.3.6.1.4.1.1.1.1.41}"
SNMP: 4.4 SEQUENCE [of], Length=16
SNMP: 5.1 OBJECT IDENTIFIER, Length=8,Value="{1.3.6.1.2.1.1.3.0}"
SNMP: 5.2 Application Primitive [3], Length=4, Data = "<0FB68C92>"
SNMP: 4.5 SEQUENCE [of], Length=12
SNMP: 5.1 OBJECT IDENTIFIER, Length=8, Value="{1.3.6.1.2.1.1.4.0}"
SNMP: 5.2 OCTET STRING, Length=0, Value = ""
SNMP: 4.6 SEQUENCE [of], Length=28
SNMP: 5.1 OBJECT IDENTIFIER, Length=8, Value="{1.3.6.1.2.1.1.5.0}"

SNMP: 5.2 OCTET STRING, Length=16, Value="XXX.XXX.XXXX.XXX"
SNMP: 4.7 SEQUENCE [of], Length=12
SNMP: 5.1 OBJECT IDENTIFIER, Length=8, Value="{1.3.6.1.2.1.1.6.0}"
SNMP: 5.2 OCTET STRING, Length=0, Value = ""
SNMP: 4.8 SEQUENCE [of], Length=13
SNMP: 5.1 OBJECT IDENTIFIER, Length=8, Value = "{1.3.6.1.2.1.1.7.0}"
SNMP: 5.2 INTEGER, Length=1, Value = "72"
SNMP:

```
ADDR   HEX                                                    ASCII
0000   08 00 20 09 00 C8 AA 00   04 00 44 86 08 00 45 00   .. ........D...E.
0010   01 0A 81 20 00 00 3B 11   73 77 84 A3 01 01 84 A3   ... ..;.sw......
0020   80 04 00 A1 0D 20 00 F6   C6 62 3081EB 02 01 00     ..... ...b0.....
0030   04 07 XX XX XX XX XX XX   XX A2 81 DC 02 01 00 02   ..XXXXXXX.......
0040   01 00 02 01 00 30 81 D0   30 10 06 08 2B 06 01 02   .....0..0...+...
0050   01 01 03 00 43 04 0F B6   8C 92 30 4A 06 08 2B 06   ....C.....0J..+.
0060   01 02 01 01 01 00 04 3E   50 6F 72 74 61 62 6C 65   .......>Portable
0070   20 49 38 30 33 38 36 20   43 20 47 61 74 65 77 61   180386 C Gatewa
0080   79 20 XX XX XX XX XX XX   XX XX XX XX XX XX XX XX   y XXX.XXX.XXXX.X
0090   XX XX 20 53 2F 4E 20 33   33 33 20 56 31 32 2E 30   XX S/N 333 V12.0
00A0   20 20 5B 20 20 5D 30 15   06 08 2B 06 01 02 01 01   [ ]0...+.....
00B0   02 00 06 09 2B 06 01 04   01 01 01 01 29 30 10 06   ....+.......)0..
00C0   08 2B 06 01 02 01 01 03   00 43 04 0F B6 8C 92 30   .+.......C.....0
00D0   0C 06 08 2B 06 01 02 01   01 04 00 04 00 30 1C 06   ...+.........0..
00E0   08 2B 06 01 02 01 01 05   00 04 10 XX XX XX XX XX   .+.........XXX.X
00F0   XX XX XX XX XX XX XX XX   XX XX XX 30 0C 06 08 2B   XX.XXXX.XXX0...+
0100   06 01 02 01 01 06 00 04   00 30 0D 06 08 2B 06 01   .........0...+..
0110   02 01 01 07 00 02 01 48                             .......H
```

We have now tackled two of the three technical subjects in our tour of the Internet network management framework: the SMI and the MIBs. The next chapter studies SNMP, which provides the communication mechanism for network management functions.

3.9. References

[3-1]   McCloghrie, K. and M.T. Rose. "Management Information Base for Network Management of TCP/IP-based Internets." RFC 1156, May 1990.

[3-2]   McCloghrie, K. and M.T. Rose. "Management Information Base for Network Management of TCP/IP-based Internets: MIB-II." RFC 1213, March 1991.

[3-3]   Rose, M. and K. McCloghrie. "Concise MIB Definitions." RFC 1212, March 1991.

[3-4]   Perkins, Dave. "How to Read and Use an SNMP MIB." *3TECH, the 3Com Technical Journal* (Spring 1991): 31–55.

[3-5]   VandenBerg, Chris. "MIB II Extends SNMP Interoperability." *Data Communications* (October 1990): 119–124.

[3-6]   LaBarre, L. "OSI Internet Management: Management Information Base." RFC 1214, April 1991.

[3-7]   Reynolds, J. and J. Postel. "Assigned Numbers." RFC 1340, July 1992.

[3-8]   Waldbusser, S. "Remote Network Monitoring Management Information Base." RFC 1271, November 1991.

[3-9]   Hurwicz, Mike. "Manage from Kansas." *LAN Magazine* (February 1992): 113–126.

[3-10] Knack, Kella. "RMON MIBs Take Off." *LAN Computing* (March 1992):3.

[3-11] Hoerth, Mark. "The RMON MIB- A New Standard for Remote Monitoring of Networks." *Telecommunications* (March 1992): S5–S9.

[3-12] Jander, Mary. "Beyond RMON: Making Sense of Remote Data" *Data Communications* (June 1992): 51–52.

[3-13] Miller, Mark A. "Scoping Out Analyzer Purchases." *Network World* (August 31, 1992): 35–43.

[3-14] Fisher, Sharon. "RMON MIB to Get Token-Ring-Specific Extensions." *Communications Week* (October 26, 1992): 48.

[3-15] Fisher, Sharon. "MIB Extensions Widen SNMP's Reach." *Communications Week* (February 17, 1992): 33.

[3-16] Burdick, Matthew J. "Continuous Monitoring of Remote Networks: The RMON MIB," *Hewlett-Packard Journal* (April 1993): 82–89.

4 The Simple Network Management Protocol

So far, this book has discussed the structure of management information (SMI) and management information bases (MIBs). This chapter completes the discussion of the Internet Network Management Framework by looking at SNMP, the protocol that communicates management information.

4.1. SNMP Objectives and Architecture

RFC 1157 states that "SNMP explicitly minimizes the number and complexity of management functions realized by the management agent itself" [Reference 4-1]. In other words, SNMP is designed to be simple. SNMP does this three ways. By reducing the development cost of the agent software, SNMP has decreased the burden on vendors who wish to support the protocol, thereby increasing the protocol's acceptance. Second, SNMP is extensible, allowing vendors to add network management functions. Third, it separates the management architecture from the architecture of hardware devices, such as hosts and routers, widening the base of multivendor support. "Network Management and the Design of SNMP" discusses additional architectural issues relating to SNMP [4-2].

SNMP has a very straightforward architecture. Figure 4-1a compares the SNMP architecture to the ISO/OSI model and the Defense Advanced Research Projects Agency (DARPA) model, around which the Internet protocols and TCP/IP were developed. Note that the four layers of the DARPA model do not map evenly to the seven layers of the OSI model.

Let's use an example to see how the processes within the SNMP architecture interact. Suppose a management console requests information about one of the managed nodes. The SNMP processes in both the manager and agent respond to the console. The ASN.1 encoding at the Application layer provides the proper syntax for the SNMP message. The remaining functions authenticate the data (attach the SNMP header) and communicate the information request.

OSI Layer	SNMP - Related Function	DARPA Layer
Application	Management Application (SNMP PDU)	Process / Application
Presentation	Structure of Management Information (ASN.1 & BER Encoding)	
Session	Authentication (SNMP Header)	
Transport	User Datagram Protocol (UDP)	Host-to-Host
Network	Internet Protocol (IP)	Internet
Data Link	LAN or WAN Interface Protocol	Network Interface
Physical		

Figure 4-1a. Comparing the SNMP architecture with the OSI and DARPA models

Because most management information does not demand the reliable delivery that connection-oriented systems provide, the communication channel between the SNMP manager and agent is connectionless. When you compare the SNMP model to the ISO/OSI model, SNMP's connectionless communication mechanism removes some of the need for a Session layer and reduces the responsibilities of the lower four layers. For most implementations, the User Datagram Protocol (UDP) performs the Transport layer functions, the

Internet Protocol (IP) provides the Network layer functions, and LANs such as Ethernet or token-ring provide the Data Link and Physical layer functions. (There are exceptions to this rule, however. RFC 1283 describes implementations that use both OSI protocols and vendor-specific protocols, such as Novell's Internetwork Packet Exchange, IPX. However, RFC 1270, called "SNMP Communication Services" [4-3], states that UDP/IP are the protocols of choice for most circumstances.)

If you compare SNMP to the Internet (or DARPA) architectural model (see Figure 4-1b), you'll notice that the DARPA model uses four layers to describe the entire communication function. In the DARPA model, SNMP would reside at the Process/Application layer. However, while the DARPA Host-to-Host layer provides end-to-end communication reliability, SNMP's use of UDP assures only proper port addressing and a checksum; it does not provide octet-by-octet error control. IP provides the Internet layer functions, such as addressing and fragmentation, necessary to deliver a SNMP message from the source to the destination. Finally, the Network Interface layer deals with the LAN or WAN hardware, such as an interface to a FDDI or Frame Relay network

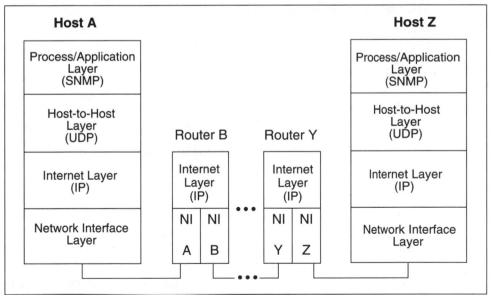

Figure 4-1b. Application-to-application connection

connection. Notice that Figure 4-1b also shows the relative complexities of the host and router functions. Hosts implement all four layers of the DARPA model, whereas routers implement only the lower two.

Comparing the SNMP architecture to the ISO/OSI and DARPA architectural models provides a theoretical basis for this discussion. But from a practical perspective, the SNMP model works as shown in Figure 4-2. This model contains several elements discussed in Chapter 1. It includes a management system that uses the SNMP manager, an SNMP agent, managed resources, and the SNMP messages communicates management information via five SNMP protocol data units (PDUs). The management application issues the Get, Get-Next, or Set PDUs. The managed system returns a GetResponse PDU. The agent may initiate a Trap (sometimes called an Event) PDU when predefined conditions are met. Section 4.3 discusses these five PDUs in detail.

4.2. SNMP Operation

The SNMP processes described in the previous sections must occur in physical devices. For example, a router must have a physical chip that implements the software acting as an SNMP agent. Two sets of logical processes occur within those physical elements: the relationships that are specified between various network management entities, and the way network management information is communicated.

4.2.1. Network management relationships

The SNMP standard, RFC 1157, and the SNMP Administrative Model, RFC 1351 [4-4], define a number of terms. Many of these definitions describe relationships between management entities:

- *Network management stations* are devices that execute the management applications that control and monitor the network elements.

- *Network elements* are devices such as hosts, bridges, routers, and hubs that contain an agent and perform the network management functions that the network management stations request.

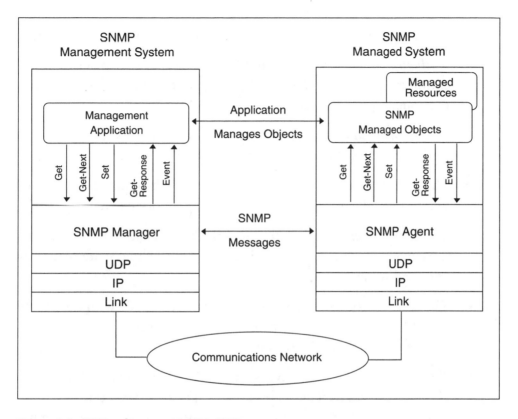

Figure 4-2. SNMP architecture *(©1990, IEEE)*

- The *SNMP* allows network management stations and the agents in the network elements to communicate.

- *SNMP application entities* reside at either a management station or a managed node, and use SNMP as a communication mechanism.

- *Protocol entities* are peer processes that implement SNMP, thus supporting the SNMP application entities.

- The *SNMP community* pairs an SNMP agent with an arbitrary set of SNMP application entities. The network administrator assigns the community a name (called the *community name*) which is essentially a password with associated rights and privileges. A management application with multiple community names may belong to multiple communities.

- *Authentic SNMP messages* are SNMP messages sent from an application entity to a specific SNMP community. The message contains the community name of interest.

- The *authentication scheme* is the method by which an SNMP message is identified as belonging to a specific SNMP community.

- The *MIB View* is the subset of MIB objects, which may be contained within several subtrees, that pertain to a network element.

- The SNMP *access mode* determines the level of access to objects that a particular application entity is allowed. The choices are read-only and read-write.

- The *community profile* pairs the SNMP access mode with the SNMP MIB View. The community profile represents specific access privileges for the variables in a MIB view.

- The SNMP *access policy* pairs an SNMP community with a SNMP community profile. The access policy represents the specific community profile that an agent permits the other members of the community to have.

- The SNMP *proxy agent* provides management functions on behalf of network elements that would otherwise be inaccessible.

Figure 4-3 illustrates some of the definitions described above.

4.2.2. Identifying and communicating object instances

SMI managed object types have an object identifier (OID) that uniquely names them and locates their place on the object tree. An instance of an object type is an occurrence of that object type, and has an assigned value. For example, the object type sysDescr {1.3.6.1.2.1.1.1.0} might have a value of "Retix Remote Bridge Model 2265M."

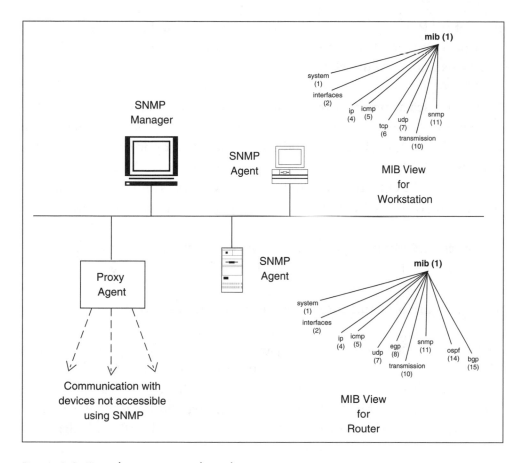

Figure 4-3. Network management relationships

Suppose a network management station wishes to retrieve an instance of a specific object. The management station must use SNMP to communicate its question to the agent.

Now, suppose multiple instances (or occurrences) of that object are possible. For example, say a router's routing table contains a number of entries. How would the network management station retrieve just the value of the third entry in the table?

RFC 1157 specifies these tasks. For these SNMP operations, a "variable name" uniquely identifies each instance of an object type. This name consists of two parts of the form *x.y*. The *x* portion is the object type defined in the MIB, and the *y* portion is an OID fragment that identifies the desired instance. The following examples should clarify this.

Consider a scalar object that has one instance. The objects contained in the System group are all scalar objects. For example, the sysServices object type has an OID of {1.3.6.1.2.1.1.7} and occurs once. The *x* portion of the variable name is the OID, and the *y* portion has been assigned to 0. You can derive this by following the OID tree down to the object sysServices and adding the appropriate instance suffix (with the suffix, or *y* portion, shown in boldface type):

iso	org	dod	internet	mgmt	mib	system	sysServices	Instance
1	3	6	1	2	1	1	7	**0**

Thus, the variable name for sysServices is {1.3.6.1.2.1.1.7.0}.

The variable name for a columnar object is more complicated because it must identify the location of a column within a row of the table. Consider the IP Address Table object type, ipAdEntBcastAddr, which specifies the value of the least significant bit (LSB) of the IP broadcast address (see Figures 4-4a and 4-4b). To begin, follow the OID tree down to ipAdEntBcastAddr:

iso	org	dod	internet	mgmt	mib	ip	ipAddrTable	ipAddrEntry	ipAdEntBcastAddr
1	3	6	1	2	1	4	20	1	4

The OID is {1.3.6.1.2.1.4.20.1.4}, consisting of the IP Group {1.3.6.1.2.1.4}, the IP Address Table (20), the ipAddrEntry (1), and the object type ipAdEntBcastAddr (4), shown in Figure 4-4a. Next, the destination route is added as a suffix, that is, a.b.c.d. (More on IP addresses and dotted decimal notation in Section 5.3.) The variable name for ipAdEntBcastAddr associated with IP Address a.b.c.d would therefore be {1.3.6.1.2.1.4.20.1.4.a.b.c.d}.

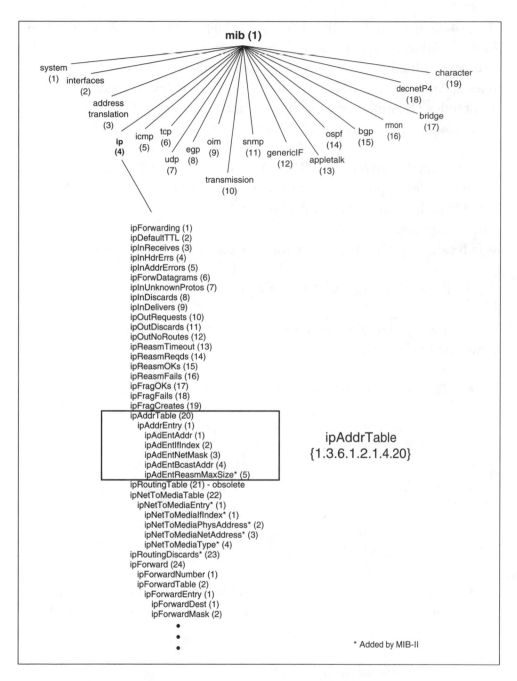

Figure 4-4a. The IP address table within the OID tree

Figure 4-4b. is a completed IP Address Table, built by retrieving all the IP Address Table variables. The column headings show the five objects, ipAdEntAddr through ipAdEntReasmMaxSize. Each row contains the values of the five variables: ipAdEntAddr [XXX.YYY.150.2], ipAdEntIfIndex (1), and so on. A different index (2) identifies the second row, and it contains different values. Additional row entries are made, as necessary, until the table is completed.

A final example (derived from RFC 1157) is from the TCP Connection Table, tcpConnTable. Suppose you wish to retrieve the state of the connection between port 575 on local address {a.b.c.d} and port 441 on remote address {w.x.y.z}. The OID for tcpConnState is {1.3.6.1.2.1.6.13.1.1}. The *y* suffix would be expressed as {a.b.c.d.575.w.x.y.z.441}. Therefore, the complete variable name would be

{1.3.6.1.2.1.6.13.1.1.a.b.c.d.575.w.x.y.z.441}

The following examples show specific variable names for both scalar and columnar object types:

- The description of this system's services:

    sysServices ::=
    {1.3.6.1.2.1.1.7.0}

- The speed of interface 3:

    ifSpeed.3 ::=
    {1.3.6.1.2.1.2.2.1.5.3}

- The physical address associated with interface 2 and IP address {a.b.c.d.} (note that the first component is a .1, which indicates an IP address [see RFC 1157, page 13]):

    atPhysAddress.2.1.a.b.c.d ::=
    {1.3.6.1.2.1.3.1.1.2.2.1.a.b.c.d}

ipAddrTable {1.3.6.1.2.1.4.20}				
ipAdEntAddr {1.3.6.1.2.1.4.20.1.1}	ipAdEntIfIndex {1.3.6.1.2.1.4.20.1.2}	ipAdEntNetMask {1.3.6.1.2.1.4.20.1.3}	ipAdEntBcastAddr {1.3.6.1.2.1.4.20.1.4}	ipAdEntReasmMaxSize {1.3.6.1.2.1.4.20.1.5}
Row 1 XXX.YYY.150.2	1	255.255.255.0	0	12000
Row 2 XXX.YYY.1.1	2	255.255.0.0	1	12000
• • • **Row n**	• • •			

Figure 4-4b. Object instances in the IP address table

- The maximum IP datagram reassembly size associated with IP address {a.b.c.d}:

    ipAdEntReasmMaxSize.a.b.c.d ::=
    {1.3.6.1.2.1.4.20.1.5.a.b.c.d}

- The number of ICMP Echo (request) messages received at this device:

    icmpInEchos ::=
    {1.3.6.1.2.1.5.8.0}

- The state of a TCP connection, between local port e, local address {a.b.c.d}, and remote port j, remote address {f.g.h.i}:

    tcpConnState.a.b.c.d.e.f.g.h.i.j ::=
    {1.3.6.1.2.1.6.13.1.1.a.b.c.d.e.f.g.h.i.j}

- Verification that a UDP listener is operational on port e of local IP address a.b.c.d:

    udpLocalAddress.a.b.c.d.e ::=
    {1.3.6.1.2.1.7.5.1.1.a.b.c.d.e}

- The neighbor state for the IP address a.b.c.d:

  egpNeighState.a.b.c.d ::=
  {1.3.6.1.2.1.8.5.1.1.a.b.c.d}

- The number of SNMP messages delivered to this device with unknown community names (a scalar):

  snmpInBadCommNames ::=
  {1.3.6.1.2.1.11.4.0}

With this background into the methods of identifying object instances, I will now discuss the SNMP protocol data units (PDUs) that carry the requests and responses for this information between Manager and Agent devices. The PDUs use the object instance examples shown here to identify the specific network management information that the manager is seeking.

4.3. SNMP Protocol Data Units (PDUs)

I will begin the discussion of PDUs by describing the position of the SNMP message within a transmitted frame. The *frame* is the unit of information transmitted between network nodes. For example, an IEEE 802.5 frame format defines the transmission between token-ring nodes, and an ANSI T1.617 format defines the transmission between Frame Relay nodes. Chapter 5 explores the various frame formats and the supporting protocols, such as IP, UDP and ICMP, that may also require analysis.

The local network header and trailers defined by the LAN or WAN protocol delimit the frame (see Figure 4-5). The transmitted data is called an *Internet Protocol (IP) datagram*. The IP datagram is a self-contained unit of information sent from the source host to its intended destination via the internetwork. Inside the datagram is a destination IP address that steers the datagram to the intended recipient. Next, the User Datagram Protocol (UDP) header identifies the higher layer protocol process (SNMP) that will process the datagram, and provides error control using a checksum. The SNMP message is the innermost part of the frame, carrying the actual data from the manager to and from the agent.

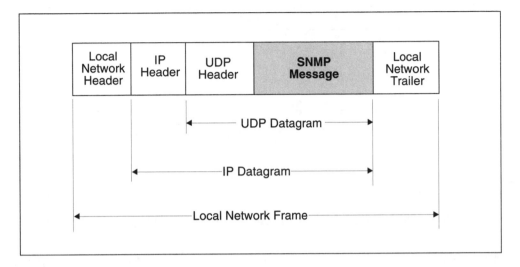

Figure 4-5. SNMP message within a transmission frame

When the IP is too long to fit inside one frame, it may be divided (or fragmented) into several frames for transmission on the LAN. For example, a datagram containing 2500 octets would require two Ethernet frames, each of which may contain a maximum of 1500 octets of higher layer data. The general structure of each frame, as shown in Figure 4-5, would remain the same.

The SNMP message itself is divided into two sections: a version identifier plus community name, and a PDU. The version identifier and community name are sometimes referred to as the SNMP *authentication header*. There are five different PDU types: GetRequest, GetNextRequest, GetResponse, SetRequest, and Trap. The Get, Set, and Response PDUs have a common format (see Figure 4-6), while the Trap PDU format is unique (Figure 4-10 later in this chapter illustrates the Trap PDU format).

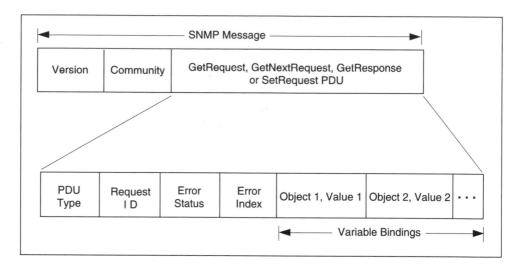

Figure 4-6. The SNMP GetRequest, GetNextRequest, GetResponse, and SetRequest PDU structures

The version number (an INTEGER type) assures that both manager and agent are using the same version of the SNMP protocol. Messages between manager and agent containing different version numbers are discarded without further processing. The community name (an OCTET STRING type) authenticates the manager before allowing access to the agent. The community name, along with the manager's IP address, is stored in the agent's community profile. If there's a difference between the manager and agent values for the community name, the agent will send an authentication failure trap message to the manager. If both the version number and community name from the manager match the one stored in the agent, the SNMP PDU begins processing.

In the following sections, I'll discuss the fields of the two PDU formats and the operation of the five PDUs. If you feel comfortable with ASN.1 notation, you may wish to refer to the SNMP definition in Section 4.5.

4.3.1. Get, Set, and Response PDU formats

The GetRequest, GetNextRequest, SetRequest, and GetResponse PDUs share a common format (see Figure 4-6). The first field, PDU Type, specifies the type of PDU the message contains:

PDU	PDU Type Field Value
GetRequest	0
GetNextRequest	1
GetResponse	2
SetRequest	3
Trap	4

The Request ID field is an INTEGER type that correlates the manager's request to the agent's response. The Error Status field is an enumerated INTEGER type that indicates normal operation (noError) or one of five error conditions. The possible values are:

Error	Value	Meaning
noError	0	Proper manager/agent operation.
tooBig	1	The size of the required GetResponse PDU exceeds a local limitation.
noSuchName	2	The requested object name did not match the names available in the relevant MIB View.
badValue	3	A SetRequest contained an inconsistent type, length, and value for the variable.
readOnly	4	Not defined in RFC 1157. (Historical footnote: this error is listed, but the description of the SetRequest PDU processing does not describe how this error is generated. The standard interpretation is that this error should not be generated, although some vendor's agents nevertheless do.)
genErr	5	Other errors, not explicitly defined, have occurred.

When an error occurs, the Error Index field identifies the entry within the variable bindings list that caused the error. For example, if a readOnly error occurred, it would return an Error Index = 4.

A Variable Binding (VarBind) pairs a variable name with its value. A *VarBindList* is a list of such pairings. Note that within the Variable Bindings fields of the SNMP PDUs (see Figures 4 through 6 and 4 through 11), the word *Object* identifies the variable name (OID encoding of object type plus the instance) for which a value is being communicated. Also note that GetRequest or GetNextRequest PDUs use a value of NULL, which is a special ASN.1 data type.

4.3.2. Using the GetRequest PDU

The manager uses the GetRequest PDU to retrieve the value of one or more object(s) from an agent. In most cases, these are scalar, not columnar, objects. To generate the GetRequest PDU, the manager assigns PDU Type = 0, a locally defined Request ID, and sets both the ErrorStatus and ErrorIndex to 0. A VarBindList, containing the requested variables, and corresponding NULL (placeholder) values, completes the PDU. Under error-free conditions, the agent generates a GetResponse PDU, which is assigned PDU Type = 2, the same value of Request ID, Error Status = noError, and Error Index = 0. The Variable Bindings now contain the values associated with each of the variables noted in the GetRequest PDU (see Figure 4-7). Recall that the term *variable* refers to an instance of a managed object.

Four error conditions are possible:

- If a variable in the Variable Bindings field does not exactly match an available object, the agent returns a GetResponse PDU with Error Status = noSuchName, and with the Error Index indicating the index of the variable in question.

- If a variable is an aggregate type, such as a row object, the agent returns a GetResponse PDU with Error Status = noSuchName, and the Error Index indicating the index of the variable in question.

- If the size of the appropriate GetReponse PDU would exceed a local limitation, then the agent returns a GetResponse PDU of identical form, with Error Status = tooBig, and Error Index = 0.

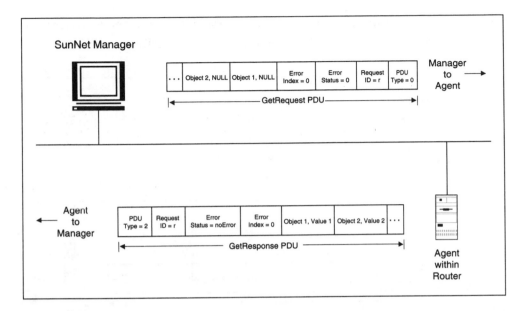

Figure 4-7. GetRequest/GetResponse PDU transmission (with no errors) *(courtesy 3Com Corp.)*

- If the value of a requested variable cannot be retrieved for any other reason, then the agent returns a GetResponse PDU, with Error Status = genErr, and the Error Index indicating the index of the variable in question.

4.3.3. Using the GetNextRequest PDU

The manager uses the GetNextRequest PDU to retrieve one or more objects and their values from an agent. In most cases, these multiple objects will reside within a table. As you can see in Figure 4-8, to generate the GetNextRequest PDU the manager assigns PDU Type = 1, a locally defined Request ID, and sets both the ErrorStatus and the ErrorIndex to 0. A VarBindList, containing the OIDs, and corresponding NULL (placeholder) values, completes the PDU. These OIDs can be any OID (which may be a variable) that immediately precedes the variable and value returned. Under error-free conditions, the agent generates a GetResponse PDU, which is assigned PDU Type = 2, the same value of Request ID, Error Status = noError, and Error Index = 0. The Variable Bindings contain the name and value associated with the lexicographical successor of each of the OIDs noted in the GetNextRequest PDU.

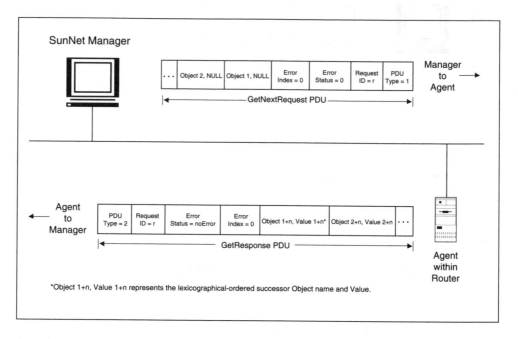

Figure 4-8. GetNextRequest/GetResponse PDU transmission (with no errors) *(courtesy 3Com Corp.)*

The key difference between the GetRequest and the GetNextRequest PDUs is the word *lexicographical*. That means that the GetNextRequest retrieves the value of the next object within the Agent's MIB View. Section 4.4.2 provides an example.

Three error conditions are possible:

- If a variable in the Variable Bindings field does not lexicographically precede the name of an object that may be retrieved (that is, an object available for Get operations and within the relevant MIB View), the agent returns a GetResponse PDU with Error Status = noSuchName, and with the Error Index indicating the index of the variable in question. This condition is called "running off the end of the MIB View."

- If the size of the appropriate GetReponse PDU exceeds a local limitation, the agent returns a GetResponse PDU of identical form, with Error Status = tooBig, and Error Index = 0.

- If the value of the lexicographical successor to a requested variable in the Variable Bindings field cannot be retrieved for any other reason, the agent returns a GetResponse PDU, with Error Status = genErr, and the Error Index indicating the index of the variable in question.

4.3.4. Using the SetRequest PDU

The manager uses the SetRequest PDU to assign a value to an object residing in the agent. As you can see in Figure 4-9, to generate that PDU the manager assigns PDU Type = 3, a locally defined Request ID, and sets both the ErrorStatus and ErrorIndex to 0. A VarBindList, containing the specified variables and their corresponding values, completes the PDU. When the agent receives the SetRequest PDU, it alters the values of the named objects to the value in the variable binding. Under error-free conditions, the agent generates a GetResponse PDU of identical form, except that the assigned PDU Type = 2, Error Status = noError, and Error Index = 0

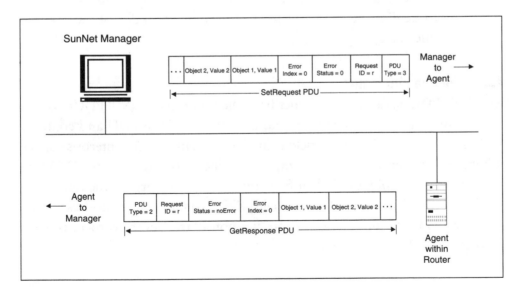

Figure 4-9. SetRequest/GetResponse PDU transmission (with no errors) *(courtesy 3Com Corp.)*

Four error conditions are possible:

- If a variable in the Variable Bindings field is not available for Set operations within the relevant MIB View, the agent returns a GetResponse PDU of identical form, with Error Status = noSuchName, and with the Error Index indicating the index of the object name in question. (Historical note: Some agent implementations return Error Status = readOnly if the object exists, but Access = read-only for that variable.)

- If the value of a variable named in the Variable Bindings field does not conform to the ASN.1 Type, Length, and Value required, the agent returns a GetResponse PDU of identical form, with Error Status = badValue and the Error Index indicating the index of the variable in question.

- If the size of the appropriate GetReponse PDU exceeds a local limitation, the agent returns a GetResponse PDU of identical form, with Error Status = tooBig, and Error Index = 0.

- If the value of a variable cannot be altered for any other reason, the agent returns a GetResponse PDU of identical form, with Error Status = genErr and the Error Index indicating the index of the variable in question.

4.3.5. The Trap PDU format

The Trap PDU has a format distinct from the four other SNMP PDUs, as you can see in Figure 4-10. The first field indicates the Trap PDU and contains PDU Type = 4. The Enterprise field identifies the management enterprise under whose registration authority the trap was defined. For example, the OID prefix {1.3.6.1.4.1.110} would identify Network General Corp. as the Enterprise sending a trap. The Agent Address field, which contains the IP address of the agent, provides further identification. If a non-IP transport protocol is used, the value 0.0.0.0 is returned.

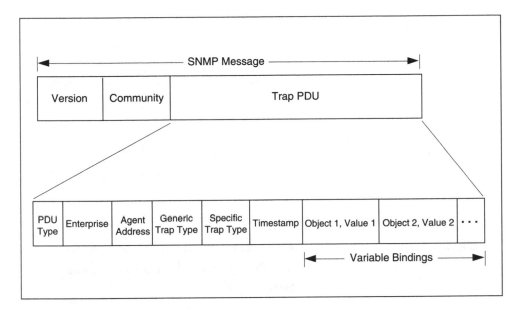

Figure 4-10. SNMP Trap PDU structure

The Generic Trap type provides more specific information on the event being reported. There are seven defined values (enumerated INTEGER types) for this field:

Trap	Value	Meaning
coldStart	0	The sending protocol entity (higher layer network management) has reinitialized, indicating that the agent's configuration nor entity implementation may be altered.
warmStart	1	The sending protocol has reinitialized, but neither the agent's configuration or the protocol entity implementation has been altered.
linkDown	2	A communication link has failed. The affected interface is identified as the first element within

		the variable bindings field: name and value of the ifIndex instance.
linkUp	3	A communication link has come up. The affected interface is identified as the first element within the variable bindings field: name and value of the ifIndex instance.
authenticationFailure	4	The agent has received an improperly authenticated SNMP message from the manager; that is, the community name was incorrect.
egpNeighborLoss	5	An EGP peer neighbor is down.
enterpriseSpecific	6	A nongeneric trap has occurred, which is further identified by the Specific Trap Type field and Enterprise field.

Two additional fields complete the Trap PDU. The Timestamp field contains the value of the sysUpTime object, representing the amount of time elapsed between the last (re-)initialization of the agent, and the generation of that Trap. The last field contains the Variable Bindings.

4.3.6. Using the Trap PDU

The agent uses the Trap PDU to alert the manager that a predefined event has occurred. To generate the Trap PDU, the agent assigns PDU Type = 4, and fills in the Enterprise, Agent Address, Generic Trap, Specific Trap Type, Timestamp fields, and the Variable Bindings list.

By definition (and convention), Traps are application-specific. Therefore, it would be difficult to cover the range of uses for this PDU. RFC 1215, "A Convention for Defining Traps for use with the SNMP", offers some guidelines for their use [4-5]. Figure 4-11 illustrates how an agent in a router could use a Trap to communicate a significant event to the manager. Section 4.4.4 provides an example of a real-world application.

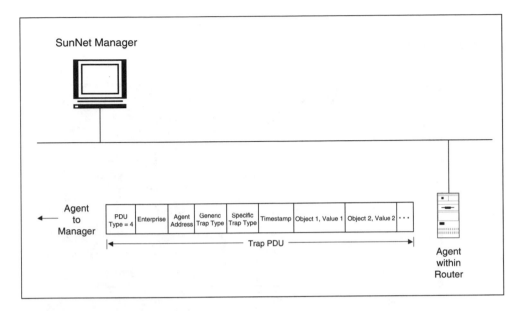

Figure 4-11. Trap PDU operation *(courtesy 3Com Corp.)*

4.3.7. SNMP PDU encoding

Recall from our discussion in Chapter 2 that the SNMP PDUs are encoded using the context-specific class, with a tag that identifies the PDU (review Figure 2-15). The Length and Value fields are then constructed to convey a particular structure and quantity of information. Now that I have discussed the structure of the SNMP PDUs, I can revisit these encodings in more detail.

Figure 4-12 shows an example of a TLV encoding of an SNMP PDU. Note that the entire encoding begins with a SEQUENCE OF type. The version is an INTEGER type, and the community name is an OCTET STRING type. A context-specific type then indicates the specific PDU and its length. Three INTEGER types provide the Request ID, Error Status, and Error Index. The VarBind list, consisting of multiple SEQUENCE OF encodings, completes the PDU. The following examples illustrate the details of this encoding structure.

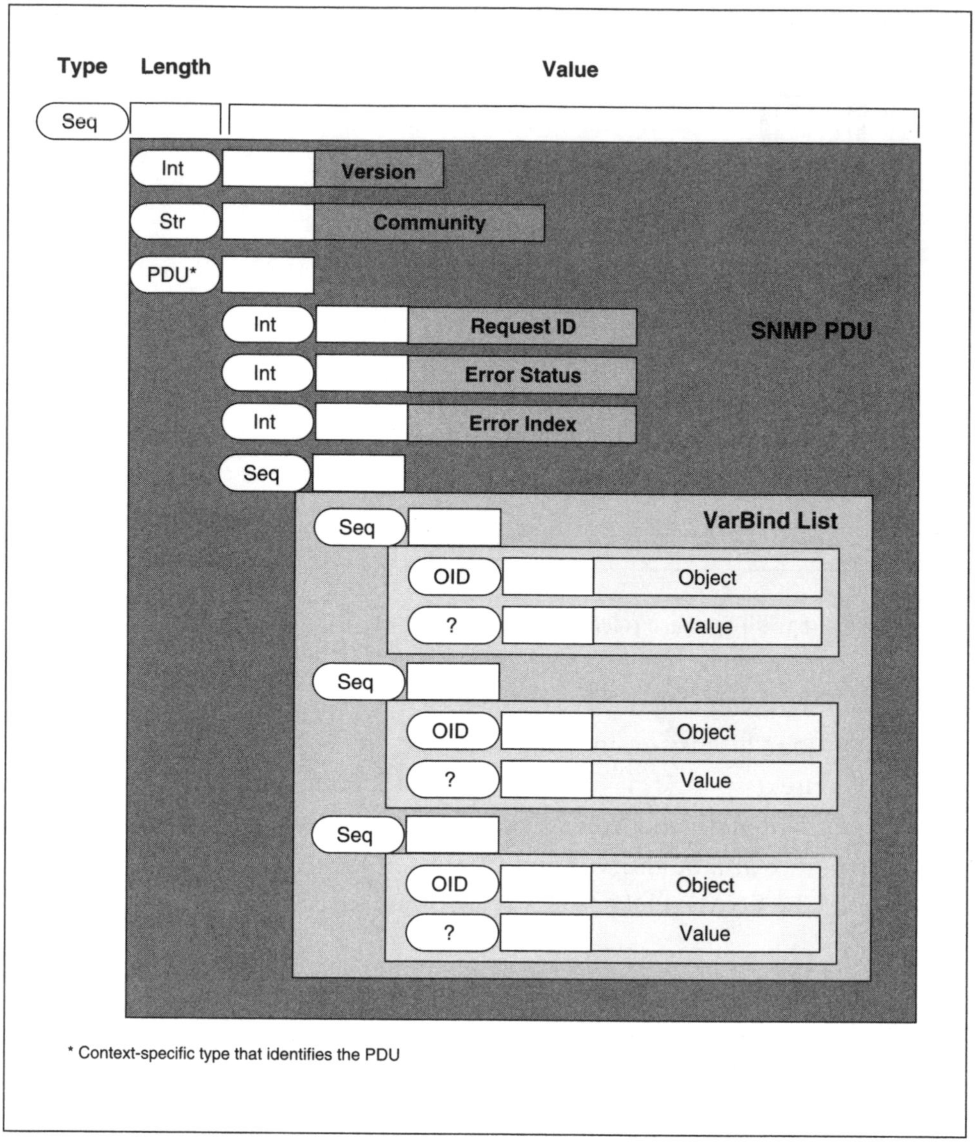

Figure 4-12. TLV Encoding of an SNMP PDU *(courtesy ProTools, Inc.)*

4.4. Application Examples

To illustrate the SNMP PDUs discussed in this chapter, the next section presents four examples of the protocol in use. The network analyzer captured each sample from an Ethernet backbone, which contained several other Ethernet segments connected by bridges and routers (see Figure 4-13). For these cases, the SNMP manager was a Sun workstation running SunNet Manager version 2.0, and a Proteon p4200+ router contained the SNMP agent. In all of these examples, I have filtered the traces to show only the SNMP protocol interaction.

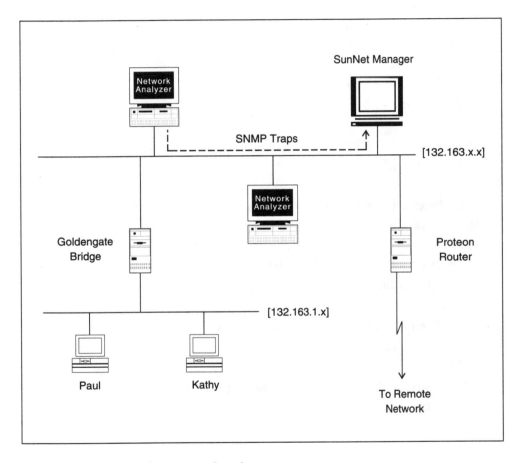

Figure 4-13. SNMP traps from a network analyzer

4.4.1. SNMP GetRequest example

Recall from our earlier discussion that the GetRequest PDU retrieves scalar objects. Trace 4.4.1 illustrates how the UDP group (review Figure 3-8) does this.

Trace 4.4.1. Retrieving scalar data using the GetRequest PDU: the UDP Group

```
Sniffer Network Analyzer data 10-Nov-92 at 11:03:08, file UDP.ENC, Pg 1
-------------------------------------------Frame 61-------------------------------------------
SNMP: ----- Simple Network Management Protocol -----
SNMP:
SNMP: Version = 0
SNMP: Community = Brutus
SNMP: Command = Get request
SNMP: Request ID = 0
SNMP: Error status = 0 (No error)
SNMP: Error index = 0
SNMP:
SNMP: Object = {1.3.6.1.2.1.1.3.0} (sysUpTime.0)
SNMP: Value  = NULL
SNMP:
SNMP: Object = {1.3.6.1.2.1.7.1.0} (udpInDatagrams.0)
SNMP: Value  = NULL
SNMP:
SNMP: Object = {1.3.6.1.2.1.7.2.0} (udpNoPorts.0)
SNMP: Value  = NULL
SNMP:
SNMP: Object = {1.3.6.1.2.1.7.3.0} (udpInErrors.0)
SNMP: Value  = NULL
SNMP:
SNMP: Object = {1.3.6.1.2.1.7.4.0} (udpOutDatagrams.0)
SNMP: Value  = NULL
SNMP:
-------------------------------------------Frame 62-------------------------------------------
SNMP: ----- Simple Network Management Protocol -----
SNMP:
SNMP: Version = 0
SNMP: Community = Brutus
SNMP: Command = Get response
```

```
SNMP: Request ID = 0
SNMP: Error status = 0 (No error)
SNMP: Error index = 0
SNMP:
SNMP: Object = {1.3.6.1.2.1.1.3.0} (sysUpTime.0)
SNMP: Value  = 263748621 hundredths of a second
SNMP:
SNMP: Object = {1.3.6.1.2.1.7.1.0} (udpInDatagrams.0)
SNMP: Value  = 573894 datagrams
SNMP:
SNMP: Object = {1.3.6.1.2.1.7.2.0} (udpNoPorts.0)
SNMP: Value  = 419103 datagrams
SNMP:
SNMP: Object = {1.3.6.1.2.1.7.3.0} (udpInErrors.0)
SNMP: Value  = 0 datagrams
SNMP:
SNMP: Object = {1.3.6.1.2.1.7.4.0} (udpOutDatagrams.0)
SNMP: Value  = 288892 datagrams
SNMP:
```

Trace 4.4.1 consists of two SNMP PDUs: the GetRequest (Frame 61) and the GetResponse (Frame 62). Both frames illustrate their respective PDU structures (as were described in Figures 4-6 and 4-7): Verson = 0, Community = Brutus, Command (PDU Type 0 or 2), Request ID = 0, Error Status = 0, and Error Index = 0.

Next, the VarBindList indicates the variables and associated values being requested or supplied. You can observe two things here. First, the SunNet Manager always asks for the sysUpTime before requesting other objects. (Other management consoles may construct the VarBindList in another fashion.) The sysUpTime provides a time-stamp update for the Sun console, and is an input to the Sun graphical display of the network management statistics. Second, the values associated with the objects in the GetRequest have a Value = NULL. Recall that NULL is the ASN.1 type used as a placeholder in the data stream. When you look at the GetResponse in Frame 62, you'll see that each NULL value has been replaced with a measured value. For example, the number of UDP datagrams that have been delivered to UDP users, udpInDatagrams {1.3.6.1.2.1.7.1.0}, has a value of 573,894 datagrams. You can interpret the rest of the VarBindList in Frame 62 in a similar manner.

4.4.2. SNMP GetNextRequest example

The GetNextRequest PDU retrieves objects from a table. Reviewing Figure 3-8, consider the UDP table, {1.3.6.1.2.7.5}. This table contains two columns, udpLocalAddress and udpLocal Port. Together, these two entries associate a local IP address with a local port number, as follows:

udpTable

udpLocalAddress	udpLocalPort
0.0.0.0	1
a.b.c.d	2
.	.
.	.
.	.

Note that the address [0.0.0.0] indicates that a UDP listener is willing to accept datagrams for any interface on this node.

In Trace 4.4.2, the SunNet Manager wishes to retrieve all the values in the UDP Table. To do so, it issues the first GetNextRequest to specify OIDs that are lexicographically immediately before any udpLocalAddress objects and before udpLocalPort objects (see Frame 33). Frame 34 returns the contents of the first row, indicating a udpLocalAddress [0.0.0.0], udpLocalPort 69, the Trivial File Transfer Protocol (TFTP) port, and object {1.3.6.1.2.1.7.5.1.1.0.0.0.0.69}. The GetNextRequest in Frame 35 is identical to the one in Frame 33, except that it requests the object returned in Frame 34, that is, the next value after

{1.3.6.1.2.1.7.5.1.1.0.0.0.0.69}. Frame 36 returns the response, which is the value of the second row: {1.3.6.1.2.1.7.5.1.1.0.0.0.0.161}, which identifies the SNMP port. Frames 37 continues the pattern, with the value of the third row identifying port 520 (a local routing port).

Note that Frame 38 reaches the end of the table, indicated by the GetResponse given in Frame 40, which moves to a different group within the OID tree. This final value is the lexicographical next item in the router's MIB, object snmpInPkts, the first object of the SNMP group. This means that the router did not have any item in the Transmission group {mib 10} in its MIB View. (These groups were in the router's MIB, however, so access to those groups using the same community name was not possible.)

The UDP table constructed from the data in Trace 4.4.2 is as follows:

udpTable

udpLocalAddress	udpLocalPort
0.0.0.0	69 (TFTP)
0.0.0.0	161 (SNMP)
0.0.0.0	520 (Router)

Trace 4.4.2. Retrieving tabular data with the GetNextRequest PDU: The udpTable

```
Sniffer Network Analyzer data  10-Nov-92 at 11:03:58, file UDT.ENC, Pg 1
---------------------------------------Frame 33---------------------------------------
SNMP: ----- Simple Network Management Protocol -----
SNMP:
SNMP: Version = 0
SNMP: Community = Brutus
SNMP: Command = Get next request
SNMP: Request ID = 0
SNMP: Error status = 0 (No error)
```

SNMP: Error index = 0
SNMP:
SNMP: Object = {1.3.6.1.2.1.1.3} (sysUpTime)
SNMP: Value = NULL
SNMP:
SNMP: Object = {1.3.6.1.2.1.7.5.1.1} (udpLocalAddress)
SNMP: Value = NULL
SNMP:
SNMP: Object = {1.3.6.1.2.1.7.5.1.2} (udpLocalPort)
SNMP: Value = NULL
SNMP:
--Frame 34--
SNMP: ----- Simple Network Management Protocol -----
SNMP:
SNMP: Version = 0
SNMP: Community = Brutus
SNMP: Command = Get response
SNMP: Request ID = 0
SNMP: Error status = 0 (No error)
SNMP: Error index = 0
SNMP:
SNMP: Object = {1.3.6.1.2.1.1.3.0} (sysUpTime.0)
SNMP: Value = 263753458 hundredths of a second
SNMP:
SNMP: Object = {1.3.6.1.2.1.7.5.1.1.0.0.0.0.69} (udpLocalAddress.0.0.0.0.69)
SNMP: Value = [0.0.0.0]
SNMP:
SNMP: Object = {1.3.6.1.2.1.7.5.1.2.0.0.0.0.69} (udpLocalPort.0.0.0.0.69)
SNMP: Value = 69
SNMP:
--Frame 35--
SNMP: ----- Simple Network Management Protocol -----
SNMP:
SNMP: Version = 0

SNMP: Community = Brutus
SNMP: Command = Get next request
SNMP: Request ID = 0
SNMP: Error status = 0 (No error)
SNMP: Error index = 0
SNMP:
SNMP: Object = {1.3.6.1.2.1.1.3} (sysUpTime)
SNMP: Value = NULL
SNMP:
SNMP: Object = {1.3.6.1.2.1.7.5.1.1.0.0.0.0.69} (udpLocalAddress.0.0.0.0.69)
SNMP: Value = NULL
SNMP:
SNMP: Object = {1.3.6.1.2.1.7.5.1.2.0.0.0.0.69} (udpLocalPort.0.0.0.0.69)
SNMP: Value = NULL
SNMP:
--Frame 36---
SNMP: ----- Simple Network Management Protocol -----
SNMP:
SNMP: Version = 0
SNMP: Community = Brutus
SNMP: Command = Get response
SNMP: Request ID = 0
SNMP: Error status = 0 (No error)
SNMP: Error index = 0
SNMP:
SNMP: Object = {1.3.6.1.2.1.1.3.0} (sysUpTime.0)
SNMP: Value = 263753461 hundredths of a second
SNMP:
SNMP: Object = {1.3.6.1.2.1.7.5.1.1.0.0.0.0.161} (udpLocalAddress.0.0.0.0.161)
SNMP: Value = [0.0.0.0]
SNMP:
SNMP: Object = {1.3.6.1.2.1.7.5.1.2.0.0.0.0.161} (udpLocalPort.0.0.0.0.161)
SNMP: Value = 161
SNMP:

```
-----------------------------------------------Frame 37--------------------------------------------------
SNMP: ----- Simple Network Management Protocol -----
SNMP:
SNMP: Version = 0
SNMP: Community = Brutus
SNMP: Command = Get next request
SNMP: Request ID = 0
SNMP: Error status = 0 (No error)
SNMP: Error index = 0
SNMP:
SNMP: Object = {1.3.6.1.2.1.1.3} (sysUpTime)
SNMP: Value  = NULL
SNMP:
SNMP: Object = {1.3.6.1.2.1.7.5.1.1.0.0.0.0.161} (udpLocalAddress.0.0.0.0.161)
SNMP: Value  = NULL
SNMP:
SNMP: Object = {1.3.6.1.2.1.7.5.1.2.0.0.0.0.161} (udpLocalPort.0.0.0.0.161)
SNMP: Value  = NULL
SNMP:
-----------------------------------------------Frame 38--------------------------------------------------
SNMP: ----- Simple Network Management Protocol -----
SNMP:
SNMP: Version = 0
SNMP: Community = Brutus
SNMP: Command = Get response
SNMP: Request ID = 0
SNMP: Error status = 0 (No error)
SNMP: Error index = 0
SNMP:
SNMP: Object = {1.3.6.1.2.1.1.3.0} (sysUpTime.0)
SNMP: Value  = 263753463 hundredths of a second
SNMP:
SNMP: Object = {1.3.6.1.2.1.7.5.1.1.0.0.0.0.520} (udpLocalAddress.0.0.0.0.520)
SNMP: Value  = [0.0.0.0]
```

```
SNMP:
SNMP: Object = {1.3.6.1.2.1.7.5.1.2.0.0.0.0.520} (udpLocalPort.0.0.0.0.520)
SNMP: Value  = 520
SNMP:
---------------------------------------------Frame 39----------------------------------------------
SNMP: ----- Simple Network Management Protocol -----
SNMP:
SNMP: Version = 0
SNMP: Community = Brutus
SNMP: Command = Get next request
SNMP: Request ID = 0
SNMP: Error status = 0 (No error)
SNMP: Error index = 0
SNMP:
SNMP: Object = {1.3.6.1.2.1.1.3} (sysUpTime)
SNMP: Value  = NULL
SNMP:
SNMP: Object = {1.3.6.1.2.1.7.5.1.1.0.0.0.0.520} (udpLocalAddress.0.0.0.0.520)
SNMP: Value  = NULL
SNMP:
SNMP: Object = {1.3.6.1.2.1.7.5.1.2.0.0.0.0.520} (udpLocalPort.0.0.0.0.520)
SNMP: Value  = NULL
SNMP:
---------------------------------------------Frame 40----------------------------------------------
SNMP: ----- Simple Network Management Protocol -----
SNMP:
SNMP: Version = 0
SNMP: Community = Brutus
SNMP: Command = Get response
SNMP: Request ID = 0
SNMP: Error status = 0 (No error)
SNMP: Error index = 0
SNMP:
SNMP: Object = {1.3.6.1.2.1.1.3.0} (sysUpTime.0)
```

```
SNMP: Value  = 263753466 hundredths of a second
SNMP:
SNMP: Object = {1.3.6.1.2.1.7.5.1.2.0.0.0.0.69} (udpLocalPort.0.0.0.0.69)
SNMP: Value  = 69
SNMP:
SNMP: Object = {1.3.6.1.2.1.11.1.0} (snmpInPkts.0)
SNMP: Value  = 116744 (counter)
SNMP:
```

4.4.3. SNMP SetRequest example

This example issues a SetRequest PDU for an object on the Proteon router, then issues a GetRequest for the same object (see Trace 4.4.3) to verify that the action was properly completed. Frames 1 and 2 retrieve the current value of ipDefaultTTL; Frames 2 and 3 set a new value for that object; Frames 5 and 6 verify the new value; Frames 7 and 8 set the value back to the original; and finally, Frames 9 and 10 verify the previous operation.

Looking at the details, notice that in Frame 1 the Value = NULL as in the previous example. The GetResponse PDU (Frame 2) contains the requested value (60) of ipDefaultTTL (the default value of the Time-to-Live field within the IP header). Frame 3 contains a SetRequest PDU, assigning Value = 64 to ipDefaultTTL. The router sends a confirming GetResponse PDU in Frame 4. Frame 5 issues a GetRequest PDU to verify that the SetRequest changed the value of ipDefaultTTL to 64 (Frame 6). Frame 7 issues a second SetRequest, this time with Value = 60, which is acknowledged in Frame 8. Frames 9 and 10 confirm that the operation was successful.

Trace 4.4.3. SNNP Set ipDefaultTTL details

```
Sniffer Network Analyzer data 11-Dec-92 at 15:16:52 file SETIPTTL.ENC Pg 1
--------------------------------------------Frame 1 --------------------------------------
SNMP: ----- Simple Network Management Protocol -----
SNMP:
SNMP: Version = 0
```

SNMP: Community = Brutus
SNMP: Command = Get request
SNMP: Request ID = 0
SNMP: Error status = 0 (No error)
SNMP: Error index = 0
SNMP:
SNMP: Object = {1.3.6.1.2.1.1.3.0} (sysUpTime.0)
SNMP: Value = NULL
SNMP:
SNMP: Object = {1.3.6.1.2.1.4.1.0} (ipForwarding.0)
SNMP: Value = NULL
SNMP:
SNMP: Object = {1.3.6.1.2.1.4.2.0} (ipDefaultTTL.0)
SNMP: Value = NULL
SNMP:
---Frame 2 ---
SNMP: ----- Simple Network Management Protocol -----
SNMP:
SNMP: Version = 0
SNMP: Community = Brutus
SNMP: Command = Get response
SNMP: Request ID = 0
SNMP: Error status = 0 (No error)
SNMP: Error index = 0
SNMP:
SNMP: Object = {1.3.6.1.2.1.1.3.0} (sysUpTime.0)
SNMP: Value = 16862273 hundredths of a second
SNMP:
SNMP: Object = {1.3.6.1.2.1.4.1.0} (ipForwarding.0)
SNMP: Value = 1 (gateway)
SNMP:
SNMP: Object = {1.3.6.1.2.1.4.2.0} (ipDefaultTTL.0)
SNMP: Value = 60
SNMP:

```
---------------------------------------------Frame 3 ---------------------------------------------
SNMP: ----- Simple Network Management Protocol -----
SNMP:
SNMP: Version = 0
SNMP: Community = Brutus
SNMP: Command = Set request
SNMP: Request ID = 0
SNMP: Error status = 0 (No error)
SNMP: Error index = 0
SNMP:
SNMP: Object = {1.3.6.1.2.1.4.2.0} (ipDefaultTTL.0)
SNMP: Value  = 64
SNMP:
---------------------------------------------Frame 4 ---------------------------------------------
SNMP: ----- Simple Network Management Protocol -----
SNMP:
SNMP: Version = 0
SNMP: Community = Brutus
SNMP: Command = Get response
SNMP: Request ID = 0
SNMP: Error status = 0 (No error)
SNMP: Error index = 0
SNMP:
SNMP: Object = {1.3.6.1.2.1.4.2.0} (ipDefaultTTL.0)
SNMP: Value  = 64
SNMP:
---------------------------------------------Frame 5 ---------------------------------------------
SNMP: ----- Simple Network Management Protocol -----
SNMP:
SNMP: Version = 0
SNMP: Community = Brutus
SNMP: Command = Get request
SNMP: Request ID = 0
SNMP: Error status = 0 (No error)
```

SNMP: Error index = 0
SNMP:
SNMP: Object = {1.3.6.1.2.1.1.3.0} (sysUpTime.0)
SNMP: Value = NULL
SNMP:
SNMP: Object = {1.3.6.1.2.1.4.1.0} (ipForwarding.0)
SNMP: Value = NULL
SNMP:
SNMP: Object = {1.3.6.1.2.1.4.2.0} (ipDefaultTTL.0)
SNMP: Value = NULL
SNMP:
--Frame 6 --
SNMP: ----- Simple Network Management Protocol -----
SNMP:
SNMP: Version = 0
SNMP: Community = Brutus
SNMP: Command = Get response
SNMP: Request ID = 0
SNMP: Error status = 0 (No error)
SNMP: Error index = 0
SNMP:
SNMP: Object = {1.3.6.1.2.1.1.3.0} (sysUpTime.0)
SNMP: Value = 16863228 hundredths of a second
SNMP:
SNMP: Object = {1.3.6.1.2.1.4.1.0} (ipForwarding.0)
SNMP: Value = 1 (gateway)
SNMP:
SNMP: Object = {1.3.6.1.2.1.4.2.0} (ipDefaultTTL.0)
SNMP: Value = 64
SNMP:
--Frame 7 --
SNMP: ----- Simple Network Management Protocol -----
SNMP:
SNMP: Version = 0

SNMP: Community = Brutus
SNMP: Command = Set request
SNMP: Request ID = 0
SNMP: Error status = 0 (No error)
SNMP: Error index = 0
SNMP:
SNMP: Object = {1.3.6.1.2.1.4.2.0} (ipDefaultTTL.0)
SNMP: Value = 60
SNMP:
---Frame 8 ---
SNMP: ----- Simple Network Management Protocol -----
SNMP:
SNMP: Version = 0
SNMP: Community = Brutus
SNMP: Command = Get response
SNMP: Request ID = 0
SNMP: Error status = 0 (No error)
SNMP: Error index = 0
SNMP:
SNMP: Object = {1.3.6.1.2.1.4.2.0} (ipDefaultTTL.0)
SNMP: Value = 60
SNMP:
---Frame 9 ---
SNMP: ----- Simple Network Management Protocol -----
SNMP:
SNMP: Version = 0
SNMP: Community = Brutus
SNMP: Command = Get request
SNMP: Request ID = 0
SNMP: Error status = 0 (No error)
SNMP: Error index = 0
SNMP:
SNMP: Object = {1.3.6.1.2.1.1.3.0} (sysUpTime.0)
SNMP: Value = NULL

SNMP:
SNMP: Object = {1.3.6.1.2.1.4.1.0} (ipForwarding.0)
SNMP: Value = NULL
SNMP:
SNMP: Object = {1.3.6.1.2.1.4.2.0} (ipDefaultTTL.0)
SNMP: Value = NULL
SNMP:
---Frame 10---
SNMP: ----- Simple Network Management Protocol -----
SNMP:
SNMP: Version = 0
SNMP: Community = Brutus
SNMP: Command = Get response
SNMP: Request ID = 0
SNMP: Error status = 0 (No error)
SNMP: Error index = 0
SNMP:
SNMP: Object = {1.3.6.1.2.1.1.3.0} (sysUpTime.0)
SNMP: Value = 16863846 hundredths of a second
SNMP:
SNMP: Object = {1.3.6.1.2.1.4.1.0} (ipForwarding.0)
SNMP: Value = 1 (gateway)
SNMP:
SNMP: Object = {1.3.6.1.2.1.4.2.0} (ipDefaultTTL.0)
SNMP: Value = 60
SNMP:

4.4.4. SNMP Trap example

The final example shows how a Trap PDU indicates an alarm condition to the network manager. In this case, the agent generating the trap is a Network General Sniffer protocol analyzer (see Figure 4-13).

One set of network statistics is *network utilization*. Network utilization is a ratio between the total number of bits transmitted in a period of time (in this case five seconds) divided by the total number of bits that could theoretically be transmitted during the same period. A typical network would have a network utilization in the 5 to 20 percent range. For this example, I set the threshold to the unrealistically low value of 1 percent over a five second period. When the network reaches that threshold, the Sniffer generates a Trap PDU and sends it to the SunNet Manager. Another Sniffer analyzer captured the results.

This transmission follows the Trap PDU structure shown in Figure 4-10. The SNMP authentication header contains the version number and community string, and the PDU Type specifies a Trap (PDU Type = 4). The Enterprise field gives the OID for the authority that defined the trap. The prefix {1.3.6.1.4.1} identifies the Private Enterprises subtree, and the 110 identifies Network General Corporation (see RFC 1340, or Appendix F). The Generic Trap field indicates an enterprise-specific trap (Trap = 6). This means that the value of the Enterprise field indicates the authority (Network General) that defined this trap.

The Specific Trap field has Type = 7, which Network General defined. The variable bindings also contain variables and values that Network General defined. The third object's value (Abs usage exceeded 1 percent) indicates the threshold set in the protocol analyzer.

Trace 4.4.4. An enterprise-specific trap: Network utilization exceeded 1 percent during a five second period.

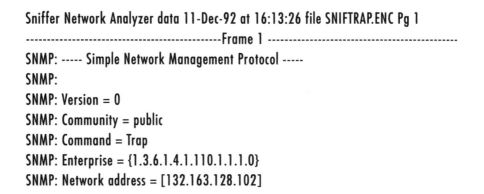

```
Sniffer Network Analyzer data 11-Dec-92 at 16:13:26 file SNIFTRAP.ENC Pg 1
-------------------------------------------Frame 1 -------------------------------------------
SNMP: ----- Simple Network Management Protocol -----
SNMP:
SNMP: Version = 0
SNMP: Community = public
SNMP: Command = Trap
SNMP: Enterprise = {1.3.6.1.4.1.110.1.1.1.0}
SNMP: Network address = [132.163.128.102]
```

SNMP: Generic trap = 6 (Enterprise specific)
SNMP: Specific trap = 7
SNMP: Time ticks = 244894900
SNMP:
SNMP: Object = {1.3.6.1.4.1.110.1.1.1.1.1.1.1.1.1}
      (Network General Corp.1.1.1.1.1.1.1.1.1)
SNMP: Value = 53 (counter)
SNMP:
SNMP: Object = {1.3.6.1.4.1.110.1.1.1.1.1.1.1.2.1}
      (Network General Corp.1.1.1.1.1.1.2.1)
SNMP: Value = 1
SNMP:
SNMP: Object = {1.3.6.1.4.1.110.1.1.1.1.1.1.1.3.1}
      (Network General Corp.1.1.1.1.1.1.3.1)
SNMP: Value = Abs usage exceeded 1%
SNMP:
SNMP: Object = {1.3.6.1.4.1.110.1.1.1.1.1.1.1.4.1}
      (Network General Corp.1.1.1.1.1.1.4.1)
SNMP: Value = 5
SNMP:
SNMP: Object = {1.3.6.1.4.1.110.1.1.1.1.1.1.1.5.1}
      (Network General Corp.1.1.1.1.1.1.5.1)
SNMP: Value = 0
SNMP:
SNMP: Object = {1.3.6.1.4.1.110.1.1.1.1.1.1.1.6.1}
      (Network General Corp.1.1.1.1.1.1.6.1)
SNMP: Value = 7
SNMP:
SNMP: Object = {1.3.6.1.4.1.110.1.1.1.1.1.1.1.7.1}
      (Network General Corp.1.1.1.1.1.1.7.1)
SNMP: Value = 724119640 (counter)
SNMP:
SNMP: Object = {1.3.6.1.4.1.110.1.1.1.1.1.1.1.8.1}
      (Network General Corp .1.1.1.1.1.1.8.1)

SNMP: Value = Global Network
SNMP:

4.5. The ASN.1 SNMP Definition

To conclude the discussion of SNMP protocol operation, Definition 4-1 is the ASN.1 definition of SNMP (from RFC 1157). Of special interest are the constructs of the various SNMP PDUs. Those constructs summarize the variables used within the PDUs, plus the values that those variables may assume.

Definition 4-1. The ASN.1 definition of SNMP

```
RFC1157-SNMP DEFINITIONS ::= BEGIN
IMPORTS
      ObjectName, ObjectSyntax, NetworkAddress, IpAddress, TimeTicks
         FROM RFC1155-SMI;

      -- top-level message
      Message ::=
              SEQUENCE {
                  version              -- version-1 for this RFC
                      INTEGER {
                          version-1(0)
                      },
                  community        -- community name
                      OCTET STRING,
                  data             -- e.g., PDUs if trivial
                      ANY          -- authentication is being used
              }

      -- protocol data units
      PDUs ::=
              CHOICE {
                      get-request
                          GetRequest-PDU,
```

```
                        get-next-request
                            GetNextRequest-PDU,
                        get-response
                            GetResponse-PDU,
                        set-request
                            SetRequest-PDU,
                        trap
                            Trap-PDU
                    }
-- PDUs
GetRequest-PDU ::=
    [0]
        IMPLICIT PDU
GetNextRequest-PDU ::=
    [1]
        IMPLICIT PDU
GetResponse-PDU ::=
    [2]
        IMPLICIT PDU
SetRequest-PDU ::=
    [3]
        IMPLICIT PDU
PDU ::=
        SEQUENCE {
            request-id
                INTEGER,
            error-status        -- sometimes ignored
                INTEGER {
                    noError(0),
                    tooBig(1),
                    noSuchName(2),
                    badValue(3),
                    readOnly(4),
                    genErr(5)
```

```
                    },
            error-index        -- sometimes ignored
                    INTEGER,
            variable-bindings -- values are sometimes ignored
                    VarBindList
        }
Trap-PDU ::=
    [4]
        IMPLICIT SEQUENCE {
            enterprise          -- type of object generating
                                -- trap, see sysObjectID in [5]

                    OBJECT IDENTIFIER,
            agent-addr          -- address of object generating
                NetworkAddress, -- trap
            generic-trap        -- generic trap type
                INTEGER {
                    coldStart(0),
                    warmStart(1),
                    linkDown(2),
                    linkUp(3),
                    authenticationFailure(4),
                    egpNeighborLoss(5),
                    enterpriseSpecific(6)
                },
            specific-trap       -- specific code, present even
                    INTEGER,    -- if generic-trap is not
                                -- enterpriseSpecific
            time-stamp          -- time elapsed between the last
                TimeTicks,      -- (re-)initialization of the
                                       network
                                -- entity and the generation of
                                       the trap
            variable-bindings -- "interesting" information
```

```
            VarBindList
    }

-- variable bindings
VarBind  ::=
        SEQUENCE {
            name
                ObjectName,
            value
                ObjectSyntax
        }
VarBindList ::=
        SEQUENCE OF
            VarBind
END
```

This chapter has explored the structure of the SNMP messages and looked at some examples of various SNMP PDUs. The Internet Engineering Task Force (IETF) continues to enhance SNMP. Such enhancements include the transmission of SNMP over other transport protocols, including OSI (RFC 1418 [4-6]), IPX (RFC 1420 [4-7]) and AppleTalk (RFC 1419 [4-8]); and work on SNMP Version 2, which Chapter 7 will discuss in detail.

Our discussion delved into the technical reasons for SNMP's popularity. It is a simple yet elegant network management solution. The trade press obviously agrees, as recent journal articles [4-9 to 4-20] attest. Another useful publication is *The Simple Times*, a bimonthly newsletter available via the Internet, which specifically addresses SNMP-related issues. For further information, send an email message to st-subscriptions@simple-times.org.

4.6. References

[4-1]   Case, J.D., M. Fedor, M.L. Schoffstall and C. Davin. "Simple Network Management Protocol (SNMP)." RFC 1157, May 1990.

[4-2]   Case, Jeffrey D., et. al. "Network Management and the Design of SNMP." *ConneXions* (March 1989): 22-26.

[4-3]   Kastenholz, F., ed. "SNMP Communication Services." RFC 1270, October 1991.

[4-4]   Davin, J., J. Galvin and K. Mcloghrie. "SNMP Administrative Model." RFC 1351, July 1992.

[4-5]   Rose, M.T. ed. "Convention for Defining Traps for Use with the SNMP." RFC 1215, March 1991.

[4-6]   M. Rose. "SNMP over OSI." RFC 1418, March 1993.

[4-7]   S. Bostock. "SNMP over IPX.", RFC 1420, March 1993.

[4-8]   G. Minshall and M. Ritter. "SNMP over AppleTalk," RFC 1419, March 1993.

[4-9]   Krall, Gary. "SNMP Opens New Lines of Sight." *Data Communications* (March 21, 1990): 45-50.

[4-10] Ben-Artzi, Amatzia, et. al. "Network Management of TCP/IP Networks: Present and Future." *IEEE Network* (July 1990): 35-43.

[4-11] Fedor, Mark S. "Case Study: Using SNMP to Manage a Large Network." *ConneXions* (August 1990): 28-33.

[4-12] Harrison, Bradford T. "SNMP Struts Its Stuff." *LAN Computing* (November 1990): 21-22.

[4-13] Simpson, David. "SNMP: Simple But Limited." *Systems Integration* (December 1990): 26-30.

[4-14] Dolan, Tom. "SNMP Streamlines Multi-Vendor Network Management." *LAN Technology* (February 1991): 29-38.

[4-15] Scott, Karyl. "Taking Care of Business with SNMP." *Data Communications* (March 21, 1990): 31-41.

[4-16] Knack, Kella. "Network Management Protocols." *LAN Computing* (May 7, 1991): 17-18.

[4-17] Ezerski, Michael B. "SNMP Completes the TCP/IP Solution." *Networking Management* (September 1991): 64-67

[4-18] Jones, Katherine. "Network Management in the World of Standards: The Role of the SNMP Protocol in Managing Networks." *International Journal of Network Management* (September 4, 1991): 5-13.

[4-19] Osmundsen, Sheila. "SNMP: The Foundation for TCP/IP Net Management." *Digital News* (March 2, 1992): 34-38.

[4-20] Wittman, Art. "Examining the Ins and Outs of SNMP." *Network Computing* (December 1992): 130-134.

5 Lower-Layer Protocol Support for SNMP

So far, this book has discussed network management applications, and the languages and protocols, such as ASN.1 and SNMP, that manage complex internetworks. An underlying communication infrastructure is also necessary for the manager and agent to communicate network management information. This infrastructure exists at the OSI Transport, Network, and Data Link layers (review Figure 4-1a), or at the DARPA Host-to-Host, Internet, and Network Interface layers.

SNMP messages fit inside the OSI Data Link layer or DARPA Local Network layer frame. To send SNMP messages, the system requires the User Datagram Protocol (UDP) and the Internet Protocol (IP), as shown in Figure 5-1. Together, the SNMP message, plus UDP and IP headers, comprise an IP datagram. This chapter discusses these supporting protocols.

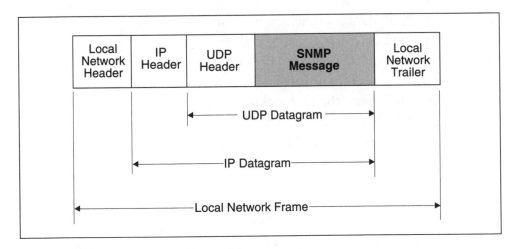

Figure 5-1. An SNMP message within a transmission frame

5.1. User Datagram Protocol (UDP)

UDP provides a connectionless host-to-host communication path for the SNMP message. A connectionless path is one in which the communication channel is not established prior to the transmission of data. Instead, the network transmits the data in a package called a *datagram*. The datagram contains all of the addressing information necessary for the SNMP message to reach its intended destination. UDP is described in RFC 768 [Reference 5-1], and is a DARPA Host-to-Host (or OSI Transport layer) protocol. UDP assumes that IP, which is also connectionless, is the underlying DARPA Internet (or OSI Network Layer) protocol.

The UDP service requires minimal overhead, and therefore uses the relatively small UDP header shown in Figure 5-2. Note in the figure that each horizontal group of bits, called a *word*, is 32 bits wide. The first two fields in the UDP header are the source and destination port numbers (each 2 octets in length) that identify the higher-layer protocol process that the datagram carries. Port number 161 (decimal) identifies SNMP messages, and port number 162 identifies SNMP traps. (Note that the SNMP agent processes use these defined ports; the manager may use these ports, or any other port. Thus, multiple managers can address the same agent process.) The Source Port field is optional, and when not used contains all ZEROs. The Length field (2 octets) is the length of the UDP datagram, which has a minimum value of 8 octets. The Checksum field (2 octets) is also optional, and is filled with all ZEROs if the upper layer protocol (ULP) process does not require a checksum. The checksum is calculated by using the Pseudo Header, which includes the source and destination IP addresses, the Protocol field obtained from the IP header, and the length of the UDP datagram. The use of the IP address to calculate the Pseudo Header assures that the UDP datagram is delivered to the correct destination network and host.

Other host processes that use UDP as the Host-to-Host protocol include the Time protocol, port number 37; the Domain Name Server (DNS), port number 53; the Bootstrap Protocol (BOOTP) server and client, port numbers 67 and 68, respectively; the Trivial File Transfer Protocol (TFTP), port number

69; and the Sun Microsystems Remote Procedure Call (SunRPC), port number 111. All of these applications are designed with the assumption that if the Host-to-Host connection fails, some higher-layer process (such as the network management application itself) would recover. Other applications require more reliable end-to-end data transmissions, and therefore use the more rigorous Transmission Control Protocol (TCP), which is discussed in detail in the companion volume *Troubleshooting TCP/IP* [5-2].

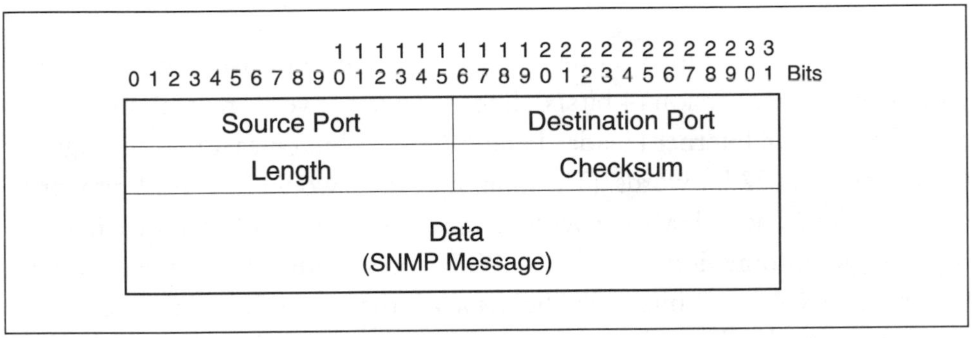

```
                        1 1 1 1 1 1 1 1 1 1 2 2 2 2 2 2 2 2 2 2 3 3
    0 1 2 3 4 5 6 7 8 9 0 1 2 3 4 5 6 7 8 9 0 1 2 3 4 5 6 7 8 9 0 1  Bits
```

Source Port	Destination Port
Length	Checksum
Data (SNMP Message)	

Figure 5-2. The User Datagram Protocol (UDP) header

5.2. Internet Protocol (IP)

IP, as defined in RFC 791 [5-3], works closely with UDP. IP handles datagram delivery. In other words, the IP destination address routes the datagram to the correct host on the specified network. The UDP port address then routes the datagram within the host to the correct host process.

To deliver datagrams, IP deals with two issues: addressing and fragmentation. The address assures that the datagram arrives at the correct destination. Datagram transmission is analogous to mailing a letter. When you mail a letter, you write a source and destination address on the envelope, place the information to be sent inside, and drop the resulting message in a mail box. With the postal service, the mailbox is a blue (or red, depending upon where you live) box. With the Internet, the mailbox service is the node where you enter the network.

Fragmentation is necessary because the sequence of LANs and WANs that any particular datagram may traverse can have differing frame sizes, and the IP datagram must fit within these varying frames (see Figure 5-1). For example, if the endpoint is attached to an IEEE 802.3 LAN with a maximum data field size of 1500 octets, IP must fragment the large IP datagram into smaller pieces (fragments) that will fit into the constraining frame. The distant node then reassembles the fragments back into a single IP datagram (sort of a reverse Humpty-Dumpty).

As you can see in Figure 5-3, the IP header contains at least 20 octets of control information. Version (4 bits) defines the current version of IP, and should be equal to four. Internet Header Length (IHL, 4 bits) measures the length of the IP header in 32-bit words. (The minimum value would be five 32-bit words, or 20 octets). The IHL also provides a measurement (or offset) for where the higher-layer information, such as the TCP header, begins within the datagram. The type of service (8 bits) tells the network the quality of service requested for this particular datagram. Values include:

Bits 0-2:	Precedence (or relative importance of this datagram)
111	Network Control
110	Internetwork Control
101	CRITIC/ECP
100	Flash Override
011	Flash
010	Immediate
001	Priority
000	Routine
Bit 3:	Delay, 0=Normal, 1=Low
Bit 4:	Throughput, 0=Normal, 1=High

Bit 5:   Reliability, 0=Normal, 1=High

Bits 6-7:   Reserved for future use (set to 0)

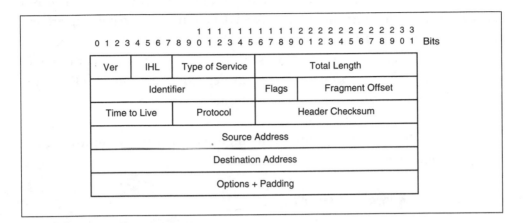

Figure 5-3. Internet Protocol (IP) header

The Total Length field (16 bits) measures the length, in octets, of the IP datagram (the IP header plus higher-layer information.) The 16-bit field allows for a datagram of up to 65,535 octets in length, although at minimum all hosts must be able to handle datagrams of 576 octets in length.

The next 32-bit word contains three fields that deal with datagram fragmentation/reassembly. The sender assigns the Identification field (16 bits) to reassemble the fragments into the datagram. Three flags indicate how the fragmentation process is to be handled:

- Bit 0: Reserved (set to 0)

- Bit 1: (DF) 0=May fragment, 1-Don't fragment

- Bit 2: (MF) 0=Last fragment, 1-More fragments

The last field within this word is a 13-bit fragment offset, which indicates where in the complete message this fragment belongs. This offset is measured in 64-bit units.

The next word in the IP header contains a time-to-live (TTL) measurement, which is the maximum amount of time that the datagram is allowed to live within the internet. When TTL=0, the datagram is destroyed. This field is a fail-safe measure that prevents misaddressed datagrams from wandering around the internet forever. TTL may be measured in either router hops or seconds, with a maximum of 255 of either measurement. If the measurement is in seconds, the maximum of 255 seconds is equivalent to 4.25 minutes (a long time to be "lost" within today's high-speed internetworks).

The Protocol field (8 bits) identifies the higher-layer protocol following the IP header. Examples include:

Decimal	Keyword	Description
1	ICMP	Internet Control Message Protocol
6	TCP	Transmission Control Protocol
17	UDP	User Datagram Protocol

RFC 1340, "Assigned Numbers" [5-4], provides a more detailed listing of the protocols defined. A 16-bit header checksum completes the third 32-bit word.

The fourth and fifth words of the IP header contain the source and destination addresses, respectively. Addressing may be implemented at several architectural layers. For example, hardware addresses are used at the DARPA Network Interface layer (or OSI Data Link layer) and are associated with a specific network interface card, usually burned into an address ROM on the card. The addresses within the IP header are the Internet layer (or OSI Network layer) addresses. The Internet address is a logical address that routes the IP datagram through the Internet to the correct host and network (LAN, MAN, or WAN).

5.3. Internet Addressing

Each 32-bit IP address is divided into Host ID and Network ID sections, and may take one of five formats, Class A through E addresses, as shown in Figure 5-4. The formats differ in the number of bits allocated to the Host and Network IDs and are identified by the first three bits. Class A addresses are designed for very large networks having many hosts and are identified by Bit 0 = 0. Bits 1 through 7 identify the network, and Bits 8 through 31 identify the specific host on that network. With a seven-bit Network ID, only 128 class A addresses are available. Of these, addresses 0 and 127 are reserved [4-8].

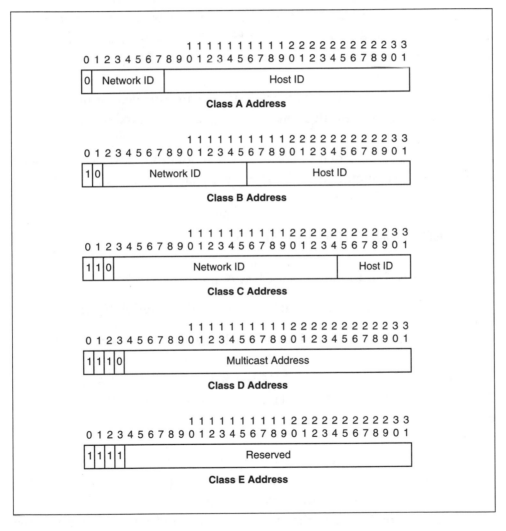

Figure 5-4. IP address formats

Class B addresses are designed for corporate internetworks having multiple LANs. Class B addresses are identified by the first two bits having a value of 10 (binary). The next 14 bits identify the Network and the remaining 16 bits identify the Host. As many as 16,384 Class B addresses are possible with addresses 0 and 16,383 reserved.

Class C addresses are generally used for smaller networks such as LANs. Class C addresses begin with a binary 110. The next 21 bits identify the Network, and the remaining 8 bits identify the Host. A total of 2,097,152 Class C addresses are possible, with addresses 0 and 2,097,151 reserved.

Class D addresses begin with a binary 1110 and are intended for multicasting. Class E addresses begin with a binary 1111 and are reserved for future use.

All IP addresses are written in dotted decimal notation, in which each octet is given a decimal number from 0 to 255. For example, network 10.55.31.84 is represented in binary as

00001010 00110111 00011111 1010100

- The first bit (0) indicates a Class A address.

- The next seven bits (0001010) represent the Network ID (decimal 10).

- The last 24 bits (00110111 00011111 1010100) represent the Host ID.

Class A addresses begin with 1-127, Class B with 128-191, Class C with 192-223, and Class D with 224-254. Thus, an address of 150.100.200.5 is easily identified as a Class B address.

IP addresses may be divided into two fields that identify a Network and a Host. A central authority assigns the Network ID, and the network administrator assigns the Host ID. Routers send a packet to a particular network (using the Network ID), and then the Network completes the delivery to the particular Host.

If an organization had two networks, it could request two Network ID assignments from the central authority. Unfortunately, this would cause the routing tables within Hosts and Routers to greatly expand. As more Network IDs were assigned, the routing tables would continue to grow. The popularity of LANs in the mid-1980s inspired the Internet community to revise the IP address structure to allow for an additional field that would identify a subnetwork within an assigned Network ID. Thus the Network, Host address has been replaced with Network, Subnetwork, Host. The space required for the Subnetwork field comes from reducing the Host field. The central authority assigns the Network ID, and the individual organization assigns the Subnetwork IDs as well as the Host IDs on each subnetwork.

5.4. Internet Control Message Protocol (ICMP)

If internetworks were flawless, datagrams would always be routed to their intended destination with no errors, excessive delays, or retransmissions. Unfortunately, this is not the case. As discussed previously, IP provides a connectionless service to the attached hosts, but requires an additional module, known as the Internet Control Message Protocol (ICMP), to report any errors that may occur in the processing of those datagrams. Examples of errors would be undeliverable datagrams or incorrect routes. The protocol is also used to test the path to a distant host (known as a PING), or to request an address mask for a particular subnet. ICMP is an integral part of IP and must be implemented in IP modules contained in hosts and routers. The standard for ICMP is RFC 792 [5-5].

IP datagrams contain ICMP messages. In other words, ICMP is a user (client) of IP, and the IP header precedes the ICMP message. The datagram would thus be IP header, ICMP header, and finally ICMP data. Protocol=1 identifies ICMP within the IP Header. A Type field within the ICMP header further identifies the purpose and format of the ICMP message. Any data required to complete the ICMP message follows the ICMP header.

Thirteen ICMP messages formats have been defined, each with a specific ICMP header format. Two of these formats (Information Request/Reply) are considered obsolete, and several others share a common message structure. The result is six unique message formats, as shown in Figure 5-5.

Network managers need to understand each of these ICMP messages because they contain valuable information about network status. All the headers share the first three fields. The Type field (1 octet) identifies one of the thirteen unique ICMP messages. These include:

Type Code	ICMP Message
0	Echo Reply
3	Destination Unreachable
4	Source Quench
5	Redirect
8	Echo
11	Time Exceeded
12	Parameter Problem
13	Timestamp
14	Timestamp Reply
15	Information Request (obsolete)
16	Information Reply (obsolete)
17	Address Mask Request
18	Address Mask Reply

The second field is labeled Code (1 octet), and elaborates on specific message types. For example, the Code field for the Destination Unreachable message indicates whether the network, host, protocol, or port was the unreachable entity. The third field is a checksum (2 octets) on the ICMP message. The ICMP message formats diverge after the third field.

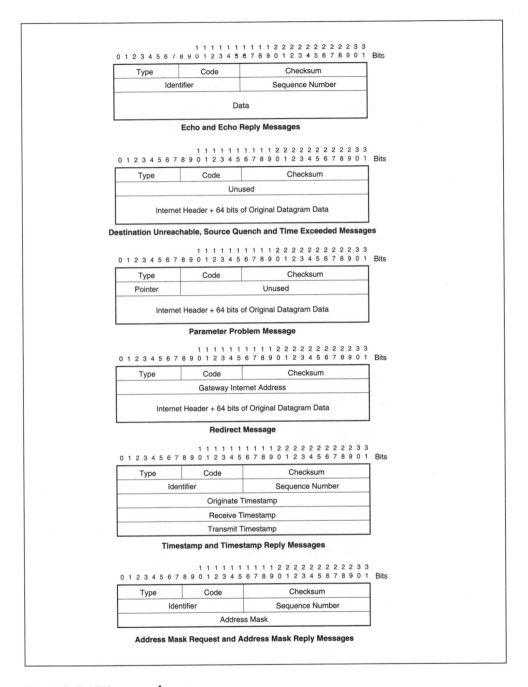

Figure 5-5. ICMP message formats.

The Echo message (ICMP Type=8) tests the communication path from a sender to receiver via the Internet. On many hosts, this function is known as PING. The sender transmits an Echo message, which may also contain an identifier (2 octets) and a sequence number (2 octets) as well as data. When the intended destination receives the message, it reverses the source and destination addresses, recomputes the checksum, and returns an echo reply (ICMP Type=0). The contents of the Data field (if any) would also return to the sender.

The Destination Unreachable message (ICMP Type=3) is used when the router or host is unable to deliver the datagram. This message is returned to the source host of the datagram in question, and its code field includes the specific reason for the delivery problem:

Code	Meaning
0	Net Unreachable
1	Host Unreachable
2	Protocol Unreachable
3	Port Unreachable
4	Fragmentation Needed and DF Set
5	Source Route Failed

Routers use codes 0, 1, 4, or 5. Hosts use codes 2 or 3. For example, when a datagram arrives at a router, it does a table lookup to determine the outgoing path to use. If the router determines that the destination network is unreachable (that is, a distance of infinite hops away), it returns a Net Unreachable message. Similarly, if a host is unable to process a datagram because the requested protocol or port is inactive, it would return a Protocol Unreachable or Port Unreachable message, respectively. Included in the Destination Unreachable message is the IP header plus the first 64 bits (8 octets) of the datagram in question. This returned data helps the host diagnose the failure in the transmission process.

The advantage of the datagram's connectionless nature is its simplicity. The disadvantage is its inability to regulate the amount of traffic into the network. As an analogy, consider the problem that your local post office faces. To handle the maximum possible number of letters, it needs enough boxes to handle the holiday rush. Building many boxes might be wasteful, however, because many of the boxes may not be used fully during the summer. If a router or host becomes congested with datagrams, it may send a Source Quench message (ICMP Type=4) asking the source of those datagrams to reduce its output. This mechanism is similar to traffic signals that regulate the flow of cars onto a freeway. The Source Quench message does not use the second 32-bit word of the ICMP header, but fills it with ZEROs. The rest of the message contains the IP header and the first 8 octets of the datagram that triggered the request.

Hosts do not always choose the correct destination address for a particular datagram, and occasionally send one to the wrong router. This scenario can occur when the host is initialized, and its routing tables are incomplete. When such a routing mistake occurs, the router receiving the datagram returns a Redirect message to the host specifying a better route. The Code field in the datagram would contain the following information:

Code	Message
0	Redirect datagrams for the network
1	Redirect datagrams for the host
2	Redirect datagrams for the type of service and network
3	Redirect datagrams for the type of service and host

The Redirect message (ICMP Type=5) contains the router (gateway) address necessary for the datagram to reach the desired destination. In addition, the IP header plus the first 8 octets of the datagram in question return to the source host to aid the diagnostic processes.

Another potential problem of connectionless networks is that datagrams can get lost within the network. Alternatively, congestion could prevent all fragments of a datagram from being reassembled within the host's required time. Either of these situations could trigger an ICMP Time Exceeded message (ICMP Type=11). This message contains two codes: time-to-live exceeded in transmit (code=0), and fragment reassembly time exceeded (code=1). The rest of the message has the same format as the Source Quench message: the second word contains all ZEROs and the rest of the message contains the IP header and first 8 octets of the offending datagram.

If a datagram cannot be processed because of errors, higher-layer processes recognize the errors and discard the datagram. Parameter problems within an IP datagram header (such an incorrect Type of Service field) would trigger the sending of an ICMP Parameter Problem message (ICMP Type=12) to the source of that datagram, identifying the location of the problem. The message contains a pointer that identifies the octet with the error. The rest of the message contains the IP datagram header plus the first 8 octets of data, as before.

The Timestamp Message (ICMP Type=13) and Timestamp Reply (ICMP Type=14) measure the round-trip transit time between two machines, or synchronize the clocks of two different machines. The first two words of the Timestamp and Timestamp Reply messages are similar to the Echo and Echo Reply messages. The next five fields contain time-stamps, measured in milliseconds since midnight, Universal Time (UT). The Timestamp requester fills in the Originate field when it transmits the request; the recipient fills in the Receive Timestamp upon its receipt. The recipient also fills in the Transmit Timestamp when it transmits the Timestamp Reply message. With this information, the requester can estimate the remote processing and round-trip transit times. (Note that these are only estimates, since network delay is a highly variable measurement.) The remote processing time is the Received Timestamp minus Transmit Timestamp. The round-trip transit time is the Timestamp Reply message arrival time minus the Originate Timestamp. With these two calculations, the two clocks can be synchronized.

The subnetting requirements (RFC 950) added the Address Mask Request (ICMP Type=17) and Address Mask Reply (ICMP Type=18) to the ICMP message set. It is assumed that the requesting host knows its own internet address. (If not, it uses RARP to discover its internet address.) The host broadcasts the Address Mask Request message to destination address 255.255.255.255 and fills the Address Mask field of the ICMP message with ZEROs, and the IP router that knows the correct address mask responds. For example, the response for a Class B network (when subnet addresses are not used) would be 255.255.0.0. A Class B network using an 8-bit subnet field would be 255.255.255.0. Section 4.2 of *Troubleshooting TCP/IP* provides additional details on subnet addresses.

5.5. Network Interface Protocols

The lowest layer of the DARPA architectural model is the Network Interface layer, which encompasses the OSI Data Link and Physical layers. This layer is responsible for the network hardware and topology, such as Ethernet, token-ring, FDDI, and so on. WAN protocols, such as dial-up or leased-line connections, X.25, or Frame Relay, can also be implemented at this layer. Because most SNMP implementations involve local, not remote manager/agent relationships, I will concentrate on the LAN protocols in this section. For more information on the WAN options, consult Chapter 3 of *Troubleshooting TC/IP* [5-2].

5.5.1. Ethernet

DEC, Intel, and Xerox (known collectively as DIX) developed Ethernet in 1973. The first version, known as Experimental Ethernet, operated at 3 Mbps, and used 8-bit addresses. This later became Ethernet Version 1, and finally Ethernet Version 2, which we use today. Ethernet Version 2 transmits at 10 Mbps and uses 48 bit addresses. Ethernet was the first LAN to achieve wide acceptance, and much of its development coincided with research into the Internet protocols. As a result, many TCP/IP-based internetworks contain Ethernet segments.

One word of caution is in order, however. In the early 1980s, the DIX Ethernet Standard became the model for IEEE 802.3, the Carrier Sense, Multiple Access Bus with Collision Detection (CSMA/CD). The IEEE improved the

DIX version and published IEEE 802.3 in 1983. The Ethernet and IEEE 802.3 standards are similar, but not identical. This section discusses Ethernet. Section 5.5.2 talks about IEEE 802.3.

The Ethernet frame format, shown in Figure 5-6, defines a length of between 64 and 1518 octets, including the header, data, and trailer. The header consists of destination and source addresses that are 6 octets (48 bits) each, plus a 2-octet field known as the Type (or Ethertype) field. The Ethernet-designated destination address for broadcast frames is all ONES (FFFFFFFFFFFFH). The type designates the higher-layer protocol in use within the data field. A number of these Ethernet Protocol Types are defined, and can be found in RFC 1340.

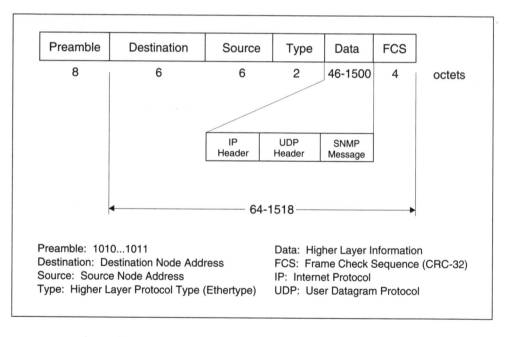

Figure 5-6. Ethernet frame with SNMP message (©1982 Digital Equipment Corp. (DEC))

The data field must be between 46 and 1500 octets in length. If an extremely short IP datagram is transmitted (less than 46 octets), the data field is padded with zeros to reach the minimum 46 octet length. (This padding is not considered part of the IP datagram length and is not counted in the Total Length field within the IP header.) The Internet Standard for Ethernet networks (RFC 894 [5-6]) and Appendix B of the IP specification (RFC 791) provide further details on the specific data formats.

5.5.2. IEEE 802.3

As I noted previously, the IEEE 802.3 standard, which is covered by the RFC 1042 [5-7] Internet standard, is similar but not identical to the DIX Ethernet. Figure 5-7 shows the IEEE 802.3 format. IEEE 802.3's destination and source address fields may be 2 or 6 octets long, although the 6 octet length, which matches the Ethernet address lengths, is most common. The Address Resolution Protocol (ARP) maps the IP address (32 bits) to the IEEE 802 address (48 bits). The ARP hardware code for IEEE 802 networks is 6. However, broadcast addresses for both Ethernet and IEEE 802 networks are consistent with all ONEs.

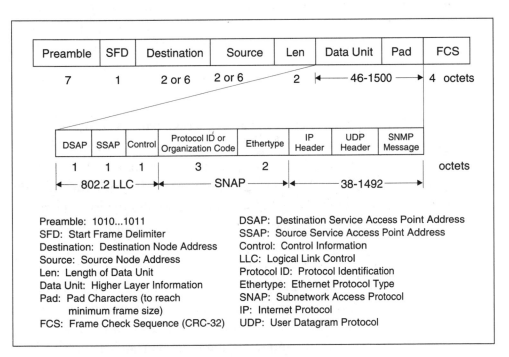

Figure 5-7. IEEE 802.3 frame with SNMP message (©1990, IEEE)

Next, the IEEE 802.3 frame defines a Length field, which specifies the length of the Data unit. Recall that, in the Ethernet frame, this was the Ethertype, indicating the higher-layer protocol in use. These two octets (the Ethertype or Length fields) distinguish whether the frame format is Ethernet or IEEE 802.3, respectively. If the Data Link layer driver mixes these up, confusion will result. For example, if the destination host expects an Ethernet frame (with an Ethertype field), it cannot respond to an IEEE 802.3 frame containing the Length field.

The Data Field contains the information from the higher layers, plus two IEEE-defined headers. The first header is the *Logical Link Control* (LLC) header defined by IEEE 802.2. The LLC header includes destination and source service access point addresses (DSAP and SSAP, respectively), and a control field. The second header is known as the *Sub-Network Access Protocol* (SNAP), defined by IEEE Standard 802-1990. This header includes a Protocol ID or Organization Code field (3 octets) and an Ethertype field (2 octets). The combination of the LLC and SNAP headers allows the higher-layer protocol in use to have both an SAP and Ethertype designation. The rest of the Data field contains the higher-layer information, such as an IP datagram.

5.5.3. IEEE 802.5

The IEEE 802.5 token-ring has enjoyed great success, partly because of strong support from major networking companies such as Apple, IBM, and Proteon, and partly because of the protocol's built-in provision for internetworking. This provision is known as *source routing* and uses the Routing Information (RI) field to connect rings via bridges. The RI field specifies the path the frame must take from its source to its destination. The mechanism for determining that path is called *route discovery*.

The IP Datagram occupies the Information field of the token-ring frame, as shown in Figure 5-8. Any necessary Routing Information precedes the Information field. Inside the Information field is the IEEE 802.2 LLC header (3 octets), SNAP header (5 octets), and the IP datagram (variable length). Given a minimum IP datagram header of 20 octets, the protocol overhead (LLC +

SNAP + IP) is 28 octets per IP datagram. The maximum length of the information field (and thus the encapsulated IP datagram) varies, depending on the "token holding time" parameter. This parameter specifies the length of time a particular node may hold the token before it must pass the token to its downstream neighbor. RFC 1042 [5-7] discusses an example token holding time of 9 milliseconds, which results in a maximum length of the IP header plus datagram of 4464 octets.

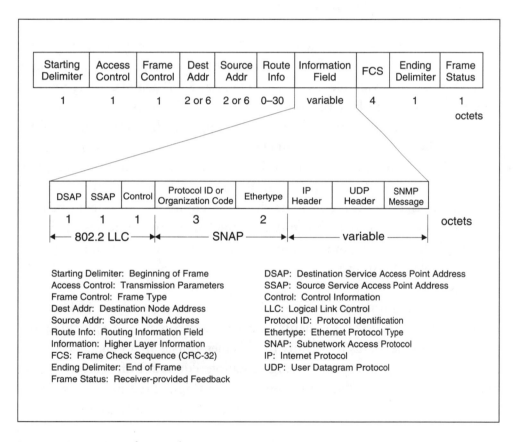

Figure 5-8. IEEE 802.5 frame with SNMP message *(©1989, IEEE)*

5.5.4. ARCNET

Datapoint Corporation developed the Attached Resource Computer Network (ARCNET) in 1977. ARCNET is a token-passing architecture that can have several Physical layer implementations, including a linear bus, a star, or a branching tree. The original version supported a transmission rate of 2.5 Mbps and up to 255 workstations, and is standardized as ANSI 878.1. In February 1992, Datapoint announced ARCNETPLUS, a 20 Mbps network which is downward-compatible with the original ARCNET.

The Internet standard for ARCNET, RFC 1201 [5-8], suggests methods for encapsulating both IP and ARP datagrams within the ARCNET frame. Three frame formats are available, as shown in Figures 5-9a, b, and c. Note that this RFC supersedes the older version (RFC 1051), and makes a number of protocol enhancements for improved TCP/IP support. The short frame format (Figure 5-9a) limits the transmitted client data to 249 octets. The long frame (Figure 5-9b) allows between 253 and 504 octets of client data. An exception frame (Figure 5-9c) is used with frames having 250 to 252 octets of client data. (Note that the frame formats shown in Figure 5-9 appear in the software buffers. The format transmitted by the hardware duplicates the Destination ID [DID], does not send the Unused and Protocol ID fields, and adds some hardware framing.)

The ARCNET frame may contain up to 512 octets, of which 504 may be client data. The sender fragments larger packets, using the Split Flag and Sequence Number fields to identify the fragments. The Split Flag takes on one of three values depending on the fragmentation required. Unfragmented packets use Split Flag = 0. The first fragment of a fragmented packet uses Split Flag = $((T-2)*2)+1$, where T = total number of expected fragments. Subsequent fragments use Split Flag = $((N-1)*2)$, where N is the number of this fragment.

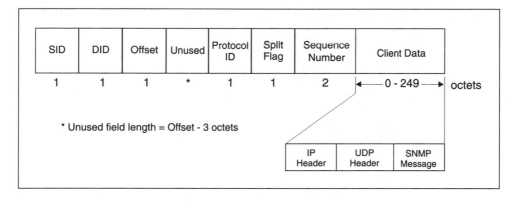

Figure 5-9a. ARCNET short frame format with SNMP message

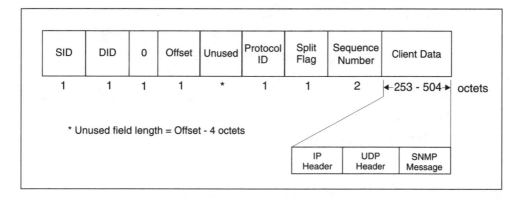

Figure 5-9b. ARCNET long frame format with SNMP message

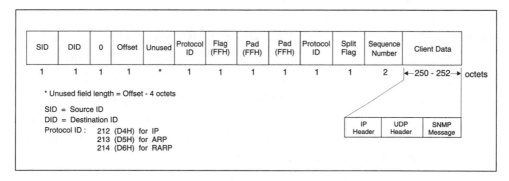

Figure 5-9c. ARCNET exception frame format with SNMP message

For example, assume that a packet requires 8 fragments. The Split Flag values would be:

Fragment	Split Flag (decimal)
1	13
2	2
3	4
4	6
5	8
6	10
7	12
8	14

Up to 120 fragments are allowed, yielding a maximum value of 238 decimal (EEH). This allows up to 60,480 octets per packet (120 * 504 = 60,480). All fragments belonging to the same packet use an identical 2-octet Sequence number.

Datapoint's ARCNETPLUS standard permits a Data field of 4224 octets in length. Currently, no Internet standard (RFC) exists that discusses the fragmentation requirements for this network.

Another unique characteristic of ARCNET and ARCNETPLUS is their addressing structures, which define an 8-bit address field and allow 255 unique hardware addresses as well as a broadcast designation (address = 0). (This address is implemented with an 8-position DIP switch, which you must set manually on each ARCNET or ARCNETPLUS card. A human error in duplicating these switch settings can cause ARCNET to fail; ARCNETPLUS offers an algorithm to detect duplicate addresses.)

5.5.5. FDDI

ANSI developed the Fiber Data Distributed Interface (FDDI) as a standard for fiber-optic data transmission. FDDI is a token-passing ring architecture that operates at 100 Mbps. (The actual data rate for FDDI is 125 Mbps, but 1 out of 5 bits handles overhead.) Because of its transmission rate, FDDI may emerge as a significant alternative to Ethernet or token-ring for local data transport. The FDDI frame structure, shown in Figure 5-10, is similar to IEEE 802.5. The maximum frame size is 4500 octets (or 9000 symbols, with 4 bits/symbol). When 6-octet addressing (the most common) is used, the MAC-layer header (preamble through source address) uses 16 octets, and the MAC-layer trailer uses 6 octets. Subtracting the headers from the maximum frame size leaves 4478 octets for data. The IEEE 802.2 LLC header requires three octets, yielding a maximum IP datagram length of 4475 octets. (Because

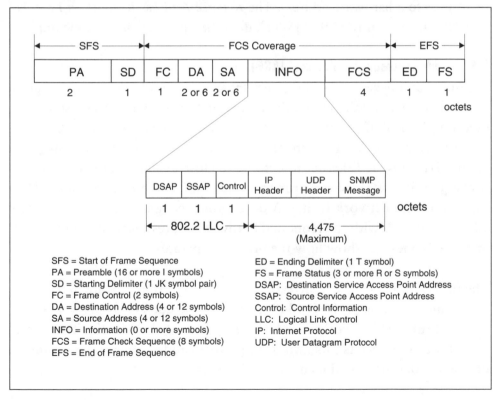

Figure 5-10. FDDI Frame with SNMP message *(courtesy American National Standards Institute)*

FDDI does not typically use SNAP, I have not shown the SNAP header, but there is no technical constraint on the use of SNAP. If present, the SNAP header would immediately follow the IEEE 802.2 header.) RFC 1188 [5-9] defines support for FDDI within TCP/IP-based internetworks.

5.6. Address Translation

In the previous two sections, I discussed the differences between the internet address, used by IP, and the local address, used by the LAN or WAN hardware. I noted that the IP address is a 32-bit logical address, but the physical hardware address depends on the hardware. For example, ARCNET has an 8-bit hardware address and Ethernet has a 48-bit hardware address. Thus, translation between the physical and logical address is necessary. The *Address Resolution Protocol* (ARP) described in RFC 826 [5-10] translates from an IP address to a hardware address. The *Reverse Address Resolution Protocol* (RARP), detailed in RFC 903 [5-11], does the opposite, as its name implies.

5.6.1. Address Resolution Protocol (ARP)

Assume that a device on an Ethernet, Host X, wishes to deliver a datagram to another device on the same Ethernet, Host Y. Host X knows Host Y's destination protocol (IP) address, but does not know Host Y's hardware (Ethernet) address. Host X would therefore broadcast an ARP packet (shown in Figure 5-11) on the Ethernet to determine Host Y's hardware address. The packet consists of 28 octets, primarily addresses, contained within the Data field of a local network frame. A device that recognizes its own protocol address responds with the requested hardware address. The individual fields of the ARP message show how the protocol operates.

The first field, Hardware (2 octets), defines the type of hardware in use. Current values are listed in RFC 1340. Examples include Hardware = 1 (Ethernet), 6 (IEEE 802 Networks), 7 (ARCNET), and 11 (LocalTalk). The second field, Protocol (2 octets), identifies the protocol address in use. For example, Protocol = 0800H would identify IP addresses.

0 1 2 3 4 5 6 7 8 9	1 1 1 1 1 1 1 1 1 1 2 2 2 2 2 2 2 2 2 2 3 3 0 1 2 3 4 5 6 7 8 9 0 1 2 3 4 5 6 7 8 9 0 1 Bits
Hardware Type	Protocol Type
HA Length	PA Length	Operation
Sender HA (octets 0-3)*	
Sender HA (octets 4-5)	Sender PA (octets 0-1)
Sender PA (octets 2-3)	Target HA (octets 0-1)
Target HA (octets 2-5)	
Target PA (octets 0-3)	

* Field lengths assume HA = 6 octets and PA = 4 octets

Figure 5-11. Address Resolution Protocol (ARP) and Reverse Address Resolution Protocol (RARP) packet formats

The next two fields allow the ARP packet to work with addressing schemes of different lengths (Figure 5-11 represents the most common scheme, where 6 octets are required for the hardware address and 4 octets are required for the protocol address). To make the protocol more adaptive, the HA Length (1 octet) and PA Length (1 octet) specify the lengths, in octets, of the addresses to be used. Figure 5-11 represents the most common scenario. Six octets (48 bits) are required for Hardware Address (HA Length=6); 4 octets (32 bits) for the Protocol Address (PA Length=4). The Operation field (2 octets) defines an ARP Request=1 or ARP Reply=2.

The next fields contain the addresses themselves. With an ARP Request message, the Target Hardware Address (HA) field is unknown and is sent filled with ZEROs. The ARP Reply packet from the target host inserts the requested address in the field. When it receives the ARP Reply, the originating station records the information in a table (known as the ARP cache) so that it doesn't need to make the same request again and again. Routers have an ARP cache with a finite lifetime so the table won't grow too large.

5.6.2. Reverse Address Resolution Protocol (RARP)

Most network hosts are intelligent enough to remember their hardware and protocol addresses. Diskless workstations, however, depend upon a server to provide much of their intelligence. The diskless workstation would know its hardware address (HA), which is coded into its ROM, but it may not know the protocol address (PA), which the server assigns. The RARP can discover the unknown PA given a known HA, and a RARP server to supply the desired answer.

The process of determining an unknown protocol address is similar to that of finding an unknown hardware address. The same packet structure is used (review Figure 5-11), with only minor modifications to the field values required. The Operation field adds two new values, 3 (RARP Request) and 4 (RARP Reply). When the RARP Request is made, the Sender HA, Sender PA, and Target HA are transmitted. The RARP Reply contains the requested Target PA.

5.7. Using SNMP with UDP and IP

This section shows how the SNMP GetRequest and GetResponse PDUs fit within the structure of an Ethernet frame (review Figure 5-1). In this section I will examine the Ethernet frame format, the IP header, the UDP header, the SNMP PDUs, and the ASN.1 encoding of the variable bindings.

Trace 5.7a shows four layers of protocol operating in two frames, 7 and 8. You can easily identify the Data Link Control (DLC) layer as Ethernet because of the Ethertype (or Type) field (review Figure 5-6). The next field, the IP Header, is 20 octets long, has routine service, and is not fragmented. The Protocol field identifies the next higher layer (UDP), while the source and destination addresses identify the origin and destination of this datagram.

The UDP header gives the source and destination port numbers. Note that the SunMgr assigns port number 3234 for SNMP, while the Retix bridge (GoldGate) uses the standard port number of 161 for SNMP.

The SNMP authentication header, containing the version number and community string, precede the SNMP PDU. We see the PDU identified (GetRequest) and the various error fields. Next comes the variable bindings, which consist of an object name and its value. The GetRequest PDU uses NULL for all the Value fields (frame 7), while the GetResponse (frame 8) contains the actual values retrieved. To review, you could return to Figure 3-2 and trace the subtree for the System Group, verifying the accuracy of the OID designation {1.3.6.1.2.1....}.

Trace 5.7a. Using SNMP with Ethernet, IP and UDP

```
Sniffer Network Analyzer data 10-Nov-92 at 10:29:36 file GOLD_SYS.ENC Pg 1
--------------------------------------Frame 7 --------------------------------------------
DLC: ----- DLC Header -----
DLC:
DLC: Frame 7 arrived at 10:29:37.30; frame size is 138 (008A hex) bytes
DLC: Destination = Station Retix 034CF1, GoldGate
DLC: Source     = Station Sun   0900C8, SunMgr
DLC: Ethertype   = 0800 (IP)
DLC:
IP:  ----- IP Header -----
IP:
IP:  Version = 4, header length = 20 bytes
IP:  Type of service = 00
IP:      000. .... = routine
IP:      ...0 .... = normal delay
IP:      .... 0... = normal throughput
IP:      .... .0.. = normal reliability
IP:  Total length = 124 bytes
IP:  Identification = 20055
IP:  Flags = 0X
IP:  .0.. .... = may fragment
IP:  ..0. .... = last fragment
IP:  Fragment offset = 0 bytes
IP:  Time to live = 60 seconds/hops
IP:  Protocol = 17 (UDP)
IP:  Header checksum = A5C5 (correct)
IP:  Source address = [XXX.YYY.128.4]
```

```
IP:   Destination address = [XXX.YYY.1.10]
IP:   No options
IP:
UDP: ----- UDP Header -----
UDP:
UDP: Source port = 3234 (SNMP)
UDP: Destination port = 161
UDP: Length = 104
UDP: No checksum
UDP:
SNMP: ----- Simple Network Management Protocol -----
SNMP:
SNMP: Version = 0
SNMP: Community = public
SNMP: Command = Get request
SNMP: Request ID = 0
SNMP: Error status = 0 (No error)
SNMP: Error index = 0
SNMP:
SNMP: Object = {1.3.6.1.2.1.1.3.0} (sysUpTime.0)
SNMP: Value  = NULL
SNMP:
SNMP: Object = {1.3.6.1.2.1.1.1.0} (sysDescr.0)
SNMP: Value  = NULL
SNMP:
SNMP: Object = {1.3.6.1.2.1.1.2.0} (sysObjectID.0)
SNMP: Value  = NULL
SNMP:
SNMP: Object = {1.3.6.1.2.1.1.3.0} (sysUpTime.0)
SNMP: Value  = NULL
SNMP:
SNMP: Object = {1.3.6.1.2.1.1.6.0} (system.6.0)
SNMP: Value  = NULL
SNMP:
```

```
------------------------------------------------Frame 8 ------------------------------------------------
DLC: ----- DLC Header -----
DLC:
DLC: Frame 8 arrived at 10:29:37.33; frame size is 195 (00C3 hex) bytes
DLC: Destination = Station Sun   0900C8, SunMgr
DLC: Source     = Station Retix 034CF1, GoldGate
DLC: Ethertype  = 0800 (IP)
DLC:
IP:  ----- IP Header -----
IP:
IP:  Version = 4, header length = 20 bytes
IP:  Type of service = 00
IP:      000. .... = routine
IP:      ...0 .... = normal delay
IP:      .... 0... = normal throughput
IP:      .... .0.. = normal reliability
IP:  Total length = 181 bytes
IP:  Identification = 0
IP:  Flags = 0X
IP:  .0.. .... = may fragment
IP:  ..0. .... = last fragment
IP:  Fragment offset = 0 bytes
IP:  Time to live = 16 seconds/hops
IP:  Protocol = 17 (UDP)
IP:  Header checksum = 1FE4 (correct)
IP:  Source address = [XXX.YYY.1.10]
IP:  Destination address = [XXX.YYY.128.4]
IP:  No options
IP:
UDP: ----- UDP Header -----
UDP:
UDP: Source port = 161 (SNMP)
UDP: Destination port = 3234
UDP: Length = 161
```

```
UDP: Checksum = 6417 (correct)
UDP:
SNMP: ----- Simple Network Management Protocol -----
SNMP:
SNMP: Version = 0
SNMP: Community = public
SNMP: Command = Get response
SNMP: Request ID = 0
SNMP: Error status = 0 (No error)
SNMP: Error index = 0
SNMP:
SNMP: Object = {1.3.6.1.2.1.1.3.0} (sysUpTime.0)
SNMP: Value  = 240267300 hundredths of a second
SNMP:
SNMP: Object = {1.3.6.1.2.1.1.1.0} (sysDescr.0)
SNMP: Value  = Retix Local Ethernet Bridge Model 2265M
SNMP:
SNMP: Object = {1.3.6.1.2.1.1.2.0} (sysObjectID.0)
SNMP: Value  = {1.3.6.1.4.1.72.8.3}
SNMP:
SNMP: Object = {1.3.6.1.2.1.1.3.0} (sysUpTime.0)
SNMP: Value  = 240267300 hundredths of a second
SNMP:
SNMP: Object = {1.3.6.1.2.1.1.6.0} (system.6.0)
SNMP: Value  =
SNMP:
```

Trace 5.7b amplifies the first trace by looking at the actual ASN.1-encoded information included within the SNMP PDUs. Frame 7 begins with a SEQUENCE OF type, code 30H, followed by the length of the encoding (94 octets, or 5E). (These two octets are shown in bold within the hexadecimal display and are the 43rd and 44th octets transmitted.) The ASN.1 encoding continues within the SNMP PDU, using the TLV (Type-Length-Value) structure discussed in Chapter 2. You can identify the first OID Value requested (line 5.1) by looking for the preceding OID. That information is the 71st octet transmitted, with an OBJECT IDENTIFIER type (06H), a Length of 8 octets (08H), and a Value of 2B 06 01 02 01 01 03 00H. Recall that the 1.3 prefix is translated into a 43 decimal (or 2BH) through the expression we studied in Section 2.5.3.3. The rest of the PDU follows in a similar manner.

The final example (see Figure 5-12), shows how the SNMP GetRequest PDU is encapsulated within the Ethernet frame. Frame 7 illustrates this with the hexadecimal characters shown below their respective fields. The data capture begins with the destination address (08 00 90 03 4C F1), which identifies the Retix bridge. Likewise, the source address (08 00 20 09 00 C8) identifies the Sun Manager. The Ethertype field (08 00) indicates that IP will be the next protocol in the Data field. You can decode the IP header, UDP header, SNMP authentication header, and SNMP GetRequest PDU (including the Variable Bindings) in a similar manner.

Trace 5.7b. ASN.1 encoding of SNMP GetRequest and GetResponse PDUs

```
Sniffer Network Analyzer data 10-Nov-92 at 10:29:36 file GOLD_SYS.ENC Pg 1
---------------------------------------------Frame 7 ---------------------------------------------
SNMP: 1.1 SEQUENCE [of], Length=94
SNMP: 2.1 INTEGER, Length=1, Value = "0"
SNMP: 2.2 OCTET STRING, Length=6, Value = "public"
SNMP: 2.3 Context-Specific Constructed [0], Length=81
SNMP: 3.1 INTEGER, Length=1, Value = "0"
SNMP: 3.2 INTEGER, Length=1, Value = "0"
SNMP: 3.3 INTEGER, Length=1, Value = "0"
SNMP: 3.4 SEQUENCE [of], Length=70
SNMP: 4.1 SEQUENCE [of], Length=12
SNMP: 5.1 OBJECT IDENTIFIER, Length=8, Value = "{1.3.6.1.2.1.1.3.0}"
SNMP: 5.2 NULL, Length=0, Value = ""
SNMP: 4.2 SEQUENCE [of], Length=12
SNMP: 5.1 OBJECT IDENTIFIER, Length=8, Value = "{1.3.6.1.2.1.1.1.0}"
SNMP: 5.2 NULL, Length=0, Value = ""
```

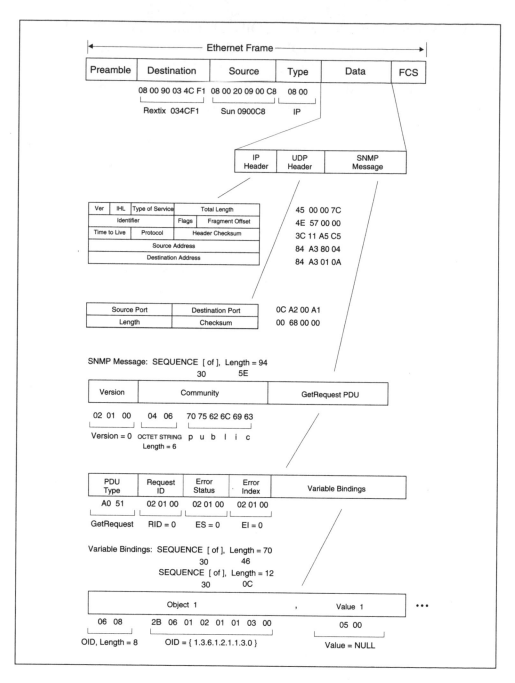

Figure 5-12. Expansion of the SNMP GetRequest PDU within an Ethernet frame

SNMP: 4.3 SEQUENCE [of], Length=12
SNMP: 5.1 OBJECT IDENTIFIER, Length=8, Value = "{1.3.6.1.2.1.1.2.0}"
SNMP: 5.2 NULL, Length=0, Value = ""
SNMP: 4.4 SEQUENCE [of], Length=12
SNMP: 5.1 OBJECT IDENTIFIER, Length=8, Value = "{1.3.6.1.2.1.1.3.0}"
SNMP: 5.2 NULL, Length=0, Value = ""
SNMP: 4.5 SEQUENCE [of], Length=12
SNMP: 5.1 OBJECT IDENTIFIER, Length=8, Value = "{1.3.6.1.2.1.1.6.0}"
SNMP: 5.2 NULL, Length=0, Value = ""
SNMP:

```
ADDR   HEX                                                  ASCII
0000   08 00 90 03 4C F1 08 00   20 09 00 C8 08 00 45 00    ....L... .....E.
0010   00 7C 4E 57 00 00 3C 11   A5 C5 84 A3 80 04 84 A3    .|NW..<.........
0020   01 0A 0C A2 00 A1 00 68   00 00 305E 02 01 00 04     .......h..0^....
0030   06 70 75 62 6C 69 63 A0   51 02 01 00 02 01 00 02    .public.Q.......
0040   01 00 30 46 30 0C 06 08   2B 06 01 02 01 01 03 00    ..0F0...+.......
0050   05 00 30 0C 06 08 2B 06   01 02 01 01 01 00 05 00    ..0...+.........
0060   30 0C 06 08 2B 06 01 02   01 01 02 00 05 00 30 0C    0...+.........0.
0070   06 08 2B 06 01 02 01 01   03 00 05 00 30 0C 06 08    ..+.........0...
0080   2B 06 01 02 01 01 06 00   05 00                      +.........
```

---Frame 8 ---

SNMP: 1.1 SEQUENCE [of], Length=150
SNMP: 2.1 INTEGER, Length=1, Value = "0"
SNMP: 2.2 OCTET STRING, Length=6, Value = "public"
SNMP: 2.3 Context-Specific Constructed [2], Length=136
SNMP: 3.1 INTEGER, Length=1, Value = "0"
SNMP: 3.2 INTEGER, Length=1, Value = "0"
SNMP: 3.3 INTEGER, Length=1, Value = "0"
SNMP: 3.4 SEQUENCE [of], Length=125
SNMP: 4.1 SEQUENCE [of], Length=16
SNMP: 5.1 OBJECT IDENTIFIER, Length=8, Value = "{1.3.6.1.2.1.1.3.0}"
SNMP: 5.2 Application Primitive [3], Length=4, Data = "<0E>RO$"
SNMP: 4.2 SEQUENCE [of], Length=51
SNMP: 5.1 OBJECT IDENTIFIER, Length=8, Value = "{1.3.6.1.2.1.1.1.0}"

SNMP: 5.2 OCTET STRING, Length=39, Value = "Retix Local Ethernet
Bridge Model 2265M"
SNMP: 4.3 SEQUENCE [of], Length=20
SNMP: 5.1 OBJECT IDENTIFIER, Length=8, Value = "{1.3.6.1.2.1.1.2.0}"
SNMP: 5.2 OBJECT IDENTIFIER, Length=8, Value = "{1.3.6.1.4.1.72.8.3}"
SNMP: 4.4 SEQUENCE [of], Length=16
SNMP: 5.1 OBJECT IDENTIFIER, Length=8, Value = "{1.3.6.1.2.1.1.3.0}"
SNMP: 5.2 Application Primitive [3], Length=4, Data = "<0E>RO$"
SNMP: 4.5 SEQUENCE [of], Length=12
SNMP: 5.1 OBJECT IDENTIFIER, Length=8, Value = "{1.3.6.1.2.1.1.6.0}"
SNMP: 5.2 OCTET STRING, Length=0, Value = ""
SNMP:

```
ADDR   HEX                                                      ASCII
0000   08 00 20 09 00 C8 08 00   90 03 4C F1 08 00 45 00       .. .......L...E.
0010   00 B5 00 00 00 00 10 11   1F E4 84 A3 01 0A 84 A3       ...............
0020   80 04 00 A1 0C A2 00 A1   64 17 30 81 96 02 01 00       .........d.0.....
0030   04 06 70 75 62 6C 69 63   A2 81 88 02 01 00 02 01       ..public........
0040   00 02 01 00 30 7D 30 10   06 08 2B 06 01 02 01 01       ....0}0...+.....
0050   03 00 43 04 0E 52 30 24   30 33 06 08 2B 06 01 02       ..C..RO$03..+...
0060   01 01 01 00 04 27 52 65   74 69 78 20 4C 6F 63 61       .....'Retix Loca
0070   6C 20 45 74 68 65 72 6E   65 74 20 42 72 69 64 67       l Ethernet Bridg
0080   65 20 4D 6F 64 65 6C 20   32 32 36 35 4D 30 14 06       e Model 2265M0..
0090   08 2B 06 01 02 01 01 02   00 06 08 2B 06 01 04 01       .+.........+....
00A0   48 08 03 30 10 06 08 2B   06 01 02 01 01 03 00 43       H..0...+.......C
00B0   04 0E 52 30 24 30 0C 06   08 2B 06 01 02 01 01 06       ..RO$0...+......
00C0   00 04 00                                                 ...
```

This chapter completes our tour of the Internet Network Management Frame-work. Chapter 6 discusses what happens when the systems (from Chapter 1) and the protocols (from Chapters 2 through 5) don't work together as designed.

5.8. References

[5-1]   Postel, J. "User Datagram Protocol." RFC 768, ISI, August 1980.

[5-2]   Miller, Mark A. *Troubleshooting TCP/IP.* San Mateo, CA: M&T Books, 1993.

[5-3]   Postel, J. "Internet Protocol." RFC 791, September 1981.

[5-4]   Reynolds, J. and J. Postel, "Assigned Numbers." RFC 1340, July 1992.

[5-5]   Postel, J. "Internet Control Message Protocol." RFC 792, September 1981.

[5-6]   Horning, Charles. "A Standard for the Transmission of IP Datagrams over Ethernet Networks." RFC 894, April 1984.

[5-7]   Postel, J. and J. Reynolds. "A Standard for the Transmission of IP Datagrams over IEEE 802 Networks." RFC 1042, February 1988.

[5-8]   Provan, D. "Transmitting IP Traffic over ARCNET Networks." RFC 1201, February 1991.

[5-9]   Katz, D. "A Proposed Standard for the Transmission of IP Datagrams over FDDI Networks." RFC 1188, October 1990.

[5-10] Plummer, D. "An Ethernet Address Resolution Protocol, or Converting Network Protocol Addresses to 48-bit Ethernet Addresses for Transmission on Ethernet Hardware." RFC 826, November 1982.

[5-11] Finlayson, R., et. al. "A Reverse Address Resolution Protocol." RFC 903, June 1984.

6 Case Studies in Implementing SNMP

So far, this book has described the technical details of SNMP. This chapter provides case studies from live networks that show how these concepts apply to the real world. These studies demonstrate actual internetwork management challenges and solutions. For consistency, all of the case studies were captured with a Network General Corp. Sniffer protocol analyzer.

6.1. Verifying Access Control with the Community Name

To warm you up to the idea of protocol analysis, I've started with a problem that has a simple solution. As Section 4.3 discussed, the SNMP message consists of an authentication header and one of five SNMP PDUs. The authentication header contains the SNMP version number and the community name. The agent uses the community name as a password to validate the identity of the manager. If the community names of the manager and agent are identical, message processing proceeds. If not, there is an authentication failure. Depending upon the agent's SNMP implementation, it will either discard the offending message, generate a trap, or both.

In the topology shown in Figure 6-1, the network administrator has set both the community name of the manager and agent to "public," a common default value. (Now is a good time to check the community name for your network devices and change this default value. Doing so will greatly increase the security on your internetwork!)

In Frame 9 of Trace 6.1a, the manager requests the IP routing table, {1.3.6.1.2.1.4.21}, using a GetNextRequest. The manager requests values for the ipRouteDest, ipRouteNextHop, ipRouteType, and ipRouteIfIndex objects

(Frame 9 of Trace 6.1b). The values of these objects are returned in Frames 10 through 54, and can be used to generate the following table:

IpRouteDest	ipRouteIfIndex	ipRouteNextHop	ipRouteType
0.0.0.0	2	128.79.3.200	4
128.79.0.0	2	128.79.3.200	3
128.79.2.0	2	128.79.3.202	4
128.79.3.0	2	128.79.3.105	3
128.79.4.0	2	128.79.3.200	4
128.79.5.0	2	128.79.3.201	4
128.79.6.0	2	128.79.3.200	4
128.79.7.0	2	128.79.3.201	4
128.79.8.0	2	128.79.3.201	4
128.79.9.0	2	128.79.3.202	4
128.79.12.0	2	128.79.3.200	4
128.79.14.0	2	128.79.3.200	4
128.79.15.0	2	128.79.3.201	4
128.79.16.0	2	128.79.3.201	4
128.79.18.0	2	128.79.3.201	4
128.79.20.0	2	128.79.3.201	4
128.79.40.0	2	128.79.3.200	4
128.79.50.0	2	128.79.3.201	4
128.79.60.0	2	128.79.3.200	4
128.79.70.0	2	128.79.3.201	4
128.79.120.0	2	128.79.3.200	4

| 128.79.180.0 | 2 | 128.79.3.201 | 4 |
| 128.79.200.0 | 2 | 128.79.3.201 | 4 |

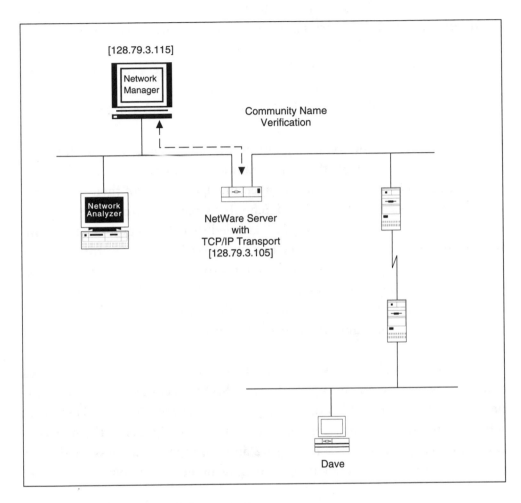

Figure 6-1. Verifying access with the community name

The ipRouteDest object contains the destination IP address for this route. The first entry is 0.0.0.0, indicating a default route. The ipRouteIfIndex identifies the local interface through which the next hop of this route may be reached. Each of these entries specifies interface number 2. The ipRouteNextHop is the IP address of the next hop of the route. The ipRouteType has one of four possible values: other (1), none of the following; invalid (2), an invalidated route; direct (3), a route to a directly connected subnetwork; and indirect (4), a route to a nonlocal (or remote) subnetwork. In the table, the second and fourth entries are direct; the remaining entries are destined for remote networks.

The GetNext operation stops in Frame 56 when the agent returns the lexicographical next object within the router's table (see Trace 6.1c): the ipRouteProto {1.3.6.1.2.1.4.21.1.9} and the ipRouteMetric1 {1.3.6.1.2.1.4.21.1.3}.

As an experiment, the network administrator changed the agent console's community name from "public" to "test." Frames 59 to 63 of Trace 6.1a show the results. In Frames 59 to 60, the manager and agent confirm their communication path by using ICMP Echo and Echo Reply messages (these messages are often called the "PING" commands). Satisfied that the communication path is working, the manager issues a GetNext request for values of three objects in the Interfaces group. The agent does not respond, so the manager retransmits the request at 5 second intervals in Frames 62 and 63. This is a fruitless exercise because the community name on the agent has been changed. The agent will not respond until the new community name is validated.

This case study illustrates several issues. First, the community name provides some access security for the agents. Second, SNMP is communicated via connectionless transport, which does not guarantee reliable delivery. Therefore, when the message did not seem to be getting across the LAN, the manager retransmitted the message in Frames 62 and 63. In fact, the message did get across the LAN, but it was not accepted because of the invalid community name.

This case study also presents a third, more subtle lesson. Recall from Section 3.3.4 that the IP routing table (MIB-II, RFC 1213) was replaced with the IP forwarding table in RFC 1354. This example shows that a manager does not conform to the current MIB standards. However, because the manager and agent MIBs were both out of date, the communication succeeds. If the manager MIB had been updated and no longer supported the IP routing table, an error would have been returned in response to the first GetNext request.

Trace 6.1a. IP routing table retrieval (Summary)

Sniffer Network Analyzer data 5-Oct-92 at 09:04:44, file NAME.ENC Pg 1

SUMMARY	Delta T	Destination	Source	Summary
9	0.0043	Agent	Manager	SNMP Next ipRouteDest .. ipRouteIfIndex (4 items)
10	0.0102	Manager	Agent	SNMP Got ipRouteDest .. ipRouteIfIndex (4 items)
11	0.0482	Agent	Manager	SNMP Next ipRouteDest .. ipRouteIfIndex (4 items)
.				
.				
.				
53	0.0662	Agent	Manager	SNMP Next ipRouteDest .. ipRouteIfIndex (4 items)
54	0.0104	Manager	Agent	SNMP Got ipRouteDest .. ipRouteIfIndex (4 items)
55	0.0687	Agent	Manager	SNMP Next ipRouteDest .. ipRouteIfIndex (4 items)
56	0.0138	Manager	Agent	SNMP Got ipRouteIfIndex .. ipRouteMetric1 (4 items)
57	65.7201	HP133ADE	HP17B65F	ARP C PA=[128.79.3.105] PRO=IP
58	0.0005	HP17B65F	HP133ADE	ARP R PA=[128.79.3.105] HA=080009133ADE PRO=IP
59	82.5076	Agent	Manager	ICMP Echo
60	0.0008	Manager	Agent	ICMP Echo reply
61	50.1077	Agent	Manager	SNMP Next ifIndex .. ifPhysAddress (3 items)
62	4.9924	Agent	Manager	SNMP Next ifIndex .. ifPhysAddress (3 items)
63	5.0003	Agent	Manager	SNMP Next ifIndex .. ifPhysAddress (3 items)

Trace 6.1b. IP routing table retrieval details (GetNext Requests)

```
Sniffer Network Analyzer data 5-Oct-92 at 09:04:44, file NAME.ENC Pg 1
----------------------------------------Frame 9 ----------------------------------------
SNMP: ----- Simple Network Management Protocol -----
SNMP:
SNMP: Version = 0
SNMP: Community = public
SNMP: Command = Get next request
SNMP: Request ID = 11386
SNMP: Error status = 0 (No error)
SNMP: Error index = 0
SNMP:
SNMP: Object = {1.3.6.1.2.1.4.21.1.1} (ipRouteDest)
SNMP: Value = NULL
SNMP:
SNMP: Object = {1.3.6.1.2.1.4.21.1.7} (ipRouteNextHop)
SNMP: Value = NULL
SNMP:
SNMP: Object = {1.3.6.1.2.1.4.21.1.8} (ipRouteType)
SNMP: Value = NULL
SNMP:
SNMP: Object = {1.3.6.1.2.1.4.21.1.2} (ipRouteIfIndex)
SNMP: Value = NULL
SNMP:
----------------------------------------Frame 10----------------------------------------
SNMP: ----- Simple Network Management Protocol -----
SNMP:
SNMP: Version = 0
SNMP: Community = public
SNMP: Command = Get response
SNMP: Request ID = 11386
SNMP: Error status = 0 (No error)
SNMP: Error index = 0
```

SNMP:
SNMP: Object = {1.3.6.1.2.1.4.21.1.1.0.0.0.0} (ipRouteDest.0.0.0.0)
SNMP: Value = [0.0.0.0]
SNMP:
SNMP: Object = {1.3.6.1.2.1.4.21.1.7.0.0.0.0} (ipRouteNextHop.0.0.0.0)
SNMP: Value = [128.79.3.200]
SNMP:
SNMP: Object = {1.3.6.1.2.1.4.21.1.8.0.0.0.0} (ipRouteType.0.0.0.0)
SNMP: Value = 4 (remote)
SNMP:
SNMP: Object = {1.3.6.1.2.1.4.21.1.2.0.0.0.0} (ipRouteIfIndex.0.0.0.0)
SNMP: Value = 2
SNMP:

Trace 6.1c. IP routing table retrieval details (End of GetNext)

Sniffer Network Analyzer data 5-Oct-92 at 09:04:44, file NAME.ENC Pg 1
---Frame 55---
SNMP: ----- Simple Network Management Protocol -----
SNMP:
SNMP: Version = 0
SNMP: Community = public
SNMP: Command = Get next request
SNMP: Request ID = 11409
SNMP: Error status = 0 (No error)
SNMP: Error index = 0
SNMP:
SNMP: Object = {1.3.6.1.2.1.4.21.1.1.128.79.200.0}
        (ipRouteDest.128.79.200.0)
SNMP: Value = NULL
SNMP:
SNMP: Object = {1.3.6.1.2.1.4.21.1.7.128.79.200.0}
        (ipRouteNextHop.128.79.200.0)
SNMP: Value = NULL

SNMP:
SNMP: Object = {1.3.6.1.2.1.4.21.1.8.128.79.200.0}
          (ipRouteType.128.79.200.0)
SNMP: Value = NULL
SNMP:
SNMP: Object = {1.3.6.1.2.1.4.21.1.2.128.79.200.0}
          (ipRouteIfIndex.128.79.200.0)
SNMP: Value = NULL
SNMP:

--Frame 56--
SNMP: ----- Simple Network Management Protocol -----
SNMP:
SNMP: Version = 0
SNMP: Community = public
SNMP: Command = Get response
SNMP: Request ID = 11409
SNMP: Error status = 0 (No error)
SNMP: Error index = 0
SNMP:
SNMP: Object = {1.3.6.1.2.1.4.21.1.2.0.0.0.0} (ipRouteIfIndex.0.0.0.0)
SNMP: Value = 2
SNMP:
SNMP: Object = {1.3.6.1.2.1.4.21.1.8.0.0.0.0} (ipRouteType.0.0.0.0)
SNMP: Value = 4 (remote)
SNMP:
SNMP: Object = {1.3.6.1.2.1.4.21.1.9.0.0.0.0} (ipRouteProto.0.0.0.0)
SNMP: Value = 2 (local)
SNMP:
SNMP: Object = {1.3.6.1.2.1.4.21.1.3.0.0.0.0} (ipRouteMetric1.0.0.0.0)
SNMP: Value = 1
SNMP:

6.2. Verifying Access Control with the Community Name and IP Address

Many network devices, such as routers, allow the network administrator to configure multiple SNMP community names for remote access. In addition, the network device can have a filter that specifies the IP address of the remote manager. Thus, the combination of the community name and IP address acts as a two-level method of remote access security.

In this example, a router was configured with two SNMP communities (see Figure 6-2). The first uses community name = abcsnmp and allows access with address [XXX.YYY.ZZZ.145]. The second uses community name = xyzsnmp and allows access with IP address [XXX.YYY.ZZZ.146]. Let's see how the router reacts to an invalid request.

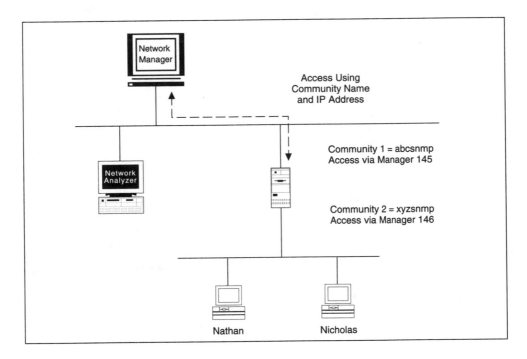

Figure 6-2. Agent access from multiple communities

In Frame 64 of Trace 6.2a, Manager 145 issues a GetRequest for the value of the sysDescr object. As you can see in Frame 64 of Trace 6.2b, that GetRequest includes the community name = abcsnmp. Since a match exists between the community name and the IP address, the router issues a GetResponse (Frame 65) containing the system description

Value = /usr3/wf/wf.rel/v5.75/wf.pj/proto.ss/ace_test.p/

In the second scenario, the manager attempts to access the router using the same IP address [XXX.YYY.ZZZ.145], but with a different community name (xyzsnmp). The GetRequest is transmitted in Frame 70 and then retransmitted in Frames 71 and 72. The router never responds. Recall that the IP address used [XXX.YYY.ZZZ.145] and the community name (xyzsnmp) are valid on the agent, but not in this combination. Thus, the association between the community name and IP address provides a second level of access security.

Trace 6.2a. Verifying access control with IP addresses (summary)

Sniffer Network Analyzer data 16-Nov-92 at 17:04:10, file 7-2.ENC, Pg 1

SUMMARY	Delta T	Destination	Source	Summary
64	0.0013	Router	Manager 145	SNMP Get sysDescr
65	0.0479	Manager 145	Router	SNMP Got sysDescr = /usr3/wf/wf.rel/v5.75 /wf.pj/proto.ss /ace_test.p/
66	4.1358	Router	Router	Ethertype=8102(Unknown)
67	5.0239	Router	Router	Ethertype=8102(Unknown)
68	5.0388	Router	Router	Ethertype=8102(Unknown)
69	5.0314	Router	Router	Ethertype=8102(Unknown)
70	1.9592	Router	Manager 145	SNMP Get sysDescr
71	0.9971	Router	Manager 145	SNMP Get sysDescr
72	2.0045	Router	Manager 145	SNMP Get sysDescr

Trace 6.2b. Verifying access control with IP addresses (details)

```
Sniffer Network Analyzer data 16-Nov-92 at 17:04:10, file 7-2.ENC, Pg 1
-------------------------------------------Frame 64-------------------------------------------
SNMP: ----- Simple Network Management Protocol -----
SNMP:
SNMP: Version = 0
SNMP: Community = abcsnmp
SNMP: Command = Get request
SNMP: Request ID = 1888324335
SNMP: Error status = 0 (No error)
SNMP: Error index = 0
SNMP:
SNMP: Object = {1.3.6.1.2.1.1.1.0} (sysDescr.0)
SNMP: Value = NULL
SNMP:
-------------------------------------------Frame 65-------------------------------------------
SNMP: ----- Simple Network Management Protocol -----
SNMP:
SNMP: Version = 0
SNMP: Community = abcsnmp
SNMP: Command = Get response
SNMP: Request ID = 1888324335
SNMP: Error status = 0 (No error)
SNMP: Error index = 0
SNMP:
SNMP: Object = {1.3.6.1.2.1.1.1.0} (sysDescr.0)
SNMP: Value = /usr3/wf/wf.rel/v5.75/wf.pj/proto.ss/ace_test.p/
SNMP:

        .
        .
        .
```

```
-----------------------------------------Frame 70-------------------------------------------
SNMP: ----- Simple Network Management Protocol -----
SNMP:
SNMP: Version = 0
SNMP: Community = xyzsnmp
SNMP: Command = Get request
SNMP: Request ID = 586726387
SNMP: Error status = 0 (No error)
SNMP: Error index = 0
SNMP:
SNMP: Object = {1.3.6.1.2.1.1.1.0} (sysDescr.0)
SNMP: Value = NULL
SNMP:
-----------------------------------------Frame 71-------------------------------------------
SNMP: ----- Simple Network Management Protocol -----
SNMP:
SNMP: Version = 0
SNMP: Community = xyzsnmp
SNMP: Command = Get request
SNMP: Request ID = 586726387
SNMP: Error status = 0 (No error)
SNMP: Error index = 0
SNMP:
SNMP: Object = {1.3.6.1.2.1.1.1.0} (sysDescr.0)
SNMP: Value = NULL
SNMP:
-----------------------------------------Frame 72-------------------------------------------
SNMP: ----- Simple Network Management Protocol -----
SNMP:
SNMP: Version = 0
SNMP: Community = xyzsnmp
SNMP: Command = Get request
SNMP: Request ID = 586726387
SNMP: Error status = 0 (No error)
```

```
SNMP: Error index = 0
SNMP:
SNMP: Object = {1.3.6.1.2.1.1.1.0} (sysDescr.0)
SNMP: Value = NULL
SNMP:
```

6.3. Verifying that a Set Command Has Been Properly Received and Implemented

The connectionless nature of SNMP's UDP transport leaves some doubt as to whether the agent has actually acted upon a Set command from the manager. Testing that the Set actually occurred requires a three-step process. In the first step, the network manager reads the current value of an object. In the second step, the network manager issues the Set command. In the third step, it rereads that value to confirm that the value was changed. This example shows these three steps in detail.

The internetwork in this example contains several Ethernet segments and is managed by a DECmcc console (see Figure 6-3). The goal is to assign a value to an object on the SynOptics hub, which contains an SNMP agent. The hub also contains a SynOptics private enterprise MIB with OID prefix {1.3.6.1.4.1.45}. To assign the value, the agent must be configured to allow access from a remote manager, as illustrated in Section 6.2. For the SynOptics hubs, the SNMP configuration parameters establish several communities, each with different access rights. The read-only community is typically named "public." The read-write community is typically named "administrator." A third community usually called "trap1" defines the devices that will receive traps.

As mentioned previously, the first step in testing the Set command, which occurs in Frames 5 to 8 (Trace 6.3a), is for the network manager to read the values of the SynOptics MIB. The SynOptics MIB is an extensive private MIB that contains objects such as the subnet mask [255.255.255.0], default gateway [XXX.YYY.170.250], boot file server address [XXX.YYY.170.20], and many others (see Frame 6 in Trace 6.3b). You should obtain documentation on private enterprise MIBs from the vendor when you initialize the network management system, so that these details will be readily available.

Note the value that we want to change is the Trap Receiver Community, OID {SynOptics 1.3.2.4.20.1.3.XXX.YYY.170.20}. From the detail of Frame 6, you can see that the fourteenth Object, Value = "public".

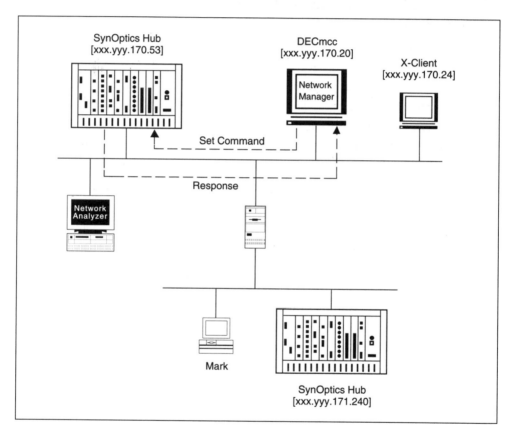

Figure 6-3. Verifying a Set command

The second step begins in Frame 9 when the manager attempts to Set the Trap community to the value "test". Frame 10 returns an authentication failure trap, which indicates that the receiver of the trap (the Hub agent) did not permit the manager to set the object's value. This failure occurred because the

Set command (Frame 9) specified a Community name = public, and that community was specified for a read-only (not read-write) operation.

When the network administrator realized his mistake, the administrator issued another Set command in Frame 21, this time with the SNMP community name = administrator, and a value for the Trap Receiver Community = trap1. This time, the SNMP Set command was authenticated and the Response (Frame 22) indicated "no error". The third step occurs in Frames 23 and 24, where a GetNext for the SynOptics private MIB objects (Frame 24) verifies that the value has been written as specified.

Trace 6.3a. Verifying a Set command (summary)

Sniffer Network Analyzer data 23-Sep-92 at 08:40:52 file SNMP71_7.ENC Pg 1

SUMMARY	Delta T	Destination	Source	Summary
5	27.1787	[XXX.YYY.170...	Manager	SNMP Next SynOptics.1.3.2.4.1.0 .. SynOptics.1.3.2.4.21.0 (16 items)
6	0.2388	Manager	Hub Agent	SNMP Got SynOptics.1.3.2.4.2.0 .. SynOptics.2.1.1.1.1.1 (16 items)
7	0.0064	Hub Agent	Manager	SNMP Next SynOptics.1.3.2.4.3.0 .. SynOptics.1.3.2.4.9.0 (7 items)
8	0.1159	Manager	Hub Agent	SNMP Got SynOptics.1.3.2.4.4.0 .. SynOptics.1.3.2.4.10.0 (7 items)
9	12.6063	Hub Agent	Manager	SNMP Set SynOptics.1.3.2.4.20.1.3 .XXX.YYY.170.20 = test

| 10 | 0.0329 | Manager | Hub Agent | SNMP Trap |
| | | | | Authentication failure |

.
.
.

21	52.8223	Hub Agent	Manager	SNMP Set
				SynOptics.1.3.2.4.20.1.3
				.XXX.YYY.170.20 = trap1
22	0.0290	Manager	Hub Agent	SNMP Got
				SynOptics.1.3.2.4.20.1.3
				.XXX.YYY.170.20 = trap1
23	6.1200	Hub Agent	Manager	SNMP Next
				SynOptics.1.3.2.4.1 ..
				SynOptics.1.3.2.4.21
				(16 items)
24	0.2185	Manager	Hub Agent	SNMP Got
				SynOptics.1.3.2.4.1.0 ..
				SynOptics.1.3.2.4.21.0
				(16 items)

Trace 6.3b. Verifying a Set command (details)

Sniffer Network Analyzer data 23-Sep-92 at 08:40:52, file SNMP71_7.ENC, Pg 1
---Frame 6 ---
SNMP: ----- Simple Network Management Protocol -----
SNMP:
SNMP: Version = 0
SNMP: Community = public
SNMP: Command = Get response
SNMP: Request ID = 717281288
SNMP: Error status = 0 (No error)
SNMP: Error index = 0
SNMP:
SNMP: Object = {1.3.6.1.4.1.45.1.3.2.4.2.0} (SynOptics.1.3.2.4.2.0)
SNMP: Value = 0

```
SNMP:
SNMP: Object = {1.3.6.1.4.1.45.1.3.2.4.11.0} (SynOptics.1.3.2.4.11.0)
SNMP: Value = [255.255.255.0]
SNMP:
SNMP: Object = {1.3.6.1.4.1.45.1.3.2.4.12.0} (SynOptics.1.3.2.4.12.0)
SNMP: Value = [XXX.YYY.170.250]
SNMP:
SNMP: Object = {1.3.6.1.4.1.45.1.3.2.4.13.0} (SynOptics.1.3.2.4.13.0)
SNMP: Value = [XXX.YYY.170.20], Manager
SNMP:
SNMP: Object = {1.3.6.1.4.1.45.1.3.2.4.14.0} (SynOptics.1.3.2.4.14.0)
SNMP: Value = /tftpboot/syn2.cfg
SNMP:
SNMP: Object = {1.3.6.1.4.1.45.1.3.2.4.15.0} (SynOptics.1.3.2.4.15.0)
SNMP: Value = 2
SNMP:
SNMP: Object = {1.3.6.1.4.1.45.1.3.2.4.16.0} (SynOptics.1.3.2.4.16.0)
SNMP: Value = 1
SNMP:
SNMP: Object = {1.3.6.1.4.1.45.1.3.2.4.17.0} (SynOptics.1.3.2.4.17.0)
SNMP: Value = 9600 (gauge)
SNMP:
SNMP: Object = {1.3.6.1.4.1.45.1.3.2.4.18.0} (SynOptics.1.3.2.4.18.0)
SNMP: Value =
SNMP:
SNMP: Object = {1.3.6.1.4.1.45.1.3.2.4.19.0} (SynOptics.1.3.2.4.19.0)
SNMP: Value =
SNMP:
SNMP: Object = {1.3.6.1.4.1.45.1.3.2.4.20.1.1.XXX.YYY.170.20}
        (SynOptics.1.3.2.4.20.1.1.XXX.YYY ...
SNMP: Value = 1
SNMP:
SNMP: Object = {1.3.6.1.4.1.45.1.3.2.4.3.0} (SynOptics.1.3.2.4.3.0)
SNMP: Value = 1
```

```
SNMP:
SNMP: Object = {1.3.6.1.4.1.45.1.3.2.4.20.1.2.XXX.YYY.170.20}
        (SynOptics.1.3.2.4.20.1.2.XXX.YYY ...
SNMP: Value = [XXX.YYY.170.20], Manager
SNMP:
SNMP: Object = {1.3.6.1.4.1.45.1.3.2.4.20.1.3.XXX.YYY.170.20}
        (SynOptics.1.3.2.4.20.1.3.XXX.YYY ...
SNMP: Value = public
SNMP:
SNMP: Object = {1.3.6.1.4.1.45.1.3.2.4.21.0} (SynOptics.1.3.2.4.21.0)
SNMP: Value = 2
SNMP:
SNMP: Object = {1.3.6.1.4.1.45.2.1.1.1.1.1} (SynOptics.2.1.1.1.1.1)
SNMP: Value = 1
SNMP:
   .
   .
   .
--------------------------------------------Frame 9 --------------------------------------------
SNMP: ----- Simple Network Management Protocol -----
SNMP:
SNMP: Version = 0
SNMP: Community = public
SNMP: Command = Set request
SNMP: Request ID = 717288552
SNMP: Error status = 0 (No error)
SNMP: Error index = 0
SNMP:
SNMP: Object = {1.3.6.1.4.1.45.1.3.2.4.20.1.3.XXX.YYY.170.20}
        (SynOptics.1.3.2.4.20.1.3.XXX.YYY ...
SNMP: Value = test
SNMP:
```

```
------------------------------------------Frame 10---------------------------------------------
SNMP: ----- Simple Network Management Protocol -----
SNMP:
SNMP: Version = 0
SNMP: Community = public
SNMP: Command = Trap
SNMP: Enterprise = {1.3.6.1.4.1.45.3.8.1}
SNMP: Network address = [XXX.YYY.170.53]
SNMP: Generic trap = 4 (Authentication failure)
SNMP: Specific trap = 0
SNMP: Time ticks = 57631330
SNMP:
    .
    .
    .

------------------------------------------Frame 21---------------------------------------------

SNMP: ----- Simple Network Management Protocol -----
SNMP:
SNMP: Version = 0
SNMP: Community = administrator
SNMP: Command = Set request
SNMP: Request ID = 717288651
SNMP: Error status = 0 (No error)
SNMP: Error index = 0
SNMP:
SNMP: Object = {1.3.6.1.4.1.45.1.3.2.4.20.1.3.XXX.YYY.170.20}
         (SynOptics.1.3.2.4.20.1.3.XXX.YYY ...
SNMP: Value = trap1
SNMP:
------------------------------------------Frame 22---------------------------------------------
SNMP: ----- Simple Network Management Protocol -----
SNMP:
SNMP: Version = 0
SNMP: Community = administrator
```

```
SNMP: Command = Get response
SNMP: Request ID = 717288651
SNMP: Error status = 0 (No error)
SNMP: Error index = 0
SNMP:
SNMP: Object = {1.3.6.1.4.1.45.1.3.2.4.20.1.3.XXX.YYY.170.20}
          (SynOptics.1.3.2.4.20.1.3.XXX.YYY ...
SNMP: Value = trap1
SNMP:
   .
   .

---------------------------------------------Frame 24---------------------------------------------
SNMP: ----- Simple Network Management Protocol -----
SNMP:
SNMP: Version = 0
SNMP: Community = public
SNMP: Command = Get response
SNMP: Request ID = 717281434
SNMP: Error status = 0 (No error)
SNMP: Error index = 0
SNMP:
SNMP: Object = {1.3.6.1.4.1.45.1.3.2.4.1.0} (SynOptics.1.3.2.4.1.0)
SNMP: Value = 2
SNMP:
SNMP: Object = {1.3.6.1.4.1.45.1.3.2.4.10.0} (SynOptics.1.3.2.4.10.0)
SNMP: Value = [XXX.YYY.170.53]
SNMP:
SNMP: Object = {1.3.6.1.4.1.45.1.3.2.4.11.0} (SynOptics.1.3.2.4.11.0)
SNMP: Value = [255.255.255.0]
SNMP:
SNMP: Object = {1.3.6.1.4.1.45.1.3.2.4.12.0} (SynOptics.1.3.2.4.12.0)
SNMP: Value = [XXX.YYY.170.250]
SNMP:
SNMP: Object = {1.3.6.1.4.1.45.1.3.2.4.13.0} (SynOptics.1.3.2.4.13.0)
```

```
SNMP: Value = [XXX.YYY.170.20], Manager
SNMP:
SNMP: Object = {1.3.6.1.4.1.45.1.3.2.4.14.0} (SynOptics.1.3.2.4.14.0)
SNMP: Value = /tftpboot/syn2.cfg
SNMP:
SNMP: Object = {1.3.6.1.4.1.45.1.3.2.4.15.0} (SynOptics.1.3.2.4.15.0)
SNMP: Value = 2
SNMP:
SNMP: Object = {1.3.6.1.4.1.45.1.3.2.4.16.0} (SynOptics.1.3.2.4.16.0)
SNMP: Value = 1
SNMP:
SNMP: Object = {1.3.6.1.4.1.45.1.3.2.4.17.0} (SynOptics.1.3.2.4.17.0)
SNMP: Value = 9600 (gauge)
SNMP:
SNMP: Object = {1.3.6.1.4.1.45.1.3.2.4.18.0} (SynOptics.1.3.2.4.18.0)
SNMP: Value =
SNMP:
SNMP: Object = {1.3.6.1.4.1.45.1.3.2.4.19.0} (SynOptics.1.3.2.4.19.0)
SNMP: Value =
SNMP:
SNMP: Object = {1.3.6.1.4.1.45.1.3.2.4.2.0} (SynOptics.1.3.2.4.2.0)
SNMP: Value = 0
SNMP:
SNMP: Object = {1.3.6.1.4.1.45.1.3.2.4.20.1.1.XXX.YYY.170.20}
        SynOptics.1.3.2.4.20.1.1.XXX.YYY ...
SNMP: Value = 1
SNMP:
SNMP: Object = {1.3.6.1.4.1.45.1.3.2.4.20.1.2.XXX.YYY.170.20}
        (SynOptics.1.3.2.4.20.1.2.XXX.YYY ...
SNMP: Value = [XXX.YYY.170.20], Manager
SNMP:
SNMP: Object = {1.3.6.1.4.1.45.1.3.2.4.20.1.3.XXX.YYY.170.20}
        (SynOptics.1.3.2.4.20.1.3.XXX.YYY ...
SNMP: Value = trap1
```

```
SNMP:
SNMP: Object = {1.3.6.1.4.1.45.1.3.2.4.21.0} (SynOptics.1.3.2.4.21.0)
SNMP: Value = 2
SNMP:
```

6.4. Verifying that the Agent Transmitted, and the Manager Received, a Trap PDU

The example in Section 6.3 showed how to verify that a Set command accomplished what it was meant to do despite UDP's connectionless transport. This case study builds on that example by verifying that another device received the agent-generated Trap message.

In this example (see Figure 6-4), the Trap transmitter is the SynOptics intelligent hub, and the manager receives the trap. An X-Windows client workstation acts as the manager's display console. A configuration table within the agent's SNMP parameters defines the IP address of the receiver. When a trap is generated, it is automatically displayed in one of the workstation's windows.

As noted previously, SNMP messages are transmitted using connectionless transport via UDP, which provides minimal error control. However, some applications, such as the X-Windows system, demand more rigorous error control and require guaranteed delivery of every octet of information, in sequence, at the proper time. The TCP Transport layer protocol addresses these requirements. Frames 1 and 2 of Trace 6.4a show the X Client and the manager exchanging information using TCP. Within the TCP header (and shown in the trace) are the destination and source port numbers (D and S, respectively), an acknowledgement number (ACK), a sequence number (SEQ), a length (LEN), and a window advertisement (WIN).

In Frame 3, the manager sends a Set command to the hub agent, and the agent responds with a trap (Authentication failure) in Frame 6. The manager then sends the trap information to the X Client for display within the alarm window (Frame 8). Upon receiving the trap, the X Client sends a TCP acknowledgement in Frame 9 and displays the trap.

236

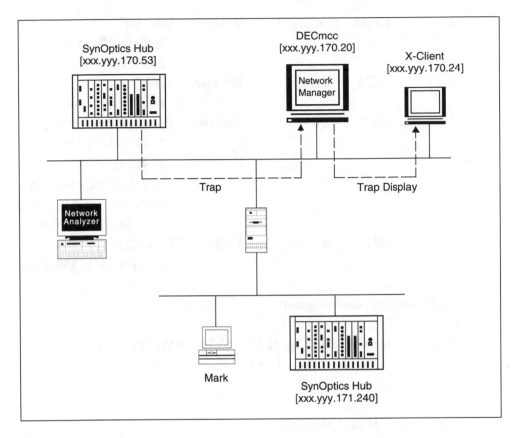

Figure 6-4. Verifying a trap

Trace 6.4a. Verifying trap reception (summary)

Sniffer Network Analyzer data 23-Sep-92 at 08:50:38, file SNMP75.ENC, Pg 1

SUMMARY	Delta T	Destination	Source	Summary
1		Manager	X Client	TCP D=4255 S=6000
				ACK=584967877
				SEQ=1899543417
				LEN=32 WIN=2920
2	0.0903	X Client	Manager	TCP D=6000 S=4255
				ACK=1899543449
				WIN=16384

3	0.4468	Hub Agent	Manager	SNMP Set SynOptics.1.3.2.4.20.1.3.XXX.YYY.170.20 = trap1
6	0.0276	Manager	Hub Agent	SNMP Trap Authentication failure
8	3.5293	X Client	Manager	XWIN C (3) Poly Text8's at 27,20 "[23-Sep-1992 08:43:23] Alarm Type[nms_trapd] from Object[snmpmg.sim.ES.COM]"; at 27,38 "TRAP [authent ...
9	0.0714	Manager	X Client	TCP D=4255 S=6000 ACK=584968457 WIN=2920

Trace 6.4b. Verifying trap reception (details)

Sniffer Network Analyzer data 23-Sep-92 at 08:50:38, file SNMP75.ENC, Pg 1

--Frame 1 --
TCP: ----- TCP header -----
TCP:
TCP: Source port = 6000 (X Windows)
TCP: Destination port = 4255
TCP: Sequence number = 1899543417
TCP: Acknowledgment number = 584967877
TCP: Data offset = 20 bytes
TCP: Flags = 18
TCP: ..0. .... = (No urgent pointer)
TCP: ...1 .... = Acknowledgment
TCP: .... 1... = Push
TCP: .... .0.. = (No reset)
TCP: .... ..0. = (No SYN)
TCP: ....0 = (No FIN)
TCP: Window = 2920
TCP: Checksum = 8A63 (correct)

TCP: No TCP options
TCP: [32 byte(s) of data]
TCP:
--Frame 2 ---
TCP: ----- TCP header -----
TCP:
TCP: Source port = 4255
TCP: Destination port = 6000 (X Windows)
TCP: Sequence number = 584967877
TCP: Acknowledgment number = 1899543449
TCP: Data offset = 20 bytes
TCP: Flags = 10
TCP: ..0. .... = (No urgent pointer)
TCP: ...1 .... = Acknowledgment
TCP: .... 0... = (No push)
TCP: .... .0.. = (No reset)
TCP: .... ..0. = (No SYN)
TCP: ....0 = (No FIN)
TCP: Window = 16384
TCP: Checksum = B7AC (correct)
TCP: No TCP options
TCP:
--Frame 3 ---
SNMP: ----- Simple Network Management Protocol -----
SNMP:
SNMP: Version = 0
SNMP: Community = public
SNMP: Command = Set request
SNMP: Request ID = 717289096
SNMP: Error status = 0 (No error)
SNMP: Error index = 0
SNMP:
SNMP: Object = {1.3.6.1.4.1.45.1.3.2.4.20.1.3.XXX.YYY.170.20}
          (SynOptics.1.3.2.4.20.1.3.XXX.YYY ...

SNMP: Value = trap1
SNMP:

--Frame 6 --
SNMP: ----- Simple Network Management Protocol -----
SNMP:
SNMP: Version = 0
SNMP: Community = trap1
SNMP: Command = Trap
SNMP: Enterprise = {1.3.6.1.4.1.45.3.8.1}
SNMP: Network address = [XXX.YYY.170.53]
SNMP: Generic trap = 4 (Authentication failure)
SNMP: Specific trap = 0
SNMP: Time ticks = 57685810
SNMP:

--Frame 8 --
XWIN: ----- X Windows -----
XWIN:
XWIN: Request opcode = 74 (Poly Text8)
XWIN: Drawable = 01D00034, Graphics context = 01D0001E
XWIN: X = 27, Y = 20
XWIN: Delta = 0
XWIN: String = "[23-Sep-1992 08:43:23] Alarm Type[nms_trapd]
        from Object[snmpmg.sim.XX.COM]"
XWIN:
XWIN: Request opcode = 74 (Poly Text8)
XWIN: Drawable = 01D00034, Graphics context = 01D0001E
XWIN: X = 27, Y = 38
XWIN: Delta = 0
XWIN: String = "TRAP [authentication failure] received, agent =
        XXX.YYY.170.53(syn2.sim.XX.COM) ...
XWIN:
XWIN: Request opcode = 74 (Poly Text8)
XWIN: Drawable = 01D00034, Graphics context = 01D0001E
XWIN: X = 27, Y = 56

```
XWIN: Delta = 0
XWIN: String = " specific-trap = 0."
XWIN:
------------------------------------------Frame 9 --------------------------------------------
TCP: ----- TCP header -----
TCP:
TCP: Source port = 6000 (X Windows)
TCP: Destination port = 4255
TCP: Sequence number = 1899543609
TCP: Acknowledgment number = 584968457
TCP: Data offset = 20 bytes
TCP: Flags = 10
TCP: ..0. .... = (No urgent pointer)
TCP: ...1 .... = Acknowledgment
TCP: .... 0... = (No push)
TCP: .... .0.. = (No reset)
TCP: .... ..0. = (No SYN)
TCP: .... ...0 = (No FIN)
TCP: Window = 2920
TCP: Checksum = E960 (correct)
TCP: No TCP options
TCP:
```

6.5. Communicating Device and Link Status with Traps

One of the most useful aspects of SNMP traps is their ability to communicate significant events to a remote network manager. This example illustrates how vendors embellish traps to provide additional information for their customers. The internetwork for this case study consists of more than 20,000 workstations, over 500 servers, and over 350 bridges and routers. Without SNMP, managing such extensive systems would be extremely difficult. In the example shown in Figure 6-5, a remote Router D and another serial link are having difficulties. This example shows how SNMP alerts the network manager to the problems.

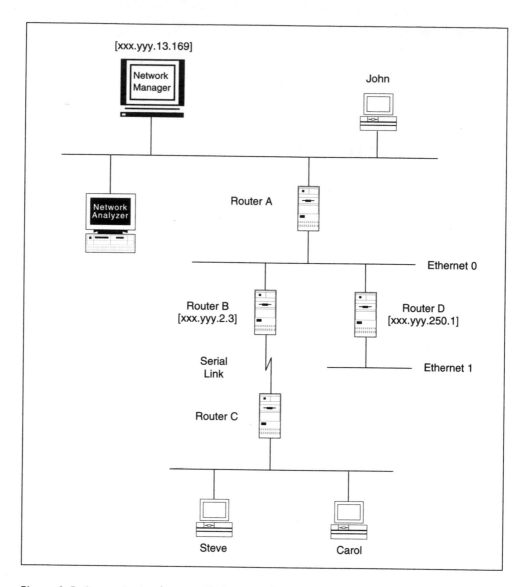

Figure 6-5. Communicating device and link status information

Router D with IP address [XXX.YYY.250.1] has a power failure, then returns to normal operation. In Frame 1 of Trace 6.5a, it signals to the manager by sending a LinkUp trap. The SNMP standard (RFC 1157) requires that the trap include the name and value of the ifIndex instance for the affected interface.

The router's manufacturer, Cisco Systems, Inc., includes additional information to further identify the interface (see Trace 6.5b.) For example, in Frame
1, the Enterprise = {1.3.6.1.4.1.9.1.1} identifies Cisco. The first three object
values transmitted come from the ifTable under the Interfaces subtree
{1.3.6.1.2.1.2}. These are the ifIndex (1 or 2); the ifDescription (Ethernet0 or
Ethernet1); and the ifType (ethernet-csmacd). The last object value, taken from
Cisco's private MIB, further identifies what happened (the link is now up).

In Frame 210, a second problem occurs on the serial link between Router B
and Router C. This failure triggers the transmission of LinkDown traps from
the router. As before, the Enterprise field identifies a Cisco device as the source
of the traps, and further identifies the failed router port by its IP address:
[XXX.YYY.2.3]. The four object values transmitted to the manager communicate the link description (serial0); the type of link (proprietary point-to-
point serial); and the reason for the trap (down).

Thus, if failures occur on other segments or communication links, which could
even be across the country from each other, SNMP traps can alert the manager that a problem exists. Further troubleshooting by using software utilities
such as ICMP Echo (PING) messages, SNMP queries (such as the IP or ICMP
groups) or test equipment (such as network analyzers) can then proceed.

Trace 6.5a. Link up and link down traps (summary)

Sniffer Network Analyzer data 23-Mar-93 at 13:08:58, file A:TRAP.ENC, Pg 1

SUMMARY	Delta T	Destination	Source	Summary
1		Manager	Router D	SNMP Trap Link up ifIndex .. cisco.2.2.1.1.20.1 (4 items)
2	0.4585	Manager	Router D	SNMP Trap Link up ifIndex .. cisco.2.2.1.1.20.2 (4 items)

.
.
.

| 210 | 27.6608 | Manager | Router B | SNMP Trap Link down ifIndex .. cisco.2.2.1.1.20.1 (4 items) |

Trace 6.5b. Link up and link down traps (details)

```
Sniffer Network Analyzer data 23-Mar-93 at 13:08:58, file A:TRAP.ENC, Pg 1
--------------------------------------------------Frame 1 --------------------------------------------------
SNMP: ----- Simple Network Management Protocol -----
SNMP:
SNMP: Version = 0
SNMP: Community = public
SNMP: Command = Trap
SNMP: Enterprise = {1.3.6.1.4.1.9.1.1}
SNMP: Network address = [XXX.YYY.12.250]
SNMP: Generic trap = 3 (Link up)
SNMP: Specific trap = 0
SNMP: Time ticks = 797
SNMP:
SNMP: Object = {1.3.6.1.2.1.2.2.1.1.1} (ifIndex.1)
SNMP: Value = 1
SNMP:
SNMP: Object = {1.3.6.1.2.1.2.2.1.2.1} (ifDescr.1)
SNMP: Value = Ethernet0
SNMP:
SNMP: Object = {1.3.6.1.2.1.2.2.1.3.1} (ifType.1)
SNMP: Value = 6 (ethernet-csmacd)
SNMP:
SNMP: Object = {1.3.6.1.4.1.9.2.2.1.1.20.1} (cisco.2.2.1.1.20.1)
SNMP: Value = up
SNMP:
```

```
-----------------------------------------------Frame 2 ----------------------------------------------------
SNMP: ----- Simple Network Management Protocol -----
SNMP:
SNMP: Version = 0
SNMP: Community = public
SNMP: Command = Trap
SNMP: Enterprise = {1.3.6.1.4.1.9.1.1}
SNMP: Network address = [XXX.YYY.12.250]
SNMP: Generic trap = 3 (Link up)
SNMP: Specific trap = 0
SNMP: Time ticks = 799
SNMP:
SNMP: Object = {1.3.6.1.2.1.2.2.1.1.2} (ifIndex.2)
SNMP: Value = 2
SNMP:
SNMP: Object = {1.3.6.1.2.1.2.2.1.2.2} (ifDescr.2)
SNMP: Value = Ethernet1
SNMP:
SNMP: Object = {1.3.6.1.2.1.2.2.1.3.2} (ifType.2)
SNMP: Value = 6 (ethernet-csmacd)
SNMP:
SNMP: Object = {1.3.6.1.4.1.9.2.2.1.1.20.2} (cisco.2.2.1.1.20.2)
SNMP: Value = up
SNMP:
-----------------------------------------------Frame 210 ----------------------------------------------------
SNMP: ----- Simple Network Management Protocol -----
SNMP:
SNMP: Version = 0
SNMP: Community = public
SNMP: Command = Trap
SNMP: Enterprise = {1.3.6.1.4.1.9.1.1}
SNMP: Network address = [XXX.YYY.2.3]
SNMP: Generic trap = 2 (Link down)
SNMP: Specific trap = 0
```

```
SNMP: Time ticks = 45039280
SNMP:
SNMP: Object = {1.3.6.1.2.1.2.2.1.1.1} (ifIndex.1)
SNMP: Value = 1
SNMP:
SNMP: Object = {1.3.6.1.2.1.2.2.1.2.1} (ifDescr.1)
SNMP: Value = Serial0
SNMP:
SNMP: Object = {1.3.6.1.2.1.2.2.1.3.1} (ifType.1)
SNMP: Value = 22 (propPointToPointSerial)
SNMP:
SNMP: Object = {1.3.6.1.4.1.9.2.2.1.1.20.1} (cisco.2.2.1.1.20.1)
SNMP: Value = down
SNMP:
```

6.6. Proper Interpretation of Private Enterprise Traps

Some vendors define traps that have meaning only within their systems. In this example, Network General Corp.'s Distributed Sniffer System is monitoring traffic on one segment of an internetwork (see Figure 6-6). The Sniffer allows the network administrator to set thresholds for various traffic parameters and transmit a trap to the Network Management console if any of these thresholds is exceeded. You'll need a copy of the vendor's MIB, such as the one from Network General Corp. shown in Definition 6-1, to properly interpret these enterprise-specific traps. This case study looks at several examples (see Trace 6.6).

Each trap sent from the Distributed Sniffer System to the management console contains nine objects. These objects are identified as belonging to the Network General private enterprises subtree, {1.3.6.1.4.1.110}, then further defined according to the private MIB (see the following table). For example, the sequence {1.3.6.1.4.1.110.1.1.1.1.1.1.3} identifies the object ngcTrText.

Like the Internet-standard MIBs described in Chapter 3, this private MIB imports definitions from other RFCs. It then defines the ngcTrapTable, which contains nine objects that are communicated via the trap. These objects are:

Object	Description
ngcTrSequence	A counter of the number of NGC alarm traps generated since the agent was last initialized.
ngcTrId	The application that generated this NGC alarm.
ngcTrText	An ASCII string describing the NGC alarm condition/cause.
ngcTrPriority	The priority level as set on the agent for this Class and Type of trap.
ngcTrClass	The Class number of the described NGC alarm.
ngcTrType	The Type number of the described NGC alarm. For each application, the alarm numbers will range from 1 to n, where n may increase as future versions of the alarm-generating applications (monitor or analyzer) detect additional network problems.
ngcTrTime	The time that the condition or event that caused the alarm occurred. This value is given in seconds since 00:00:00 Greenwich mean time (GMT) January 1, 1970.
ngcTrSuspect	An ASCII string describing the host that caused the NGC alarm. (Note: The current version of Expert Analyzer generates a null string for this field.)
ngcTrDiagId	An integer identifying the diagnosis that triggered this NGC alarm.

Trace 6.6 shows three traps defined by the third object, ngcTrText, that the Distributed Sniffer System generated. The first trap defines a Broadcast storm (Frame 1), indicating that an excessive number of messages addressed to a broadcast address have been identified and that routine network traffic has been disrupted. The second indicates a slow server (Frame 2). The third (Frame 3) identifies excessive requests denied for a specific workstation address.

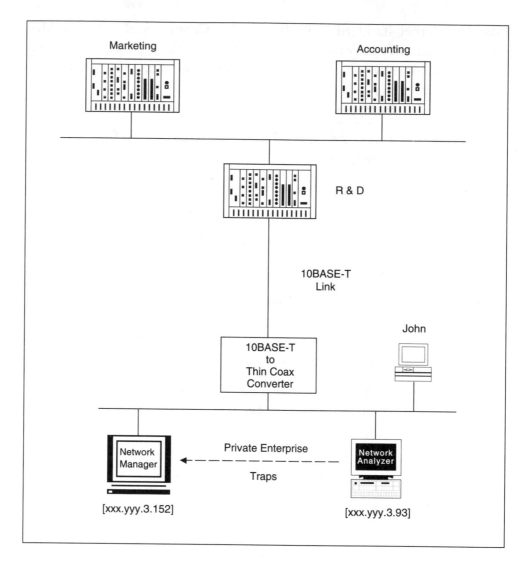

Figure 6-6. Using private enterprise traps

The agent sends each trap as an SNMP trap PDU. THE PDU header contains the fields shown at the beginning of the trace (Version, Community, Command, Enterprise, and so on). The field labeled "Enterprise" contains the OID of the product transmitting the trap. The number {1.3.6.1.4.1} represents {iso.org.dod.internet.private.enterprises}. The next number, 110, which was assigned by a central registration authority, represents Network General Corporation. Companies pay for a subtree under "enterprises" and are granted the right to administer the numbers under this subtree. If you are using an SNMP library or network-management platform, look for something like an "enterprises" file that lists these numbers and meanings. Network General assigns the rest of the object identifier beyond the 110 in its MIB. In this case, the 110 is followed by 1.1.1.0, which means ngcSystems.ngcServers.ngcMonitor.0, where the final zero indicates an instance of this object. This sequence, as you can see in Definition 6-1, represents a Network General Distributed Sniffer System (DSS) Server.

The SNMP header also indicates the Generic Trap type. All enterprise-specific traps, such as the three in this trace, include a specific trap field. For Network General Distributed Sniffer System Server traps, the specific trap field is the same as the ngcTrType variable in the trap and indicates the type of problem being reported.

The traps in Frames 1 through 3 were sent by a DSS Server running the analyzer application (ngcTrId = 3) in the sequence shown (notice ngcTrSequence objects = 2, 3, 4, which are the first objects transmitted in each frame). The ngcTrTime object (the seventh object in each frame, Value = 723941239, 723941240, 72394140) indicates that all three of these traps were sent in response to problems detected within one second of each other at 10:47 PM on December 9, 1992 GMT. You figure out how to translate the value into the actual time that the traps were sent by referencing the Network General MIB in Definition 6-1. The MIB also provides a text description of the problem (ngcTrText), a numerical index for the problem type (ngcTrType), and a configured priority (ngcPriority).

The types of problems that Network General DSS Servers can report vary by the type of network (such as Ethernet or token ring) and the release date of the product. You can expect new product releases to report new problems, although a particular value of the ngcTrType field always indicates the same problem. Check the DSS Server documentation for a list of possible traps and the specific trap numbers assigned to them. In the current release (DSS 2.0), these numbers are listed in the Server Installation and Operations Manual.

Enterprise-specific traps can be quite useful for network managers, but you'll need copies of the MIB and other vendor documentation to properly interpret these traps.

Trace 6.6. Interpreting enterprise-specific traps

```
Sniffer Network Analyzer data 9-Dec-92 at 14:47:18 file NGCTRAP.ENC, Pg 1
----------------------------------------------Frame 1 ----------------------------------------------
SNMP: ----- Simple Network Management Protocol -----
SNMP:
SNMP: Version = 0
SNMP: Community = public
SNMP: Command = Trap
SNMP: Enterprise = {1.3.6.1.4.1.110.1.1.1.0}
SNMP: Network address = [161.69.3.93]
SNMP: Generic trap = 6 (Enterprise specific)
SNMP: Specific trap = 15
SNMP: Time ticks = 18000
SNMP:
SNMP: Object = {1.3.6.1.4.1.110.1.1.1.1.1.1.1.1}
        (Network General Corp.1.1.1.1.1.1.1.1)
SNMP: Value = 2 (counter)
SNMP:
SNMP: Object = {1.3.6.1.4.1.110.1.1.1.1.1.1.2.1}
        (Network General Corp.1.1.1.1.1.1.2.1)
SNMP: Value = 3
SNMP:
SNMP: Object = {1.3.6.1.4.1.110.1.1.1.1.1.1.3.1}
        (Network General Corp.1.1.1.1.1.1.3.1)
SNMP: Value = Broadcast storm
SNMP:
```

SNMP: Object = {1.3.6.1.4.1.110.1.1.1.1.1.4.1}
        (Network General Corp.1.1.1.1.1.1.4.1)
SNMP: Value = 3
SNMP:
SNMP: Object = {1.3.6.1.4.1.110.1.1.1.1.1.5.1}
        (Network General Corp.1.1.1.1.1.1.5.1)
SNMP: Value = 0
SNMP:
SNMP: Object = {1.3.6.1.4.1.110.1.1.1.1.1.6.1}
        (Network General Corp.1.1.1.1.1.1.6.1)
SNMP: Value = 16
SNMP:
SNMP: Object = {1.3.6.1.4.1.110.1.1.1.1.1.7.1}
        (Network General Corp.1.1.1.1.1.1.7.1)
SNMP: Value = 723941239 (counter)
SNMP:
SNMP: Object = {1.3.6.1.4.1.110.1.1.1.1.1.8.1}
        (Network General Corp.1.1.1.1.1.1.8.1)
SNMP: Value =
SNMP:
SNMP: Object = {1.3.6.1.4.1.110.1.1.1.1.1.9.1}
        (Network General Corp.1.1.1.1.1.1.9.1)
SNMP: Value = -322681743
SNMP:
---Frame 2 ---
SNMP: ----- Simple Network Management Protocol -----
SNMP:
SNMP: Version = 0
SNMP: Community = public
SNMP: Command = Trap
SNMP: Enterprise = {1.3.6.1.4.1.110.1.1.1.0}
SNMP: Network address = [161.69.3.93]
SNMP: Generic trap = 6 (Enterprise specific)
SNMP: Specific trap = 2

```
SNMP: Time ticks = 18000
SNMP:
SNMP: Object = {1.3.6.1.4.1.110.1.1.1.1.1.1.1.1}
        (Network General Corp.1.1.1.1.1.1.1.1)
SNMP: Value = 3 (counter)
SNMP:
SNMP: Object = {1.3.6.1.4.1.110.1.1.1.1.1.1.2.1}
        (Network General Corp.1.1.1.1.1.1.2.1)
SNMP: Value = 3
SNMP:
SNMP: Object = {1.3.6.1.4.1.110.1.1.1.1.1.1.3.1}
        (Network General Corp.1.1.1.1.1.1.3.1)
SNMP: Value = Slow server: 000000000001
SNMP:
SNMP: Object = {1.3.6.1.4.1.110.1.1.1.1.1.1.4.1}
        (Network General Corp.1.1.1.1.1.1.4.1)
SNMP: Value = 4
SNMP:
SNMP: Object = {1.3.6.1.4.1.110.1.1.1.1.1.1.5.1}
        (Network General Corp.1.1.1.1.1.1.5.1)
SNMP: Value = 0
SNMP:
SNMP: Object = {1.3.6.1.4.1.110.1.1.1.1.1.1.6.1}
        (Network General Corp.1.1.1.1.1.1.6.1)
SNMP: Value = 3
SNMP:
SNMP: Object = {1.3.6.1.4.1.110.1.1.1.1.1.1.7.1}
        (Network General Corp.1.1.1.1.1.1.7.1)
SNMP: Value = 723941240 (counter)
SNMP:
SNMP: Object = {1.3.6.1.4.1.110.1.1.1.1.1.1.8.1}
        (Network General Corp.1.1.1.1.1.1.8.1)
SNMP: Value =
SNMP:
```

SNMP: Object = {1.3.6.1.4.1.110.1.1.1.1.1.1.9.1}
        (Network General Corp.1.1.1.1.1.1.9.1)
SNMP: Value = -322681872
SNMP:
---Frame 3 ---
SNMP: ----- Simple Network Management Protocol -----
SNMP:
SNMP: Version = 0
SNMP: Community = public
SNMP: Command = Trap
SNMP: Enterprise = {1.3.6.1.4.1.110.1.1.1.0}
SNMP: Network address = [161.69.3.93]
SNMP: Generic trap = 6 (Enterprise specific)
SNMP: Specific trap = 4
SNMP: Time ticks = 18000
SNMP:
SNMP: Object = {1.3.6.1.4.1.110.1.1.1.1.1.1.1.1}
        (Network General Corp.1.1.1.1.1.1.1.1)
SNMP: Value = 4 (counter)
SNMP:
SNMP: Object = {1.3.6.1.4.1.110.1.1.1.1.1.1.2.1}
        (Network General Corp.1.1.1.1.1.1.2.1)
SNMP: Value = 3
SNMP:
SNMP: Object = {1.3.6.1.4.1.110.1.1.1.1.1.1.3.1}
        (Network General Corp.1.1.1.1.1.1.3.1)
SNMP: Value = Excessive requests denied for 0000928039D3
SNMP:
SNMP: Object = {1.3.6.1.4.1.110.1.1.1.1.1.1.4.1}
        (Network General Corp.1.1.1.1.1.1.4.1)
SNMP: Value = 2
SNMP:
SNMP: Object = {1.3.6.1.4.1.110.1.1.1.1.1.1.5.1}
        (Network General Corp.1.1.1.1.1.1.5.1)

```
SNMP: Value = 0
SNMP:
SNMP: Object = {1.3.6.1.4.1.110.1.1.1.1.1.1.6.1}
        (Network General Corp.1.1.1.1.1.1.6.1)
SNMP: Value = 5
SNMP:
SNMP: Object = {1.3.6.1.4.1.110.1.1.1.1.1.1.7.1}
        (Network General Corp.1.1.1.1.1.1.7.1)
SNMP: Value = 723941240 (counter)
SNMP:
SNMP: Object = {1.3.6.1.4.1.110.1.1.1.1.1.1.8.1}
        (Network General Corp.1.1.1.1.1.1.8.1)
SNMP: Value =
SNMP:
SNMP: Object = {1.3.6.1.4.1.110.1.1.1.1.1.1.9.1}
        (Network General Corp.1.1.1.1.1.1.9.1)
SNMP: Value = -322681873
SNMP:
```

Definition 6-1:

```
-------------------------------------------------------------------------------------
--    NGC.ASN:  Network General Corporation MIB extensions for
--        Network Monitor/Analyzer products.
--
--            Network General Corporation
--            4200 Bohannon Drive
--            Menlo Park, CA 94025
--            (415) 473-2000
--
--             March 26, 1993
--             Rev (Special Revision)
-------------------------------------------------------------------------------------
        NGCMONITOR-MIB DEFINITIONS ::= BEGIN
```

```
      IMPORTS
            enterprises, NetworkAddress, IpAddress,
            Counter                 FROM RFC1155-SMI
            DisplayString           FROM RFC1158-MIB
            OBJECT-TYPE             FROM RFC1212;
            TRAP-TYPE               FROM RFC1215;


--          This MIB module uses the extended OBJECT-TYPE macro as defined
--          in RFC 1212 and the TRAP-TYPE macro as defined in RFC 1215


--          Network General Corporation enterprise
            ngc                     OBJECT IDENTIFIER ::= { enterprises 110 }
            ngcSystems              OBJECT IDENTIFIER ::= { ngc 1 }
            ngcServers              OBJECT IDENTIFIER ::= { ngcSystems 1 }
            ngcMonitor              OBJECT IDENTIFIER ::= { ngcServers 1 }


--          Groups in ngcMonitor
            ngcTrap                 OBJECT IDENTIFIER ::= { ngcMonitor 1 }


--          The ngcTrap group. This group contains objects describing
--          the last Network General 'alarm' resulting in transmission
--          of a SNMP trap message.
ngcTrapTable OBJECT-TYPE
      SYNTAX SEQUENCE OF NgcTrapEntry
      ACCESS not-accessible
      STATUS mandatory
      DESCRIPTION
            "The agent's table of NGC alarm information."
      ::= { ngcTrap 1 }
ngcTrapEntry OBJECT-TYPE
      SYNTAX NgcTrapEntry
      ACCESS not-accessible
      STATUS mandatory
   DESCRIPTION
```

```
        "Information about the last NGC alarm trap generated
        by the agent."
     INDEX  { 1 }
     ::= { ngcTrapTable 1 }
  NgcTrapEntry ::=
     SEQUENCE {
       ngcTrSequence
         Counter,
       ngcTrId
         INTEGER,
       ngcTrText
         DisplayString (SIZE (0..80)),
       ngcTrPriority
         INTEGER,
       ngcTrClass
         INTEGER,
       ngcTrType
         INTEGER,
       ngcTrTime
         Counter,
       ngcTrSuspect
         DisplayString (SIZE (0..32)),
       ngcTrDiagId
         INTEGER
     }
  ngcTrSequence OBJECT-TYPE
     SYNTAX Counter
     ACCESS read-only
     STATUS mandatory
     DESCRIPTION
       "A counter of the number of NGC alarm traps generated
       since the agent was last initialized."
     ::= { ngcTrapEntry 1 }
  ngcTrId OBJECT-TYPE
```

```
SYNTAX INTEGER {
    monitor(1),
    analyzer(3)
    }
ACCESS read-only
STATUS mandatory
DESCRIPTION
 "The application which generated this NGC alarm."
::= { ngcTrapEntry 2 }
ngcTrText OBJECT-TYPE
SYNTAX DisplayString (SIZE (0..80))
ACCESS read-only
STATUS mandatory
DESCRIPTION
 "An ASCII string describing the NGC alarm condition/cause."
::= { ngcTrapEntry 3 }
ngcTrPriority OBJECT-TYPE
SYNTAX INTEGER {
    inform(1),
    warning(2),
    minor(3),
    major(4),
    critical(5)
    }
ACCESS read-only
STATUS mandatory
DESCRIPTION
 "The priority level as set on the agent for
 this Class and Type of trap."
::= { ngcTrapEntry 4 }
ngcTrClass OBJECT-TYPE
SYNTAX INTEGER
ACCESS read-only
STATUS mandatory
```

DESCRIPTION
  "The Class number of the described NGC alarm."
  ::= { ngcTrapEntry 5 }
ngcTrType OBJECT-TYPE
  SYNTAX INTEGER
  ACCESS read-only
  STATUS mandatory
  DESCRIPTION
   "The Type number of the described NGC alarm. For each
   application the alarm numbers will range from 1 to n,
   where n may increase as future versions of the alarm-
   generating applications (monitor or analyzer) detect
   additional network problems. (See separate list
   of alarm types generated by current versions of these
   applications.)"
  ::= { ngcTrapEntry 6 }
ngcTrTime OBJECT-TYPE
  SYNTAX Counter
  ACCESS read-only
  STATUS mandatory
  DESCRIPTION
   "The time that the condition or event occurred which
   caused generation of this alarm. This value is given
   in seconds since 00:00:00 Greenwich mean time (GMT)
   January 1, 1970."
  ::= { ngcTrapEntry 7 }
ngcTrSuspect OBJECT-TYPE
  SYNTAX DisplayString (SIZE (0..32))
  ACCESS read-only
  STATUS mandatory
  DESCRIPTION
   "An ASCII string describing the host which caused the
   NGC alarm. (Note: current version of Expert Analyzer
   generates a null string for this field.)"

```
    ::= { ngcTrapEntry 8 }
ngcTrDiagId OBJECT-TYPE
  SYNTAX INTEGER
  ACCESS read-only
  STATUS mandatory
  DESCRIPTION
    "An integer identifying the diagnosis which triggered
    this NGC alarm.
    ::= { ngcTrapEntry 9 }


— Network General Corporation Enterprise-Specific Traps
ngcMonitorAlarm TRAP-TYPE
  ENTERPRISE { ngc }
  VARIABLES { ngcTrSequence, ngcTrId, ngcTrText, ngcTrPriority,
        ngcTrClass, ngcTrType, ngcTrTime, ngcTrSuspect,
        ngcTrDiagId }
  DESCRIPTION
    "The SNMP trap that is generated when the monitor has
    recognized the presence of an alarm condition."
    ::= 1


END
```

6.7. Incompatible Private Enterprise MIBs

SNMP's popularity has encouraged numerous vendors to incorporate the protocol and its functions into their products. Unfortunately, any time more than one vendor gets involved in a system, incompatibilities can arise, as illustrated in this example (see Figure 6-7).

The manager in this case is a Hewlett-Packard OpenView console, and the agent is a Novell file server running NetWare v3.11 with the TCP/IP and SNMP options. The manager requests the value of a specific object from the agent in Frame 1, and the response is "no such name." The details of the captured frames identify what happened (see Trace 6.7).

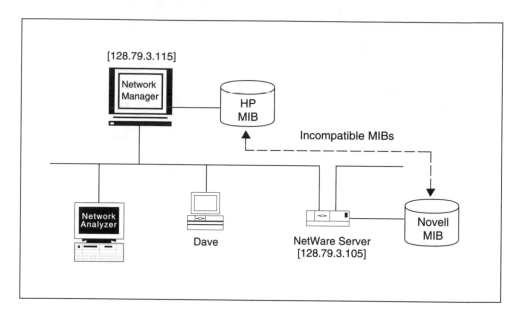

Figure 6-7. Incompatible private enterprise MIBs

In the first IP datagram (Frame 1), the manager's SNMP process includes Identification = 29913 to identify the message. Note that the HP manager assigned Source port = 4837 on its host, and used the Destination port = 161, the standard SNMP port, for the agent's host. Also note that the Community name = public. The SNMP GetRequest PDU has a Request ID = 1840, which is used to correlate this request with the agent's response. The object in question is from the private enterprise tree, {1.3.6.1.4.1}, and is further identified as belonging to the Hewlett-Packard enterprise {1.3.6.1.4.1.11}. The specific object is {1.3.6.1.4.1.11.2.3.1.1.3.0} or {HP 2.3.1.1.3.0}, which identifies the CPU utilization. (Note that the network analyzer is programmed to identify the HP subtree {1.3.6.1.4.1.11}, but not the exact object. We know that this object is CPU utilization from looking into the details of HP's private MIB.)

The agent responds in Frame 2. Note that the agent uses a different Identification (22662) for the IP datagram. This is not a problem, since IP processes of the manager and agent are independent. The agent correctly designates the Destination port (4837) within its UDP header, which sends the SNMP reply to the manager's SNMP process. The agent's message contains the community name (public), and the Request ID (1840) that correlate with the manager's request. The last two fields provide a clue to the problem: the Error Status = 2 (no such name) and the Error Index = 1. These specify that the object name given in the GetRequest was unknown to the agent, and that the first object specified contained the error. When you consider that the HP manager was asking a Novell server for its CPU utilization, the confusion isn't surprising. Thus, while both manager and agent support MIB-II, their private enterprise MIBs are incompatible. Another example of standards-based, yet incompatible, systems.

Trace 6.7. Inconsistent private enterprise MIBs

```
Sniffer Network Analyzer data 5-Oct-92 at 09:42:54, file PRVMIB2.ENC Pg 1
-------------------------------------------Frame 1 --------------------------------------------
DLC: ----- DLC Header -----
DLC:
DLC: Frame 1 arrived at 09:43:20.8073; Frame size is 87 (0057 hex) bytes.
DLC: Destination = Station H-P  133ADE
DLC: Source   = Station H-P  17B65F
DLC: Ethertype = 0800 (IP)
DLC:
IP:  ----- IP Header -----
IP:
IP: Version = 4, header length = 20 bytes
IP: Type of service = 00
IP:    000. .... = routine
IP:    ...0 .... = normal delay
IP:    .... 0... = normal throughput
IP:    .... .0.. = normal reliability
IP: Total length = 73 bytes
IP: Identification = 29913
IP: Flags = 0X
IP: .0.. .... = may fragment
```

IP: ..0. .... = last fragment
IP: Fragment offset = 0 bytes
IP: Time to live = 30 seconds/hops
IP: Protocol = 17 (UDP)
IP: Header checksum = 2051 (correct)
IP: Source address = [128.79.3.115], Manager
IP: Destination address = [128.79.3.105], Agent
IP: No options
IP:
UDP: ----- UDP Header -----
UDP:
UDP: Source port = 4837 (SNMP)
UDP: Destination port = 161
UDP: Length = 53
UDP: Checksum = CBCC (correct)
UDP:
SNMP: ----- Simple Network Management Protocol -----
SNMP:
SNMP: Version = 0
SNMP: Community = public
SNMP: Command = Get request
SNMP: Request ID = 1840
SNMP: Error status = 0 (No error)
SNMP: Error index = 0
SNMP:
SNMP: Object = {1.3.6.1.4.1.11.2.3.1.1.3.0} (HP.2.3.1.1.3.0)
SNMP: Value = NULL
SNMP:
---Frame 2 ---
DLC: ----- DLC Header -----
DLC:
DLC: Frame 2 arrived at 09:43:20.8093; Frame size is 88 (0058 hex) bytes.
DLC: Destination = Station H-P 17B65F
DLC: Source   = Station H-P 133ADE

DLC: Ethertype = 0800 (IP)
DLC:
IP: ----- IP Header -----
IP:
IP: Version = 4, header length = 20 bytes
IP: Type of service = 00
IP: 000. .... = routine
IP: ...0 .... = normal delay
IP: .... 0... = normal throughput
IP: .... .0.. = normal reliability
IP: Total length = 73 bytes
IP: Identification = 22662
IP: Flags = 0X
IP: .0.. .... = may fragment
IP: ..0. .... = last fragment
IP: Fragment offset = 0 bytes
IP: Time to live = 128 seconds/hops
IP: Protocol = 17 (UDP)
IP: Header checksum = DAA3 (correct)
IP: Source address = [128.79.3.105], Agent
IP: Destination address = [128.79.3.115], Manager
IP: No options
IP:
UDP: ----- UDP Header -----
UDP:
UDP: Source port = 161 (SNMP)
UDP: Destination port = 4837
UDP: Length = 53
UDP: No checksum
UDP:
SNMP: ----- Simple Network Management Protocol -----
SNMP:
SNMP: Version = 0
SNMP: Community = public

```
SNMP: Command = Get response
SNMP: Request ID = 1840
SNMP: Error status = 2 (No such name)
SNMP: Error index = 1
SNMP:
SNMP: Object = {1.3.6.1.4.1.11.2.3.1.1.3.0} (HP.2.3.1.1.3.0)
SNMP: Value = NULL
SNMP:
```

6.8. Proper Handling of an Invalid Object Identifier (OID)

Chapters 2 and 3 discussed the ASN.1 encodings for objects within the SNMP MIBs. These encodings are based upon a tree structure, and specific object identifiers (OIDs) locate the position of objects on the tree. Since these OIDs are sequences of numbers, a mistake of just one digit renders the sequence invalid. This example shows how an agent responds to a manager's mistake.

In this example, the manager wishes to obtain the value of the system description (see Figure 6-8 and Trace 6.8a). The first time the request is made (Frame 1), a correct response is returned (Frame 3). The second request (Frame 4) is unsuccessful (Frame 5). The details of the SNMP messages (Trace 6.8b) reveal that an invalid OID caused the problem.

In the first GetRequest (Frame 1 of Trace 6.8b), the OID given for sysDescr is {1.3.6.1.2.1.1.1.0}. This OID consists of the prefix {1.3.6.1.2.1.1.1} and an instance (.0). Recall that an instance of .0 indicates a scalar object, that is, one that occurs only once. (Columnar objects may have multiple instances, requiring a suffix of .2, .3, .4, and so on. In these cases, the suffix identifies the specific instance of interest.) In Frame 3, you can see that the GetResponse returns Value = /usr3/wf/wf.rel/v5.75/wf.pj/proto.ss/ace_test.p/. So far, so good.

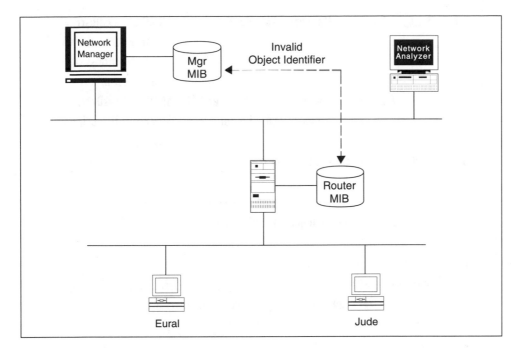

Figure 6-8. Invalid Object Identifier (OID)

Now, as an experiment, the network administrator issues another GetRequest (Frame 4) which returns an error (Frame 5). The details show why this problem occurred. The GetRequest contains an invalid OID, {1.3.6.1.3.1.1.1.1}, otherwise known as sysDescr.1. Since this is a scalar, not a tabular object, the ASN.1 syntax is invalid. The response returned in Frame 5 indicates this error: No such name. Thus, the agent provided a proper response for an OID that was not within its MIB.

Trace 6.8a. Handling an invalid object identifier (summary)

Sniffer Network Analyzer data 16-Nov-92 at 17:43:32, file 7-15.ENC, Pg 1

SUMMARY	Delta T	Destination	Source	Summary
1		Router	Manager 146	SNMP Get sysDescr
2	0.0488	Router	SGI 020C5D	ARP R PA=[XXX.YYY.3.146] HA=080069020C5D PRO=IP

3	0.0031	Manager 146	Router	SNMP Got sysDescr = /usr3/wf/wf.rel/v5.75 /wf.pj/proto.ss /ace_test.p/
4	7.2153	Router	Manager 146	SNMP Get sysDescr
5	0.0421	Manager 146	Router	SNMP Got No such name sysDescr

Trace 6.8b. Handling an invalid object identifier (details)

```
-------------------------------------------Frame 1 ---------------------------------------------
SNMP: ----- Simple Network Management Protocol -----
SNMP:
SNMP: Version = 0
SNMP: Community = xyzsnmp
SNMP: Command = Get request
SNMP: Request ID = 13227000
SNMP: Error status = 0 (No error)
SNMP: Error index = 0
SNMP:
SNMP: Object = {1.3.6.1.2.1.1.1.0} (sysDescr.0)
SNMP: Value = NULL
SNMP:
-------------------------------------------Frame 3 ---------------------------------------------
SNMP: ----- Simple Network Management Protocol -----
SNMP:
SNMP: Version = 0
SNMP: Community = xyzsnmp
SNMP: Command = Get response
SNMP: Request ID = 13227000
SNMP: Error status = 0 (No error)
SNMP: Error index = 0
SNMP:
SNMP: Object = {1.3.6.1.2.1.1.1.0} (sysDescr.0)
SNMP: Value = /usr3/wf/wf.rel/v5.75/wf.pj/proto.ss/ace_test.p/
```

SNMP:

\--Frame 4 --

SNMP: ----- Simple Network Management Protocol -----

SNMP:

SNMP: Version = 0

SNMP: Community = xyzsnmp

SNMP: Command = Get request

SNMP: Request ID = 1094416166

SNMP: Error status = 0 (No error)

SNMP: Error index = 0

SNMP:

SNMP: Object = {1.3.6.1.2.1.1.1.1} (sysDescr.1)

SNMP: Value = NULL

SNMP:

\--Frame 5 --

SNMP: ----- Simple Network Management Protocol -----

SNMP:

SNMP: Version = 0

SNMP: Community = xyzsnmp

SNMP: Command = Get response

SNMP: Request ID = 1094416166

SNMP: Error status = 2 (No such name)

SNMP: Error index = 1

SNMP:

SNMP: Object = {1.3.6.1.2.1.1.1.1} (sysDescr.1)

SNMP: Value = NULL

SNMP:

6.9 Supporting the RMON MIB with a Network Monitor

One of the significant enhancements to distributed network management has been the Remote Monitoring MIB (RMON). Both Ethernet and token-ring versions of RMON are available (as discussed in Sections 3.4 and 3.5). RMON extends the reach of the network manager to remote LAN segments located anywhere on that internetwork. The RMON agent can be a simple device that connects to a local LAN segment and gathers statistics on that segment's performance. RMON agents can also be built into internetworking devices such bridges, routers, and intelligent hubs. The RMON manager could be a software application running on the network management console.

For example, Network General Corp. (Menlo Park, CA) makes an agent called the RMON Option Kit that consists of a network interface card and software and can be installed in any DOS-compatible workstation. An example of RMON network management software would be the Armon package from Armon Networking, Ltd. (Tel Aviv, Israel), which runs as an application on the SunNet manager platform. This example shows sample statistics that this Ethernet RMON agent can tabulate for the manager (see Figure 6-9).

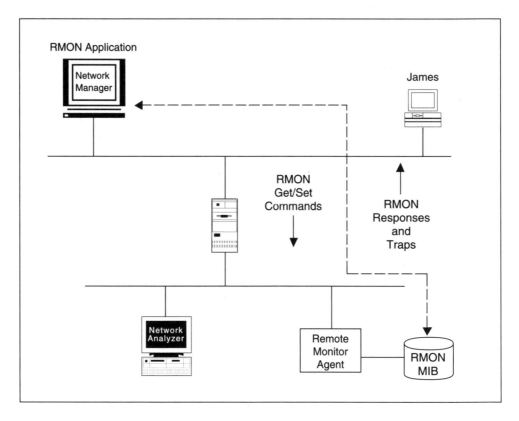

Figure 6-9. Retrieving remote information using the RMON MIB

The Ethernet RMON MIB contains nine groups (review Figure 3-12). The first group maintains a table of statistics, measured on the agent's segment. The second group contains historical information about significant network events. In Trace 6.9a, the manager wishes to retrieve the statistics table and check its values. Frames 86 and 88 transmit the Manager's GetNextRequests, and Frame 87 and 89 contain the RMON agent's responses. Note that only one instance of the etherStatsTable exists, as all of the OIDs in the GetResponse messages (Frames 87 and 89) end with the suffix .1.

The details of the agent's response show the statistics that are maintained (see Trace 6.9b). Of particular interest are the number of errored frames (fragments, jabbers, and collisions), counted by objects {1.3.6.1.2.1.16.1.1.1.11}, 12 and 13, respectively. Both Frames 87 and 89 reveal values of 21,389 fragments, 4 jabbers, and 163 collisions, respectively, for those objects. (Review the Statistics group of Figure 3-12, the RMON Ethernet MIB).

Next, the manager issues a Set command followed by a Get for confirmation to store configuration entries in the History Control table, {1.3.6.1.2.1.16.2.1}. This table contains various parameters that control the periodic sampling of statistics. The sampled values are stored in the Ether History table, {1.3.6.1.2.1.16.2.2}. A two-step process stores the configuration entries. In the first step (Frames 90 and 91), the manager picks a random instance number between 1 and 65535 (52021 in this case), and issues a Set to the historyControlStatus object {1.3.6.1.2.1.16.2.1.1.7.52021 with Value = 2 (createRequest). The instance number (52021) identifies the table, and prevents another manager from creating the same table with the same instance. This SetRequest succeeded, as the GetResponse (Frame 91) was returned with Error Status = 0 (No error).

The second step (Frame 92) stores the configuration entries. Among the values set are the buckets requested (100), the control interval (five seconds), and the control owner (Armon). The RMON agent confirms these values in Frame 93, and indicates a value of 1 (valid) for the historyControlStatus object, {1.3.6.1.2.1.16.2.1.1.7.52021}. To confirm the creation of the table, the manager issues a GetRequest for the table objects in Frame 94, which are returned with their values in Frame 95. All objects were created as indicated in the SetRequest command.

In summary, the RMON MIB provides a way to manage remote and directly connected network devices. As support for this MIB becomes more widespread, the effectiveness of remote network management will also increase.

Trace 6.9a. RMON MIB objects (summary)

Sniffer Network Analyzer data 30-Mar-93 at 15:01:14, RMON3.ENC, Pg 1

SUMMARY	Delta T	Destination	Source	Summary
86	3.1904	RMON Agent	Manager	SNMP Next sysUpTime .. mib.16.1.1.1.21 (22 items)
87	0.0079	Manager	RMON Agent	SNMP Got sysUpTime .. mib.16.1.1.1.21.1 (22 items)
88	0.0813	RMON Agent	Manager	SNMP Next sysUpTime .. mib.16.1.1.1.21.1 (22 items)
89	0.0301	Manager	RMON Agent	SNMP Got sysUpTime .. mib.16.2.1.1.1.1 (22 items)
90	0.2267	RMON Agent	Manager	SNMP Set mib.16.2.1.1.7.52021 = 2
91	0.0019	Manager	RMON Agent	SNMP Got mib.16.2.1.1.7.52021 = 2
92	0.3165	RMON Agent	Manager	SNMP Set mib.16.2.1.1.2.52021 .. mib.16.2.1.1.7.52021 (5 items)

93	0.0025	Manager	RMON Agent	SNMP Got mib.16.2.1.1.2.52021 .. mib.16.2.1.1.7.52021 (5 items)
94	0.4172	RMON Agent	Manager	SNMP Get sysUpTime .. mib.16.2.1.1.7.52021 (8 items)
95	0.0025	Manager	RMON Agent	SNMP Got sysUpTime .. mib.16.2.1.1.7.52021 (8 items)

Trace 6.9b. RMON MIB objects (details)

Sniffer Network Analyzer data 30-Mar-93 at 15:01:14, RMON3.ENC, Pg 1
--Frame 86--
SNMP: ----- Simple Network Management Protocol -----
SNMP:
SNMP: Version = 0
SNMP: Community = armon
SNMP: Command = Get next request
SNMP: Request ID = 0
SNMP: Error status = 0 (No error)
SNMP: Error index = 0
SNMP:
SNMP: Object = {1.3.6.1.2.1.1.3} (sysUpTime)
SNMP: Value = NULL
SNMP:
SNMP: Object = {1.3.6.1.2.1.16.1.1.1.1} (mib.16.1.1.1.1)
SNMP: Value = NULL
SNMP:
SNMP: Object = {1.3.6.1.2.1.16.1.1.1.2} (mib.16.1.1.1.2)
SNMP: Value = NULL
SNMP:
SNMP: Object = {1.3.6.1.2.1.16.1.1.1.3} (mib.16.1.1.1.3)
SNMP: Value = NULL

SNMP:
SNMP: Object = {1.3.6.1.2.1.16.1.1.1.4} (mib.16.1.1.1.4)
SNMP: Value = NULL
SNMP:
SNMP: Object = {1.3.6.1.2.1.16.1.1.1.5} (mib.16.1.1.1.5)
SNMP: Value = NULL
SNMP:
SNMP: Object = {1.3.6.1.2.1.16.1.1.1.6} (mib.16.1.1.1.6)
SNMP: Value = NULL
SNMP:
SNMP: Object = {1.3.6.1.2.1.16.1.1.1.7} (mib.16.1.1.1.7)
SNMP: Value = NULL
SNMP:
SNMP: Object = {1.3.6.1.2.1.16.1.1.1.8} (mib.16.1.1.1.8)
SNMP: Value = NULL
SNMP:
SNMP: Object = {1.3.6.1.2.1.16.1.1.1.9} (mib.16.1.1.1.9)
SNMP: Value = NULL
SNMP:
SNMP: Object = {1.3.6.1.2.1.16.1.1.1.10} (mib.16.1.1.1.10)
SNMP: Value = NULL
SNMP:
SNMP: Object = {1.3.6.1.2.1.16.1.1.1.11} (mib.16.1.1.1.11)
SNMP: Value = NULL
SNMP:
SNMP: Object = {1.3.6.1.2.1.16.1.1.1.12} (mib.16.1.1.1.12)
SNMP: Value = NULL
SNMP:
SNMP: Object = {1.3.6.1.2.1.16.1.1.1.13} (mib.16.1.1.1.13)
SNMP: Value = NULL
SNMP:
SNMP: Object = {1.3.6.1.2.1.16.1.1.1.14} (mib.16.1.1.1.14)
SNMP: Value = NULL
SNMP:

SNMP: Object = {1.3.6.1.2.1.16.1.1.1.15} (mib.16.1.1.1.15)
SNMP: Value = NULL
SNMP:
SNMP: Object = {1.3.6.1.2.1.16.1.1.1.16} (mib.16.1.1.1.16)
SNMP: Value = NULL
SNMP:
SNMP: Object = {1.3.6.1.2.1.16.1.1.1.17} (mib.16.1.1.1.17)
SNMP: Value = NULL
SNMP:
SNMP: Object = {1.3.6.1.2.1.16.1.1.1.18} (mib.16.1.1.1.18)
SNMP: Value = NULL
SNMP:
SNMP: Object = {1.3.6.1.2.1.16.1.1.1.19} (mib.16.1.1.1.19)
SNMP: Value = NULL
SNMP:
SNMP: Object = {1.3.6.1.2.1.16.1.1.1.20} (mib.16.1.1.1.20)
SNMP: Value = NULL
SNMP:
SNMP: Object = {1.3.6.1.2.1.16.1.1.1.21} (mib.16.1.1.1.21)
SNMP: Value = NULL
SNMP:
---Frame 87---
SNMP: ----- Simple Network Management Protocol -----
SNMP:
SNMP: Version = 0
SNMP: Community = armon
SNMP: Command = Get response
SNMP: Request ID = 0
SNMP: Error status = 0 (No error)
SNMP: Error index = 0
SNMP:
SNMP: Object = {1.3.6.1.2.1.1.3.0} (sysUpTime.0)
SNMP: Value = 10132171 hundredths of a second
SNMP:

SNMP: Object = {1.3.6.1.2.1.16.1.1.1.1.1} (mib.16.1.1.1.1.1)
SNMP: Value = 1
SNMP:
SNMP: Object = {1.3.6.1.2.1.16.1.1.1.2.1} (mib.16.1.1.1.2.1)
SNMP: Value = {1.3.6.1.2.1.2.2.1.1.1}
SNMP:
SNMP: Object = {1.3.6.1.2.1.16.1.1.1.3.1} (mib.16.1.1.1.3.1)
SNMP: Value = 0 (counter)
SNMP:
SNMP: Object = {1.3.6.1.2.1.16.1.1.1.4.1} (mib.16.1.1.1.4.1)
SNMP: Value = 1557016926 (counter)
SNMP:
SNMP: Object = {1.3.6.1.2.1.16.1.1.1.5.1} (mib.16.1.1.1.5.1)
SNMP: Value = 7705082 (counter)
SNMP:
SNMP: Object = {1.3.6.1.2.1.16.1.1.1.6.1} (mib.16.1.1.1.6.1)
SNMP: Value = 272349 (counter)
SNMP:
SNMP: Object = {1.3.6.1.2.1.16.1.1.1.7.1} (mib.16.1.1.1.7.1)
SNMP: Value = 20682 (counter)
SNMP:
SNMP: Object = {1.3.6.1.2.1.16.1.1.1.8.1} (mib.16.1.1.1.8.1)
SNMP: Value = 2082 (counter)
SNMP:
SNMP: Object = {1.3.6.1.2.1.16.1.1.1.9.1} (mib.16.1.1.1.9.1)
SNMP: Value = 0 (counter)
SNMP:
SNMP: Object = {1.3.6.1.2.1.16.1.1.1.10.1} (mib.16.1.1.1.10.1)
SNMP: Value = 0 (counter)
SNMP:
SNMP: Object = {1.3.6.1.2.1.16.1.1.1.11.1} (mib.16.1.1.1.11.1)
SNMP: Value = 21389 (counter)
SNMP:
SNMP: Object = {1.3.6.1.2.1.16.1.1.1.12.1} (mib.16.1.1.1.12.1)

SNMP: Value = 4 (counter)
SNMP:
SNMP: Object = {1.3.6.1.2.1.16.1.1.1.13.1} (mib.16.1.1.1.13.1)
SNMP: Value = 163 (counter)
SNMP:
SNMP: Object = {1.3.6.1.2.1.16.1.1.1.14.1} (mib.16.1.1.1.14.1)
SNMP: Value = 2425300 (counter)
SNMP:
SNMP: Object = {1.3.6.1.2.1.16.1.1.1.15.1} (mib.16.1.1.1.15.1)
SNMP: Value = 3309942 (counter)
SNMP:
SNMP: Object = {1.3.6.1.2.1.16.1.1.1.16.1} (mib.16.1.1.1.16.1)
SNMP: Value = 448315 (counter)
SNMP:
SNMP: Object = {1.3.6.1.2.1.16.1.1.1.17.1} (mib.16.1.1.1.17.1)
SNMP: Value = 94386 (counter)
SNMP:
SNMP: Object = {1.3.6.1.2.1.16.1.1.1.18.1} (mib.16.1.1.1.18.1)
SNMP: Value = 1019509 (counter)
SNMP:
SNMP: Object = {1.3.6.1.2.1.16.1.1.1.19.1} (mib.16.1.1.1.19.1)
SNMP: Value = 386237 (counter)
SNMP:
SNMP: Object = {1.3.6.1.2.1.16.1.1.1.20.1} (mib.16.1.1.1.20.1)
SNMP: Value = monitor
SNMP:
SNMP: Object = {1.3.6.1.2.1.16.1.1.1.21.1} (mib.16.1.1.1.21.1)
SNMP: Value = 1
SNMP:
---Frame 88---
SNMP: ----- Simple Network Management Protocol -----
SNMP:
SNMP: Version = 0
SNMP: Community = armon

SNMP: Command = Get next request
SNMP: Request ID = 0
SNMP: Error status = 0 (No error)
SNMP: Error index = 0
SNMP:
SNMP: Object = {1.3.6.1.2.1.1.3} (sysUpTime)
SNMP: Value = NULL
SNMP:
SNMP: Object = {1.3.6.1.2.1.16.1.1.1.1.1} (mib.16.1.1.1.1.1)
SNMP: Value = NULL
SNMP:
SNMP: Object = {1.3.6.1.2.1.16.1.1.1.2.1} (mib.16.1.1.1.2.1)
SNMP: Value = NULL
SNMP:
SNMP: Object = {1.3.6.1.2.1.16.1.1.1.3.1} (mib.16.1.1.1.3.1)
SNMP: Value = NULL
SNMP:
SNMP: Object = {1.3.6.1.2.1.16.1.1.1.4.1} (mib.16.1.1.1.4.1)
SNMP: Value = NULL
SNMP:
SNMP: Object = {1.3.6.1.2.1.16.1.1.1.5.1} (mib.16.1.1.1.5.1)
SNMP: Value = NULL
SNMP:
SNMP: Object = {1.3.6.1.2.1.16.1.1.1.6.1} (mib.16.1.1.1.6.1)
SNMP: Value = NULL
SNMP:
SNMP: Object = {1.3.6.1.2.1.16.1.1.1.7.1} (mib.16.1.1.1.7.1)
SNMP: Value = NULL
SNMP:
SNMP: Object = {1.3.6.1.2.1.16.1.1.1.8.1} (mib.16.1.1.1.8.1)
SNMP: Value = NULL
SNMP:
SNMP: Object = {1.3.6.1.2.1.16.1.1.1.9.1} (mib.16.1.1.1.9.1)
SNMP: Value = NULL

SNMP:
SNMP: Object = {1.3.6.1.2.1.16.1.1.1.10.1} (mib.16.1.1.1.10.1)
SNMP: Value = NULL
SNMP:
SNMP: Object = {1.3.6.1.2.1.16.1.1.1.11.1} (mib.16.1.1.1.11.1)
SNMP: Value = NULL
SNMP:
SNMP: Object = {1.3.6.1.2.1.16.1.1.1.12.1} (mib.16.1.1.1.12.1)
SNMP: Value = NULL
SNMP:
SNMP: Object = {1.3.6.1.2.1.16.1.1.1.13.1} (mib.16.1.1.1.13.1)
SNMP: Value = NULL
SNMP:
SNMP: Object = {1.3.6.1.2.1.16.1.1.1.14.1} (mib.16.1.1.1.14.1)
SNMP: Value = NULL
SNMP:
SNMP: Object = {1.3.6.1.2.1.16.1.1.1.15.1} (mib.16.1.1.1.15.1)
SNMP: Value = NULL
SNMP:
SNMP: Object = {1.3.6.1.2.1.16.1.1.1.16.1} (mib.16.1.1.1.16.1)
SNMP: Value = NULL
SNMP:
SNMP: Object = {1.3.6.1.2.1.16.1.1.1.17.1} (mib.16.1.1.1.17.1)
SNMP: Value = NULL
SNMP:
SNMP: Object = {1.3.6.1.2.1.16.1.1.1.18.1} (mib.16.1.1.1.18.1)
SNMP: Value = NULL
SNMP:
SNMP: Object = {1.3.6.1.2.1.16.1.1.1.19.1} (mib.16.1.1.1.19.1)
SNMP: Value = NULL
SNMP:
SNMP: Object = {1.3.6.1.2.1.16.1.1.1.20.1} (mib.16.1.1.1.20.1)
SNMP: Value = NULL
SNMP:

SNMP: Object = {1.3.6.1.2.1.16.1.1.1.21.1} (mib.16.1.1.1.21.1)
SNMP: Value = NULL
SNMP:

--Frame 89--
SNMP: ----- Simple Network Management Protocol -----
SNMP:
SNMP: Version = 0
SNMP: Community = armon
SNMP: Command = Get response
SNMP: Request ID = 0
SNMP: Error status = 0 (No error)
SNMP: Error index = 0
SNMP:
SNMP: Object = {1.3.6.1.2.1.1.3.0} (sysUpTime.0)
SNMP: Value = 10132180 hundredths of a second
SNMP:
SNMP: Object = {1.3.6.1.2.1.16.1.1.1.2.1} (mib.16.1.1.1.2.1)
SNMP: Value = {1.3.6.1.2.1.2.2.1.1.1}
SNMP:
SNMP: Object = {1.3.6.1.2.1.16.1.1.1.3.1} (mib.16.1.1.1.3.1)
SNMP: Value = 0 (counter)
SNMP:
SNMP: Object = {1.3.6.1.2.1.16.1.1.1.4.1} (mib.16.1.1.1.4.1)
SNMP: Value = 1557018586 (counter)
SNMP:
SNMP: Object = {1.3.6.1.2.1.16.1.1.1.5.1} (mib.16.1.1.1.5.1)
SNMP: Value = 7705087 (counter)
SNMP:
SNMP: Object = {1.3.6.1.2.1.16.1.1.1.6.1} (mib.16.1.1.1.6.1)
SNMP: Value = 272349 (counter)
SNMP:
SNMP: Object = {1.3.6.1.2.1.16.1.1.1.7.1} (mib.16.1.1.1.7.1)
SNMP: Value = 20682 (counter)
SNMP:

SNMP: Object = {1.3.6.1.2.1.16.1.1.1.8.1} (mib.16.1.1.1.8.1)
SNMP: Value = 2082 (counter)
SNMP:
SNMP: Object = {1.3.6.1.2.1.16.1.1.1.9.1} (mib.16.1.1.1.9.1)
SNMP: Value = 0 (counter)
SNMP:
SNMP: Object = {1.3.6.1.2.1.16.1.1.1.10.1} (mib.16.1.1.1.10.1)
SNMP: Value = 0 (counter)
SNMP:
SNMP: Object = {1.3.6.1.2.1.16.1.1.1.11.1} (mib.16.1.1.1.11.1)
SNMP: Value = 21389 (counter)
SNMP:
SNMP: Object = {1.3.6.1.2.1.16.1.1.1.12.1} (mib.16.1.1.1.12.1)
SNMP: Value = 4 (counter)
SNMP:
SNMP: Object = {1.3.6.1.2.1.16.1.1.1.13.1} (mib.16.1.1.1.13.1)
SNMP: Value = 163 (counter)
SNMP:
SNMP: Object = {1.3.6.1.2.1.16.1.1.1.14.1} (mib.16.1.1.1.14.1)
SNMP: Value = 2425301 (counter)
SNMP:
SNMP: Object = {1.3.6.1.2.1.16.1.1.1.15.1} (mib.16.1.1.1.15.1)
SNMP: Value = 3309943 (counter)
SNMP:
SNMP: Object = {1.3.6.1.2.1.16.1.1.1.16.1} (mib.16.1.1.1.16.1)
SNMP: Value = 448315 (counter)
SNMP:
SNMP: Object = {1.3.6.1.2.1.16.1.1.1.17.1} (mib.16.1.1.1.17.1)
SNMP: Value = 94388 (counter)
SNMP:
SNMP: Object = {1.3.6.1.2.1.16.1.1.1.18.1} (mib.16.1.1.1.18.1)
SNMP: Value = 1019510 (counter)
SNMP:
SNMP: Object = {1.3.6.1.2.1.16.1.1.1.19.1} (mib.16.1.1.1.19.1)

SNMP: Value = 386237 (counter)
SNMP:
SNMP: Object = {1.3.6.1.2.1.16.1.1.1.20.1} (mib.16.1.1.1.20.1)
SNMP: Value = monitor
SNMP:
SNMP: Object = {1.3.6.1.2.1.16.1.1.1.21.1} (mib.16.1.1.1.21.1)
SNMP: Value = 1
SNMP:
SNMP: Object = {1.3.6.1.2.1.16.2.1.1.1.1} (mib.16.2.1.1.1.1)
SNMP: Value = 1
SNMP:
--Frame 90--
SNMP: ----- Simple Network Management Protocol -----
SNMP:
SNMP: Version = 0
SNMP: Community = armon
SNMP: Command = Set request
SNMP: Request ID = 0
SNMP: Error status = 0 (No error)
SNMP: Error index = 0
SNMP:
SNMP: Object = {1.3.6.1.2.1.16.2.1.1.7.52021} (mib.16.2.1.1.7.52021)
SNMP: Value = 2
SNMP:
--Frame 91--
SNMP: ----- Simple Network Management Protocol -----
SNMP:
SNMP: Version = 0
SNMP: Community = armon
SNMP: Command = Get response
SNMP: Request ID = 0
SNMP: Error status = 0 (No error)
SNMP: Error index = 0
SNMP:

SNMP: Object = {1.3.6.1.2.1.16.2.1.1.7.52021} (mib.16.2.1.1.7.52021)
SNMP: Value = 2
SNMP:
--Frame 92--
SNMP: ----- Simple Network Management Protocol -----
SNMP:
SNMP: Version = 0
SNMP: Community = armon
SNMP: Command = Set request
SNMP: Request ID = 0
SNMP: Error status = 0 (No error)
SNMP: Error index = 0
SNMP:
SNMP: Object = {1.3.6.1.2.1.16.2.1.1.2.52021} (mib.16.2.1.1.2.52021)
SNMP: Value = {1.3.6.1.2.1.2.2.1.1.1}
SNMP:
SNMP: Object = {1.3.6.1.2.1.16.2.1.1.3.52021} (mib.16.2.1.1.3.52021)
SNMP: Value = 100
SNMP:
SNMP: Object = {1.3.6.1.2.1.16.2.1.1.5.52021} (mib.16.2.1.1.5.52021)
SNMP: Value = 5
SNMP:
SNMP: Object = {1.3.6.1.2.1.16.2.1.1.6.52021} (mib.16.2.1.1.6.52021)
SNMP: Value = Armon
SNMP:
SNMP: Object = {1.3.6.1.2.1.16.2.1.1.7.52021} (mib.16.2.1.1.7.52021)
SNMP: Value = 1
SNMP:
--Frame 93--
SNMP: ----- Simple Network Management Protocol -----
SNMP:
SNMP: Version = 0
SNMP: Community = armon
SNMP: Command = Get response

SNMP: Request ID = 0
SNMP: Error status = 0 (No error)
SNMP: Error index = 0
SNMP:
SNMP: Object = {1.3.6.1.2.1.16.2.1.1.2.52021} (mib.16.2.1.1.2.52021)
SNMP: Value = {1.3.6.1.2.1.2.2.1.1.1}
SNMP:
SNMP: Object = {1.3.6.1.2.1.16.2.1.1.3.52021} (mib.16.2.1.1.3.52021)
SNMP: Value = 100
SNMP:
SNMP: Object = {1.3.6.1.2.1.16.2.1.1.5.52021} (mib.16.2.1.1.5.52021)
SNMP: Value = 5
SNMP:
SNMP: Object = {1.3.6.1.2.1.16.2.1.1.6.52021} (mib.16.2.1.1.6.52021)
SNMP: Value = Armon
SNMP:
SNMP: Object = {1.3.6.1.2.1.16.2.1.1.7.52021} (mib.16.2.1.1.7.52021)
SNMP: Value = 1
SNMP:
--Frame 94--
SNMP: ----- Simple Network Management Protocol -----
SNMP:
SNMP: Version = 0
SNMP: Community = armon
SNMP: Command = Get request
SNMP: Request ID = 0
SNMP: Error status = 0 (No error)
SNMP: Error index = 0
SNMP:
SNMP: Object = {1.3.6.1.2.1.1.3.0} (sysUpTime.0)
SNMP: Value = NULL
SNMP:
SNMP: Object = {1.3.6.1.2.1.16.2.1.1.1.52021} (mib.16.2.1.1.1.52021)
SNMP: Value = NULL

SNMP:
SNMP: Object = {1.3.6.1.2.1.16.2.1.1.2.52021} (mib.16.2.1.1.2.52021)
SNMP: Value = NULL
SNMP:
SNMP: Object = {1.3.6.1.2.1.16.2.1.1.3.52021} (mib.16.2.1.1.3.52021)
SNMP: Value = NULL
SNMP:
SNMP: Object = {1.3.6.1.2.1.16.2.1.1.4.52021} (mib.16.2.1.1.4.52021)
SNMP: Value = NULL
SNMP:
SNMP: Object = {1.3.6.1.2.1.16.2.1.1.5.52021} (mib.16.2.1.1.5.52021)
SNMP: Value = NULL
SNMP:
SNMP: Object = {1.3.6.1.2.1.16.2.1.1.6.52021} (mib.16.2.1.1.6.52021)
SNMP: Value = NULL
SNMP:
SNMP: Object = {1.3.6.1.2.1.16.2.1.1.7.52021} (mib.16.2.1.1.7.52021)
SNMP: Value = NULL
SNMP:
---Frame 95---
SNMP: ----- Simple Network Management Protocol -----
SNMP:
SNMP: Version = 0
SNMP: Community = armon
SNMP: Command = Get response
SNMP: Request ID = 0
SNMP: Error status = 0 (No error)
SNMP: Error index = 0
SNMP:
SNMP: Object = {1.3.6.1.2.1.1.3.0} (sysUpTime.0)
SNMP: Value = 10132279 hundredths of a second
SNMP:
SNMP: Object = {1.3.6.1.2.1.16.2.1.1.1.52021} (mib.16.2.1.1.1.52021)
SNMP: Value = 52021

```
SNMP:
SNMP: Object = {1.3.6.1.2.1.16.2.1.1.2.52021} (mib.16.2.1.1.2.52021)
SNMP: Value = {1.3.6.1.2.1.2.2.1.1.1}
SNMP:
SNMP: Object = {1.3.6.1.2.1.16.2.1.1.3.52021} (mib.16.2.1.1.3.52021)
SNMP: Value = 100
SNMP:
SNMP: Object = {1.3.6.1.2.1.16.2.1.1.4.52021} (mib.16.2.1.1.4.52021)
SNMP: Value = 100
SNMP:
SNMP: Object = {1.3.6.1.2.1.16.2.1.1.5.52021} (mib.16.2.1.1.5.52021)
SNMP: Value = 5
SNMP:
SNMP: Object = {1.3.6.1.2.1.16.2.1.1.6.52021} (mib.16.2.1.1.6.52021)
SNMP: Value = Armon
SNMP:
SNMP: Object = {1.3.6.1.2.1.16.2.1.1.7.52021} (mib.16.2.1.1.7.52021)
SNMP: Value = 1
SNMP:
```

6.10. Comparing Network Management Alternatives: Accessing Remote Bridge Parameters with TELNET and SNMP

To summarize the examples discussed in this chapter, this section looks at two alternatives for accessing the configuration parameters and operational statistics of a remote bridge. One alternative is to access the bridge with a workstation and to access the bridge's configuration menus using the Telecommunication Network Protocol (TELNET). TELNET allows a remote user to access a host or device as if it were a local terminal. The second alternative is to access the bridge with the management console using SNMP and retrieve the appropriate MIB information. Let's compare these two methods.

In the first method, a Sun Workstation initiates a TELNET session with the 3Com bridge (see Figure 6-10). The network administrator uses commands defined by 3Com to retrieve the system parameters and statistics. Each of these commands is then sent from the workstation to the bridge in a TEL-NET message, and the bridge returns a corresponding response. For example, in Frame 1 (see Trace 6.10a), the system version is requested using the 3Com *show -sys ver* command. The bridge responds with: "SW/NBII-BR-5.0.1, booted on Mon Mar 22 12:05 from local floppy" (see Trace 6.10b).

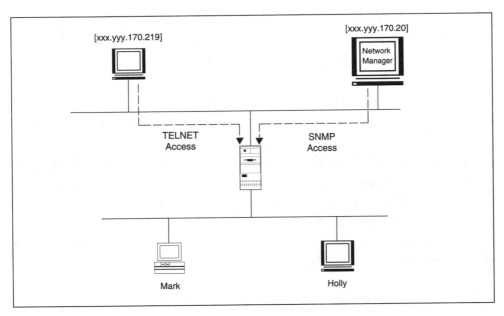

Figure 6-10. Remote device configuration using TELNET and SNMP

Subsequent requests obtain the system contact (Frames 7 through 10), the system location (Frames 11 through 14), and the system name (Frames 15 through 18). The network administrator next accesses the IP Address Translation (ARP) table (Frames 19 through 53), and the IP table (Frames 54 through 65). The final operation retrieves the Path Statistics, such as the number of packets transmitted and received, collisions, and network utilization (Frames 66 through 99). The TELNET method requires the transmission of a total of 99 frames, including 8,599 octets of information.

The second method uses the network management console to access the bridge's MIB using SNMP (see Trace 6.10c). The administrator queries the System group (Frames 1 through 4), the Address Translation group (Frames 5 through 18), the IP group (Frames 19 through 22), and the Interfaces group (Frames 23 through 42). The details of these transactions reveal almost identical information as that discovered earlier (see Trace 6.10d). The SNMP method required the transmission of a total of 42 frames and 8,910 octets of information.

The question, then, is which of these two methods is best? From a network traffic point of view, the results are almost identical: 8,599 octets transmitted using TELNET, and 8,910 octets using SNMP.

From a practical angle, however, SNMP has an advantage. TELNET requires the network manager to have a workstation available, understand TELNET commands, and understand the product-specific parameters, menus, configuration screens, and so on, that are part of that managed system. SNMP does not require these details. The administrator simply goes to the management console, accesses the device in question (the 3Com bridge), and enters well-known SNMP commands. Few details of that bridge's internal configuration are necessary. What's more, SNMP may also use vendor-specific traps to alert the administrator to significant events.

In summary, great synergies can come from using an open network management platform instead of a multitude of vendor-specific solutions. Perhaps this is one reason that SNMP has achieved its great popularity!

Trace 6.10a. Accessing bridge parameters with a TELNET session (summary)

Sniffer Network Analyzer data 26-Mar-93 at 13:52:54, file DIG1.ENC, Pg 1

SUMMARY	Delta T	Destination	Source	Summary
1		3Com Bridge	Sun Station	Telnet C PORT=2200 show -sys ver<0D0A>
2	0.0031	Sun Station	3Com Bridge	Telnet R PORT=2200 SW/NBII-BR-5.0.1, booted on Mon Mar 22

3	0.0005	Sun Station	3Com Bridge	Telnet R PORT=2200
				nb2 REM: 1.0.2
				<0D0A>
4	0.0007	Sun Station	3Com Bridge	Telnet R PORT=2200
				Copyright 1985-1992
				3Com Corporation<0D0A>
5	0.0015	Sun Station	3Com Bridge	Telnet R PORT=2200
				[24]nbii650b#
6	0.1308	3Com Bridge	Sun Station	TCP D=23 S=2200
				ACK=344321989 WIN=4096
7	9.9600	3Com Bridge	Sun Station	Telnet C PORT=2200
				show -sys scon<0D0A>
8	0.0029	Sun Station	3Com Bridge	Telnet R PORT=2200
				SysCONtact =
				"John Doe"<0D0A>
9	0.0014	Sun Station	3Com Bridge	Telnet R PORT=2200
				[25]nbii650b#
10	0.0357	3Com Bridge	Sun Station	TCP D=23 S=2200
				ACK=344322028 WIN=4096
11	4.8660	3Com Bridge	Sun Station	Telnet C PORT=2200
				show -sys sloc<0D0A>
12	0.0030	Sun Station	3Com Bridge	Telnet R PORT=2200
				SysLOCation =
				"650 Computer
				Room"<0D0A>
13	0.0015	Sun Station	3Com Bridge	Telnet R PORT=2200
				[26]nbii650b#
14	0.1295	3Com Bridge	Sun Station	TCP D=23 S=2200
				ACK=344322077 WIN=4096
15	4.8946	3Com Bridge	Sun Station	Telnet C PORT=2200
				show -sys snam<0D0A>
16	0.0029	Sun Station	3Com Bridge	Telnet R PORT=2200
				SysNAMe =
				"nbii650b"<0D0A>

17	0.0015	Sun Station	3Com Bridge	Telnet R PORT=2200
				[27]nbii650b#
18	0.1011	3Com Bridge	Sun Station	TCP D=23 S=2200
				ACK=344322113 WIN=4096
19	4.4364	3Com Bridge	Sun Station	Telnet C PORT=2200
				show -ip addr<0D0A>
20	0.0029	Sun Station	3Com Bridge	Telnet R PORT=2200
				---IP Address Trans...
				XXX.YYY.170.214
.				
.				
.				
54	5.2126	3Com Bridge	Sun Station	Telnet C PORT=2200
				show -ip netaddr<0D0A>
55	0.0030	Sun Station	3Com Bridge	Telnet R PORT=2200
				--IP Directly Conn..
56	0.0010	Sun Station	3Com Bridge	Telnet R PORT=2200 IP
				Address Port
				Subnet Mask Status...
.				
.				
.				
66	15.9375	3Com Bridge	Sun Station	Telnet C PORT=2200
				show stat -path<0D0A>
67	0.0046	Sun Station	3Com Bridge	Telnet R PORT=2200
				ACCUMULATED
				VALUES<0D0A>
68	0.0006	Sun Station	3Com Bridge	Telnet R PORT=2200
				<0D0A>
69	0.0010	Sun Station	3Com Bridge	Telnet R PORT=2200
				== PATH statistic...
70	0.0007	Sun Station	3Com Bridge	Telnet R PORT=2200
71	0.0010	Sun Station	3Com Bridge	Telnet R PORT=2200
.				

96	0.0010	Sun Station	3Com Bridge	Telnet R PORT=2200
				Byte/Sec
				Rcv Good: Packets
				29885492 2732272...
97	0.0009	Sun Station	3Com Bridge	Telnet R PORT=2200
				Xmit Bad: Pkt/Sec
98	0.0014	Sun Station	3Com Bridge	Telnet R PORT=2200
				[30]nbii650b#
99	0.1944	3Com Bridge	Sun Station	TCP D=23 S=2200
				ACK=344324928 WIN=4096

Trace 6.10b. Accessing bridge parameters with a TELNET session (details)

Sniffer Network Analyzer data 26-Mar-93 at 13:52:54, file DIG1.ENC, Pg 1
--Frame 1 --
Telnet:----- Telnet data -----
Telnet:
Telnet:show -sys ver<0D0A>
Telnet:
--Frame 2 --
Telnet:----- Telnet data -----
Telnet:
Telnet:SW/NBII-BR-5.0.1, booted on Mon Mar 22 12:05 from local floppy<0D0A>
Telnet:
--Frame 3 --
Telnet:----- Telnet data -----
Telnet:
Telnet:nb2 REM: 1.0.2 <0D0A>
Telnet:
--Frame 4 --
Telnet:----- Telnet data -----
Telnet:

```
Telnet:Copyright 1985-1992, 3Com Corporation<0D0A>
Telnet:
--------------------------------------------Frame 5 --------------------------------------------
Telnet:----- Telnet data -----
Telnet:
Telnet:[24]nbii650b#
Telnet:
--------------------------------------------Frame 7 --------------------------------------------
Telnet:----- Telnet data -----
Telnet:
Telnet:show -sys scon<0D0A>
Telnet:
--------------------------------------------Frame 8 --------------------------------------------
Telnet:----- Telnet data -----
Telnet:
Telnet:SysCONtact = "John Doe"<0D0A>
Telnet:
--------------------------------------------Frame 9 --------------------------------------------
Telnet:----- Telnet data -----
Telnet:
Telnet:[25]nbii650b#
Telnet:
```

Trace 6.10c. Accessing remote bridge parameters with SNMP (summary)

Sniffer Network Analyzer data 26-Mar-93 at 13:55:46, file DIG2.ENC, Pg 1

SUMMARY	Delta T	Destination	Source	Summary
1		3Com Bridge	Manager	SNMP Next sysDescr .. sysServices (7 items)
2	0.0035	Manager	3Com Bridge	SNMP Got sysDescr .. sysServices (7 items)
.				
.				
.				

| 5 | 1.2927 | 3Com Bridge | Manager | SNMP Next atIfIndex .. atNetAddress (3 items) |
| 6 | 0.0038 | Manager | 3Com Bridge | SNMP Got atIfIndex .. atNetAddress (3 items) |

.
.
.

| 19 | 2.6261 | 3Com Bridge | Manager | SNMP Next ipAdEntAddr .. ipAdEntReasmMaxSize (5 items) |
| 20 | 0.0034 | Manager | 3Com Bridge | SNMP Got ipAdEntAddr .. ipAdEntReasmMaxSize (5 items) |

.
.
.

| 23 | 2.3142 | 3Com Bridge | Manager | SNMP Next ifIndex .. ifOutOctets (16 items) |
| 24 | 0.0106 | Manager | 3Com Bridge | SNMP Got ifIndex .. ifOutOctets (16 items) |

.
.
.

| 41 | 0.0045 | 3Com Bridge | Manager | SNMP Next ifOutUcastPkts .. ifSpecific (6 items) |
| 42 | 0.0058 | Manager | 3Com Bridge | SNMP Got ifOutNUcastPkts .. atIfIndex (6 items) |

Trace 6.10d. Accessing remote bridge parameters with SNMP (summary)

```
Sniffer Network Analyzer data 26-Mar-93 at 13:55:46, file DIG2.ENC, Pg 1
------------------------------------------Frame 1 ----------------------------------------------
SNMP: ----- Simple Network Management Protocol -----
SNMP:
SNMP: Version = 0
SNMP: Community = public
SNMP: Command = Get next request
SNMP: Request ID = 733178616
SNMP: Error status = 0 (No error)
SNMP: Error index = 0
SNMP:
SNMP: Object = {1.3.6.1.2.1.1.1} (sysDescr)
SNMP: Value = NULL
SNMP:
SNMP: Object = {1.3.6.1.2.1.1.2} (sysObjectID)
SNMP: Value = NULL
SNMP:
SNMP: Object = {1.3.6.1.2.1.1.3} (sysUpTime)
SNMP: Value = NULL
SNMP:
SNMP: Object = {1.3.6.1.2.1.1.4} (sysContact)
SNMP: Value = NULL
SNMP:
SNMP: Object = {1.3.6.1.2.1.1.5} (sysName)
SNMP: Value = NULL
SNMP:
SNMP: Object = {1.3.6.1.2.1.1.6} (sysLocation)
SNMP: Value = NULL
SNMP:
SNMP: Object = {1.3.6.1.2.1.1.7} (sysServices)
SNMP: Value = NULL
SNMP:
```

```
---------------------------------------------Frame 2 ---------------------------------------------
SNMP: ----- Simple Network Management Protocol -----
SNMP:
SNMP: Version = 0
SNMP: Community = public
SNMP: Command = Get response
SNMP: Request ID = 733178616
SNMP: Error status = 0 (No error)
SNMP: Error index = 0
SNMP:
SNMP: Object = {1.3.6.1.2.1.1.1.0} (sysDescr.0)
SNMP: Value = SW/NBII-BR-5.0.1
SNMP:
SNMP: Object = {1.3.6.1.2.1.1.2.0} (sysObjectID.0)
SNMP: Value = {1.3.6.1.4.1.43.1.4}
SNMP:
SNMP: Object = {1.3.6.1.2.1.1.3.0} (sysUpTime.0)
SNMP: Value = 35594870 hundredths of a second
SNMP:
SNMP: Object = {1.3.6.1.2.1.1.4.0} (sysContact.0)
SNMP: Value = John Doe
SNMP:
SNMP: Object = {1.3.6.1.2.1.1.5.0} (sysName.0)
SNMP: Value = nbii650b
SNMP:
SNMP: Object = {1.3.6.1.2.1.1.6.0} (sysLocation.0)
SNMP: Value = 650 Computer Room
SNMP:
SNMP: Object = {1.3.6.1.2.1.1.7.0} (sysServices.0)
SNMP: Value = 74
SNMP:

    .
    .
    .
```

```
----------------------------------------------Frame 5 --------------------------------------------
SNMP: ----- Simple Network Management Protocol -----
SNMP:
SNMP: Version = 0
SNMP: Community = public
SNMP: Command = Get next request
SNMP: Request ID = 733178619
SNMP: Error status = 0 (No error)
SNMP: Error index = 0
SNMP:
SNMP: Object = {1.3.6.1.2.1.3.1.1.1} (atIfIndex)
SNMP: Value = NULL
SNMP:
SNMP: Object = {1.3.6.1.2.1.3.1.1.2} (atPhysAddress)
SNMP: Value = NULL
SNMP:
SNMP: Object = {1.3.6.1.2.1.3.1.1.3} (atNetAddress)
SNMP: Value = NULL
SNMP:
----------------------------------------------Frame 6 --------------------------------------------
SNMP: ----- Simple Network Management Protocol -----
SNMP:
SNMP: Version = 0
SNMP: Community = public
SNMP: Command = Get response
SNMP: Request ID = 733178619
SNMP: Error status = 0 (No error)
SNMP: Error index = 0
SNMP:
SNMP: Object = {1.3.6.1.2.1.3.1.1.1.0.1.XXX.YYY.170.0}
(atIfIndex.0.1.XXX.YYY.170.0)
SNMP: Value = 0
SNMP:
SNMP: Object = {1.3.6.1.2.1.3.1.1.2.0.1.XXX.YYY.170.0}
```

(atPhysAddress.0.1.XXX.YYY.170.0)
SNMP: Value = FFFFFFFFFFFF, Broadcast
SNMP:
SNMP: Object = {1.3.6.1.2.1.3.1.1.3.0.1.XXX.YYY.170.0}
(atNetAddress.0.1.XXX.YYY.170.0)
SNMP: Value = [XXX.YYY.170.0]
SNMP:
.
.
.

--Frame 19--
SNMP: ----- Simple Network Management Protocol -----
SNMP:
SNMP: Version = 0
SNMP: Community = public
SNMP: Command = Get next request
SNMP: Request ID = 733178620
SNMP: Error status = 0 (No error)
SNMP: Error index = 0
SNMP:
SNMP: Object = {1.3.6.1.2.1.4.20.1.1} (ipAdEntAddr)
SNMP: Value = NULL
SNMP:
SNMP: Object = {1.3.6.1.2.1.4.20.1.2} (ipAdEntIfIndex)
SNMP: Value = NULL
SNMP:
SNMP: Object = {1.3.6.1.2.1.4.20.1.3} (ipAdEntNetMask)
SNMP: Value = NULL
SNMP:
SNMP: Object = {1.3.6.1.2.1.4.20.1.4} (ipAdEntBcastAddr)
SNMP: Value = NULL
SNMP:
SNMP: Object = {1.3.6.1.2.1.4.20.1.5} (ipAdEntReasmMaxSize)
SNMP: Value = NULL
SNMP:

```
---------------------------------------------Frame 20---------------------------------------------
SNMP: ----- Simple Network Management Protocol -----
SNMP:
SNMP: Version = 0
SNMP: Community = public
SNMP: Command = Get response
SNMP: Request ID = 733178620
SNMP: Error status = 0 (No error)
SNMP: Error index = 0
SNMP:
SNMP: Object = {1.3.6.1.2.1.4.20.1.1.XXX.YYY.170.214}
        (ipAdEntAddr.XXX.YYY.170.214)
SNMP: Value = [XXX.YYY.170.214], 3Com Bridge
SNMP:
SNMP: Object = {1.3.6.1.2.1.4.20.1.2.XXX.YYY.170.214}
        (ipAdEntIfIndex.XXX.YYY.170.214)
SNMP: Value = 0
SNMP:
SNMP: Object = {1.3.6.1.2.1.4.20.1.3.XXX.YYY.170.214}
        (ipAdEntNetMask.XXX.YYY.170.214)
SNMP: Value = [255.255.255.0]
SNMP:
SNMP: Object = {1.3.6.1.2.1.4.20.1.4.XXX.YYY.170.214}
        (ipAdEntBcastAddr.XXX.YYY.170.214)
SNMP: Value = 0
SNMP:
SNMP: Object = {1.3.6.1.2.1.4.20.1.5.XXX.YYY.170.214}
        (ipAdEntReasmMaxSize.XXX.YYY.170.214)
SNMP: Value = 65535
SNMP:
    .
    .
    .
```

```
-------------------------------------Frame 23----------------------------------------
SNMP: ----- Simple Network Management Protocol -----
SNMP:
SNMP: Version = 0
SNMP: Community = public
SNMP: Command = Get next request
SNMP: Request ID = 733178622
SNMP: Error status = 0 (No error)
SNMP: Error index = 0
SNMP:
SNMP: Object = {1.3.6.1.2.1.2.2.1.1} (ifIndex)
SNMP: Value = NULL
SNMP:
SNMP: Object = {1.3.6.1.2.1.2.2.1.2} (ifDescr)
SNMP: Value = NULL
SNMP:
SNMP: Object = {1.3.6.1.2.1.2.2.1.3} (ifType)
SNMP: Value = NULL
SNMP:
SNMP: Object = {1.3.6.1.2.1.2.2.1.4} (ifMtu)
SNMP: Value = NULL
SNMP:
SNMP: Object = {1.3.6.1.2.1.2.2.1.5} (ifSpeed)
SNMP: Value = NULL
SNMP:
SNMP: Object = {1.3.6.1.2.1.2.2.1.6} (ifPhysAddress)
SNMP: Value = NULL
SNMP:
SNMP: Object = {1.3.6.1.2.1.2.2.1.7} (ifAdminStatus)
SNMP: Value = NULL
SNMP:
SNMP: Object = {1.3.6.1.2.1.2.2.1.8} (ifOperStatus)
SNMP: Value = NULL
SNMP:
```

SNMP: Object = {1.3.6.1.2.1.2.2.1.9} (ifLastChange)
SNMP: Value = NULL
SNMP:
SNMP: Object = {1.3.6.1.2.1.2.2.1.10} (ifInOctets)
SNMP: Value = NULL
SNMP:
SNMP: Object = {1.3.6.1.2.1.2.2.1.11} (ifInUcastPkts)
SNMP: Value = NULL
SNMP:
SNMP: Object = {1.3.6.1.2.1.2.2.1.12} (ifInNUcastPkts)
SNMP: Value = NULL
SNMP:
SNMP: Object = {1.3.6.1.2.1.2.2.1.13} (ifInDiscards)
SNMP: Value = NULL
SNMP:
SNMP: Object = {1.3.6.1.2.1.2.2.1.14} (ifInErrors)
SNMP: Value = NULL
SNMP:
SNMP: Object = {1.3.6.1.2.1.2.2.1.15} (ifInUnknownProtos)
SNMP: Value = NULL
SNMP:
SNMP: Object = {1.3.6.1.2.1.2.2.1.16} (ifOutOctets)
SNMP: Value = NULL
SNMP:
--Frame 24--
SNMP: ----- Simple Network Management Protocol -----
SNMP:
SNMP: Version = 0
SNMP: Community = public
SNMP: Command = Get response
SNMP: Request ID = 733178622
SNMP: Error status = 0 (No error)
SNMP: Error index = 0
SNMP:

SNMP: Object = {1.3.6.1.2.1.2.2.1.1.1} (ifIndex.1)
SNMP: Value = 1
SNMP:
SNMP: Object = {1.3.6.1.2.1.2.2.1.2.1} (ifDescr.1)
SNMP: Value = 3Com NETBuilderETH/1-1
SNMP:
SNMP: Object = {1.3.6.1.2.1.2.2.1.3.1} (ifType.1)
SNMP: Value = 6 (ethernet-csmacd)
SNMP:
SNMP: Object = {1.3.6.1.2.1.2.2.1.4.1} (ifMtu.1)
SNMP: Value = 1500 octets
SNMP:
SNMP: Object = {1.3.6.1.2.1.2.2.1.5.1} (ifSpeed.1)
SNMP: Value = 10000000 bits per second
SNMP:
SNMP: Object = {1.3.6.1.2.1.2.2.1.6.1} (ifPhysAddress.1)
SNMP: Value = Bridge034ACD
SNMP:
SNMP: Object = {1.3.6.1.2.1.2.2.1.7.1} (ifAdminStatus.1)
SNMP: Value = 1 (up)
SNMP:
SNMP: Object = {1.3.6.1.2.1.2.2.1.8.1} (ifOperStatus.1)
SNMP: Value = 1 (up)
SNMP:
SNMP: Object = {1.3.6.1.2.1.2.2.1.9.1} (ifLastChange.1)
SNMP: Value = 1995 hundredths of a second
SNMP:
SNMP: Object = {1.3.6.1.2.1.2.2.1.10.1} (ifInOctets.1)
SNMP: Value = 1611173470 octets
SNMP:
SNMP: Object = {1.3.6.1.2.1.2.2.1.11.1} (ifInUcastPkts.1)
SNMP: Value = 13162801 packets
SNMP:
SNMP: Object = {1.3.6.1.2.1.2.2.1.12.1} (ifInNUcastPkts.1)

SNMP: Value = 8368939 packets
SNMP:
SNMP: Object = {1.3.6.1.2.1.2.2.1.13.1} (ifInDiscards.1)
SNMP: Value = 0 packets
SNMP:
SNMP: Object = {1.3.6.1.2.1.2.2.1.14.1} (ifInErrors.1)
SNMP: Value = 579 packets
SNMP:
SNMP: Object = {1.3.6.1.2.1.2.2.1.15.1} (ifInUnknownProtos.1)
SNMP: Value = 6620842 packets
SNMP:
SNMP: Object = {1.3.6.1.2.1.2.2.1.16.1} (ifOutOctets.1)
SNMP: Value = -1258921820 octets
SNMP:

   .
   .
   .

---Frame 41---
SNMP: ----- Simple Network Management Protocol -----
SNMP:
SNMP: Version = 0
SNMP: Community = public
SNMP: Command = Get next request
SNMP: Request ID = 733178609
SNMP: Error status = 0 (No error)
SNMP: Error index = 0
SNMP:
SNMP: Object = {1.3.6.1.2.1.2.2.1.17.4} (ifOutUcastPkts.4)
SNMP: Value = NULL
SNMP:
SNMP: Object = {1.3.6.1.2.1.2.2.1.18.4} (ifOutNUcastPkts.4)
SNMP: Value = NULL
SNMP:
SNMP: Object = {1.3.6.1.2.1.2.2.1.19.4} (ifOutDiscards.4)

SNMP: Value = NULL
SNMP:
SNMP: Object = {1.3.6.1.2.1.2.2.1.20.4} (ifOutErrors.4)
SNMP: Value = NULL
SNMP:
SNMP: Object = {1.3.6.1.2.1.2.2.1.21.4} (ifOutQLen.4)
SNMP: Value = NULL
SNMP:
SNMP: Object = {1.3.6.1.2.1.2.2.1.22.4} (ifSpecific.4)
SNMP: Value = NULL
SNMP:
---Frame 42---
SNMP: ----- Simple Network Management Protocol -----
SNMP:
SNMP: Version = 0
SNMP: Community = public
SNMP: Command = Get response
SNMP: Request ID = 733178609
SNMP: Error status = 0 (No error)
SNMP: Error index = 0
SNMP:
SNMP: Object = {1.3.6.1.2.1.2.2.1.18.1} (ifOutNUcastPkts.1)
SNMP: Value = 10078921 packets
SNMP:
SNMP: Object = {1.3.6.1.2.1.2.2.1.19.1} (ifOutDiscards.1)
SNMP: Value = 0 packets
SNMP:
SNMP: Object = {1.3.6.1.2.1.2.2.1.20.1} (ifOutErrors.1)
SNMP: Value = 409 packets
SNMP:
SNMP: Object = {1.3.6.1.2.1.2.2.1.21.1} (ifOutQLen.1)
SNMP: Value = 0 packets
SNMP:
SNMP: Object = {1.3.6.1.2.1.2.2.1.22.1} (ifSpecific.1)

```
SNMP: Value = {0}
SNMP:
SNMP: Object = {1.3.6.1.2.1.3.1.1.1.0.1.XXX.YYY.170.0}
        (atIfIndex.0.1.XXX.YYY.170.0)
SNMP: Value = 0
SNMP:
```

This chapter has looked at various issues that network administrators may encounter when implementing SNMP. Many of these problems come as the result of vendor-specific implementations that may be incompatible with each other. Regardless of the problems discovered in these case studies, I found that all of the vendors had a common benchmark: the same version of SNMP.

In our final, and concluding section, we will explore the next generation of the Internet network management protocol, SNMP version 2 (SNMPv2). Since this protocol is in its infancy stage, it is impossible to predict the implementation issues that will facenetwork administrators as they seek to integrate SNMP and SNMPv2. As we will see, however, the developers of SNMPv2 have made significant efforts to remove any incompatibilities. Experience will tell if these efforts have been successful.

7 SNMP Version 2

The original version of SNMP (SNMPv1) was derived from the Simple Gateway Monitoring Protocol (SGMP) and published as an RFC in 1988. At that time, the industry agreed that SNMP would be an interim solution until OSI-based network management using CMIS/CMIP became more mature. Since then, however, SNMP has become more popular while the OSI solution has been less widely adopted than was anticipated originally. As a result, it became appropriate to revise and improve SNMPv1.

In March of 1992, the IETF solicited proposals to enhance SNMPv1. A team consisting of Jeffrey Case, Keith McCloghrie, Marshall Rose, and Steven Waldbusser prepared a proposal called the *Simple Management Protocol* (SMP). At about the same time, the IETF initiated another effort aimed at enhancing SNMP security. These two research efforts merged and became known as version 2 of the Internet-Standard Network Management Framework, or simply the SNMPv2 framework. The new documentation comprises more than 400 pages in twelve documents (RFCs 1441 to 1452). The first document, "An Introduction to SNMPv2" [7-1], provides an overview of the remaining standards. This chapter discusses the key enhancements in the SNMPv2 framework, and refers you to the appropriate source for further details.

7.1. The SNMPv2 Structure of Management Information

As Chapter 2 discussed, MIB modules provide a mechanism for grouping similar objects. The SMI for SNMPv2 [7-2] defines the subset of the ASN.1 language that describes various MIB modules. SNMPv2 has two documents that support the SMI: the Conformance Statements and the Textual Conventions. The conformance statements provide a implementation baseline and would include, for example, a lower bound on what agents must support [7-3]. The textual conventions define the data types used within these MIB modules and make it easier to read the modules [7-4]. The SMI also defines two new branches of the Internet OID tree, security {1.3.6.1.5} and snmpV2 {1.3.6.1.6}. Under snmpV2 are the Transport domains, snmpDomains; Transport proxies, snmp-Proxys; and Module identities, snmpModules. Defined under the snmpMod-ules are the SNMPv2 MIB, snmpMIB; the Manager to Manager MIB, snmpM2M; and the Party MIB, partyMIB. Figure 7-1a. illustrates the positions of these new elements of the OID tree.

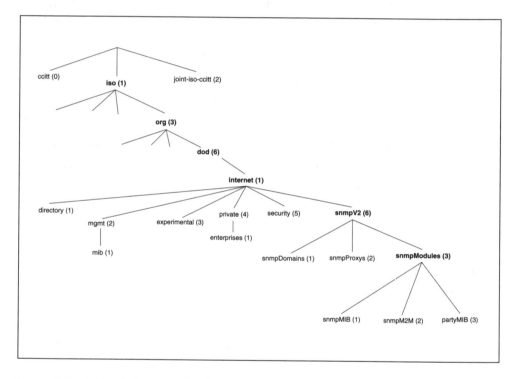

Figure 7-1a. SNMPv2 elements within the OID tree

Section 7.1.1 considers the data types and macros that make up the SMI and Conformance Statements; Section 7.2 discusses the Textual Conventions, including transport, domains, and module identities.

7.1.1. SNMPv2 data types

The SNMPv2 SMI has added support for ASN.1 data types that SNMPv1 did not use, and has also defined new data types. ASN.1 data types that remain unchanged from RFC 1155 include INTEGER, OCTET STRING, and OBJECT IDENTIFIER. Defined data types from RFC 1155 that have not changed are IpAddress, TimeTicks, and Opaque. New SNMPv2 data types include

Data Type	Description
BIT STRING	An ASN.1 type that enumerates named bits, each having a specific meaning. This data type can be used for a sequence of flag bits, each representing a different value.
Integer32	A defined type that represents integer-valued information between -2^{31} and 2^{31}-1 inclusive (-2147483648 and 2147483647 decimal). (Note: This type is indistinguishable from the INTEGER type, although the INTEGER type may have different numerical constraints.)
Counter32	A defined type that represents a non-negative integer that monotonically increases until it reaches a maximum value of 2^{32}-1 (4294967295 decimal) when it wraps around and starts increasing again from zero.
Gauge32	A defined type that represents a non-negative integer, which may increase or decrease, but never exceeds a maximum value (2^{32}-1, as above).
NsapAddress	A defined type that represents an OSI address as a variable-length OCTET STRING.
Counter64	A defined type that represents a non-negative integer that monotonically increases until it reaches a maximum value of 2^{64}-1 (18446744073709551615 decimal), then wraps around and starts increasing again from zero. Counter64 is used for objects for which the 32-bit counter (Counter32) is too small, or which would wrap around too quickly. The SMI document [7-2] states that the

Counter64 type may be used only if the information being modeled would wrap in less than one hour using the Counter32 type.

UInteger32   A defined type that represents integer-valued information between 0 and $2^{32}-1$ inclusive (0 to 4294967295 decimal). Note: Integer32 is a signed number and UInteger32 is an unsigned number.

7.1.2. ASN.1 macros

The SNMPv2 SMI extends the OBJECT-TYPE macro (discussed in Section 3.2.3), and also defines four new ASN.1 macros. The new macros are NOTI-FICATION-TYPE, MODULE-COMPLIANCE, OBJECT-GROUP, and AGENT-CAPABILITIES. Because of the OBJECT-TYPE macro's global significance, this section describes it in detail. This section also summarizes the functions of the other macros and refers readers to the appropriate document for implementation details.

The OBJECT-TYPE macro conveys the syntax and semantics of a managed object:

```
OBJECT-TYPE MACRO ::=
BEGIN
  TYPE NOTATION ::=
        "SYNTAX" type(Syntax)
        UnitsPart
        "MAX-ACCESS" Access
        "STATUS" Status
        "DESCRIPTION" Text
        ReferPart
        IndexPart
        DefValPart
  VALUE NOTATION ::=
        value(VALUE ObjectName)
  UnitsPart ::=
        "UNITS" Text
        | empty
```

```
Access ::=
    "not-accessible"
    | "read-only"
    | "read-write"
    | "read-create"
Status ::=
    "current"
    | "deprecated"
    | "obsolete"
ReferPart ::=
    "REFERENCE" Text
    | empty
IndexPart ::=
    "INDEX"  "{" IndexTypes "}"
    | "AUGMENTS" "{" Entry   "}"
    | empty
IndexTypes ::=
    IndexType
    | IndexTypes "," IndexType
IndexType ::=
    "IMPLIED" Index
    | Index
Index ::=
    -- use the SYNTAX value of the
    -- correspondent OBJECT-TYPE
    -- invocation
    value(Indexobject ObjectName)
Entry ::=
    -- use the INDEX value of the
    -- correspondent OBJECT-TYPE
    -- invocation
    value(Entryobject ObjectName)
DefValPart ::=
    "DEFVAL" "{" value(Defval
```

```
       Syntax) "}"
        | empty
   -- uses the NVT ASCII character set
    Text ::= """" string """"
   END
```

The OBJECT-TYPE macro has been enhanced from versions defined in RFC 1155 and RFC 1212. In the TYPE NOTATION, a new UNITS clause contains a textual definition of the units associated with that object. Examples include "packets", "messages", or "seconds". The MAX-ACCESS clause defines the maximum level of access for an object. In other words, this clause determines whether it makes sense within the proper operation of the protocol to read, write, and/or create an instance of an object. The values are ordered from least to greatest accessibility: not-accessible, read-only, read-write, and read-create (where read-create is a superset of read-write).

The revised STATUS clause of the OBJECT-TYPE macro eliminates the "optional" value in earlier versions of the macro. The DESCRIPTION clause is now mandatory, and the REFERENCE clause can provide a textual cross reference to another module. The INDEX clause, which identifies instances of columnar objects within a table, can now be replaced with the AUGMENTS clause if the object corresponds to a conceptual row. The AUGMENTS clause thus augments (or extends) a conceptual row within a table. Finally, the DEF-VAL clause defines a default value for the object.

The SNMPv2 SMI's new NOTIFICATION-TYPE macro defines the information contained within the unsolicited transmission of management information. This includes a SNMPv2-Trap-PDU or an Inform-Request-PDU. The SNMP Protocol Operations document (RFC 1448) contains details of the use of the NOTIFICATION-TYPE macro.

The three remaining new ASN.1 macros are defined in the Conformance Statements document [7-3]. The OBJECT-GROUP macro defines collections of related, managed objects. The MODULE-COMPLIANCE macro conveys a minimum set of requirements for implementing one or more MIB modules. In other words, the MODULE-COMPLIANCE macro conveys the minimum conformance specification, including the objects and groups required, which may come from different MIB modules.

The AGENT-CAPABILITIES macro describes the capabilities of an SNMPv2 agent. It defines the MIB modules, objects, and values implemented within the agent. An OBJECT IDENTIFIER value is associated with this macro, which is used as the value of the agent's sysObjectID object. When the manager retrieves the value of sysObjectID, it can use it to identify the agent's capabilities.

7.2. The SNMPv2 Textual Conventions

SNMPv2 defines a textual convention for the convenience of human readers of MIB modules. The textual convention consists of a data type with a specific name, and associated syntax and semantics. For example, the textual convention MacAddress represents an IEEE 802 MAC address, an OCTET STRING of size 6.

The TEXTUAL-CONVENTION macro that follows defines the Textual conventions. Of particular interest is the DISPLAY-HINT clause, which tells the reader how the value of the object will be displayed. It uses abbreviations such as x (hexadecimal), d (decimal), o (octal), and b (binary). The textual conventions definitions are:

```
SNMPv2-TC DEFINITIONS ::= BEGIN
IMPORTS
   ObjectSyntax, Integer32, TimeTicks
     FROM SNMPv2-SMI;
-- definition of textual conventions
TEXTUAL-CONVENTION MACRO ::=
BEGIN
   TYPE NOTATION ::=
       DisplayPart
```

```
        "STATUS" Status
        "DESCRIPTION" Text
        ReferPart
        "SYNTAX" type(Syntax)
VALUE NOTATION ::=
        value(VALUE Syntax)
DisplayPart ::=
        "DISPLAY-HINT" Text
        | empty
Status ::=
        "current"
        | "deprecated"
        | "obsolete"
ReferPart ::=
        "REFERENCE" Text
        | empty
-- uses the NVT ASCII character set
Text ::= """" string """"
END
```

The following textual conventions have been defined for use with SNMPv2
[7-4]:

Convention	Description
DisplayString	Represents textual information taken from the NVT ASCII character set.
PhysAddress	Represents Media- or Physical-level addresses (originally from RFC 1213).
MacAddress	An 802 MAC address represented in the "canonical" order defined by IEEE 802.1a; that is, it is represented as if it were transmitted least significant bit first, even though 802.5

requires MAC addresses to be transmitted most significant bit first. (Originally from RFCs 1230 and 1231.)

TruthValue | Represents a boolean value. (Originally from RFC 1253.)

TestAndIncr | Represents integer-valued information for atomic operations. Atomic operations are self-contained, but performed in a specific order or sequence. The TestAndIncr assures that these required sequences are maintained.

AutonomousType | Represents an independently extensible type identification value. It may, for example, indicate a particular subtree with further MIB definitions, or define a particular type of protocol or hardware. (Originally from RFC 1316.)

InstancePointer | A pointer to a row of a MIB table in the managed device. By convention, it is the name of the first columnar object in the conceptual row. Note that the term "conceptual row" defines all of the objects having the same instance value in a MIB table. The terms "conceptual row" and "row" are generally used interchangeably. (Originally from RFC 1316.)

RowStatus | Creates and deletes conceptual rows, and is used as the value of the SYNTAX clause for the status column of a conceptual row (see the SMI document for further details; originally from RFC 1271, the RMON MIB).

7.3. The SNMPv2 MIB

SNMPv2 provides three MIB documents (review Figure 7-1a). The first describes a MIB module for SNMPv2 objects [7-5], and is identified by {snmp-Modules 1}. The second coordinates multiple management stations, and is therefore called the Manager-to-Manager MIB. It is identified as {snmpModules 2} [7-6]. The third module supports the SNMPv2 security protocols and is called the Party MIB, {snmpModules 3} [7-12].

The MIB for SNMPv2 objects, {snmpMIB 1}, contains six groups. These groups are shown in Figure 7-1b and include:

Group Objects	Description
SNMPv2 Statistics	Provide basic performance measurements for the SNMPv2 entity. Examples include packets received, messages received with invalid encodings, and messages received with authentication errors.
SNMPv1 Statistics	Provide basic instrumentation for a SNMPv2 entity that also implements SNMPv1. Examples would include SNMPv1 messages delivered to a SNMPv2 entity that had unknown community names or disallowed operations.
Object Resource	Allow an SNMPv2 entity acting as an agent to describe its dynamically configurable object resources. These objects are analogous to the sysObjectID and sysDescr objects for SNMPv1.
Traps	Allow the SNMPv2 entity, when acting in an agent role, to generate SNMPv2-Trap PDUs. Included in this group is a table that tracks the number of traps sent to each SNMPv2 entity.
Well-Known Traps	Describe the six well-known traps from SNMPv1: coldStart, warmStart, linkDown, linkUp, authenticationFailure, and egp-NeighborLoss.
Set	Allow several cooperating SNMPv2 entities, all acting in a manager role, to coordinate their use with a SNMPv2 Set operation.

Also included in the SNMPv2 MIB is an additional group, {snmpMIBConformance}, shown at the bottom of Figure 7-1b. This group provides a formal mechanism to define which objects an agent must implement in order for that agent to comply with (or conform to) the MIB.

```
              snmpModules (3)
                snmpMIB (1)
                  snmpMIBObjects (1)
                    snmpStats (1)
                      snmpStatsPackets (1)
                      snmpStats30Something (2)
                      snmpStatsEncodingErrors (3)
                      snmpStatsUnknownDstParties (4)
                      snmpStatsDstPartyMismatches (5)
                      snmpStatsUnknownSrcParties (6)
                      snmpStatsBadAuths (7)
                      snmpStatsNotInLifetimes (8)
                      snmpStatsWrongDigestValues (9)
                      snmpStatsUnknownContexts (10)
                      snmpStatsBadOperations (11)
                      snmpStatsSilentDrops (12)
                    snmpV1 (2)
                      snmpV1BadCommunityNames (1)
                      snmpV1BadCommunityUses (2)
                    snmpOR (3)
                      snmpORLastChange (1)
                      snmpORTable (2)
                        snmpOREntry (1)
                          snmpORIndex (1)
                          snmpORID (2)
                          snmpORDescr (3)
                    snmpTrap (4)
                      snmpTrapOID (1)
                      snmpTrapTable (2)
                        snmpTrapEntry (1)
                          snmpTrapNumbers (1)
                      snmpTrapEnterprise (3)
                      snmpV2EnableAuthenTraps (4)
                    snmpTraps (5)
                      coldStart (1)
                      warmStart (2)
                      linkDown (3)
                      linkUp (4)
                      authenticationFailure (5)
                      egpNeighborLoss (6)
                    snmpSet (6)
                      snmpSetSerialNo (1)
                  snmpMIBConformance (2)
                    snmpMIBCompliances (1)
                    snmpMIBGroups (2)
                      snmpStatsGroup (1)
                      snmpV1Group (2)
                      snmpORGroup (3)
                      snmpTrapGroup (4)
                      snmpSetGroup (5)
                snmpM2M (2)
                partyMIB (3)
```

Figure 7-1b. SNMPv2 snmpMIB object tree

313

7.4. The SNMPv2 Manager-to-Manager MIB

One of the significant enhancements to SNMPv2 is the ability to configure entities as both managers and agents. The Manager-to-Manager MIB (M2M MIB), defined in [7-6], describes how an entity can act in both roles. Such a configuration would be appropriate for a very large, distributed internetwork. For example, each local segment could have a network manager, which would, in turn, act as an agent to a more global manager (see Figure 7-2). This is called a dual role for the SNMPv2 entity. When the entity receives management requests, it acts as an agent; when performing the requested services, it acts as a manager.

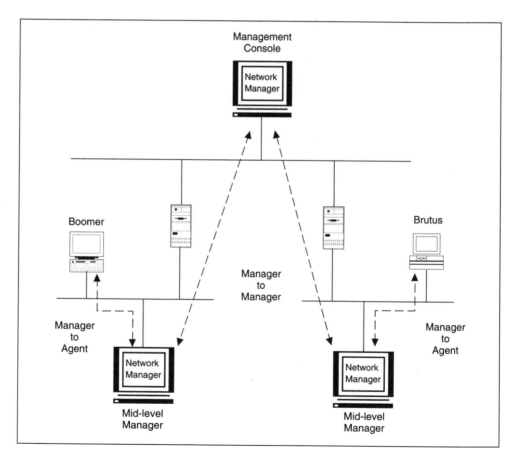

Figure 7-2. SNMPv2 Manager-to-Manager communication

The M2M MIB module, {snmpModules 2}, defines procedures for one management station to request information from another management station. To support those procedures, the M2M MIB module defines three new concepts: alarms, events, and notifications. These concepts generalize ones introduced in the RMON MIB. An *alarm* is a specific condition that occurs when the value of a particular variable is exceeded. The alarm triggers an *event*, which in turn may cause one or more *notifications* to be reported to management stations. The Inform-Request PDU, which is discussed in the next section, performs those notifications.

The M2M MIB (see Figure 7-3) contains three tables and scalar objects, in two groups. These groups are:

Group Objects	Description
Alarm	Provide descriptive and configuration information about threshold alarms from a SNMPv2 entity acting in a dual role. The alarm mechanism periodically takes statistical samples from SNMPv2 variables and compares them to preconfigured thresholds. The Alarm table stores these configuration entries, including the variable, polling period, and threshold parameters. When samples cross the threshold values, the alarm generates events.
Event	Provide descriptive and configuration information regarding events from an SNMPv2 entity acting in a dual role. The Event table associates an event type with the notification method and associated parameters. The Notification table is also part of this group, and defines notifications that should occur when an associated event is fired.

The M2M MIB also includes compliance and conformance information.

```
snmpModules (3)
  snmpMIB (1)
  snmpM2M (2)
    snmpM2MObjects (1)
      snmpAlarm (1)
        snmpAlarmNextIndex (1)
        snmpAlarmTable (2)
          snmpAlarmEntry (1)
            snmpAlarmIndex (1)
            snmpAlarmVariable (2)
            snmpAlarmInterval (3)
            snmpAlarmSampleType (4)
            snmpAlarmValue (5)
            snmpAlarmStartupAlarm (6)
            snmpAlarmRisingThreshold (7)
            snmpAlarmFallingThreshold (8)
            snmpAlarmRisingEventIndex (9)
            snmpAlarmFallingEventIndex (10)
            snmpAlarmUnavailableEventIndex (11)
            snmpAlarmStatus (12)
        snmpAlarmNotification (3)
          snmpRisingAlarm (1)
          snmpFalling Alarm (2)
          snmpObjectUnavailableAlarm (3)
      snmpEvent (2)
        snmpEventNextIndex (1)
        snmpEventTable (2)
          snmpEventEntry (1)
            snmpEventIndex (1)
            snmpEventID (2)
            snmpEventDescription (3)
            snmpEventEvents (4)
            snmpEventLastTimeSent (5)
            snmpEventStatus (6)
        snmpEventNotifyMinInterval (3)
        snmpEventNotifyMaxRetransmissions (4)
        snmpEventNotifyTable (5)
          snmpEventNotifyEntry (1)
            snmpEventNotifyIntervalRequested (1)
            snmpEventNotifyRetransmissionsRequested (2)
            snmpEventNotifyLifetime (3)
            snmpEventNotifyStatus (4)
    snmpM2MConformance (2)
      snmpM2MCompliances (1)
      snmpM2MGroups (2)
        snmpAlarmGroup (1)
        snmpEventGroup (2)
  partyMIB (3)
```

Figure 7-3. SNMPv2 snmpM2M object tree

7.5. SNMPv2 Protocol Operations

When it comes to processing protocol messages, SNMPv2 entities may act as an agent, manager, or both. The entity acts as an agent when it responds to protocol messages (other than the Inform notification, which is reserved for managers), or when it sends Trap notifications. The entity acts as a manager when it initiates protocol messages or responds to Trap or Inform notifications. The entity may also act as a proxy agent.

SNMPv2 provides three types of access to network management information, which are determined by the network management entity's role, and relate to the Manager-to-Manager capabilities. The first type of interaction is called request-response, where an SNMPv2 manager sends a request to an SNMPv2 agent, which responds. The second type of interaction is a request-response where both entities are SNMPv2 managers. The third type is an unconfirmed interaction where an SNMPv2 agent sends an unsolicited message, or trap, to the manager and no response is returned.

SNMPv2 has significantly enhanced the PDUs that convey this management information (see Figure 7-4). SNMPv2 offers new PDUs and adds error codes and exception responses. The latter allows a management application to easily determine why a management operation failed.

7.5.1. SNMPv2 PDUs

SNMPv2 defines eight PDU types, of which three are new: the GetBulkRequest, the InformRequest, and the SNMPv2-Trap. The following is a list of all the SNMPv2 PDUs, along with their assigned tag numbers:

PDU/Tag Number	Description
GetRequest [0]	Retrieves values of objects listed within the variable bindings field.
GetNextRequest [1]	Retrieves values of objects that are the lexicographical successors of the variables, up to the end of the MIB view of this request.

Response [2]   Generated in response to a GetRequest, GetNextRequest, Get-
                        BulkRequest, SetRequest, or InformRequest PDU.

SetRequest [3]   Establishes the value of a variable.

GetBulkRequest [5]   Retrieves a large amount of data, such as the contents of a
                        large table.

InformRequest [6]   Allows one manager to communicate information in its MIB
                        view to another manager.

SNMPv2-Trap [7]   Used by an SNMPv2 agent to provide information regarding
                        an exceptional condition. The destination of the SNMPv2-Trap
                        is determined by consulting the aclTable within the Party
                        MIB. The Trap PDU, defined for SNMPv1 with tag [4], is now
                        considered obsolete. Section 7.8 discusses conversion from
                        the Trap PDU to the SNMPv2-Trap PDU.

The PDUs that the SNMPv2 entity generates or receives depend on its role as
an agent or manager:

SNMPv2 PDU	Agent Generate	Agent Receive	Manager Generate	Manager Receive
GetRequest		X	X	
GetNextRequest		X	X	
Response	X		X	X
SetRequest		X	X	
GetBulkRequest		X	X	
InformRequest			X	X
SNMPv2-Trap	X			X

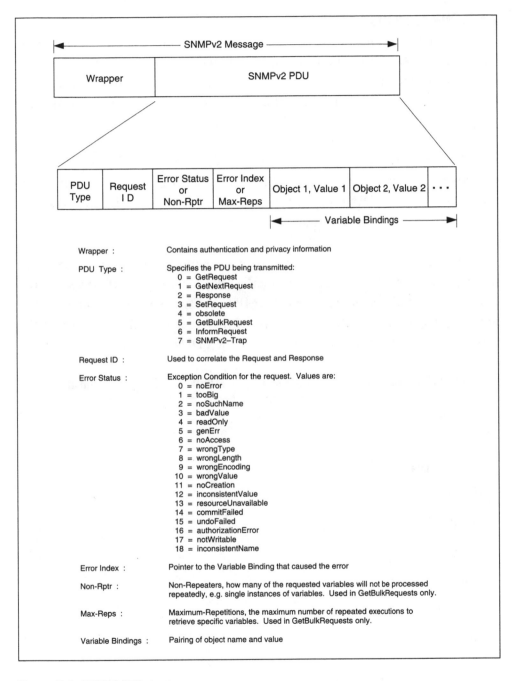

Figure 7-4. SNMPv2 PDU structure

7.5.2. SNMPv2 PDU syntax

The SNMPv2 message consists of the wrapper, which contains the authentication and privacy information, and the PDU. The syntax of the SNMPv2 PDUs is similar to the structures defined in SNMPv1. Significant enhancements include error status codes that detail why protocol operations were unsuccessful.

The PDU consists of four fields—the PDU Type field, the Request ID field, the Error Status field, and the Error Index field (see Figure 7-4)—plus the variable bindings. The PDU Type field specifies one of the seven PDUs being transmitted. The Request ID correlates the request and response PDUs.

The Error Status field includes new exception conditions. When errors occur in the processing of the GetRequest, GetNextRequest, GetBulkRequest, SetRequest, or InformRequest PDUs, the SNMPv2 entity prepares a Response PDU with the error status field set to help the manager identify and correct the problem. The following table shows how the PDUs use these error codes:

SNMPv2 Error	Get	GetNext	GetBulk	Set	Inform
noError	X	X	X	X	X
tooBig	X	X		X	X
noSuchName*					
badValue*					
readOnly*					
genErr	X	X	X	X	
noAccess				X	
wrongType				X	
wrongLength				X	

* Never generated by a SNMPv2 entity, as discussed in the Coexistence document, [7-13].

wrongEncoding				X	
wrongValue				X	
noCreation				X	
inconsistentValue				X	
resourceUnavailable				X	
commitFailed				X	
undoFailed				X	
authorizationError	X	X	X	X	X
notWritable				X	
inconsistentName				X	

The Error Index field is used with the Error Status code. When errors occur in the processing of the variable bindings, the Error Index field identifies the binding that caused the error. An error in the first binding would have Index = 1, an error in the second binding would have Index = 2, and so on.

7.5.2.1. The GetBulkRequest PDU

The GetBulkRequest (which some literature calls the "awesome GetBulkRequest") retrieves large amounts of data. The GetBulkRequest PDU enhances the GetNext PDU, and essentially executes multiple GetNext requests (lexicographically ordered) with a single PDU. The structure of the GetBulkRequest PDU resembles that of the other PDUs, but changes the syntax of two fields. It replaces Error Status with Non-Repeaters, and Error Index with Max-Repetitions.

The values of the Non-Repeaters and Max Repetitions fields indicate the processing requested. The Non-Repeaters field defines the number of requested variables that will not be processed repeatedly, and is used when some of the variables are scalar objects with only one variable. The Max-Repetitions field defines the maximum number of repeated executions that retrieve specific variables.

The retrieved variables return in the Response PDU that corresponds to the request. One variable binding in the Response PDU is requested for the first N variable bindings in the GetBulkRequest. M variable bindings are requested for each of the R remaining variable bindings in the GetBulkRequest. The following expression gives the total number of requested variable bindings:

> Total Variable Bindings = $N + (M * R)$, where
> N = the minimum of
>   (a) the value of the Non-Repeaters field
>   and
>   (b) the number of variable bindings in the GetBulkRequest
> M = the value of the Max-Repetitions field in the GetBulkRequest
> R = the minimum of
>   (a) the number of variable bindings in the GetBulkRequest less N
>   and
>   (b) zero

Processing continues until all of the requested variables have been retrieved, or the maximum size of the Response PDU is reached. The maximum size is determined by the smallest maximum message size that the source can generate or by the maximum message size that the destination can accept. The Response PDU then returns with the variables that the GetBulk requested.

7.5.2.2. InformRequest PDU

The InformRequest PDU performs manager-to-manager, not agent-to-manager, communication. An application may request a specific destination for the InformRequest PDU, or may find those destinations in the snmpEvent-NotifyTable, defined in the M2M MIB. The first two variable bindings that the PDU transmits are the sysUpTime.0 (from MIB-II), and the snmpEventID.i (from the SNMP Event table in the M2M MIB). Subsequent variable bindings contain information in the MIB view of a party, which is local to the manager that transmitted the InformRequest.

7.5.2.3. SNMPv2-Trap PDU

In SNMP version 1, the syntax of the Trap PDU differed from the other PDUs. With SNMPv2, the SNMPv1 Trap is now obsolete, and has been replaced by the SNMPv2-Trap PDU, which maintains a structure consistent with the other SNMPv2 PDUs. Agents transmit SNMPv2 PDUs when an exceptional situation occurs. Object values in the access control list (acl) or aclTable of the Party MIB define the intended destination(s) for these traps. The first variable in the SNMPv2-Trap is sysUpTime.0, from MIB-II. The second variable is snmpTrapOID.0, from the Traps group within the SNMPv2 MIB, which contains the administratively assigned name of the notification. Subsequent variables provide more information on the Trap.

7.5.3. SNMPv2 PDU definitions

For your reference, the following is a list of definitions for the SNMP PDUs, taken from the SNMPv2 Protocol Operations document [7-7]:

```
SNMPv2-PDU DEFINITIONS ::= BEGIN
IMPORTS
    ObjectName, ObjectSyntax, Integer32
    FROM SNMPv2-SMI;

-- protocol data units
PDUs ::=
    CHOICE {
    get-request
        GetRequest-PDU,
    get-next-request
        GetNextRequest-PDU,
    get-bulk-request
        GetBulkRequest-PDU,
    response
        Response-PDU,
    set-request
        SetRequest-PDU,
```

```
        inform-request
            InformRequest-PDU,
        snmpV2-trap
            SNMPv2-Trap-PDU
        }

-- PDUs
GetRequest-PDU ::=
    [0]
            IMPLICIT PDU
GetNextRequest-PDU ::=
    [1]
            IMPLICIT PDU
Response-PDU ::=
    [2]
            IMPLICIT PDU
SetRequest-PDU ::=
    [3]
            IMPLICIT PDU
-- [4] is obsolete
GetBulkRequest-PDU ::=
    [5]
            IMPLICIT BulkPDU
InformRequest-PDU ::=
    [6]
            IMPLICIT PDU
SNMPv2-Trap-PDU ::=
    [7]
            IMPLICIT PDU

max-bindings
    INTEGER ::= 2147483647
PDU ::
    SEQUENCE {
```

```
        request-id
            Integer32,
        error-status                    -- sometimes ignored
            INTEGER {
        noError(0),
                tooBig(1),
                noSuchName(2),          -- for proxy compatibility
                badValue(3),            -- for proxy compatibility
                readOnly(4),            -- for proxy compatibility
                genErr(5),
                noAccess(6),
                wrongType(7),
                wrongLength(8),
                wrongEncoding(9),
                wrongValue(10),
                noCreation(11),
                inconsistentValue(12),
                resourceUnavailable(13),
                commitFailed(14),
                undoFailed(15),
                authorizationError(16),
                notWritable(17),
                inconsistentName(18)
            },
        error-index                     -- sometimes ignored
            INTEGER (0..max-bindings),
        variable-bindings               -- values are sometimes ignored
            VarBindList
    }

BulkPDU ::=                             -- MUST be identical in
    SEQUENCE {                          -- structure to PDU
        request-id
            Integer32,
```

```
                non-repeaters
                    INTEGER (0..max-bindings),
                max-repetitions
                    INTEGER (0..max-bindings),
                variable-bindings              -- values are ignored
                    VarBindList
        }
-- variable binding
VarBind ::=
    SEQUENCE {
        name
            ObjectName,
        CHOICE {
            value
                ObjectSyntax,
            unSpecified                 -- in retrieval requests
                    NULL,

                                        -- exceptions in responses
                noSuchObject[0]
                        IMPLICIT NULL,
            noSuchInstance[1]
                        IMPLICIT NULL,
            endOfMibView[2]
                        IMPLICIT NULL
        }
    }
-- variable-binding list
VarBindList ::=
    SEQUENCE (SIZE (0..max-bindings)) OF
        VarBind
END
```

7.6. SNMPv2 Transport Mappings

SNMP version 1 was originally defined for transmission over UDP and IP. Subsequent research explored the use of SNMP with other transport protocols, including OSI transport (RFC 1418), AppleTalk's Datagram Delivery Protocol (DDP) (RFC 1419), and Novell's Internetwork Packet Exchange (IPX) (RFC 1420). SNMPv2 formally defines implementations over these other transports in the Transport Mapping document, RFC 1449 [7-8] (see Figure 7-5). The Transport Mapping document also includes instructions to provide proxy to SNMPv1, and use of the Basic Encoding Rules (BER).

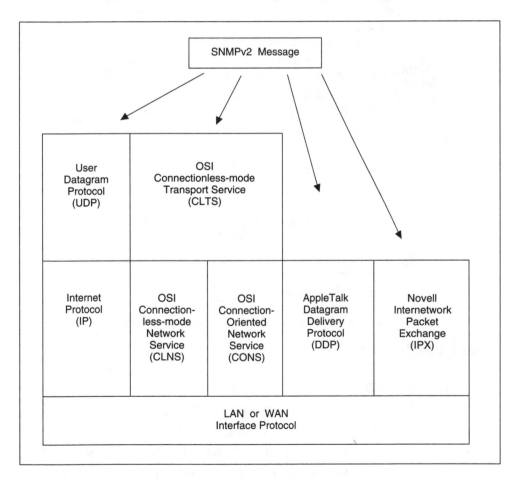

Figure 7-5. Transport mappings for SNMPv2

7.6.1. SNMPv2 over UDP

SNMPv2 over UDP is the preferred transport mapping. UDP provides compatibility with SNMPv1 at both the Transport and Network layers, although other higher-layer issues, such as SNMPv2 PDU structures, remain. RFC 1340 also suggests that SNMPv2 agents continue the practice of listening on UDP port 161, and that notifications listen on UDP port 162. (UDP port 162 was previously defined for SNMP traps.) Figure 7-6 illustrates the details of the UDP header, which precedes the SNMP message within the transmitted frame.

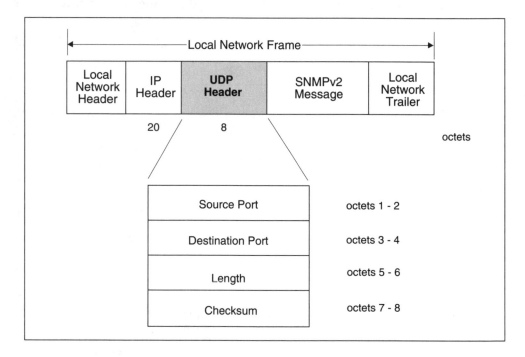

Figure 7-6. SNMPv2 over UDP

7.6.2. SNMPv2 over OSI

RFC 1449 defines two options for transmitting SNMPv2 messages over OSI protocols. Both send the SNMPv2 message in a single transport service data unit (TSDU), using the provisions of the OSI Connectionless-mode Transport Service (CLTS). Then at the Network layer, either a Connectionless-mode Network Service (CLNS) or a Connection-oriented Network Service (CONS) may be used.

When you use connectionless-mode network service, you would use the OSI Connectionless Network Protocol (CLNP) as the Network layer protocol. Figure 7-7 shows details of the CLNP header, the position of the CLTS header, and the SNMPv2 message within the transmission frame.

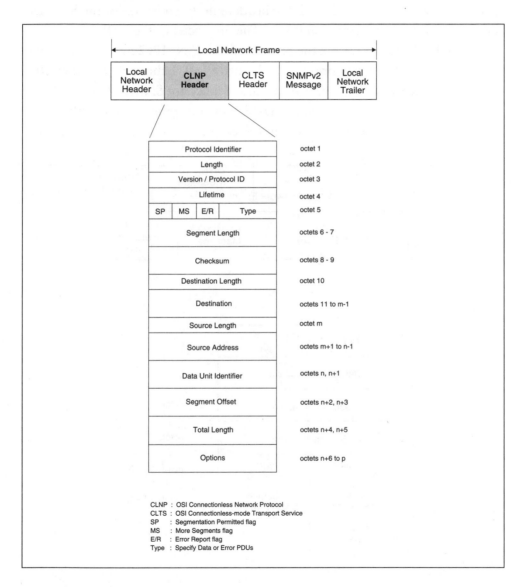

Figure 7-7. SNMPv2 over ISO CLNP

7.6.3. SNMPv2 over AppleTalk DDP

Apple Computer's AppleTalk protocol suite is another option available for SNMPv2 transport. The SNMPv2 message is sent in a single Datagram Delivery Protocol (DDP) datagram, which operates at the OSI Network layer. Figure 7-8 shows the details of the DDP header and the position of the SNMPv2 message within the transmission frame. The final octet of the DDP header specifies the DDP Type, indicating the protocol in use. SNMPv2 messages use DDP Type = 8, since Apple has previously defined types 1 through 7. Other DDP parameters, such as socket numbers, are also defined for SNMPv2 use. SNMPv2 entities acting in the agent role use DDP socket number 8, and *notification sinks*, which are entities receiving a notification, use DDP socket number 9.

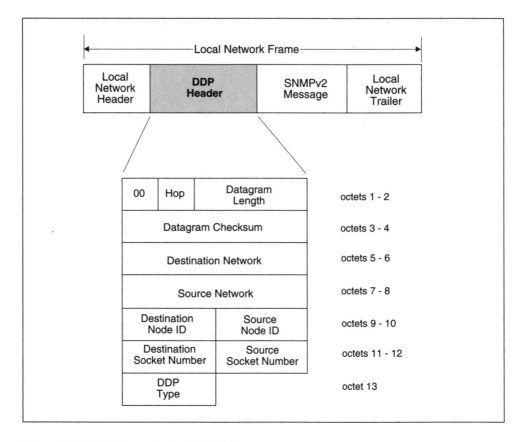

Figure 7-8. SNMPv2 over the AppleTalk DDP

7.6.4. SNMPv2 over Novell IPX

Novell Inc.'s NetWare protocol suite defines the Internetwork Packet Exchange (IPX) protocol at the Network layer. SNMPv2 messages are serialized into a single IPX datagram, shown in Figure 7-9. Within the IPX header is a Packet Type parameter that specifies the protocol in use. SNMPv2 messages use Packet Type = 4, which is defined as a Packet Exchange Protocol packet. SNMPv2 entities acting in the agent role listen on IPX socket number 36879 (900FH), while notification sinks listen on socket 36880 (9010H).

7.6.5. SNMPv2 transport mapping definitions

For your reference, this section reproduces the following transport mapping definitions from RFC 1449 [7-8]. Note the use of the TEXTUAL-CONVENTIONS macro, and the DISPLAY-HINT within each type, which provides information about how the different types of addresses are to be displayed. Recall the following abbreviations:

Abbreviation	Meaning
x	hexadecimal
d	decimal
o	octal
b	binary

The transport mapping definitions are:

```
SNMPv2-TM DEFINITIONS ::= BEGIN
IMPORTS
      snmpDomains, snmpProxys
            FROM SNMPv2-SMI
      TEXTUAL-CONVENTION
            FROM SNMPv2-TC;
```

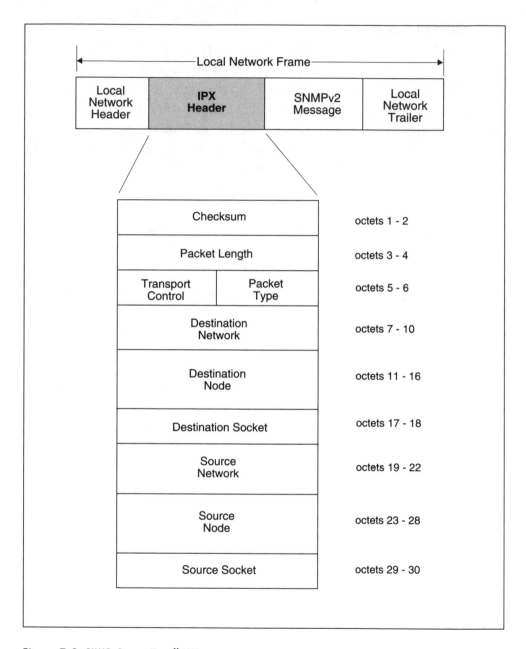

Figure 7-9. SNMPv2 over Novell IPX

```
-- SNMPv2 over UDP
snmpUDPDomain OBJECT IDENTIFIER ::= { snmpDomains 1 }
-- for a SnmpUDPAddress of length 6:
--
-- octets      contents           encoding
-- 1-4         IP-address         network-byte order
-- 5-6         UDP-port           network-byte order
--
SnmpUDPAddress ::= TEXTUAL-CONVENTION
     DISPLAY-HINT "1d.1d.1d.1d/2d"
     STATUS        current
     DESCRIPTION
         "Represents a UDP address."
     SYNTAX        OCTET STRING (SIZE (6))
-- SNMPv2 over OSI
snmpCLNSDomain OBJECT IDENTIFIER ::= { snmpDomains 2 }
snmpCONSDomain OBJECT IDENTIFIER ::= { snmpDomains 3 }
-- for a SnmpOSIAddress of length m:
--
-- octets      contents           encoding
-- 1           length of NSAP     "n" as an unsigned-integer
--                                   (either 0 or from 3 to 20)
-- 2..(n+1)    NSAP               concrete binary representation
-- (n+2)..m    TSEL               string of (up to 64) octets
--
SnmpOSIAddress ::= TEXTUAL-CONVENTION
     DISPLAY-HINT "*1x:/1x:"
     STATUS        current
     DESCRIPTION
         "Represents an OSI transport-address."
     SYNTAX        OCTET STRING (SIZE (1 | 4..85))

-- SNMPv2 over DDP
```

333

```
snmpDDPDomain OBJECT IDENTIFIER ::= { snmpDomains 4 }
-- for a SnmpNBPAddress of length m:
--
-- octets          contents          encoding
--  1              length of object  "n" as an unsigned integer
-- 2..(n+1)        object            string of (up to 32) octets
-- n+2             length of type    "p" as an unsigned integer
-- (n+3)..(n+2+p)  type              string of (up to 32) octets
--  n+3+p          length of zone    "q" as an unsigned integer
-- (n+4+p)..m      zone              string of (up to 32) octets
--
-- for comparison purposes, strings are case-insensitive
--
-- all strings may contain any octet other than 255 (hex ff)
--
SnmpNBPAddress ::= TEXTUAL-CONVENTION
    STATUS      current
    DESCRIPTION
        "Represents an NBP name."
    SYNTAX      OCTET STRING (SIZE (3..99))

-- SNMPv2 over IPX
snmpIPXDomain OBJECT IDENTIFIER ::= { snmpDomains 5 }
-- for a SnmpIPXAddress of length 12:
--
-- octets     contents          encoding
-- 1-4        network-number    network-byte order
-- 5-10       physical-address  network-byte order
-- 11-12      socket-number     network-byte order
--
SnmpIPXAddress ::= TEXTUAL-CONVENTION
    DISPLAY-HINT "4x.1x:1x:1x:1x:1x:1x.2d"
    STATUS   current
```

```
DESCRIPTION
    "Represents an IPX address."
    SYNTAX      OCTET STRING (SIZE (12))

-- for proxy to community-based SNMPv1 (RFC 1157)
rfc1157Proxy      OBJECT IDENTIFIER  ::= { snmpProxys 1 }
-- uses SnmpUDPAddress
rfc1157Domain     OBJECT IDENTIFIER  ::= { rfc1157Proxy 1 }
-- the community-based noAuth
rfc1157noAuth     OBJECT IDENTIFIER  ::= { rfc1157Proxy 2 }
END
```

7.7. SNMPv2 Security

When SNMPv1 was first published (circa 1988), the community name and the version number in the SNMP header provided the only message security capabilities. This provision, known as the *trivial protocol*, assured that both agent and manager recognized the same community name before proceeding with network management operations.

Additional research into security issues yielded three documents on the subject, all released in July 1992:

RFC	Title
1351	"SNMP Administrative Model"
1352	"SNMP Security Protocols"
1353	"Definitions for Managed Objects for Administration of SNMP Parties"

New versions of these documents have come out for SNMPv2; see references [7-9], [7-10], and [7-12]. These new standards assure the authentication and privacy of network management communication. Authentication assures the appropriate origin of the message, while privacy protects the messages from disclosure.

7.7.1. SNMPv2 Administrative Model

SNMPv2's Administrative Model defines the relationships between the SNMPv2 entities exchanging network management messages. The basis for this model is the SNMPv2 Party, which is defined as "a conceptual, virtual execution environment whose operation is restricted (for security or other purposes) to an administratively defined subset of all possible operations of a particular SNMPv2 entity." The standard goes on to state that each SNMPv2 Party comprises a single, unique party identity, a logical network location, a single authentication protocol, and a single privacy protocol.

The Party MIB [7-12], discussed in Section 7.7.3, contains the following ASN.1 definition for the SNMPv2 party:

```
PartyEntry ::=
    SEQUENCE {
        partyIdentity    Party,
        partyIndex       INTEGER,
        partyTDomain     OBJECT IDENTIFIER,
        partyTAddress    TAddress,
        partyMaxMessageSize INTEGER,
        partyLocal       TruthValue,
        partyAuthProtocol  OBJECT IDENTIFIER,
        partyAuthClock    Clock,
        partyAuthPrivate  OCTET STRING,
        partyAuthPublic   OCTET STRING,
        partyAuthLifetime INTEGER,
        partyPrivProtocol OBJECT IDENTIFIER,
        partyPrivPrivate  OCTET STRING,
        partyPrivPublic   OCTET STRING,
        partyCloneFrom    Party,
        partyStorageType  StorageType,
        partyStatus       RowStatus
    }
```

Thus, the SNMPv2 party contains extensive information about that entity. For example, the partyIdentity is an OBJECT-IDENTIFIER assigned to the party. The partyTDomain identifies the transport domain through which the party receives its network management information, such as snmpUDPDomain (SNMPv2 over UDP). Also of interest are the partyAuthProtocol, which identifies the authentication protocol, and the partyPrivProtocol, which identifies the privacy protocol. Consult the SNMPv2 Administrative Model document for more information on parties.

To summarize, secure SNMP messages are communicated between two parties. An SNMPv2 entity can, however, define multiple parties, each having different parameters. For example, different parties could use different authentication and/or privacy protocols. For communication to occur, all party parameters and related protocol parameters, such as encryption keys, must be validated.

Recall from our earlier discussion of the SNMPv2 PDU types that a "wrapper" precedes the PDU within the SNMPv2 message. That management communication may consist of both authentication and privacy components (see Figure 7-10). This management communication is defined as follows:

```
SnmpMgmtCom ::= [2] IMPLICIT SEQUENCE {
    dstParty
        OBJECT IDENTIFIER,
    srcParty
        OBJECT IDENTIFIER,
    context
        OBJECT IDENTIFIER,
    pdu
        PDUs
    }
```

- The dstParty component is called the destination and identifies the SNMPv2 party to which the communication is directed.

- The srcParty component is called the source and identifies the SNMPv2 party from which the communication is originated.

- The context component identifies the SNMPv2 context containing the management information referenced by the communication.

- The PDU component has the form and significance defined in the Protocol Operations document.

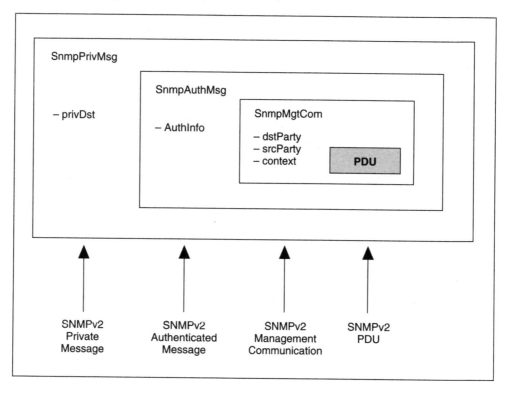

Figure 7-10. SNMPv2 PDU with security wrappers

Thus, the first component of the "wrapper" defines the source and destination parties, as well as the context, local or remote, in which the objects are to be interpreted.

An authenticated management communication reliably identifies the integrity of the originating SNMPv2 party, and is defined as

```
SnmpAuthMsg ::= [1] IMPLICIT SEQUENCE {
 authInfo
  ANY, -- defined by authentication protocol
 authData
  SnmpMgmtCom
 }
```

- The authInfo component is called the authentication information and represents information necessary to support the authentication protocol used by the SNMPv2 party originating the message.

- The authData component is called the authentication data and represents a SNMPv2 management communication (SnmpMgmtCom from above).

Thus, the SNMPv2 authenticated message adds authentication information to the "wrapper" (review Figure 7-10).

Finally, privacy information may be included in the SNMPv2 message to protect it from disclosure:

```
SnmpPrivMsg ::= [1] IMPLICIT SEQUENCE {
 privDst
  OBJECT IDENTIFIER,
 privData
  [1] IMPLICIT OCTET STRING
 }
```

- The privDst component is called the privacy destination and identifies the SNMPv2 party to which the communication is directed.

- The privData component is called the privacy data and represents the (possibly encrypted) serialization (according to the conventions of the Transport Mappings) of a SNMPv2 authenticated management communication.

Thus, the private SNMPv2 message includes privacy information to protect that message from unauthorized disclosure.

7.7.2. SNMPv2 Security Protocols

A SNMPv2 party, defined by the SNMPv2 Administrative Model, is associated with a single authentication protocol and a single privacy protocol. The authentication protocol provides a way to reliably identify the originator of the message. The privacy protocol provides a way to protect the message from disclosure. The privacy protocol defined in the Security Protocols document [7-10] further stipulates that only authenticated messages may be protected from disclosure. In other words, authentication is required for privacy.

In the ASN.1 definition of the SNMPv2 party, two components, partyAuth-Protocol and partyPrivProtocol, identify the authentication and privacy protocols, respectively. If authentication or privacy are not used, special values of these components are used. If the partyAuthProtocol component has a value of noAuth, then the message's integrity and origin are not authenticated. Likewise, if the partyPrivProtocol has a value of noPriv, then the message is not protected from disclosure.

The SNMPv2 Security document discusses two primary protocols, the Digest Authentication Protocol and the Symmetric Privacy Protocol. The digest authentication protocol verifies message integrity (that the message received is the same as the message sent) and message origin. The data integrity is protected with a message digest calculated according to the MD5 message-digest algorithm [7-11]. This digest is a 128-bit sequence calculated over the designated portion of the SNMPv2 message, then sent with the message to the receiver. The receiver, in turn, verifies the message digest. Before the digest is calculated, a secret value, known only to the message originator and the intended recipient, is prefixed to the message. After the digest verifies message integrity, the secret value verifies the origin of the message.

The symmetric privacy protocol assures message privacy. This protocol depends on the message's encryption using a secret key known only to the originator and recipient. In addition, the encrypted message must be authenticated as described above. The algorithm uses the Data Encryption Standard (DES) in the Cipher Block Chaining mode of operation. Both NIST [7-12] and ANSI have documented this standard.

Both the authentication protocol and the privacy protocol depend upon the existence of loosely synchronized clocks and shared secret values. The security protocols document [7-10] describe methods for distributing these values.

7.7.3. The Party MIB

The Party MIB [7-13] defines the managed objects that correspond to the properties of the SNMPv2 parties, contexts, and access control policies. This MIB is the third MIB module defined for SNMPv2 and is identified as {snmp-Modules 3}.

The Party MIB is divided into three major sections (see Figure 7-11). The first contains administrative assignments, partyAdmin, designated {partyMIB 1}, and defines the security protocols, temporal (current) domains, and initial configurations for parties and contexts. The second contains the Party MIB objects, partyMIBObjects, designated {partyMIB 2}, and contains four groups, including the Party Database group, Contexts Database group, Access Privileges Database group, and View Database group. The final section contains conformance information, designated partyMIBConformance, {partyMIB 3}.

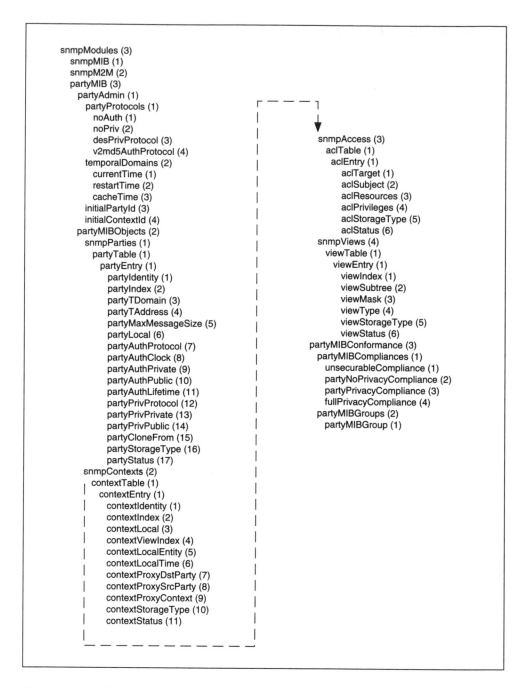

```
snmpModules (3)
  snmpMIB (1)
  snmpM2M (2)
  partyMIB (3)
    partyAdmin (1)
      partyProtocols (1)
        noAuth (1)
        noPriv (2)
        desPrivProtocol (3)
        v2md5AuthProtocol (4)
      temporalDomains (2)
        currentTime (1)
        restartTime (2)
        cacheTime (3)
      initialPartyId (3)
      initialContextId (4)
    partyMIBObjects (2)
      snmpParties (1)
        partyTable (1)
          partyEntry (1)
            partyIdentity (1)
            partyIndex (2)
            partyTDomain (3)
            partyTAddress (4)
            partyMaxMessageSize (5)
            partyLocal (6)
            partyAuthProtocol (7)
            partyAuthClock (8)
            partyAuthPrivate (9)
            partyAuthPublic (10)
            partyAuthLifetime (11)
            partyPrivProtocol (12)
            partyPrivPrivate (13)
            partyPrivPublic (14)
            partyCloneFrom (15)
            partyStorageType (16)
            partyStatus (17)
      snmpContexts (2)
        contextTable (1)
          contextEntry (1)
            contextIdentity (1)
            contextIndex (2)
            contextLocal (3)
            contextViewIndex (4)
            contextLocalEntity (5)
            contextLocalTime (6)
            contextProxyDstParty (7)
            contextProxySrcParty (8)
            contextProxyContext (9)
            contextStorageType (10)
            contextStatus (11)

                              snmpAccess (3)
                                aclTable (1)
                                  aclEntry (1)
                                    aclTarget (1)
                                    aclSubject (2)
                                    aclResources (3)
                                    aclPrivileges (4)
                                    aclStorageType (5)
                                    aclStatus (6)
                              snmpViews (4)
                                viewTable (1)
                                  viewEntry (1)
                                    viewIndex (1)
                                    viewSubtree (2)
                                    viewMask (3)
                                    viewType (4)
                                    viewStorageType (5)
                                    viewStatus (6)
                      partyMIBConformance (3)
                        partyMIBCompliances (1)
                          unsecurableCompliance (1)
                          partyNoPrivacyCompliance (2)
                          partyPrivacyCompliance (3)
                          fullPrivacyCompliance (4)
                        partyMIBGroups (2)
                          partyMIBGroup (1)
```

Figure 7-11. SNMPv2 partyMIB object tree

7.8 Coexistence of SNMPv1 and SNMPv2

With more than 400 pages of documentation defining SNMPv2, migrating from SNMPv1 to SNMPv2 would be a reasonable concern. The Coexistence document [7-14] presents a number of guidelines that outline the modifications necessary for successful coexistence. From a practical point of view, two methods are defined to achieve coexistence: a proxy agent and a bi-lingual manager.

The proxy agent translates between SNMPv1 to/from SNMPv2 messages (see Figure 7-12). When translating from SNMPv2 to SNMPv1, GetRequest, GetNextRequest, or SetRequest PDUs from the manager are passed directly to the SNMPv1 agent. GetBulkRequest PDUs are translated into GetNextPDUs. For translating from SNMPv1 to SNMPv2, the GetResponse PDU is passed unaltered to the manager. A SNMPv1 Trap PDU is mapped to a SNMPv2-Trap PDU, with the two new variable bindings, sysUpTime.0 and snmpTrapOID.0, prepended to the variable bindings field.

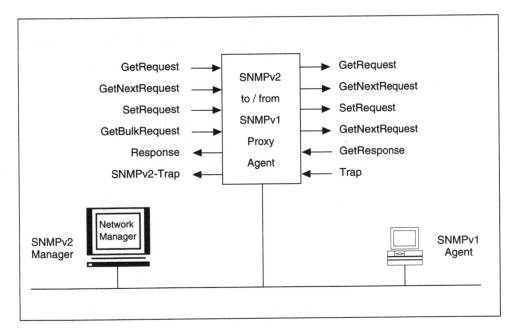

Figure 7-12. SNMPv1/SNMPv2 proxy agent operation

The second alternative is a bi-lingual manager, which incorporates both the SNMPv1 and SNMPv2 protocols. When the manager needs to communicate with an agent, it selects the protocol appropriate for the application.

7.9. Surveying the Future of SNMP

The last question is the viability of this new architecture. If the popularity of SNMPv1 is any indication, SNMPv2 will be a rousing success. And if the current interest in SNMPv2 from the trade press is any indication, numerous vendors will migrate their products to the new protocol (see references [7-14] through [7-19]). However, one key factor in the acceptance of the SNMPv2 framework will be the industry's willingness to implement the protocol's complex security enhancements.

But the most important indicator of the new framework's success will be user and vendor acceptance. Let's get together in a few years and see if my predictions of success have come true.

7.10. References

[7-1]   Case, J.D. and K. McCloghrie, M.T. Rose, S.L. Waldbusser, "Introduction to version 2 of the Network Management Framework." RFC 1441, April 1993.

[7-2]   Case, J.D. and K. McCloghrie, M.T. Rose, S.L. Waldbusser, "Structure of Management Information for version 2 of the Simple Network Management Protocol (SNMPv2)." RFC 1442, April 1993.

[7-3]   Case, J.D. and K. McCloghrie, M.T. Rose, S.L. Waldbusser, "Conformance Statements for version 2 of the Simple Network Management Protocol (SNMPv2)." RFC 1444, April 1993.

[7-4]   Case, J.D. and K. McCloghrie, M.T. Rose, S.L. Waldbusser, 'Textual Conventions for version 2 of the Simple Network Management Protocol (SNMPv2)." RFC 1443, April 1993.

[7-5]   Case, J.D. and K. McCloghrie, M.T. Rose, S.L. Waldbusser, "Management Information Base for version 2 of the Simple Network Management Protocol (SNMPv2)." RFC 1450, April 1993.

[7-6]   Case, J.D. and K. McCloghrie, M.T. Rose, S.L. Waldbusser, "Manager to Manager Management Information Base." RFC 1451, April 1993.

[7-7]   Case, J.D. and K. McCloghrie, M.T. Rose, S.L. Waldbusser, "Protocol Operations for version 2 of the Simple Network Management Protocol (SNMPv2)." RFC 1448, April 1993.

[7-8]   Case, J.D. and K. McCloghrie, M.T. Rose, S.L. Waldbusser, "Transport Mappings for version 2 of the Simple Network Management Protocol (SNMPv2)." RFC 1449, April 1993.

[7-9]   Davin, J.R and J.M. Galvin, K. McCloghrie. "Administrative Model for version 2 of the Simple Network Management Protocol (SNMPv2)." RFC 1445, April 1993.

[7-10] Galvin, J.M. K. McCloghrie, J.R. Davin. "Security Protocols for version 2 of the Simple Network Management Protocol (SNMPv2)." RFC 1446, April 1993.

[7-11] R.L. Rivest. "The MD5 Message-Digest Algorithm." RFC 1321, April 1992.

[7-12] Data Encryption Standard, National Institute of Standards and Technology. Federal Information Processing Standard (FIPS) Publication 46-1. Supersedes FIPs Publication 46, (January, 1977; reaffirmed January, 1988).

[7-13] McCloghrie, K and J.R. Davin, J.M. Galvin. "Party MIB for version 2 of the Simple Network Management Protocol (SNMPv2)." RFC 1447, April 1993.

[7-14] Case, J.D. and K. McCloghrie, M.T. Rose, S.L. Waldbusser. "Coexistence between version 1 and version 2 of the Internet-standard Network Management Framework." RFC 1452, April 1993.

[7-15] Case, Jeff et. al. "The Simple Management Protocol and Framework." *ConneXions, The Interoperability Report* (October 1992):16-23.

[7-16] Jander, Mary. "Coming Soon to a Network Near You." Data Communications (November 1992):66-76.

[7-17] Huntington-Lee, Jill. "New SNMP Version Heads for Fast-Track Acceptance." Open Systems Today (December 7, 1992):26-29.

[7-18] Malloy, Maureen. "On the Winding Road to SNMP Version 2." Network World (January 4, 1993):17-20.

[7-19] Musich, Paula. "SNMP V2 is Clearing Standards Hurdles." PC Week (January 11, 1993):49-56.

[7-20] Caron, Jerimiah. "SNMP Approaches a Crossroad." LAN Times (March 8, 1993):1-96.

Appendix A: Addresses of Standards Organization

AT&T Publications

AT&T Technologies Commercial
   Sales
P.O. Box 19901
Indianapolis, IN 46219
317/322-6557
800/432-6600

Bellcore Standards

Bell Communications Research
Information Management Services
8 Corporate Place, 3A-184
Piscataway, NJ 08854-4196
908/699 5800
800/521-2673

CCITT Recommendations and Federal Information Processing Standards (FIPS)

U.S. Department of Commerce
National Technical Information
   Service
5285 Port Royal Road
Springfield, VA 22161
703/487-4650

CSA Standards

Canadian Standards Association
178 Rexdale Boulevard
Rexdale, ONT M9W 1R3
CANADA
416/747-4363

ECMA Standards

European Computer Manufacturers
   Association
114 Rue de rhone CH-1204
Geneva
SWITZERLAND
41 22 735-3634

ECSA Standards

Exchange Carriers Standards
   Association
1200 G Street NW, Suite 500
Washington, DC 20005
202/628-6380

EIA Standards

Electronic Industries Association
Standards Sales
2001 Pennsylvania Avenue NW
Washington, DC 20006
202/457-4966
800/854-7179

IEEE Standards

Institute of Electrical and
    Electronics Engineers
445 Hoes Lane
P.O. Box 1331
Piscataway, NJ 08855-1331
908/981-1393
800/678-4333

Internet Standards

DDN Network Information Center
Government Systems, Inc.
14200 Park Meadow Drive
Suite 200
Chantilly, VA 22021
703/802-4535
800/365-3642
(See Appendix D for further
    information.)

ISO and ANSI Standards

American National Standards
    Institute
11 West 42nd Street, 13th floor
New York, NY 10036
212/642-4900

ISO Standards

International Organization for
    Standardization
1, Rue de varembe
CH-1211
Geneva 20
SWITZERLAND
41 22 749-0111

Military Standards Sales

Naval Publications and Forms
    Center
Commanding Officer
NPFC 43
5801 Tabor Avenue
Philadelphia, PA 19120
215/697-3321

National Institute of Standards and Technology

Technology Building 225,
    Room B-64
Gaithersburg, MD 20899
301/975-2816

Appendix B: Acronyms and Abbreviations

A	ampere
AARP	AppleTalk Address Resolution Protocol
ABP	alternate bipolar
ACK	acknowledgement
ACS	asynchronous communication server
ACTLU	activate logical unit
ACTPU	activate physical unit
ADSP	AppleTalk Data Stream Protocol
AEP	AppleTalk Echo Protocol
AFP	AppleTalk Filing Protocol
AFRP	ARCNET Fragmentation Protocol
AGS	asynchronous gateway server
AI	artificial intelligence
AMI	alternate mark inversion
AMT	address mapping table
ANSI	American National Standards Institute
API	applications program interface
APPC	Advanced Program-to-Program Communication
ARE	all routes explorer
ARI	address recognized indicator bit
ARP	Address Resolution Program
ARPA	Advanced Research Projects Agency
ARPANET	Advanced Research Projects Agency Network
ASCE	Association Control Service Element
ASCII	American Standard Code for Information Interchange
ASN.1	Abstract Syntax Notation One
ASP	AppleTalk Session Protocol

ATM	Asynchronous Transfer Mode
ATP	AppleTalk Transaction Protocol
B8ZS	bipolar with 8 ZERO substitution
BC	block check
BER	Basic Encoding Rules
BIOS	Basic Input/Output System
BITNET	Because It's Time NETwork
BIU	basic information unit
BOC	Bell Operating Company
BOOTP	Bootstrap Protocol
BPDU	bridge protocol data unit
bps	bits per second
BPV	bipolar violations
BRI	basic rate interface
BSC	binary synchronous communication
BSD	Berkeley Software Distribution
BTU	basic transmission unit
CCIS	common channel interoffice signaling
CCITT	International Telegraph and Telephone Consultative Committee
CCR	commitment, concurrency, and recovery
CICS	customer information communication system
CLNP	Connectionless Network Protocol
CLNS	Connectionless-mode Network Services
CLTP	Connectionless Transport Protocol
CMIP	Common Management Information Protocol
CMIS	Common Management Information Service
CMISE	Common Management Information Service Element
CMOL	CMIP on IEEE 802.2 Logical Link Control
CMOT	Common Management Information Protocol over TCP/IP
CONS	Connection-mode Network Services
COS	Corporation for Open Systems
CPE	customer premises equipment
CPE	convergence protocol entity

CRC	cyclic redundancy check
CREN	The Corporation for Research and Educational Networking
CRS	configuration report server
CSMA/CD	Carrier Sense Multiple Access with Collision Detection
CSNET	computer+science network
CSU	channel service unit
CTERM	Command Terminal Protocol
DAP	Data Access Protocol
DARPA	Defense Advanced Research Projects Agency
DAT	duplicate address test
DCA	Defense Communications Agency
DCC	Data Country Code
DCE	data circuit-terminating equipment
DDCMP	Digital Data Communications Message Protocol
DDN	Defense Data Network
DDP	Datagram Delivery Protocol
DECmcc	DEC Management Control Center
DEMPR	DEC multiport repeater
DIX	DEC, Intel, and Xerox
DL	data link
DLC	data link control
DMA	direct memory access
DNIC	Data Network Identification Code
DNS	Domain Name System
DOD	Department of Defense
DPA	demand protocol architecture
DRP	DECnet Routing Protocol
DSAP	destination service access point
DSU	data service unit
DSU/CSU	Data service unit/channel service unit
DTE	data terminal equipment
DTR	data terminal ready
EBCDIC	Extended Binary Coded Decimal Interchange Code
ECL	End Communication layer

ECSA	Exchange Carriers Standards Association
EDI	electronic data interchange
EGA	enhanced graphics array
EGP	Exterior Gateway Protocol
EIA	Electronic Industries Association
ELAP	EtherTalk Link Access Protocol
EOT	end of transmission
ESF	extended superframe format
ES-IS	End System to Intermediate System Protocol
FAL	file access listener
FAT	file access table
FCC	Federal Communications Commission
FCI	frame copied indicator bit
FCS	frame check sequence
FDDI	fiber data distributed interface
FDM	frequency division multiplexing
FID	format identifer
FIPS	Federal Information Processing Standard
FM	function management
FMD	function management data
FT1	fractional T1
FTAM	File Transfer Access and Management
FTP	File Transfer Protocol
G	giga-
GB	gigabyte
GHz	gigahertz
GOSIP	Government OSI profile
GUI	graphical user interface
HA	hardware address
HDLC	high-level data link control
HEMS	high-level entity management system
HLLAPI	High-level language API
Hz	hertz
IAB	Internet Activities Board

IANA	Internet Assigned Numbers Authority
ICD	international code designator
ICMP	Internet Control Message Protocol
ICP	Internet Control Protocol
IDP	Internetwork Datagram Protocol
IEEE	Institute of Electrical and Electronics Engineers
IETF	Internet Engineering Task Force
I/G	individual/group
IGP	Interior Gateway Protocol
IGRP	Internet Gateway Routing Protocol
IMPS	interface message processors
I/O	input/output
IOC	inter-office channel
IP	Internet Protocol
IPC	Interprocess Communications Protocol
IPX	Internetwork Packet Exchange Protocol
IR	Internet router
IRTF	Internet Research Task Force
ISDN	Integrated Services Digital Network
IS-IS	Intermediate System to Intermediate System Protocol
ISO	International Organization for Standardization
ISODE	ISO Development Environment
ITU	International Telecommunication Union
IXC	inter-exchange carrier
Kbps	kilo bits per second
KHz	kilohertz
LAA	locally administered address
LAN	local area network
LAP	link access procedure
LAPB	Link Access Procedure Balanced
LAPD	Link Access Procedure D Channel
LAT	Local Area Transport
LATA	local access transport area
LAVC	local area VAX cluster

LEC	local exchange carrier
LEN	length
LF	largest frame
LLAP	LocalTalk Link Access Protocol
LLC	Logical Link Control
LME	layer management entity
LMI	layer management interface
LMMP	LAN/MAN Management Protocol
LMMPE	LAN/MAN Management Protocol Entity
LMMS	LAN/MAN Management Service
LMMU	LAN/MAN Management User
LPP	Lightweight Presentation Protocol
LSB	least significant bit
LSL	Link Support layer
MAC	medium access control
MAN	metropolitan area network
Mbps	megabits per second
MHS	message handling service
MHz	megahertz
MIB	management information base
MILNET	MILitary NETwork
MIOX	Multiprotocol Interconnect over X.25
MIPS	millions instructions per second
MIS	management information systems
MLID	multiple link interface driver
MNP	Microcom Networking Protocol
MOP	Maintenance Operations Protocol
MSAU	multistation access unit
MSB	most significant bit
MTA	message transfer agent
MTBF	mean time between failures
MTTR	mean time to repair
MTU	maximum transmission unit
MUX	multiplex, multiplexor

NACS	NetWare Asynchronous Communications Server
NAK	negative acknowledgement
NASI	NetWare Asynchronous Service Interface
NAU	network addressable unit
NAUN	nearest active upstream neighbor
NBP	Name Binding Protocol
NCP	Network Control Program
NCP	NetWare Core Protocol
NCSI	network communications services interface
NDIS	Network Driver Interface Standard
NetBEUI	NetBIOS Extended User Interface
NetBIOS	Network Basic Input/Output System
NFS	Network File System
NIC	network information center
NIC	network interface card
NICE	network information and control exchange
NIS	names information socket
NIST	National Institute of Standards and Technology
NLM	netware loadable module
NMS	network management station
NOC	network operations center
NOS	network operating system
NSF	National Science Foundation
NSP	Network Services Protocol
NT	network termination
OC1	optical carrier, level 1
ODI	Open Data Link Interface
OID	object identifier
OIM	OSI Internet management
OSF	Open Software Foundation
OSI	Open Systems Interconnection
OSI-RM	Open Systems Interconnection Reference Model
OSPF	Open Shortest Path First
PA	protocol address

PABX	private automatic branch exchange
PAD	packet assembler and disassembler
PAP	Printer Access Protocol
PBX	private branch exchange
PCI	protocol control information
PCM	pulse code modulation
PDN	public data network
PDU	protocol data unit
PEP	Packet Exchange Protocol
PLEN	protocol length
POP	point of presence
POSIX	Portable Operating System Interface-UNIX
POTS	plain old telephone service
PPP	Point-to-Point Protocol
PSN	packet switch node
PSP	presentation services process
PSPDN	packet switched public data network
PTP	point-to-point
PUC	Public Utility Commission
RARP	Reverse Address Resolution Protocol
RBOC	Regional Bell Operating Company
RC	routing control
RD	route descriptor
RFC	request for comments
RFS	remote file system
RH	request/response header
RI	routing information
RII	route information indicator
RIP	Routing Information Protocol
RJE	remote job entry
ROSE	Remote Operations Service Element
RMON	remote monitoring
RPC	remote procedure call
RPS	ring parameter server

RSX	Realtime Resource-Sharing eXecutive
RT	routing type
RU	request/response unit
SABME	set asynchronous balanced mode extended
SAP	service access point
SAP	Service Advertising Protocol
SCS	system communication services
SDLC	Synchronous Data Link Control
SDN	software defined network
SEQ	sequence
SGMP	Simple Gateway Management Protocol
SLIP	Serial Line IP
SMB	server message block
SMDS	Switched Multimegabit Data Service
SMI	structure of management information
SMI	system management interface
SMTP	Simple Mail Transfer Protocol
SNA	System Network Architecture
SNADS	Systems Network Architecture Distribution Services
SNAP	sub-network access protocol
SNMP	Simple Network Management Protocol
SOH	start of header
SONET	Synchronous Optical Network
SPP	Sequenced Packet Protocol
SPX	Sequenced Packet Exchange protocol
SR	source routing
SRF	specifically routed frame
SRI	Stanford Research Institute
SRT	source routing transparent
SSAP	source service access point
STE	spanning tree explorer
SUA	stored upstream address
SVC	switched virtual circuit
TB	terabyte

TCP	Transmission Control Protocol
TCP/IP	Transmission Control Protocol/Internet Protocol
TDM	time division multiplexing
TELNET	Telecommunications Network Protocol
TFTP	Trivial File Transfer Protocol
TH	transmission header
TLAP	TokenTalk Link Access Protocol
TLI	Transport Layer Interface
TLV	Type-Length-Value encoding
TP	Transport Protocol
TSR	terminate-and-stay resident
UA	unnumbered acknowledgement
UA	user agent
UDP	User Datagram Protocol
U/L	universal/local
ULP	Upper Layer Protocols
UNMA	unified network management architecture
UT	universal time
UTP	unshielded twisted pair
UUCP	UNIX to UNIX copy program
V	volt
VAN	value added network
VAP	value-added process
VARP	VINES Address Resolution Protocol
VFRP	VINES Fragmentation Protocol
VGA	video graphics array
VICP	VINES Internet Control Protocol
VINES	Virtual Networking System
VIP	VINES Internet Protocol
VIPC	VINES Interprocess Communications
VLSI	very large-scale integration
VMS	virtual memory system
VRTP	VINES Routing Update Protocol
VSPP	VINES Sequenced Packet Protocol

VT	virtual terminal
WAN	wide area network
WIN	window
XDR	External data representation
XID	exchange identification
XMP	X/Open Management Protocol
XNS	Xerox Network System
ZIP	Zone Information Protocol
ZIS	Zone Information Socket
ZIT	Zone Information Table

Appendix C: Selected Manufacturers of SNMP-Related Internetworking Products

Accton Technology Corp.
46750 Fremont Blvd. #104
Fremont, CA 94538
(510) 226-9800
(800) 926-9288
Fax: (510) 226-9833

ACSYS Inc.
20 Burlington Mal Rd. Suite 400
Burlington, MA 01803
(617) 270-5566
Fax: (617) 270-5575

ADAX, Inc.
614 Bancroft Way
Berkeley, CA 94710
(510) 548-7047
Fax: (510) 548-5526

ADC Kentrox
P.O. Box 10704
Portland, OR 97210
(503) 643-1681
(800) 733-5511
Fax: (503) 641-3341

ADI Systems
2115 Ringwood Ave.
San Jose, CA 95131
(408) 944-0100
(800) 228-0530
Fax: (408) 944-0300

Advanced Computer Communications (ACC)
10261 Bubb Rd.
Cupertino, CA 95014
(408) 864-0600
(800) 444-7854
Fax: (408) 446-5234

Advanced Logic Research

9401 Jeronimo
Irvine, CA 92718
(714) 581-6770
(800) 444-4257
Fax: (714) 581-9240

The AG Group

2540 Camino Diablo #202
Walnut Creek, CA 94596
(510) 937-7900
Fax: (510) 937-2479

Alantec

2380 Bering Dr.
San Jose, CA 95131
(408) 955-9500
(800) 252-6832
Fax: (408) 955-9500

Alcatel Network Systems

2912 Wake Forest Road
Raleigh, NC 27609
(919) 850-6000
Fax: (919) 850-6171

Alisa Systems, Inc.

221 E. Walnut, Suite 175
Pasadena, CA 91101
(818) 792-9474
(800) 992-5472
Fax: (818) 792-4068

Allen-Bradley

555 Briarwood Circle
Ann Arbor, MI 48108
(313) 998-2000
Fax: (313) 668-2922

Alliant Computer Systems Corp.

One Monarch Drive
Littleton, MA 01460
(508) 486-4950

Allied Telesis, Inc.

575 E. Middlefield Road
Mountain View, CA 94043
(415) 964-2771
Fax: (415) 964-0944

American Power Conversion Corp.

132 Fairgrounds Rd.
West Kingston, RI 02892
(401) 789-5735
(800) 800-4272
Fax: (401) 789-3710

AMP

P.O. Box 3608
Harrisburg, PA 17105
(717) 564-0100
(800) 522-6752
Fax: (717) 986-7575

Andrew Corporation
23610 Telo Ave.
Torrance, CA 90505
(310) 784-8000
(800) 733-0331
Fax: (310) 784-8093

Anixter Brothers, Inc.
6602 Owens Drive, Suite 300
Pleasanton, CA 94588
(510) 463-1223
Fax: (510) 463-1255

Apple Computer, Inc.
20525 Mariani Avenue
Cupertino, CA 95014
(408) 996-1010
(800) 776-2333
Fax: (408) 974-6726

Applied Computing Devices Inc.
100 So. Campus Dr.
Terre Haute IN 47802
(812) 232 6051
Fax: (812) 231 5280

Applitek Corporation
100 Brickstone Square
Andover, MA 01810
(508) 475-4050
(800) 526-2489
Fax: (508) 475-0550

APT Communications, Inc.
9607 Dr. Perry Rd.
Ijamsville, MD 21754
(301) 831-1182
(800) 842-0626
Fax: (301) 874-5255

Armon Networking Limited
Tel Aviv Israel
972 3 490702
Fax: 972 3 490701

Asante Technologies
404 Tasman Drive
Sunnyvale, CA 94089
(408) 752-8388
(800) 662-9686
Fax: (408) 734-4864

Ascom Timeplex Inc.
400 Chestnut Ridge Road
Woodcliff Lake, NJ 07675
(201) 391-1111
Fax: (201) 573-6470

AT&T Computer Systems
Gatehall Drive
Parsippany, NJ 07054
(201) 397-4800
Fax: (201) 397-4918

AT&T EasyLink Services

400 Interspace Pkwy.
Parsippany, NJ 07054
(800) 779-1111
Fax (201) 818-6534

Attachmate Corp.

13617 131st Ave.SE.
Bellevue, WA 98006
(206) 644-4010
(800) 426-6283
Fax: (206) 747-9924

Auspex Systems Inc.

2952 Bunker Hill Lane
Santa Clara, CA 95054
(408) 492-0900
Fax: (408) 492-0909

Autotrol Technology

12500 N. Washington
Denver, CO 80241
(303) 452-4919
(800) 233 2882
Fax: (303) 252 2249

Avatar

65 South St.
Hopkinton, MA 01748
(508) 435-3000
(800) 282-3270
Fax: (508) 435-2470

Aydin Computer & Monitor Systems

700 Dresher Rd.
Horsham, PA 19044
(215) 657-8600
Fax: (215) 657-5470

Banyan Systems, Inc.

115 Flanders Road #5
Westboro, MA 01581
(508) 898-1000
(800) 828-2404
Fax: (508) 836-1810

BBN Communications Corp.

150 Cambridge Park Dr.
Cambridge, MA 02140
(617) 873-2000
Fax: (617) 873-2509

Beame & Whiteside Software

P.O. Box 8130
Dundas, Ontario, Canada L9H 5E7
(416) 765-0822
(800) 463-6637
Fax: (416) 765-0815

Bear Computer Systems Inc.

9584 Topanga Canyon Blvd.
Chatsworth CA 91311
(818) 341-0403
(800) 255 0662
Fax: (818) 341-1831

Bell Atlantic Software Systems
14 Washington Rd. Bldg. 2
Princeton Junction, NJ 08550
(609) 936-2900
Fax: (609) 936-2859

Bellcore
331 Newman Springs Road
Red Bank, NJ 07701-7030
(908) 758-2032
(800) 521-2673

BGL Technology Corporation
451 Constitution Avenue
Camarillo, CA 93012
(805) 987-7305
Fax: (805) 987-7346

Black Box Corporation
1000 Park Drive
P.O. Box 12800
Pittsburgh, PA 15241
(412) 746-5500
Fax: (412) 746-0746

BRIO Technology Inc.
444 Castro St., Suite 700
Mountain View, CA 94041
(415) 961-4110
(800) 486-2746
Fax: (415) 961-4572

Brixton Systems
185 Alewise Pkwy
Cambridge, MA 02138
(617) 876-5359
Fax: (617) 547-9820

Bull HN Information Systems
Technology Park
2 Wall Street
Billerica, MA 01821
(508) 294-6000
Fax: (508) 294-6440

Bytex
4 Technology Dr.
Westborough MA 01581
(508) 366-8000
(800) 227-1145
Fax: (508) 366-7977

Cabletron Systems, Inc.
P.O. Box 5005
Rochester, NH 03867-0505
(603) 332-9400
Fax: (603) 332-4616

CACI Products
3344 N. Torey Pines Ct.
La Jolla, CA 92037
(619) 457-9681
Fax: (619) 457-1184

Cactus Computer, Inc.
1120 Metrocrest Dr., Ste. 103
Carrollton, TX 75006
(214) 416-0525
Fax: (214) 416-7151

California Microwave
985 Almanor Ave.
Sunnyvale, CA 94086
(408) 732-4000
(800) 772-5465
Fax: (408) 732-4244

Castle Rock Computing
20863 Stevens Creek Blvd.
   Suite 530
Cupertino, CA 95014
(408) 867-6492
(800) 331-7667
Fax: (408) 432-0892

Cayman Systems, Inc.
26 Landsdowne St.
Cambridge, MA 02139
(617) 494-1999
(800) 473-4776
Fax: (617) 494-9270

CBIS, Inc.
5875 Peachtree Industrial Blvd.
Bldg 100/170
Norcross, GA 30092
(404) 446-1332
Fax: (404) 446-9164

Cheyenne Software Inc.
55 Bryant Ave.
Roslyn, NY 11576
(516) 484-5110
(800) 243-9462
Fax: (516) 484-3446

Chipcom Corporation
118 Turnpike Rd.
Southborough, MA 01772
(508) 460-8900
(800) 228-9930
Fax: (508) 460-8950

Cisco Systems Inc.
1525 O'Brien Drive
Menlo Park, CA 94025
(415) 326-1941
(800) 553-6387
Fax: (415) 326-1989

Claflin & Clayton, Inc.
203 S.W. Cutoff
Northboro, MA 01532
(508) 393-7979
Fax: (508) 393-8788

Clearpoint Research Corporation
35 Parkwood Drive
Hopkinton, MA 01848
(508) 435-2000
Fax: (508) 435-7530

CMC/Rockwell International
125 Cremona Dr.
Santa Barbara, CA 93117
(805) 968-4262
(800) 262-8023
Fax: (805) 968-6478

Codenoll Technology
1086 N. Broadway
Yonkers, NY 10701
(914) 965-6300
Fax: (914) 965-9811

Codex/Motorola
20 Cabot Blvd.
Mansfield, MA 02048
(508) 261-4000
Fax: (508) 261-7105

Comdisco Systems, Inc.
919 E. Hillsdale Blvd. #300
Foster City, CA 94404
(415) 574-5800
Fax: (415) 358-3601

Comlink, Inc.
44790 S. Grimmer Blvd., Suite 207
Fremont, CA 94538
(510) 490-4690
Fax: (415) 490-4664

Compatible Systems Corporation
P.O. Drawer 17220
Boulder, CO 80308
(303) 444-9532
(800) 356-0283
Fax: (303) 444-9595

COMPAQ Computer Corporation
P.O. Box 692000
Houston, TX 77269
(713) 370-0670
(800) 345-1518
Fax: (713) 374-1740

Computer Logics
31200 Carter St.
Solon, OH 44139
(800) 828-0311
Fax: (216) 349-8620

Computer Network Technology
6500 Wedgwood Rd.
Maple Grove, MN 55369
(612) 550-8000
Fax: (612) 550-8800

Concord Communications Inc.
753 Forest St.
Marlborough, MA 01752
(508) 460-4646
Fax: (508) 481-9772

Concurrent Computer Corporation

One Technology Way
Westford, MA 01886
(508) 692-6200
Fax:(508) 692-7864

Control Data Corporation

4201 N. Lexington Avenue
Arden Hills, MN 55126
(612) 482-3030
Fax: (612) 482-4203

Coral Network Corporation

8 Technology Dr.
Westborough MA 01581
(508) 366-3600
Fax: (508) 870-1777

Corvus Systems

160 Great Oaks Blvd.
San Jose, CA 95119-1347
(408) 281-4100
Fax: (408) 578-4102

Cray Communications Inc.

9020 Junction Dr.
Annapolis, MD 20701
(301) 317-7710
(800) 359-7710
Fax: (301) 317-7220

Cray Research, Inc.

655 Lone Oak Drive
Egan, MN 55121
(612) 683-7100
Fax: (612) 683-7199

Crescendo Communications, Inc.

710 Lakeway Drie, Suite 200
Sunnyvale, CA 94086
(408) 732-4400
Fax: (408) 732-4604

CrossComm Corporation

450 Donald Lynch Blvd.
Marlborough MA 01752
(508) 481-4060
(800) 388-1200
Fax: (508) 490-5535

Crystal Point, Inc.

22122 20th Ave. S.E. #148
Bothell, WA 98021
(206) 487-3656
(800) 982-0628
Fax: (206) 487-3773

CXR/Digilog

900 Business Center Dr. #200
Horsham, PA 19044-3453
(215) 956-9570
(800) 344-4564
Fax: (215) 956-0108

Dalcon Computer Services
1321 Murfreesboro Rd.
Nashville, TN 37217
(615) 366-4300
Fax: (615) 361-3800

Datability, Inc.
One Palmer Terrace
Carlstadt, NJ 07072
(201) 438-2400
Fax: (201) 438-2688

Data General Corporation
4400 Computer Drive
Westboro, MA 01580
(508) 366-8911
(800) 328-2436
Fax: (508) 366-1744

Data Interface Systems, Corp.
8701 N. MoPac Expressway #415
Austin, TX 78759
(512) 346-5641
(800) 351-4244
Fax: (512) 346-4035

Datapoint Corporation
8400 Datapoint Drive
San Antonio, TX 78229-8500
(512) 593-7900
(800) 733-1500
Fax: (512) 593-7472

David Systems Inc.
615 Tasman Dr.
Sunnyvale, CA 94088-3718
(408) 541-6000
(800) 762-7848
Fax: (408) 541-6985

Daystar Digital, Inc.
5556 Atlanta Hwy.
Flowery Branch, GA 30542
(404) 967-2077
(800) 962-2077
Fax: (404) 967-3018

DCA 10Net Communications
7887 Washington Village Drive
  Suite 200
Dayton, OH 45459
(513) 433-2238
(800) 782-1010
Fax: (513) 434-6305

Demax Software Inc.
999 Baker Way, Ste. 500
San Mateo, CA 94404
(415) 341-9017
(800) 283-3629
Fax: (415) 341-5809

Dickens Data Systems

1175 Northmeadow Parkway, Suite 150
Roswell, GA 30076
(404) 475-8860
Fax: (404) 442-7525

Digital Analysis Corporation

1889 Preston White Drive
Reston, VA 22091
(703) 476-5900
Fax: (703) 476-1918

Digital Communications Associates (DCA)

1000 Alderman Dr.
Alpharetta, GA 30201
(404) 442-4000
(800) 348-3221
Fax: (404) 442-4366

Digital Equipment Corporation (DEC)

146 Main St.
Maynard, MA 01754
(508) 493-5111
(800) 344-4825
Fax: (508) 493-8787

Digital Link

217 Humboldt Ct.
Sunnyvale, CA 94089
(408) 745-6200
(800) 441-1142
Fax: (408) 745-6250

Digital Technology

2300 Edwin C. Moses Blvd.
Dayton, OH 45408
(513) 443-0412
(800) 852-1252
Fax: (513) 226-0511

Digitech Industries

55 Kenosha Ave.
Danbury, CT 06813
(203) 797-2676
Fax: (203) 797-2682

Distinct Corporation

P.O. Box 3410
Saratoga, CA 95070
(408) 741-0781
Fax: (408) 741-0795

D-Link Systems

5 Musick
Irvine, CA 92718
(714) 455-1688
Fax: (714) 455-2521

DMA

1776 E. Jericho Tpke.
Huntington, NY 11743
(516) 462-0440
Fax: (516) 462-6652

Dove Computer
1200 N. 23rd St.
Wilmington, NC 28405
(919) 763-7918
(800) 788-3683
Fax: (919) 251-9441

Eicon Technology Corporation
2196 32nd Ave.
Montreal, QUE Canada H8T 3H7
(514) 631-2592
Fax: (514) 631-3092

Emerging Technologies Inc.
900 Walt Whitman Rd.
Melville, NY 11747
(516) 271-4525
Fax: (516) 271-4814

Emerson Computer Power Inc.
9650 Jeronimo Rd.
Irvine, CA 92718
(714) 457-3600
(800) 222-5877
Fax: (714) 457-3788

Empirical Tools & Technologies
517 C Mission Street
Santa Cruz, CA 95060
(408) 427-5280
Fax: (408) 427-5281

Emulex Corporation
3545 Harbor Blvd.
Costa Mesa, CA 92626
(714) 662-5600
Fax: (714) 241-0792

Encore Computer Systems Division
6901 W. Sunrise Blvd.
Plantation, FL 33313
(305) 587-2900
Fax: (305) 797-5793

Eon Systems
19091 Pruneridge Ave.
Cupertino, CA 95014
(800) 752-0900

Epilogue Technology Corporation
11116 Desert Classic Ln. NE
Albuquerque NM 87111
(505) 271-9933
Fax: (505) 271-9798

Equinox Systems
6851 W. Sunrise Blvd.
Plantation, FL 33313
(305) 791-6061
(800) 275-3500
Fax: (305) 253-0003

Essex Systems Inc.
One Central Street
Middleton MA 01949
(508) 750-6200
Fax: (508) 750-4699

Experdata
10301 Toledo Ave. S.
Bloomington, MN 55437
(612) 831-2122
Fax:(612) 835-0700

Fairfield Software Inc.
200 W. Lowe St.
Fairfield, IA 52556
(515) 472-7077
Fax: (515) 472-7198

Falcon Microsystems, Inc
1100 Mercantile Ln.
Landover, MD 20785-5326
(301) 341-0146
Fax: (301) 386-3583

Farallon Computing Inc.
2470 Mariner Sq. Loop
Alameda, CA 94501
(510) 814-5100
Fax: (510) 814-5020

FEL Computing
10 Main Street
P.O. Box 72
Williamsville, VT 05362
(802) 348-7171
(800) 639-4110
Fax: (802) 348-7124

FiberCom Inc.
3353 Orange Ave. N.E.
Roanoke, VA 24012
(703) 342-6700
(800) 423-1183
Fax: (703) 342-5961

Fibermux Corporation
9310 Topanga Canyon Blvd.
Chatsworth, CA 91311
(818) 709-6000
(800) 800-4624
Fax: (818) 709-1556

Fibronics International Inc.
33 Riverside Dr.
Pembroke, MA 02359
(617) 826-0099
(800) 327-9526
Fax: (617) 826-7745

Frederick Engineering Inc.
10200 Old Columbia Road
Columbia, MD 21046
(410) 290-9000
Fax: (410) 381-7180

Frontier Software Development Inc.
1501 Main St., Suite 40
Tewksbury, MA 01876
(508) 851-8872
Fax: (508) 851-6956

Frontier Technologies Inc.
10201 N. Port Washington Rd. 13 West
Mequon, WI 53092
(414) 241-4555
Fax: (414) 241-7084

FTP Software, Inc.
2 High St.
No. Andover, MA 01845
(508) 685-4000
Fax: (508) 794-4477

Gandalf Data Inc.
9 No. Olney Ave.
Cherry Hill, NJ 08083
(609) 424-9400
(800) 426-3253
Fax: (609) 751-4374

Gateway Communications, Inc.
2941 Alton Avenue
Irvine, CA 92714
(714) 553-1555
(800) 367-6555
Fax: (714) 553-1616

General DataCom, Inc.
1579 Straits Turnpike
Middlebury, CT 06762-1299
(203) 574-1118
Fax: (203) 758-8507

Glasgal Communications Inc.
151 Veterans Drive
Northvale, NJ 07647
(201) 768-8082
Fax: (201) 768-2947

Grafpoint Inc.
1485 Saratoga Ave.
San Jose, CA 95129
(408) 446-1919
(800) 426-2230
Fax: (408) 446-0666

Gupta Technologies
1060 Marsh Rd.
Menlo Park, CA 94025
(415) 321-9500
(800) 876-3267
Fax: (415) 321-5471

Halley Systems, Inc.
1590 Oakland Rd.
San Jose, CA 95131
(408) 253-3718
Fax: (408) 441-2199

Harris Computer Systems Division

2101 W. Cypress Creek Road
Fort Lauderdale, FL 33309
(305) 974-1700
(800) 666-4544
Fax: (305) 977-5580

Hayes Microcomputer Products, Inc.

P.O. Box 105203
Atlanta, GA 30348
(404) 840-9200
Fax: (404) 447-0178

Helios Systems

1996 Lundy Avenue
San Jose, CA 95131
(408) 432-0292
Fax: (408) 432-7323

Hewlett-Packard Company

3000 Hanover St.
Palo Alto, CA 94304
(415) 857-1501
(800) 752-0900

Hewlett-Packard

Colorado Telecommunications
   Division
5070 Centennial Blvd.
Colorado Springs, CO 80919
(719) 531-4000
Fax: (719) 531-4505

Hewlett-Packard Business Computing Systems

19091 Pruneridge Ave.
Cupertino, CA 95014
(800) 752-0900

Honeywell Information Systems

Federal Systems Divisions
7900 West Park Drive
McLean, VA 22102
(703) 827-3894
Fax: (703) 827-3729

Hughes LAN Systems Inc.

1225 Charleston Road
Mountain View, CA 94043
(415) 966-7300
(800) 395-5267
Fax: (415) 960-3738

IBM

Old Orchard Road
Armonk, NY 10504
(914) 765-1900
(800) 426-2468
Fax: (800) 232-9426

IDEAssociates Inc.

29 Dunham Road
Billerica, MA 01821
(508) 663-6878
Fax: (508) 663-8851

IMC Networks
16931 Milliken Avenue
Irvine, CA 92714
(714) 724-1070
(800) 624-1070
Fax: (714) 724-1020

Independence Technologies
42705 Lawrence Pl.
Fremont, CA 94538
(510) 438-2000
Fax: (510) 438-2034

Information Presentation Technologies
555 Chorro Street, Suite A
San Luis Obispo, CA 93405
(805) 541-3000
Fax: (805-541-3037

Informix Software, Inc.
16011 College Blvd.
Lenexa, KS 66219
(913) 599-7100
(800) 331-1763
Fax: (913) 599-8590

IN-NET Corporation
15150 Ave. of Science #100
San Diego, CA 92128
(619) 487-3693
(800) 283-3334
Fax: (619) 487-3697

Intel Corporation
2402 W. Beardsley Road
Phoenix, AZ 85027
(602) 869-4647
(800) 538-3373
Fax: (800) 525-3019

Intellicom
20415 Nordhoff St.
Chatsworth, CA 91311
(818) 407-3900
Fax: (818) 882-2404

InterComputer Communication Corp.
8230 Montgomery Rd.
Cincinnati, OH 45236
(513) 745-0500
Fax: (513) 745-0327

InterCon Systems Corporation
950 Herndon Pkwy., Ste. 420
Herndon, VA 22070
(703) 709-9890
Fax: (703) 709-9896

InterConnections Incorporated
14711 N.E. 29th Place
Bellevue, WA 98007
(206) 881-5773
(800) 950-5774
Fax: (206) 867-5022

Interlink Computer Sciences, Inc.
47370 Fremont Blvd.
Fremont, CA 94538
(510) 657-9800
(800) 422-3711
Fax: (510) 659-6381

International Data Sciences
501 Jefferson Blvd.
Warwick, RI 02886
(401) 737-9900
(800) 437-3282
Fax: (401) 737-9911

Interphase
13800 Senlac
Dallas, TX 75234
(214) 919-9000
Fax: (214) 919-9200

Ipswitch, Inc.
580 Main St.
Reading, MA 01867
(617) 942-0621
Fax: (617) 942-0823

Itoshu Technology Inc.
2515 McCabe Way
Irvine, CA 92714
(714) 660-0506
Fax: (714) 757-4423

J & L Information Systems
9238 Deering Avenue
Chatsworth, CA 91311
(818) 709-1778
Fax: (818) 882-1424

Lanera Corporation
516 Valley Way
Milpitas, CA 95035
(408) 956-8344
Fax: (408) 956-8343

Lanmaster
1401 North 14th St.
P.O. Box 845
Temple, TX 76503
(817) 771-2124
Fax: (817) 771-2379

Lannet Data Communications Inc.
7711 Center Ave. #600
Huntington Beach, CA 92647
(714) 891-5580
Fax: (714) 891-7788

Lantronix
26072 Merit Circle, Suite 113
Laguna Hills, CA 92853
(714) 367-0050
Fax: (714) 367-0287

Lanwan Technologies

1566 La Pradera Drive
Campbell, CA 95008
(408) 374-8190
Fax: (408) 741-0152

Larse Corporation

4600 Patrick Henry Drive
P.O. Box 58138
Santa Clara, CA 95052
(408) 988-6600
Fax: (408) 986-8690

Legent Corporation

711 Powell Ave. SW
Renton, WA 98055-1291
(206) 228-8980
Fax: (206) 235-7560

Lexcel

4905 East La Palma Ave.
Anaheim, CA 92807
(714) 970-0300
(800) 925-2623
Fax: (714) 970-5743

Livingston Enterprises, Inc.

6920 Koll Center Pkwy, Suite 220
Pleasanton, CA 94566
(510) 426-0770
Fax: (510) 426-8951

Loral Command & Control

9970 Federal Drive
Colorado Springs, CO 80921
(719) 594-1000
Fax: (719) 594-1305

Luxcom Inc.

3249 Laurelview Ct.
Fremont, CA 94538
(510) 770-3300
Fax: (510) 770-3399

Madge Networks, Inc.

2310 North 1st St.
San Jose, CA 95131
(408) 955-0700
(800) 876-2343
Fax: (408) 955-0970

McData Corporation

310 Interlocken Pkwy.
Broomfield, CO 80021
(303) 460-9200
(800) 752-0388
Fax: (303) 465-4996

MCI Communications Corp.

8003 W. Park Drive
McLean, VA 22102
(800) 888-0800
Fax: (703) 260-7099

Mesa Graphics Inc.
P.O. Box 600
Los Alamos, NM 87544
(505) 672-1998

Micom Systems, Inc.
4100 Los Angeles Ave.
Simi Valley, CA 93063
(805) 583-8600
(800) 642-6687
Fax: (805) 583-1997

Microcom, Inc.
500 River Ridge Drive
Norwood, MA 02062-5028
(617) 551-1000
(800) 822-8224
Fax: (617) 551-1006

Micro Decisionware
2995 Wilderness Pl.
Boulder, CO 80301
(303) 443-2706
(800) 423-8737
Fax: (303) 443-2797

Micro Integration
215 Paca Street
Cumberland, MD 21502
(301) 777-3307
(800) 832-4526
Fax: (301) 777-3462

Microsoft Corporation
One Microsoft Way
Redmond, WA 98052-6399
(206) 882-8080
(800) 227-4679
Fax: (206) 635-6100

Micro Technology
4905 E. La Palma Ave.
Anaheim, CA 92807
(714) 970-0300
(800) 999-9684
Fax: (714) 970-5413

Micro Tempus Corporation
440 Rene-Levesque West
   Suite 1700
Montreal Quebec Canada H22 1V7
(617) 899-4046
Fax: (514) 397-9465

Microtest, Inc.
4747 No. 22nd St.
Phoenix, AZ 85016
(602) 952-6400
(800) 526-9675
Fax: (602) 952-6401

Miramar Systems
201 N. Salsipuedes St. #204
Santa Barbara, CA 93103
(805) 966-2432
Fax: (805) 965-1824

The Mitre Corporation
7525 Colshire Drive
McLean, VA 22102
(703) 883-6728
Fax: (703) 883-3315

Mitsubishi
201 Broadway
Cambridge, MA 02139
(617) 621-7500
Fax: (617) 621-7550

Momentum Software Corp.
401 S. Van Brunt St.
Englewood, NJ 07631
(800) 767-1462
(201) 871-0077
Fax: (201) 871-0807

Morning Star Technologies, Inc.
1760 Zollinger Road
Columbus, OH 43221
(614) 451-1883
Fax: (614) 459-5054

Motorola Codex
20 Cabot Blvd.
Mansfield, MA 02048
(508) 261-4000
(800) 544-0062
Fax: (508) 261-7118

Mt. Xinu, Inc.
2560 9th Street, Suite 312
Berkeley, CA 94710
(510) 644-0146
Fax: (510) 644-2680

Multi-Tech Systems
2205 Woodale Dr.
Mounds View, MN 55112
(612) 785-3500
(800) 328-9717
Fax: (612) 785-9874

Mux Lab
165 Graveline Rd.
St. Laurent, Quebec H4T 1R3
CANADA
(514) 735-2741
(800) 361-1965
Fax: (514) 735-8057

National Semiconductor
2900 Semiconductor Dr. 16-195 M/S
Santa Clara, CA 95052
(408) 721-5020
(800) 538-8510
Fax:(408) 721-7662

NCR Comten
2700 Snelling Ave N.
St. Paul, MN 55113
(612) 638-7777
Fax: (612) 638-8573

NCR Corporation
1700 S. Patterson Blvd.
Dayton, OH 45479
(513) 445-5000
(800) 225-5627
Fax: (513) 445-1847

NCR Corporation
3245 Platte Springs Road
W. Columbia, SC 29170
(803) 796-9740
Fax: (803) 739-7745

NEC America
1525 Walnut Hill Ln.
Irving, TX 75038
(214) 518-5000
(800) 222-4632
Fax: (214) 518-5572

Neon Software, Inc.
3685 Mt.Diablo Blvd. Suite 203
Lafayette, CA 94549
(510) 283-9771
Fax: (510) 283-6507

NetFrame Systems
1545 Barber Lane
Milpitas, CA 95035
(408) 944-0600
(800) 852-3726
Fax: (408) 434-4190

NetLabs Inc.
4920 El Camino Real
Los Altos, CA 94022
(415) 961-9500
(800) 447-9300
Fax: (415) 961-9300

Netlink
3214 Spring Forest Road
Raleigh, NC 27604
((919) 878-8612
(800) 638-5465
Fax: (919) 872-2132

NetManage, Inc.
20823 Stevens Creek Blvd. #100
Cupertino, CA 95014
(408) 973-7171
Fax: (408) 257-6405

Netwise
2477 55th St.
Boulder, CO 80301
(303) 442-8280
(800) 733-7722
Fax: (303) 442-3798

Network Application Technology Inc.
1686 Dell Ave.
Campbell, CA 95008
(408) 370-4300
(800) 543-8887
Fax: (408) 370-4222

Network Computing Inc.
1950 Stemmons Freeway Suite 3016
Dallas, TX 75027
(214) 746-4949
(800) 736-3012
Fax: (214) 746-4955

Network Equipment Technologies Inc.
800 Saginaw Dr.
Redwood City, CA 94063
(415) 366-4400
(800) 234-4638
Fax: (415) 366-5675

Network General
4200 Bohannon Drive
Menlo Park, CA 94025
(415) 473-2000
(800) 395-3151
Fax: (415) 321-0855

Network Integrators Assoc.
6007 Meridian Ave.
San Jose, CA 95120
(408) 927-0412
Fax: (408) 927-0412

Network Managers
73 Princeton St. Suite 305
N. Chelmsford, MA 01863
(508) 251-4111
(800) 821-5466
Fax: (508) 251-8562

Network Monitoring Inc.
46750 Fremont Blvd. Suite 108
Fremont, CA 94538
(510) 770-9390
Fax: (510) 770-9213

Network Peripherals, Inc.
1371 McCarthy Blvd.
Milpitas, CA 95035
(408) 321-7300
Fax: (408) 321-9218

Network Research Corp.
4000 Via Pescador
Camarillo, CA 93012
(805) 484-2128
Fax: (805) 484-3929

Network Resources Corp. (NRC)
61 E. Daggett Dr.
San Jose, CA 95134
(408) 383-9300
Fax: (408) 383-0136

Network Systems Corporation
7600 Boone Ave. N.
Minneapolis, MN 55428
(612) 424-4888
(800) 248-8777
Fax: (612) 424-1661

Networth, Inc.
8404 Esters Blvd.
Irving, TX 75063
(214) 929-1700
(800) 544-5255
Fax: (214) 929-1720

Newbridge Networks
593 Herndon Pkwy.
Herndon, VA 22070-5241
(703) 834-3600
(800) 332-1080
Fax: (703) 471-7080

Newport Systems Solutions, Inc.
4019 Westerly Pl., Suite 103
Newport Beach, CA 92660
(714) 752-1511
(800) 368-6533
Fax: (714) 752-8389

Novell, Inc.
122 East 1700 South
Provo, UT 84606
(801) 429-7000
(800) 638-9273
Fax: (801) 429-5155

Novell, Inc.
2180 Fortune Drive
San Jose, CA 95131
(408) 473-8333
(800) 243-8526
Fax: (408) 435-1706

Novell Desktop Product Group
70 Garden Ct.
Monterey, CA 93940
(408) 649-3896
(800) 274-4374
Fax: (408) 646-6248

Nynex Information Solutions Group Inc.
Four W. Red Oak Lane
White Plains, NY 10604
(914) 644-6000
Fax: (914) 694-2609

Objective Systems Integrators
1002 River Rock Dr. Suite 221
Folsom, CA 95630
(916) 989-7340
Fax: (916) 989-7363

OpenConnect Systems Inc.
2711 LBJ Freeway Suite 800
Dallas, TX 75234
(214) 484-5200
Fax: (214) 484-6100

Optical Data Systems (ODS)
1101 E. Arapaho Road
Richardson, TX 75081
(214) 234-6400
Fax: (214) 234-4059

Oracle Corp.
500 Oracle Pkwy.
Redwood Shores, CA 94065
(415) 506-7000
(800) 392-2999
Fax: (415) 506-7255

Pacer Software Inc.
7911 Herschel Ave. #402
La Jolla, CA 92037
(619) 454-0565
Fax: (619) 454-6267

Panda Programming
6158 Lariat Loop NE
Bainbridge Island, WA 98110
(206) 842-6506

Paramax Defense Systems/ Division of Unisys
5151 Camino Ruiz
Camarillo, CA 93011
(805) 987-6811
Fax: (805) 388-7790

Penril DataComm Networks
1300 Quince Orchard Blvd.
Gaithersburg, MD 20878
(301) 921-8600
(800) 473-6745
Fax: (301) 921-8376

Performance Technology
7800 IH-10 West, Ste. 800
San Antonio, TX 78230
(210) 349-2000
(800) 327-8526
Fax: (210) 366-0123

Persoft Inc.
465 Science Dr.
Madison, WI 53711
(608) 273-6000
(800) 368-5283
Fax: (608) 273-8227

Plexcom
2255 Agate Ct.
Simi Valley, CA 93065
(805) 522-3333
Fax: (805) 583-4764

Process Software Corporation
959 Concord Street
Framingham, MA 01701
(508) 879-6994
Fax: (508) 879-0042

Proteon, Inc.
2 Technology Drive
Westborough, MA 01581
(508) 898-2800
(800) 545-7464
Fax: (508) 366-8901

ProTools Inc.
14976 N.W. Greenbrier Pkwy.
Beaverton, OR 97006
(503) 645-5400
(800) 743-4335
Fax: (503) 645-3577

PSI
165 Jordan Road
Troy, NY 12180
(518) 283-8860
Fax: (518) 283-8904

PureData
180 W. Beaver Creek Rd.
Richmond Hill, Ontario L4B 1B4
CANADA
(416) 731-6444
Fax: (416) 731-7017

Pyramid Technology Corporation
3860 No. 1st St.
San Jose, CA 95134
(408) 428-9000
Fax: (408) 327-5691

QMS Corporation
2650 San Tomas Expressway
Santa Clara, CA 95051
(408) 986-9400
Fax: (408) 727-3725

Rabbit Software Corp.
7 Great Valley Pkwy. E.
East Malvern, PA 19355
(215) 647-0440
(800) 722-2482
Fax: (215) 640-1379

Racal-Datacom, Inc.
155 Swanson Road
Boxborough, MA 01719
(508) 263-9929
(800) 526-8255
Fax: (508) 263-8655

Racal Data Communications
1601 N. Harrison Pkwy.
Sunrise, FL 33323-2899
(305) 846-1601
(800) 722-2555
Fax: (305) 846-5510

Racore Computer Products
170 Knowles Dr. #204
Los Gatos, CA 95030
(408) 374-8290
(800) 635-1274
Fax: (408) 374-6653

RAD Data Communications Inc.
900 Corporate Dr.
Mahwah, NJ 07430
(201) 529-1100
Fax: (201) 529-5777

RAD Network Devices Inc.
7711 Center Ave., Suite 270
Huntington Beach, CA 92647
(714) 891-1446
Fax: (714) 891-1764

Remedy Corp.
1965 Landings Dr.
Mountain View, CA 94043
(415) 903-5200
Fax: (415) 903-9001

Republic Telcom Systems Corp.
6150 Lookout Road
Boulder, CO 80301
(303) 530-8600
(800) 621-0236
Fax: (303) 530-8625

Research Triangle Institute
3040 Cornwallis Road
Research Triangle Park, NC 27709-2194
(919) 541-6000
Fax: (919) 541-5985

Retix
2401 Colorado Ave. Suite 200
Santa Monica, CA 90404
(310) 828-3400
(800) 255-2333
Fax: (310) 828-2255

RFI Communications & Security
360 Turtle Creek Court
San Jose, CA 95125-1389
(408) 298-5400
Fax: (408) 275-0156

RTMX-Uniflex
800 Eastowne Dr., Suite 111
Chapel Hill, NC 27514
(919) 493-1451
Fax: (919) 490) 2903

SAIC
170 Knowles Dr.
Los Gatos, CA 95030
(408) 374-2500
Fax: (408) 374-1680

Samsung Software America
One Corporate Drive
Andover, MA 01810
(508) 685-7200
Fax: (508) 685-4940

The Santa Cruz Operation
400 Encinal Street P.O. Box 1900
Santa Cruz, CA 95061-1900
(408) 425-7222
Fax: (408) 458-4227

SBE, Inc.
4550 No. Canyon Rd.
San Ramon, CA 94583
(510) 355-2000
(800) 925-2666
Fax: (510) 355-2020

SCI Systems
1300 S. Memorial Parkway
Huntsville, AL 35803
(205) 882-4304
Fax: (205) 882-4305 or 4871

SCOPE Incorporated
1860 Michael Faraday Drive
Reston, VA 22090
(703) 471-5600
Fax: (703) 471-1715

Shany
2680 Bayshore Parkway Suite 104
Mountain View, CA 94043
(415) 694-7410
Fax: (415) 694-4728

Shiva Corporation
One Cambridge Center
Cambridge, MA 02142
(617) 252-6300
(800) 458-3550
Fax: (617) 252-6852

Siemens Stromberg-Carlson
900 Broken Sound Pkwy.
Boca Raton, FL 33487
(407) 955-6144
Fax: (407) 955-6538

Silicon Graphics Inc
2011 N. Shoreline Blvd.
Mountain View, CA 94043
(415) 960-1980
(800) 326-1020
Fax: (415) 961-0595

Simpact Associates, Inc.
9210 Sky Park Court
San Diego, CA 92123
(619) 565-1865
(800) 275-1860
Fax: (619) 292-8015

Simware Inc.
2 Gurdwara Rd.
Ottawa, Ontario K2E 1A2
(613) 727-1779
(800) 267-7588 or 9991
Fax: (613) 727-8797

Sirius Systems, Inc.
Box 2202
Petersburg, VA 23804
(804) 733-7944
Fax: (804) 861-0358

SMC Mass Inc.
25 Walkers Brook Dr.
Reading, MA 01867
(617) 942-0200
(800) 647-4462
Fax: (617) 942-0825

Smith Micro Software
51 Columbia
Eliso Viejo, CA 92656
(714) 362-5800
(714) 362-2300

SNMP Research
3001 Kimberlin Heights Road
Knoxville, TN 37920
(615) 573-1434
Fax: (615) 573-9197

Softronics
5085 List Drive
Colorado Springs, CO 80919
(719) 593-9540
(800) 225-8590
Fax: (719) 548-1878

SoftSwitch Inc.
640 Lee Rd. #200
Wayne, PA 19087
(215) 640-9600
Fax: (215) 640-7550

Software AG of North America, Inc.
11190 Sunrise Valley Drive
Reston, VA 22091
(703) 860-5050
Fax: (703) 391-6975

Software Kinetics Ltd.
65 Iber Road
Stittsville, Ontario, Canada K2S 1E7
(613) 831-0888
Fax: (613) 831-1836

SONY Corporation
677 River Oaks Parkway
San Jose, CA 95134
(408) 432-1600
Fax: (408) 432-1874
Fax: 81-3-3448-7461

Standard Microsystems Corp. (SMC)
35 Marcus Blvd.
Hauppauge, NY 11788
(516) 273-3100
(800) 992-4762
Fax: (516) 273-7935

StarNine Technologies

2550 9th St Suite 112
Berkeley, CA 94710
(510) 548-0391
Fax: (510) 548-0393

Star Tek Inc.

71 Lyman St.
Northborough, MA 01532
(508) 393-9393
(800) 225-8528
Fax: (508) 393-6934

Sun Microsystems Inc.

2550 Garcia Ave.
Mountain View, CA 94043-1100
(415) 960-1300
(800) 872-4786
Fax: (415) 856-2114

SunSelect

2060 Challenger Dr.
Alameda, CA 94501
(510) 769-9669
(800) 445-8677
Fax: (510) 769-8773

Sybase Inc.

6475 Christie Ave.
Emeryville, CA 94608
(510) 596-3500
Fax: (510) 658-9441

Synergy Software

2457 Perkiomen Ave.
Reading, PA 19606
(215) 779-0522
Fax: (215) 370-0548

Synernetics Inc.

85 Rangeway Rd.
North Billerica, MA 01862
(508) 670-9009
(800) 992-2446
Fax: (508) 670-9015

SynOptics Communications, Inc.

P.O. Box 58185
4401 Great America Pkwy.
Santa Clara, CA 95052-8185
(408) 988-2400
Fax: (408) 988-5525

Syntax, Inc.

840 So. 333rd St.
Federal Way, WA 98003
(206) 833-2525
Fax: (206) 838-9836

Syskonnect Inc.

12930 Saratoga Ave. Suite D-1
Saratoga, CA 95070
(408) 725-4650
(800) 752-3334
Fax: (408) 725-4654

Systems Center Inc.
1800 Alexander Bell Dr.
Reston, VA 22091
(703) 264-8000
(800) 533-5128
Fax: (703) 264-1308

T3plus Networking Inc.
2840 San Tomas Expressway
Santa Clara, CA 95051
(408) 727-4545
(800) 477-7050
Fax: (408) 727-4545

Tandem Computers, Inc.
14231 Tandem Blvd.
Austin, TX 78728-6699
(512) 244-8359
Fax: (512) 244-8037

Tangent Computer Inc.
197 Airport Blvd.
Burlingame, CA 94010
(800) 800-6060
Fax: (415) 342-9388

Technically Elite Concepts Inc.
2615 Pacific Coast Highway #322
Hermosa Beach, CA 90254
(310) 379-2505
(800) 659-6975
Fax: (310) 379-5985

Tecmar
6225 Cochran Road
Solon, OH 44139-3377
(216) 349-0600
(800) 624-8560
Fax: (216) 349-0851

Technology Exchange Company
One Jacob Way
Reading, MA 01867
(800) 333-5177
Fax: (617) 944-3700

Tekelec
26580 W. Agoura Rd.
Calabasas, CA 91302
(818) 880-5656
(800) 835-3532
Fax: (818) 880-6993

TEKnique
911 N. Plum Grove Road
Schaumburg, IL 60173
(708) 706-9700
Fax: (708) 706-9735

Tektronix, Inc.
625 SE Salmon
Redmond, OR 97756
(503) 923-0333
(800) 833-9200
Fax: (503) 923-4434

Telco Systems Inc./Magnalink Communications

63 Nahatan St.
Norwood, MA 02062
(617) 255-9400
Fax: (617) 255-5885

Telebit Corporation

1315 Chesapeake Terrace
Sunnyvale, CA 94089
(408) 734-4333
(800) 835-3248
Fax: (408) 734-4333

Telecommunications Techniques Corp.

20400 Observation Dr.
Germantown, MD 20874
(301) 353-1550
(800) 638-2049
Fax: (301) 353-0731

Telematics International, Inc.

1201 Cypress Creek Road
Ft. Lauderdale, FL 33309
(305) 772-3070
Fax: (305) 351-4405

Tenon Intersystems

1123 Chapala Street Suite 202
Santa Barbara, CA 93101
(805) 963-6983
Fax: (805) 962-8202

TGV, Inc.

603 Mission Street
Santa Cruz, CA 95060
(408) 427-4366
(800) 848-3440
Fax: (408) 427-4365

Themis Computer

6681 Owens Drive
Pleasanton, CA 94588
(510) 734-0870
Fax: (510) 734-0873

Thomas-Conrad Corporation

1908-R Kramer Ln.
Austin, TX 78758
(512) 836-1935
(800) 332-8683
Fax: (512) 836-2840

3Com Corporation

5400 Bayfront Plaza
Santa Clara, CA 95052
(408) 562-6400
(800) 638-3266
Fax: (408) 764-5001

Tiara Computer Systems

1091 Shoreline Blvd.
Mountain View, CA 94043
(415) 965-1700
(800) 638-4272
Fax: (415) 965-2677

Tri-Data Systems, Inc.
3270 Scott Blvd.
Santa Clara, CA 94054
(408) 727-3270
(800) 874-3282
Fax: (408) 980-6565

Triticom
11800 Single Tree Ln. Suite 310
Eden Prairie, MN 55344
(612) 937-0772
Fax: (612) 937-1998

TRW Inc.
1760 Glenn Curtiss St.
Carson, CA 90746
(310) 764-9467
Fax: (213) 764-9491

UDS Motorola, Inc.
5000 Bradford Drive
Huntsville, AL 35805-1993
(205) 430-8000
(800) 451-2369
Fax: (205) 430-7265

Ultra Network Technologies
101 Daggett Drive
San Jose, CA 95134
(408) 922-0100
Fax: (408) 433-9287

Ungermann-Bass, Inc.
3990 Freedom Circle
Santa Clara, CA 95052-8030
(408) 496-0111
(800) 873-6381
Fax: (408) 727-4456

UniSoft Systems
6121 Hollis Street
Emeryville, CA 94608-2092
(510) 420-6400
Fax: (510) 420-6499

Unisys
Township Line and Union Mtg. Rd.
Blue Bell, PA 19422
(215) 986-4011
Fax: (215) 986-6850

UNIX Systems Laboratories, Inc.
190 River Road
Summit, NJ 07901
(908) 522-5006
Fax: (908) 522-5463

U.S. Robotics Software
8100 N. McCormick Blvd.
Skokie, IL 60076-2920
(504) 923-0888
(800) 292-2988

UUNET Technologies/AlterNet
3110 Fairview Park Dr., #570
Falls Church, VA 22042
(703) 204-8000
Fax: (703) 204-8001

Verilink Corp.
145 Baytech Drive
San Jose, CA 95134
(408) 945-1199
(800) 543-1008
Fax: (408) 946-5124

VisiSoft
2700 Northeast Expressway B-700
Atlanta, GA 30345
(404) 320 0077
Fax: (404) 320-0450

Vitalink Communications Corp.
48761 Kato Rd.
Fremont, CA 94538
(510) 226-6500
(800) 443-5740
Fax: (510) 440-2380

Walker Richer and Quinn, Inc.
2815 Eastlake Ave. E.
Seattle, WA 98102
(206) 324-0407
(800) 872-2829
Fax: (206) 322-8151

Wall Data, Inc.
17769 NE 78th Place
Redmond, WA 98052-4992
(206) 883-4777
(800) 487-8622
Fax: (206) 861-3175

Wandel and Goltermann
2200 Gateway Centre Blvd.
Morrisville, NC 27560
(919) 460-3300
(800) 346-6332
Fax: (919) 481-4372

Wang Laboratories
1 Industrial Ave.
Lowell, MA 01851
(508) 459-5000
(800) 225-0654
Fax: (508) 967-7020

Webster Computer Corporation
2109 O'Toole Ave., Ste. J
San Jose, CA 95131
(408) 954-8054
(800) 457-0903
Fax: (408) 954-1832

WellFleet Communications Corp.
8 Federal St.
Billerica, MA 01821
(508) 670-8888
Fax: (508) 436-3658

White Pine Software, Inc.
40 Simon St., Ste. 201
Nashua, NH 03060
(603) 886-9050
Fax: (603) 886-9051

Wilcom Products
Rt. 3 Daniel Webster Hwy.
Laconia, NH 03246
(603) 524-2622
Fax: (603) 528-3804

Wingra Software Inc.
450 Science Dr. 1 West
Madison, WI 53711
(608) 238-8637
Fax: (608) 238-8986

The Wollongong Group, Inc.
1129 San Antonio Road
Palo Alto, CA 94303
(415) 962-7100
(800) 872-8649
Fax: (415) 969-5547

Xerox Corporation
100 Clinton Ave. S.,
Rochester, NY 14644
(716) 423-5090
Fax: (716) 423-5733

Xinetron Inc.
2302 Walsh Ave..
Santa Clara, CA 95051
(408) 727-5509
(800) 345-4415
Fax: (408) 727-6499

Xircom
26025 Mureau Road
Calabasas, CA 91302
(800) 874-7875
(818) 878-7600
Fax: (818) 878-7630

Xylogics
53 Third Ave.
Burlington, MA 01803
(617) 272-8142
(800) 225-3317
Fax: (617) 273-5392

Xyplex, Inc.
330 Codman Hill Rd.
Boxborough, MA 01719
(508) 264-9900
(800) 338-5316
Fax: (508) 264-9930

Zenith Electronics Corporation
Communication Products Division
1000 Milwaukee Avenue
Glenview, IL 60025
(708) 391-8000
(800) 788-7244
Fax: (708) 391-8919

Appendix D: Obtaining Internet Information

The Network Information Center (NIC) is the central repository of Internet information. Publications include Request for Comments (RFC) documents, FYI documents, the *DDN Protocol Implementations and Vendors Guide,* the *DDN Protocol Handbook,* and others. The NIC's address is

> DDN Network Information Center
> Government Systems, Inc.
> 14200 Park Meadow Drive
> Suite 200
> Chantilly, VA 22021
> (703) 802-4535
> (800) 365-3642
> Fax: (703) 802-8376
> Internet: 192.112.36.5 (NIC.DDN.MIL)

Obtaining RFCs

You can obtain hard copies of RFCs from the NIC for a small fee. You can also obtain them online via the Internet. To do so, use FTP to log in to NIC.DDN.MIL with name = anonymous and password = guest. The RFCs are located in subdirectory RFC, file name RFC*nnnn*.TXT or RFC*nnnn*.PS, where *nnnn* represents the RFC number (i.e., RFC1175). Both ASCII (TXT suffix) and PostScript (PS suffix) files are available. FYI documents may be obtained in a similar manner. The subdirectory is FYI, and the file names are FYI*nn*.TXT or FYI*nn*.PS.

Other repositories of RFCs are also available. These include:

- FTP.NISC.SRI.COM (directory RFC, file name RFC*nnnn*.TXT or RFC*nnnn*.PS)

- NIS.NSF.NET (directory RFC, file name RFC*nnnn*.TXT-1)

- VENERA.ISI.EDU (directory in-notes, file name RFC*nnnn*.TXT or RFC*nnnn*.PS)

Note that some systems require leading zeros in the RFC number. In other words, if RFC868.TXT does not work, try RFC0868.TXT.

A second method of obtaining RFCs is to use electronic mail. (The following is an excerpt from the HELP file, which can be obtained via the Internet using this method.) This automated mail service is provided by the DDN Network Information Center. It allows access to NIC documents and information via ordinary electronic mail. The automated mail service is especially useful for people who do not have access to the NIC via a direct Internet link, such as BITNET, CSNET, and UUCP sites.

To use the mail service, send a mail message to SERVICE@NIC.DDN.MIL. In the SUBJECT field, request the type of service you wish. You may add any needed arguments. The message body is normally ignored. However, if the SUBJECT field is empty, the first line of the message body will be used as the request. Large files will be broken into smaller, separate messages. However, a few files are too large to be sent through the mail system. Requests are processed automatically once a day.

The following services are currently available:

Service	Description
HELP	A list of current services.
HOST *xxx*	Returns information about host *xxx*.

WHOIS xxx	Used to get more details about a host.
IEN nnn	nn is the IEN number or the word INDEX.
IETF xxx	xx is a file name.
INDEX	Returns the master list of available index files.
INTERNET-DRAFTS xxx	xxx is a file name.
NETINFO xxx	xxx is a file name or the word INDEX.
RFC nnn	nnn is the RFC number or the word INDEX.
RFC nnn.PS	Used to retrieve an available Postcript RFC. Check RFC INDEX for the form of the RFC.
FYI nnn	nnn is the FYI number or the word INDEX.
FYI nnn.PS	Used to retrieve PostScript versions of FYI files.
SEND xxx	xxx is a fully specified file name.
WHOIS xxx	Returns information about xxx from the WHOIS service. Use WHOIS HELP for information on how to use WHOIS.

Some example SUBJECT lines are:

```
HELP
RFC 822
RFC INDEX
RFC 1119.PS
FYI 1
IETF 1IETF-DESCRIPTION.TXT
INTERNET-DRAFTS 1ID-ABSTRACTS.TXT
NETINFO DOMAIN-TEMPLATE.TXT
SEND RFC: RFC-BY-AUTHOR.TXT
SEND IETF/1WG-SUMMARY.TXT
SEND INTERNET-DRAFTS/DRAFT-IETF-NETDATA-NETDATA-00.TXT
HOST DIIS
WHOIS KOSTERS, MARK
```

Send comments or suggestions to SUGGESTIONS@NIC.DDN.MIL. Send questions and bug reports to BUG-SERVICE@NIC.DDN.MIL.

Note that a space is required between the document type and the document number. In other words, RFC 1187 will work, but RFC1187 will not work.

The RFC-Info Service

A new service to assist users with Internet information was announced in the March 1992 issue of *ConneXions, the Interoperability Report*. Following is the text detailing the new service, which was obtained by using Help:Help, which is described below.

RFC-Info is an electronic mail-based service for locating and retrieving RFCs and FYIs. Users can ask for "lists" of all RFCs and FYIs that have certain attributes, or "filters," such as IDs, keywords, titles, authors, issuing organizations, and dates. Once an RFC is uniquely identified (e.g., by its RFC number) it may also be retrieved.

To use the service, send e-mail to RFC-INFO@ISI.EDU with your requests in the body of the message. Feel free to put anything in the SUBJECT because the system ignores it. (All is case-independent, obviously.)

To get started, you may send a message to RFC-INFO@ISI.EDU with a request or requests. Following are some examples of requests. The right-hand column explains what the requests are.

Request	Explanation
Help: Help	Gets help information.
List: FYI	List the FYI notes.
List: RFC keywords: window	Lists RFCs with window as the keyword or in the title.

List: FYI keywords: window	Lists FYIs about windows.
List: * keywords: window	Lists both RFCs and FYIs about windows.
List: RFC title: ARPA*NET	Lists RFCs about ARPANET, ARPA NETWORK, etc.

List: RFC
   organization: MITRE
   dated-after: Jul-01-1991
   dated-before: Aug-31-1991
	Lists RFCs issued by MITRE, dated 7 and 8/1991.

List: RFC obsoletes: RFC0010	Lists RFCs obsoleting a given RFC.
List: RFC Author: Bracken*	Lists RFCs by authors starting with Bracken. The asterisk is a wildcard that matches everything.

List: RFC
   Authors: J. Postel
   Authors: R. Gillman
	Lists RFCs by both Postel and Gillman. Note: the "filters" are ANDed.

List: RFC Authors: Crocker	Lists RFCs by any Crocker.
List: RFC Authors: S.D. Crocker	Lists only RFCs by S.D. Crocker.
List: RFC Authors: D. Crocker	Lists only RFCs by D. Crocker.
Retrieve: RFC Doc-ID: RFC0822	Retrieve RFC-822. Note: there are always four digits in an RFC number.
Help: Manual	Retrieves the long user manual, which is over 30 pages long.
Help: List	This is a LIST request.

399

Help: Retrieve	Shows how to use the RETRIEVE request.
Help: Topics	Lists topics for which help is available.
Help: Dates	Dates is an example of a topic for which help is available.
List: keywords	This lists the keywords in use.
List: organizations	Lists the organizations known to the system.

Please try using this service. Report problems to RFC-MANAGER@ISI.EDU.

Internet Mailing Lists

A number of mailing lists are maintained on the Internet for the purposes of soliciting information and discussions on specific subjects. In addition, a number of Internet Engineering Task Force (IETF) working groups maintain a list for the exchange of information that is specific to their group.

For example, the IETF maintains two lists, the IETF General Discussion list and the IETF Announcement list. To join the IETF Announcement list, send a request to

  ietf-announce-request@cnri.reston.va.us

To join the IETF General Discussion, send a request to

  ietf-request@cnri.reston.va.us

A number of other mailing lists are available. An up-to-date tabulation of lists that address network management topics can be found in each issue of *The Simple Times* (see later in this Appendix). To join a mailing list, send a message to the associated request list

  listname-request@*listhost*

(See the example for the IETF lists given above.)

Following are some mailing lists and their e-mail addresses:

Mailing List Subject	E-Mail Address
SNMP General Discussion	snmp@psi.com
SNMPv2 Working Group	snmp2@thumper.bellcore.com
SNMP Security Working Group	snmp-sec-dev@tis.com
Bridge MIB Working Group	bridge-mib@decwrl.dec.com
Ethernet MIB Working Group	enet_mib@ftp.com
FDDI MIB Working Group	fddi-mib@cs.utk.edu
Host MIB Working Group	hostmib@andrew.cmu.edu
UPS MIB Working Group	ups-mib@cs.utk.edu

Magazines and Journals

The Simple Times is a bimonthly newsletter that details various topics relevant to SNMP. It is freely distributed in electronic form via the Internet, and is also available in hard copy form through various SNMP-related vendors. The electronic version is available in PostScript, MIME (Multimedia Internet Mail Extension), and Richtext, a page description language. For further information, send a message to

st-subscriptions@simple-times.org

with the word *help* in the subject line. For additional information, contact

The Simple Times
c/o Dover Beach Consulting
420 Whisman Court
Mountain View, CA 94043-2186
(415) 968-1052
Fax: (415) 968-2510
Internet: st-editorial@simple-times.org

As a final note, announcements of new RFCs and other Internet-related technical issues are published in *ConneXions, the Interoperability Report*. Subscriptions to *ConneXions* may be obtained from

> Interop, Inc.
> 480 San Antonio Road
> Suite 100
> Mountain View, CA 94040
> (415) 941-3399
> (800) 468-3767
> Fax: (415) 949-1779
> Internet: connexions@interop.com

Appendix E: Network Management RFCs

RFC	Subject	Date
1052	IAB Recommendations for the Development of Internet Network Management Standards	April 1988
1089	SNMP Over Ethernet	February 1989
1109	Report of the Second Ad Hoc Network Management Review Group	August 1989
1147	FYI on a Network Management Tool Catalog	April 1990
1155	Structure and Identification of Management Information for TCP/IP-Based Internets	May 1990
1156	Management Information Base—MIB I (Historical)	May 1990
1157	Simple Network Management Protocol (SNMP) of TCP/IP-Based Internets: MIB-II	May 1990
1187	Bulk Table Retrieval with the SNMP	October 1990
1189	Common Management Information Services and Protocols for the Internet (CMOT and CMIP)	October 1990
1212	Concise MIB Definitions	March 1991

1213	Management Information Base—MIB II	March 1991
1214	OSI Internet Management—MIB (Historical)	April 1991
1215	Convention for Defining Traps for Use with SNMP	March 1991
1224	Managing Asychronously-Generated Alerts	May 1991
1227	SNMP MUX Protocol and MIB	May 1991
1228	SNMP-DPI:SNMP Distributed Program Interface	May 1991
1229	Extensions to the Generic Interface MIB	May 1991
1230	IEEE 802.4 Token Bus Interface Type MIB	May 1991
1231	IEEE 802.5 Token Ring Interface Type MIB	May 1991
1238	CLNS MIB	June 1991
1239	Reassignment of Experimental MIBs to Standard MIBs	June 1991
1243	AppleTalk MIB	July 1991
1253	OSPF Version 2 MIB	August 1991
1269	BGP Version 3 MIB	October 1991
1270	SNMP Communications Services	October 1991
1271	Remote Network Monitoring MIB	November 1991

1285	FDDI MIB	January 1992
1286	Bridge MIB	December 1991
1289	DECnet Phase IV MIB	December 1991
1303	A Convention for Describing SNMP-Based Agents	February 1992
1304	SMDS Interface Protocol (SIP) MIB	February 1992
1315	Frame Relay DTE Interface Type MIB	April 1992
1316	Character Device MIB	April 1992
1317	RS-232 Interface Type MIB	April 1992
1318	Parallel Printer Interface Type MIB	April 1992
1321	MD5 Message Digest Algorithm	April 1992
1351	SNMP Administrative Model *(Historic)*	July 1992
1352	SNMP Security Protocols *(Historic)*	July 1992
1353	SNMP Party MIB *(Historic)*	July 1992
1354	IP Forwarding Table MIB	July 1992
1368	IEEE 802.3 Repeater MIB	October 1992
1381	SNMP MIB Extension for X.25 LAPB	November 1992
1382	SNMP MIB Extension for the X.25 Packet Layer	November 1992

1389	RIP Version 2 MIB Extensions	January 1993
1398	Ethernet-like Interface Type MIB	January 1993
1406	DS1/E1 Interface MIB	January 1993
1407	DS3/E3 Interface Type MIB	January 1993
1414	Identification MIB	January 1993
1418	SNMP over OSI	February 1993
1419	SNMP over AppleTalk	February 1993
1420	SNMP over IPX	February 1993
1441	Introduction to SNMPv2	April 1993
1442	Structure of Management Information for SNMPv2	April 1993
1443	Textual Conventions for SNMPv2	April 1993
1444	Conformance Statements for SNMPv2	April 1993
1445	Administrative Model for SNMPv2	April 1993
1446	Security Protocols for SNMPv2	April 1993
1447	Party MIB for SNMPv2	April 1993
1448	Protocol Operations for SNMPv2	April 1993
1449	Transport Mappings for SNMPv2	April 1993

Appendix F: Network Management Parameters from RFC 1340

The "Assigned Numbers" document, currently RFC 1340, contains a number of network management parameters. This Appendix is an excerpt from that document.

For the management of hosts and gateways (routers) on the Internet, a data structure for the information has been defined. The data structure is the Structure and Indentification of Management Information for TCP/IP-based Internets (SMI), RFC 1155, and the Management Information Base for Network Management of TCP/IP-based Internets (MIB-II).

The SMI includes the provision for parameters or codes to indicate experimental or private data structures. These parameter assignments are listed here. The older simple gateway monitoring protocol (SGMP) (see RFC 1028) also defined a data structure. The parameter assignments used with SGMP are included here for historical completeness.

Object Identifiers

The network management object identifiers are under the iso (1), org (3), dod (6), internet (1), or 1.3.6.1, branch of the name space.

SMI Network Management Directory Codes

Prefix: 1.3.6.1.1.

Decimal	Name	Description
all	Reserved	Reserved for future use

SMI Network Management MGMT Codes

Prefix: 1.3.6.1.2

Decimal	Name	Description
0	Reserved	
1	MIB	

Prefix: 1.3.6.1.2.1 (mib-2)

Decimal	Name	Description
0	Reserved Reserved	
1	system System	
2	interfaces	Interfaces
3	at	Address Translation
4	ip	Internet Protocol
5	icmp	Internet Control Message
6	tcp	Transmission Control Protocol
7	udp	User Datagram Protocol
8	egp	Exterior Gateway Protocol
9	cmot	CMIP over TCP
10	transmission	Transmission
11	snmp	Simple Network Management
12	GenericIF	Generic Interface Extensions
13	Appletalk	Appletalk Networking
14	ospf	Open Shortest Path First
15	bgp	Border Gateway Protocol

16	rmon	Remote Network Monitoring
17	bridge	Bridge Objects
18	DecnetP4	Decnet Phase 4
19	Character	Character Streams

Prefix: 1.3.6.1.2.1.10 (transmission)

Decimal	Name	Description
7	IEEE802.3	CSMACD-like Objects
8	IEEE802.4	Token Bus-like Objects
9	IEEE802.5	Token-Ring-like Objects
15	FDDI	FDDI Objects
18	DS1/E1	DS1 Interface Objects
30	DS3	DS3 Interface Objects
31	SIP	SMDS Interface Objects
32	FRAME-RELAY	Frame Relay Objects
33	RS-232	RS-232 Objects
34	Parallel	Parallel Printer Objects
38	MIOX	Multiprotocol Interconnect over X.25

SMI Network Management Experimental Codes

Prefix: 1.3.6.1.3.

Decimal	Name	Description
0	Reserved	
1	CLNS	ISO CLNS Objects
2*	T1-Carrier	T1 Carrier Objects
3*	IEEE802.3	Ethernet-like Objects
4*	IEEE802.5	Token-Ring-like Objects
5*	DECNet-PHIV	DECNet Phase IV
6*	Interface	Generic Interface Objects
7*	IEEE802.4	Token Bus-like Objects
8*	FDDI	FDDI Objects
9	LANMGR-1	LAN Manager V1 Objects
10	LANMGR-TRAPS	LAN Manager Trap Objects
11	Views	SNMP View Objects
12	SNMP-AUTH	SNMP Authentication Objects
13*	BGP	Border Gateway Protocol
14*	Bridge	Bridge MIB
15*	DS3	DS3 Interface Type
16*	SIP	SMDS Interface Protocol
17*	Appletalk	Appletalk Networking
18	PPP	PPP Objects
19*	Character MIB	Character MIB
20*	RS-232 MIB	RS-232 MIB
21*	Parallel MIB	Parallel MIB
22	atsign-proxy	Proxy via Community
23*	OSPF	OSPF MIB
24	Alert-Man	Alert-Man

25	FDDI-Synoptics	FDDI-Synoptics
26*	Frame Relay	Frame Relay MIB
27*	rmon	Remote Network Management
28	IDPR	IDPR MIB
29	HUBMIB	IEEE 802.3 Hub MIB
30	IPFWDTBLMIB	IP Forwarding Table MIB
31	LATM MIB	
32	SONET MIB	
33	IDENT	
34	MIME-MHS	

* obsoleted

SMI Network Management Private Enterprise Codes

These codes are available via anonymous FTP on host: venera.isi.edu, directory: mib, file: snmp-vendors-contacts.

Prefix: 1.3.6.1.4.1.

Decimal	Name
0	Reserved
1	Proteon
2	IBM
3	CMU
4	Unix
5	ACC
6	TWG
7	CAYMAN
8	PSI
9	cisco
10	NSC
11	HP

12	Epilogue
13	U of Tennessee
14	BBN
15	Xylogics, Inc.
16	Timeplex
17	Canstar
18	Wellfleet
19	TRW
20	MIT
21	EON
22	Spartacus
23	Excelan
24	Spider Systems
25	NSFNET
26	Hughes LAN Systems
27	Intergraph
28	Interlan
29	Vitalink Communications
30	Ulana
31	NSWC
32	Santa Cruz Operation
33	Xyplex
34	Cray
35	Bell Northern Research
36	DEC
37	Touch
38	Network Research Corp.
39	Baylor College of Medicine
40	NMFECC-LLNL

41	SRI
42	Sun Microsystems
43	3Com
44	CMC
45	SynOptics
46	Cheyenne Software
47	Prime Computer
48	MCNC/North Carolina Data Network
49	Chipcom
50	Optical Data Systems
51	gated
52	Cabletron Systems
53	Apollo Computers
54	DeskTalk Systems, Inc.
55	SSDS
56	Castle Rock Computing
57	MIPS Computer Systems
58	TGV, Inc.
59	Silicon Graphics, Inc.
60	University of British Columbia
61	Merit
62	FiberCom
63	Apple Computer Inc
64	Gandalf
65	Dartmouth
66	David Systems
67	Reuter
68	Cornell
69	LMS

70	Locus Computing Corp.
71	NASA
72	Retix
73	Boeing
74	AT&T
75	Ungermann-Bass
76	Digital Analysis Corp.
77	LAN Manager
78	Netlabs
79	ICL
80	Auspex Systems
81	Lannet Company
82	Network Computing Devices
83	Raycom Systems
84	Pirelli Focom Ltd.
85	Datability Software Systems
86	Network Application Technology
87	LINK (Lokales Informatik-Netz Karlsruhe)
88	NYU
89	RND
90	InterCon Systems Corporation
91	LearningTree Systems
92	Webster Computer Corporation
93	Frontier Technologies Corporation
94	Nokia Data Communications
95	Allen-Bradley Company
96	CERN
97	Sigma Network Systems, Inc.
98	Emerging Technologies, Inc.

99	SNMP Research
100	Ohio State University
101	Ultra Network Technologies
102	Microcom
103	Martin Marietta Astronautic Group
104	Micro Technology
105	Process Software Corporation
106	Data General Corporation
107	Bull Company
108	Emulex Corporation
109	Warwick University Computing Services
110	Network General Corporation
111	Oracle
112	Control Data Corporation
113	Hughes Aircraft Company
114	Synernetics, Inc.
115	Mitre
116	Hitachi, Ltd.
117	Telebit
118	Salomon Technology Services
119	NEC Corporation
120	Fibermux
121	FTP Software Inc.
122	Sony
123	Newbridge Networks Corporation
124	Racal-Milgo Information Systems
125	CR SYSTEMS
126	DSET Corporation
127	Computone

128	Tektronix, Inc.
129	Interactive Systems Corporation
130	Banyan Systems Inc.
131	Sintrom Datanet Limited
132	Bell Canada
133	Crosscomm Corporation
134	Rice University
135	T3Plus Networking, Inc.
136	Concurrent Computer Corporation
137	Basser
138	Luxcom
139	Artel
140	Independence Technologies, Inc. (ITI)
141	Frontier Software Development
142	Digital Computer Limited
143	Eyring, Inc.
144	Case Communications
145	Penril DataComm, Inc.
146	American Airlines
147	Sequent Computer Systems
148	Bellcore
149	Konkord Communications
150	University of Washington
151	Develcon
152	Solarix Systems
153	Unifi Communications Corp.
154	Roadnet
155	Network Systems Corp.
156	ENE (European Network Engineering)

157	Dansk Data Elektronik A/S
158	Morning Star Technologies
159	Dupont EOP
160	Legato Systems, Inc.
161	Motorola SPS
162	European Space Agency (ESA)
163	BIM
164	Rad Data Communications Ltd.
165	Intellicom
166	Shiva Corporation
167	Fujikura America
168	Xlnt Designs INC (XDI)
169	Tandem Computers
170	BICC
171	D-Link Systems, Inc.
172	AMP, Inc.
173	Netlink
174	C. Itoh Electronics
175	Sumitomo Electric Industries (SEI)
176	DHL Systems, Inc.
177	Network Equipment Technologies
178	APTEC Computer Systems
179	Schneider & Koch & Co., Datensysteme GmbH
180	Hill Air Force Base
181	ADC Kentrox
182	Japan Radio Co.
183	Versitron
184	Telecommunication Systems
185	Interphase

186	Toshiba Corporation
187	Clearpoint Research Corp.
188	Ascom Gfeller Ltd.
189	Fujitsu America
190	NetCom Solutions, Inc.
191	NCR
192	Dr. Materna GmbH
193	Ericsson Business Communications
194	Metaphor Computer Systems
195	Patriot Partners
196	The Software Group Limited (TSG)
197	Kalpana, Inc.
198	University of Waterloo
199	CCL/ITRI
200	Coeur Postel
201	Mitsubish Cable Industries, Ltd.
202	SMC
203	Crescendo Communication, Inc.
204	Goodall Software Engineering
205	Intecom
206	Victoria University of Wellington
207	Allied Telesis, Inc.
208	Dowty Network Systems A/S
209	Protools
210	Nippon Telegraph and Telephone Corp.
211	Fujitsu Limited
212	Network Peripherals Inc.
213	Netronix, Inc.
214	University of Wisconsin - Madison

215	NetWorth, Inc.
216	Tandberg Data A/S
217	Technically Elite Concepts, Inc.
218	Labtam Australia Pty. Ltd.
219	Republic Telcom Systems, Inc.
220	ADI Systems, Inc.
221	Microwave Bypass Systems, Inc.
222	Pyramid Technology Corp.
223	Unisys Corp.
224	LANOPTICS LTD. Israel
225	NKK Corporation
226	MTrade UK Ltd.
227	Acals
228	ASTEC, Inc.
229	Delmarva Power
230	Telematics International, Inc.
231	Siemens Nixdorf Informations Syteme AG
232	Compaq
233	NetManage, Inc.
234	NCSU Computing Center
235	Empirical Tools and Technologies
236	Samsung Group
237	Takaoka Electric Mfg. Co., Ltd.
238	Netrix Systems Corporation
239	WINDATA
240	RC International A/S
241	Netexp Research
242	Internode Systems Pty Ltd
243	netCS Informationstechnik GmbH

244	Lantronix
245	Avatar Consultants
246	Furukawa Electoric Co. Ltd.
247	AEG Electrcom
248	Richard Hirschmann GmbH & Co.
249	G2R Inc.
250	University of Michigan
251	Netcomm, Ltd.
252	Sable Technology Corporation
253	Xerox
254	Conware Computer Consulting GmbH
255	Compatible Systems Corp.
256	Scitec Communications Systems Ltd.
257	Transarc Corporation
258	Matsushita Electric Industrial Co., Ltd.
259	ACCTON Technology
260	Star-Tek, Inc.
261	Codenoll Tech. Corp.
262	Formation, Inc.
263	Seiko Instruments, Inc. (SII)
264	RCE (Reseaux de Communication d'Entreprise SA.)
265	Xenocom, Inc.
266	AEG KABEL
267	Systech Computer Corporation
268	Visual
269	SDD (Scandinavian Airlines Data Denmark A/S)
270	Zenith Electronics Corporation
271	TELECOM FINLAND
272	BinTec Computersystems

273	EUnet Germany
274	PictureTel Corporation
275	Michigan State University
276	GTE Telecom Incorporated
277	Cascade Communications Corp.
278	Hitachi Cable, Ltd.
279	Olivetti
280	Vitacom Corporation
281	INMOS
282	AIC Systems Laboratories Ltd.
283	Cameo Communications, Inc.
284	Diab Data AB
285	Olicom A/S
286	Digital-Kienzle Computersystems
287	CSELT (Centro Studi E Laboratori Telecomunicazioni)
288	Electronic Data Systems
289	McData Corporation
290	Harris Computer Systems Division (HCSD)
291	Technology Dynamics, Inc.
292	DATAHOUSE Information Systems Ltd.
293	DSIR Network Group
294	Texas Instruments
295	PlainTree Systems Inc.
296	Hedemann Software Development
297	Fuji Xerox Co., Ltd.
298	Asante Technology
299	Stanford University
300	Digital Link
301	Raylan Corporation

302	Datacraft
303	Hughes
304	Farallon Computing, Inc.
305	GE Information Services
306	Gambit Computer Communications
307	Livingston Enterprises, Inc.
308	Star Technologies
309	Micronics Computers Inc.
310	Basis, Inc.
311	Microsoft
312	US West Advance Technologies
313	University College London
314	Eastman Kodak Company
315	Network Resources Corporation
316	Atlas Telecom
317	Bridgeway
318	American Power Conversion Corp.
319	DOE Atmospheric Radiation Measurement Project
320	VerSteeg CodeWorks
321	Verilink Corp
322	Sybus Corportation
323	Tekelec
324	NASA Ames Research Center
325	Simon Fraser University
326	Fore Systems, Inc.
327	Centrum Communications, Inc.
328	NeXT Computer, Inc.
329	Netcore, Inc.
330	Northwest Digital Systems

331	Andrew Corporation
332	DigiBoard
333	Computer Network Technology Corp.
334	Lotus Development Corp.
335	MICOM Communication Corporation
336	ASCII Corporation
337	PUREDATA Research/USA
338	NTT DATA
339	Empros Systems International
340	Kendall Square Research (KSR)
341	Martin Marietta Energy Systems
342	Network Innovations
343	Intel Corporation
344	Proxar
345	Epson Research Center
346	Fibernet
347	Box Hill Systems Corporation
348	American Express Travel Related Services
349	Compu-Shack
350	Parallan Computer, Inc.
351	Stratacom
352	Open Networks Engineering, Inc.
353	ATM Forum
354	SSD Management, Inc.
355	Automated Network Management, Inc.
356	Magnalink Communications Corporation
357	TIL Systems, Ltd.
358	Skyline Technology, Inc.
359	Nu-Mega Technologies, Inc.

360	Morgan Stanley & Co. Inc.
361	Integrated Business Network
362	L & N Technologies, Ltd.
363	Cincinnati Bell Information Systems, Inc.
364	OSCOM International
365	MICROGNOSIS
366	Datapoint Corporation
367	RICOH Co. Ltd.
368	Axis Communications AB
369	Pacer Software
370	Axon Networks Inc.
371	Brixton Systems, Inc.
372	GSI
373	Tatung Co., Ltd.
374	DIS Research LTD
375	Quotron Systems, Inc.
376	Dassault Electronique
377	Corollary, Inc.
378	SEEL, Ltd.
379	Lexcel
380	W.J. Parducci & Associates, Inc.
381	OST
382	Megadata Pty Ltd.
383	LLNL Livermore Computer Center
384	Dynatech Communications
385	Symplex Communications Corp.
386	Tribe Computer Works
387	Taligent, Inc.
388	Symbol Technology, Inc.

389	Lancert
390	Alantec
391	Ridgeback Solutions
392	Metrix, Inc.
393	Excutive Systems/XTree Company
394	NRL Communication Systems Branch
395	I.D.E. Corporation
396	Matsushita Electric Works, Ltd.
397	MegaPAC
398	Pilkington Communication Systems
440	Amnet, Inc.
441	Chase Research
442	PEER Networks
443	Gateway Communications, Inc.
444	Peregrine Systems
445	Daewoo Telecom
446	Norwegian Telecom Research
447	WilTel
448	Ericsson-Camtec
449	Codex
450	Basis
451	AGE Logic
452	INDE Electronics
453	ISODE Consortium
454	J.I. Case
455	Trillium Digital Systems
456	Bacchus Inc.
457	MCC
458	Stratus Computer

459	Quotron
460	Beame & Whiteside
461	Cellular Technical Services
462	Shore Microsystems, Inc.
463	Telecommunications Techniques Corp.
464	DNPAP (Technical University Delft)
465	Plexcom, Inc.
466	Tylink
467	Brookhaven National Laboratory
468	Computer Communication Systems
469	Norand Corporation
470	Max-Lab
471	Premisys Communications, Inc.
472	Bell South Telecommunications
473	J. Stainsbury PLC
474	Ki Research Inc.
475	Wandel and Goltermann Technologies
476	Emerson Computer Power
477	Network Software Associates
478	Procter and Gamble
479	Meridian Technology Corporation
480	QMS, Inc.
481	Network Express
482	LANcity Corporation
483	Dayna Communications, Inc.
484	kn-X Ltd.
485	Sync Research, Inc.
486	PremNet
487	SIAC

488	New York Stock Exchange
489	American Stock Exchange
490	FCR Software, Inc.
491	National Medical Care, Inc.
492	Dialogue Communication Systemes, S.A.
493	NorTele
494	Madge Networks, Inc.
495	Teleglobe Communications
496	CTON Nick Hennenfent
497	Leap Technology, Inc.
498	General DataComm, Inc.
499	ACE Communications, Ltd.
500	Automatic Data Processing (ADP)
501	Programa SPRITEL
502	Adacom
503	Metrodata Ltd
504	Ellemtel Telecommunication Systems Laboratories
505	Arizona Public Service
506	NETWIZ, Ltd.
507	Science and Engineering Research Council (SERC)
508	The First Boston Corporation
509	Hadax Electronics Inc.
510	VTKK
511	North Hills Israel Ltd.
512	TECSIEL
513	Bayerische Motoren Werke (BMW)
514	CNET Technologies
515	MCI
516	Human Engineering AG (HEAG)

517	FileNet Corporation
518	NFT-Ericsson
519	Dun & Bradstreet
520	Intercomputer Communications
521	Defense Intelligence Agency
522	Telesystems SLW Inc.
523	APT Communications
524	Delta Airlines
525	California Microwave
526	Avid Technology Inc.
527	Integro Advanced Computer Systems
528	RPTI
529	Ascend Communications Inc.
530	Eden Computer Systems Inc.
531	Kawasaki-Steel Corp.
532	Barclays
533	B.U.G., Inc.
534	Exide Electronics
535	Superconducting Supercollider Lab.
536	Triticom
537	Universal Instruments Corp.
538	Information Resources, Inc.
539	Applied Innovation, Inc.
540	Crypto AG
541	Infinite Networks, Ltd.
542	Rabbit Software
543	Apertus Technologies
544	Equinox Systems, Inc.
545	Hayes Microcomputer Products

546	Empire Technologies Inc.
547	Glaxochem, Ltd.
548	KPY Network Partners, Corp.
549	Agent Technology, Inc.
550	Dornier GMBH
551	Telxon Corporation
552	Entergy Corporation
553	Garrett Communications Inc.
554	Agile Networks, Inc.
555	Larse Corporation
556	Stock Equipment
557	ITT Corporation
558	Universal Data Systems, Inc.
559	Sonix Communications, Ltd.
560	Paul Freeman Associates, Inc.
561	John S. Barnes, Corp.
562	Northern Telecom
563	CAP Debris
564	Telco Systems NAC
565	Tosco Refining Co.
566	Russell Info Sys
567	University of Salford
568	NetQuest Corp.
569	Armon Networking Ltd.
570	IA Corporation
571	AU-System Communication AB
572	GoldStar Information & Communications, Ltd.
573	SECTRA AB
574	ONEAC Corporation

575	Tree Technologies
576	GTE Government Systems
577	Denmac Systems, Inc.
578	Interlink Computer Sciences, Inc.
579	Bridge Information Systems, Inc.
580	Leeds and Northrup Australia (LNA)
581	BHA Computer
582	Newport Systems Solutions, Inc.
583	Atrium Technologies
584	ROBOTIKER
585	PeerLogic Inc.
586	Digital Transmission Systems
587	Far Point Communications
588	Xircom
589	Mead Data Central
590	Royal Bank of Canada
591	Advantis, Inc.
592	Chemical Banking Corp.
593	Eagle Technology
594	British Telecom
595	Radix BV
596	TAINET Communication System Corp.
597	Comtek Services Inc.
598	Fair Issac
599	AST Research, Inc.
600	Soft*Star s.r.l
601	Bancomm
602	Trusted Information Systems, Inc.
603	Harris & Jeffries, Inc.

604	Axel Technology Corp.
605	GN Navtel, Inc.
606	CAP debis
607	Lachman Technology, Inc.
608	Galcom Networking Ltd.
609	BAZIS
610	SYNAPTEL
611	Investment Management Services, Inc.
612	Taiwan Telecommunication Lab
613	Anagram Corporation
614	Univel
615	University of California, San Diego
616	CompuServe
617	Telstra - OTC Australia
618	Westinghouse Electric Corp.
619	DGA Ltd.
620	Elegant Communications Inc.
621	Experdata
622	Unisource Business Networks
623	Molex, Inc.
624	Quay Financial Software
625	VMX Inc.
626	Hypercom, Inc.
627	University of Guelph
628	DIaLOGIKa
629	NBASE Switch Communication
630	Anchor Datacomm B.V.
631	PACDATA
632	University of Colorado

633	Tricom Communications Limited
634	Santix Software GmbH
635	FastComm Communications Corp.
636	The Georgia Institute of Technology
637	Alcatel Data Networks
638	GTECH Corporation
639	UNOCAL Corporation
640	First Pacific Network
641	Lexmark International
642	Qnix Computer
643	Jigsaw Software Concepts (Pty) Ltd.
644	VIR, Inc.
645	SFA Datacomm Inc.
646	SEIKO Telecommunication Systems, Inc.
647	Unified Management
648	RADLINX Ltd.
649	Microplex Systems Ltd.
650	Objecta Elektronik & Data AB
651	Phoenix Microsystems
652	Distributed Systems International, Inc.
653	Evolving Systems, Inc.
654	SAT GmbH
655	CeLAN Technology, Inc.
656	Landmark Systems Corp.
657	Netone Systems Co., Ltd.
658	Loral Data Systems
659	Cellware Broadband Technology
660	ccmail, Inc.
661	IMC Networks Corp.

662	Octel Communications Corp.
663	RIT Technologies LTD.
664	Adtran
665	PowerPlay Technologies, Inc.
666	Oki Electric Industry Co., Ltd.
667	Specialix International
668	INESC
669	Globalnet Communications
670	Product Line Engineer SVEC Computer Corp.
671	Printer Systems Corp.
672	Contec Micro Electronics USA
673	Unix Integration Services
674	Dell Computer Corporation
675	Whittaker Electronic Systems
676	QPSX Communications
677	Loral WDI
678	Federal Express Corp.

SGMP Vendor-Specific Codes (Obsolete)

Prefix: 1,255

Decimal	Name
0	Reserved
1	Proteon
2	IBM
3	CMU
4	Unix
5	ACC
6	TWG
7	CAYMAN

8	NYSERNET
9	cisco
10	BBN
11	Unassigned
12	MIT
13-254	Unassigned
255	Reserved

Appendix G: Management Information Bases

This appendix provides a summary of the objects contained in various management information bases (MIBs), including the Internet Standard MIB (MIB-II) (see RFC 1213), the Remote Network Monitoring MIB (see RFC 1271), and various MIBs that have been defined for specific functions, such as the AppleTalk or DECnet protocols. Within each MIB, the object identifier (OID) of each major group is also noted.

Groups in MIB II

MIB-II is the Internet-standard MIB. That MIB contains the following groups (see Figure 3-1):

- System provides demographic information about the managed node's configuration, location, etc.

- Interfaces is a table containing information about the managed node's interfaces.

- Address Translation is used to convert IP to Physical addresses (now deprecated).

- IP contains Internet Protocol-related statistics and tables.

- ICMP contains Internet Control Message Protocol-related input/output statistics.

- TCP contains Transmission Control Protocol-related connection information and statistics.

- UDP contains User Datagram Protocol-related information and datagram statistics.

- EGP contains Exterior Gateway Protocol-related message statistics and table of neighbor information.

- OIM contains OSI Internet Management-related information (given an arc within MIB-II, but not used with SNMP).

- Transmission contains information about the physical transmission medium.

- SNMP contains Simple Network Management Protocol-related information and statistics.

The System group {1.3.6.1.2.1.1}

The System group provides a textual description of the entity in printable ASCII characters. Descriptions include a system description, OID, the length of time since its network management entity was reinitialized, plus other administrative details. Implementation of the System group is mandatory. Objects within this group (see Figure 3-2) include:

- sysDescr is a textual description of the entity in printable ASCII characters.

- sysObjectID is the vendor's identification of the object.

- sysUpTime is the amount of time (measured in hundredths of seconds) since the network management portion of the system was last reinitialized.

- sysContact is the textual identification of the contact person for this managed node.

- sysName is an administratively assigned name for this node, i.e., the domain name.

- sysLocation is the physical location of the node.

- sysServices is the set of services that the entity primarily provides.

The Interfaces group {1.3.6.1.2.1.2}

Information about the various hardware interfaces on a managed device is provided by the Interfaces group and presented in a table format (see Figure 3-3) . The first object (ifNumber) indicates the number of interfaces on that device. For each interface, a row is made in the table, with 22 column entries per row. The column entries provide information regarding those interfaces:

- ifNumber is the number of network interfaces present on this system.

- ifTable is a list of interface entries, with the number of entries given by the value of ifNumber.

  - ifEntry is an interface entry containing objects at the subnetwork layer and below for a particular interface.

    - ifIndex is a unique value, between 1 and the value of ifNumber, for each interface.

    - ifDescr is a text string containing information about the interface.

    - ifType is the specific type of interface, such as Ethernet, token ring, FDDI, frame-relay, etc. (RFC 1213 lists the values for this object.)

    - ifMTU is the largest IP datagram, measured in octets, that can be sent/received on this interface.

    - ifSpeed is an estimate of the interface's current bandwidth measured in bits per second.

    - ifPhysAddress is the interface's address at the protocol layer immediately below IP.

    - ifAdminStatus is the desired state of the interface.

    - ifOperStatus is the current operational state of the interface.

    - ifLastChange is the value of sysUpTime at the time that the interface entered its current operational state.

- ifInOctets is the total number of octets received on the interface.

- ifInUcastPkts is the number of subnetwork-unicast packets delivered to a higher-layer protocol.

- ifInNUcastPkts is the number of subnetwork non-unicast packets delivered to a higher-layer protocol.

- ifInDiscards is the number of inbound packets that were discarded for reasons other than errors.

- ifInErrors is the number of inbound packets that contained errors, preventing their delivery to a higher-layer protocol.

- ifInUnknownProtos is the number of packets received but discarded because of an unknown or unsupported protocol.

- ifOutOctets is the total number of octets transmitted out of the interface.

- ifOutUcastPkts is the total number of packets that higher-level protocols requested be transmitted to a subnet-unicast address, including those that were discarded or not sent.

- ifOutNUcastPkts is the total number of packets that higher-level protocols requested be transmitted to a non-unicast (i.e. subnetwork broadcast or subnetwork multicast) address, including those that were discarded or not sent.

- ifOutDiscards is the number of outbound packets that were discarded for reasons other than errors.

- ifOutErrors is the number of outbound packets that could not be transmitted because of errors.

- ifOutQLen is the length, in packets, of the output packet queue.

- ifSpecific is a reference to MIB definitions specific to the particular media being used to realize the interface. This value provides additional information on that interface.

The Address Translation group {1.3.6.1.2.1.3}

The Address Translation group (see Figure 3-4) was included in MIB-I, but deprecated in MIB-II. The purpose of the Address Translation group was to provide a table that translated between IP addresses and physical (hardware) addresses. In MIB-II and future releases, each protocol group will contain its own translation tables. The Address Translation group contains the following objects:

- atTable is comprised of the Address Translation tables containing NetworkAddress to physical address equivalences.

    - atEntry, where each entry contains one NetworkAddress to physical address equivalence.

        - atIfIndex is an interface identifier that has the same value as ifIndex.

        - atPhysAddress is the media-dependent physical address.

        - atNetAddress is the NetworkAddress (IP address) that corresponds to the physical address.

The IP group {1.3.6.1.2.1.4}

The IP (Internet Protocol) group (see Figure 3-5) provides specific information on the usage of that protocol by the various hosts and routers, and is mandatory for all managed nodes. Three tables are included in this group: an address table (ipAddrTable), an IP to physical address translation table (ipNetToMediaTable), and an IP forwarding table (ipForwardTable, which is defined in RFC 1354). The IP forwarding table replaces and obsoletes the IP route table that was included in MIB-II. The IP subtree contains the following objects:

- ipForwarding indicates whether or not this entity is acting as an IP router (a gateway, in Internet terminology).

- ipDefaultTTL is the default value inserted in the IP header's time-to-live field.

- ipInReceives is the total number of input datagrams received.

- ipInHdrErrors is the number of input datagrams discarded due to errors in their IP headers.

- ipInAddrErrors is the number of input datagrams discarded because the IP address in their IP header's destination field was not a valid address to be received at this entity.

- ipForwDatagrams is the number of IP datagrams for which this entity was not their final destination, and forwarding to another entity was required.

- ipInUnknownProtos is the number of datagrams received but discarded because of an unknown or unsupported protocol.

- ipInDiscards is the number of input datagrams received but discarded for reasons other than errors.

- ipInDelivers is the total number of input datagrams successfully delivered to IP user protocols, including ICMP.

- ipOutRequests is the total number of IP datagrams that local IP user-protocols (including ICMP) supplied to IP in request for transmission.

- ipOutDiscards is the number of output IP datagrams that were discarded for reasons other than errors.

- ipOutNoRoutes is the number of IP datagrams discarded because no route could be found to transmit them to their destination.

- ipReasmTimeout is the maximum number of seconds that received fragments are held while the are awaiting reassembly at this entity.

- ipReasmReqds is the number of IP fragments received that needed to be reassembled at this entity.

- ipReasmOKs is the number of IP datagrams successfully reassembled.

- ipReasmFails is the number of failures detected by the IP reassembly algorithm.

- ipFragOKs is the number of IP datagrams that have been successfully fragmented at this entity.

- ipFragFails is the number of IP datagrams that have been discarded at this entity because they could not be fragmented.

- ipFragCreates is the number of IP datagram fragments that have been created as a result of fragmentation at this entity.

- ipAddrTable is the table of addressing information relevant to this entry's IP addresses. There are five columns in this table.

  - ipAddrEntry is the addressing information for one of this entity's IP addresses.

    - ipAdEntAddr is the IP address to which this entry's addressing information pertains.

    - ipAdEntIfIndex is the index value that identifies the interface to which this entry applies, and has the same value as ifIndex.

    - ipAdEntNetMask is the subnet mask associated with the IP address of this entry.

    - ipAdEntBcastAddr is the value of the least significant bit in the IP broadcast address.

    - ipAdEntReasmMaxSize is the size of the largest IP datagram that this entity can reassemble.

- ipRoutingTable has been replaced and obsoleted by the ipForward-Table, {ip 24}, below.

- ipNetToMediaTable is the IP translation table used for mapping from IP addresses to physical addresses. This table contains the four columns below.

  - ipNetToMediaEntry, where each entry contains one IPAddress to physical address equivalence.

- ipNetToMediaIfIndex is the interface on which this entry's equivalence is effective, and which has the same value as ifIndex.

- ipNetToMediaPhysAddress is the media-dependent physical address.

- ipNetToMediaNetAddress is the IpAddress corresponding to the media-dependent physical address.

- ipNetToMediaType is the type of mapping.

- ipRoutingDiscards is the number of routing entries that were chosen to be discarded even though they are valid.

- ipForward is the IP forwarding table.

  - ipForwardNumber is the number of current ipForwardTable entries that are not invalid.

  - ipForwardTable is this entity's IP routing table, containing 15 columns.

    - ipForwardEntry is a particular route to a particular destination.

      - ipForwardDest is the destination IP address of this route.

      - ipForwardMask contains the subnet mask.

      - ipForwardPolicy is the general set of conditions that would cause the selection of one multipath route.

      - ipForwardNextHop, on remote routes, is the address of the next system en route.

      - ipForwardIfIndex is the ifIndex value that identifies the local interface through which the next hop of this route should be reached.

      - ipForwardType is the type of route.

      - ipForwardProto is the routing mechanism by which this route was learned.

- ipForwardAge is the number of seconds since this route was last updated.

- ipForwardInfo is a reference to MIB definitions specific to the particular routing protocol which is responsible for this route.

- ipForwardNextHopAS is the Autonomous System number of the next hop.

- ipForwardMetric1 is the primary routing metric for this route.

- ipForwardMetric2 is an alternate routing metric for this route.

- ipForwardMetric3 is an alternate routing metric for this route.

- ipForwardMetric4 is an alternate routing metric for this route.

- ipForwardMetric5 is an alternate routing metric for this route.

The ICMP group {1.3.6.1.2.1.5}

The ICMP (Internet Control Message Protocol) group (see Figure 3-6) is mandatory for all implementations. This group represents various operations of ICMP within the managed entity and contains 26 scalar objects.

- icmpInMsgs is the total number of ICMP messages that the entity received.

- icmpInErrors is the number of ICMP messages that the entity received but determined as having ICMP-specific errors.

- icmpInDestUnreachs is the number of ICMP Destination Unreachable messages received.

- icmpInTimeExcds is the number of ICMP Time Exceeded messages received.

- icmpInParmProbs is the number of ICMP Parameter Problem messages received.

445

- icmpInSrcQuenchs is the number of ICMP Source Quench messages received.

- icmpInRedirects is the number of ICMP Redirect messages received.

- icmpInEchos is the number of ICMP Echo (request) messages received.

- icmpInEchoReps is the number of ICMP Echo Reply messages received.

- icmpInTimestamps is the number of ICMP Timestamp (request) messages received.

- icmpInTimestampReps is the number of ICMP Timestamp Reply messages received.

- icmpInAddrMasks is the number of ICMP Address Mask Request messages received.

- icmpInAddrMaskReps is the number of ICMP Address Mask Reply messages received.

- icmpOutMsgs is the total number of ICMP messages that this entity attempted to send.

- icmpOutErrors is the number of ICMP messages that this entity did not send because of ICMP-related problems.

- icmpOutDestUnreachs is the number of ICMP Destination Unreachable messages sent.

- icmpOutTimeExcds is the number of ICMP Time Exceeded messages sent.

- icmpOutParmProbs is the number of ICMP Parameter Problem messages sent.

- icmpOutSrcQuenchs is the number of ICMP Source Quence messages sent.

- icmpOutRedirects is the number of ICMP Redirect messages sent.

- icmpOutEchos is the number of ICMP Echo (request) messages sent.

- icmpOutEchoReps is the number of ICMP Echo Reply messages sent.

- icmpOutTimestamps is the number of ICMP Timestamp (request) messages sent.

- icmpOutTimestampReps is the number of ICMP Timestamp Reply messages sent.

- icmpOutAddrMasks is the number of ICMP Address Mask Request messages sent.

- icmpOutAddrMaskReps is the number of ICMP Address Mask Reply messages sent.

The TCP group {1.3.6.1.2.1.6}

The TCP (Transmission Control Protocol) group (see Figure 3-7) is mandatory and provides information regarding TCP operation and connections. This group contains one table with the connection information (tcpConnTable) and 14 scalars.

- tcpRtoAlgorithm is the algorithm used to determine the timeout value used for retransmitting unacknowledged octets.

- tcpRtoMin is the minimum value (measured in milliseconds) permitted by a TCP implementation for the retransmission timeout.

- tcpRtoMax is the maximum value (measured in milliseconds) permitted by a TCP implementation for the retransmission timeout.

- tcpMaxConn is the limit on the total number of TCP connections the entity can support.

- tcpActiveOpens is the number of times TCP connections have made a transition to the SYN-SENT state from the CLOSED state.

- tcpPassiveOpens is the number of times TCP connections have made a direct transition to the SYN-REVD state from the LISTEN state.

- tcpAttemptFails is the number of failed connection attempts.

- tcpEstabResets is the number of resets that have occurred.

- tcpCurrEstab is the number of TCP connections having a current state of either ESTABLISHED or CLOSE-WAIT.

- tcpInSegs is the total number of segments received.

- tcpOutSegs is the total number of segments sent.

- tcpRetransSegs is the total number of segments retransmitted.

- tcpConnTable is a table containing information about this entity's existing TCP connections. There are five columns in this table (see below).

  - tcpConnEntry has information about a particular current TCP connection.

    - tcpConnState is the state of this TCP connection.

    - tcpConnLocalAddress is the local IP address for this TCP connection.

    - tcpConnLocalPort is the local port number for this TCP connection.

    - tcpConnRemAddress is the remote IP address for this TCP connection.

    - tcpConnRemPort is the remote port number for this TCP connection.

- tcpInErrs is the total number of segments received in error.

- tcpOutRsts is the number of TCP segments sent containing the RST flag.

The UDP group {1.3.6.1.2.1.7}

The UDP (User Datagram Protocol) group (see Figure 3-8) is mandatory and provides information regarding UDP operation. This group is much smaller than the TCP group, given that UDP is a connectionless protocol unlike TCP's connection orientation. Therefore, no connection attempt, establishment, reset, etc. information needs to be compiled. The UDP group contains four scalars and one table (udpTable).

- udpInDatagrams is the total number of UDP datagrams delivered to UDP users.

- udpNoPorts is the total number of received UDP datagrams for which there was not application at the destination port.

- udpInErrors is the number of received UDP datagrams that could not be delivered for reasons other than the lack of an application at the destination port.

- udpOutDatagrams is the total number of UDP datagrams sent from this entity.

- udpTable is a table containing UDP listener information, providing details about the UDP end points that are accepting datagrams.

  - udpEntry contains information about a particular UDP listener. There are two columns in this table, as shown below.

    - udpLocalAddress is the local IP address for this UDP listener.

    - udpLocalPort is the local port number for this UPD listener.

The EGP group {1.3.6.1.2.1.8}

The EGP (Exterior Gateway Protocol) group is mandatory for all systems that implement the EGP. This protocol is used for communication between autonomous (i.e., self-contained) systems, and is described in detail in RFC 904. This group (see Figure 3-9) includes five scalar objects and one table containing EGP neighbor information.

- egpInMsgs is the number of EGP messages received without error.

- egpInErrors is the number of EGP messages received that proved to be in error.

- egpOutMsgs is the total number of locally generated EGP messages.

- egpOutErrors is the number of locally generated EGP messages not sent due to resource limitations within an EGP entity.

- egpNeighTable is the EGP neighbor table.

  - egpNeighEntry contains information about this entity's relationship with a particular EGP neighbor. This table contains 15 columns, listed below.

    - egpNeighState is the EGP state of the local systems with respect to this entry's EGP neighbor.

    - egpNeighAddr is the IP address of this entry's EGP neighbor.

    - egpNeighAs is the autonomous system of this EGP peer.

    - egpNeighInMsgs is the number of EGP messages received without error from this EGP peer.

    - egpNeighInErrs is the number of EGP messages received from this EGP peer that contain errors.

    - egpNeighOutMsgs is the number of locally generated EGP messages to this EGP peer.

    - egpNeighOutErrs is the number of locally generated EGP messages not sent to this EGP peer due to resource limitations within an EGP entity.

    - egpNeighInErrMsgs is the number of EGP-defined error messages received from this EGP peer.

    - egpNeighOutErrMsgs is the number of EGP-defined error messages sent to this EGP peer.

    - egpNeighStateUps is the number of EGP state transitions to the UP state with this EGP peer.

- egpNeighStateDowns is the number of EGP state transitions from the UP state to any other state with this EGP peer.

- egpNeighIntervalHello is the interval (measured in hundredths of a second) between EGP Hello command retransmissions.

- egpNeighIntervalPoll is the interval (measured in hundredths of a second) between EGP poll command retransmissions.

- egpNeighMode is the polling mode of this EGP entity.

- egpNeighEventTrigger is a control variable used to trigger operator-initiated Start and Stop events.

- egpAs is the autonomous system number of this EGP entity.

The CMOT (OIM) group {1.3.6.1.2.1.9}

The CMOT (Common Management Information Protocol [CMIP] over TCP/IP) group is given a placeholder in MIB-II. At one time in the development of the Internet Network Management Framework, an effort was underway to use SNMP as an interim step, with CMOT as the long-term and OSI-compliant solution. As a result, this CMOT group was placed within MIB-II. The details of that subtree are given in RFC 1214, which specifies the OSI Internet Management (OIM) MIB. At the present time, it has a "historical" status.

The Transmission group {1.3.6.1.2.1.10}

The Transmission group (see Figure 3-10) contains objects that relate to the transmission of the data. None of these objects are explicitly defined in RFC 1213. Mention is made in that document, however, of these transmission objects residing in the experimental subtree (1.3.6.1.3) until such time that they are "proven." The "Assigned Numbers" document (currently RFC 1340) lists the following objects under the transmission group:

- {1.3.6.1.2.1.10.5}, X.25 Packet Layer objects (RFC 1382)

- {1.3.6.1.2.1.10.7}, CSMA/CD-like objects (RFC 1284)

- {1.3.6.1.2.1.10.8}, Token Bus-like objects (RFC 1230)

- {1.3.6.1.2.1.10.9}, Token Ring-like objects (RFC 1231)

- {1.3.6.1.2.1.10.15}, FDDI objects (RFC 1285)

- {1.3.6.1.2.1.10.16}, X.25 LAPB objects (RFC 1381)

- {1.3.6.1.2.1.10.18}, T1 Carrier objects (RFC 1232)

- {1.3.6.1.2.1.10.30}, DS3 Interface objects (RFC 1233)

- {1.3.6.1.2.1.10.31}, SMDS Interface objects (RFC 1304)

- {1.3.6.1.2.1.10.32}, Frame Relay objects (RFC 1315)

- {1.3.6.1.2.1.10.33}, RS-232 objects (RFC 1317)

- {1.3.6.1.2.1.10.34}, Parallel printer objects (RFC 1318)

The SNMP group {1.3.6.1.2.1.11}

The SNMP group (see Figure 3-11) provides information on SNMP objects. There are a total of 30 scalar objects in this group.

- snmpInPkts is the total number of messages delivered to the SNMP entity from the transport service.

- snmpOutPkts is the total number of SNMP messages that were passed from the SNMP protocol entity to the transport service.

- snmpInBadVersions is the total number of SNMP messages that were for an unsupported SNMP version.

- snmpInBadCommunityNames is the total number of SNMP messages that used an SNMP community name not known to that entity.

- snmpInBadCommunityUses is the total number of SNMP messages that represented an SNMP operation that was not allowed by the SNMP community name in the message.

- snmpInASNParseErrs is the total number of ASN.1 or BER errors encountered.

- {snmp 7}. This is not used.

- snmpInTooBigs is the total number of SNMP PDUs received with the "tooBig" error-status field.

- snmpInNoSuchNames is the total number of SNMP PDUs received with the "noSuchName" error-status field.

- snmpInBadValues is the total number of SNMP PDUs received with the "badValue" error-status field.

- snmpInReadOnlys is the total number of SNMP PDUs received with the "readOnly" error-status field.

- snmpInGenErrs is the total number of SNMP PDUs received with the "genErr" error-status field.

- snmpInTotalReqVars is the total number of MIB objects that have been retrieved.

- snmpInTotalSetVars is the total number of MIB objects that have been altered.

- snmpInGetRequests is the total number of SNMP Get-Request PDUs accepted and processed.

- snmpInGetNexts is the total number of SNMP Get-Next PDUs received.

- snmpInSetRequests is the total number of SNMP Set-Request PDUs received.

- snmpInGetResponses is the total number of SNMP Get-Response PDUs received.

- snmpInTraps is the total number of SNMP Trap PDUs received.

- snmpOutTooBigs is the total number of SNMP PDUs sent with the "tooBig" error-status field.

- snmpOutNoSuchNames is the total number of SNMP PDUs sent with the "noSuchName" error-status field.

- snmpOutBadValues is the total number of SNMP PDUs sent with the "badValue" error-status field.

- {snmp 23}. This is not used.

- snmpOutGenErrs is the total number of SNMP PDUs sent with the "genErr" error-status field.

- snmpOutGetRequests is the total number of SNMP Get-Request PDUs sent.

- snmpOutGetNexts is the total number of SNMP Get-Next PDUs sent.

- snmpOutSetRequests is the total number of SNMP Set-Request PDUs sent.

- snmpOutGetResponses is the total number of SNMP Get-Response PDUs sent.

- snmpOutTraps is the total number of SNMP Trap PDUs sent.

- snmpEnableAuthenTraps indicates whether the SNMP agent process is permitted to generate authentication-failure traps.

Extensions to the Generic-Interface MIB {1.3.6.1.2.1.12}

RFC 1229 defines extensions to the generic interfaces structure contained in MIB-II. The Interfaces group is designed to apply to all network interfaces, irrespective of the communication media or protocols used. The extensions provide additional objects relating to interfaces. This MIB contains three tables: the Generic Interface table, the Generic Interface Test table, and the Generic Receive Address table.

The AppleTalk MIB {1.3.6.1.2.1.13}

RFC 1243 defines objects for managing AppleTalk networks. The MIB consists of nine groups, which are arranged according to the port or protocol in use. These groups include: the LocalTalk Link Access Protocol (LLAP) group, the AppleTalk Address Resolution Protocol (AARP) group, the AppleTalk Port (ATPort) group, the Datagram Delivery Protocol (DDP) group, the Routing Table Maintenance Protocol (RTMP) group, the Kinetics Internet Protocol (KIP) group, the Zone Information Protocol (ZIP) group, the Name Binding Protocol (NBP) group, and the AppleTalk Echo Protocol (ATEcho) group.

The OSPF Version 2 MIB {1.3.6.1.2.1.14}
Open Shortest Path First (OSPF) version 2 is a protocol described in RFC 1247, and it is used for inter-router communication. RFC 1253 defines a MIB that supports OSPF version 2. This MIB consists of the following sections: General Variables, Area Data Structure, Area Stub Metric Table, Link State Database, Address Range Table, Host Table, Interface Table, Interface Metric Table, Virtual Interface Table, Neighbor Table, and Virtual Neighbor Table.

The BGP Version 3 MIB {1.3.6.1.2.1.15}
The Border Gateway Protocol (BGP) version 3 is a protocol described in RFC 1267. This protocol is used for inter-autonomous system routing. In other words, BGP is used to exchange network reachability information with other BGP systems. RFC 1269 defines the MIB in support of the BGP. This MIB contains two tables, the BGP Peer table and the BGP Received Path Attribute table.

The Ethernet RMON MIB {1.3.6.1.2.1.16}
The Remote Network Monitoring (RMON) MIB was developed for the purpose of standardizing the management information that is sent to and from remote network monitoring probes, and is presented in RFC 1271. SNMP agents supporting the RMON MIB can be located in a variety of distributed internetwork hardware, such as bridges or routers. The RMON MIB contains nine groups (see Figure 3-12). All of these groups are considered optional (not mandatory), but the implementation of certain groups also requires the use of other groups. For example, implementing the Filter group also requires the Packet Capture group. The nine Ethernet groups are summarized as follows:

- Statistics contains probe-measured statistics, such as the number and sizes of packets, broadcasts, collisions, etc.

455

- History records periodic statistical samples over time that can be used for trend analysis.

- Alarms compares statistical samples with preset thresholds, generating alarms when a particular threshold is crossed.

- Host maintains statistics of the hosts on the network, including the MAC addresses of the active hosts.

- HostTopN provides reports that are sorted by host table statistics, indicating which hosts are at the top of the list in a particular category.

- Matrix stores statistics in a traffic matrix regarding conversations between pairs of hosts.

- Filter allows packets to be matched according to a filter equation.

- Packet Capture allows packets to be captured after they pass through a logical channel.

- Event controls the generation and notification of events, which may also include the use of SNMP trap messages.

The Ethernet RMON Statistics group {1.3.6.1.2.1.16.1}

The Statistics group is optional and contains a table of statistics that are measured by the probe. This information is available for each interface on the managed device. Each etherStatsEntry is a row in the table, containing 21 columns of information, with the following objects.

- etherStatsTable is a list of Ethernet statistics entries.

  - etherStatsEntry is a collection of statistics kept for a particular Ethernet interface.

    - etherStatsIndex is an identifier of the etherStats entry.

    - etherStatsDataSource is an identifier of the source of the data, i.e., the particular interface.

- etherStatsDropEvents is the total number of events that packets were dropped by the probe due to lack of resources.

- etherStatsOctets is the total number of octets of data received on the network.

- etherStatsPkts is the total number of packets received.

- etherStatsBroadcastPkts is the total number of good packets received that were directed to the broadcast address.

- etherStatsMulticastPkts is the total number of good packets received that were directed to a multicast address.

- etherStatsCRCAlignErrors is the total number of packets received that had alignment or Frame Check Sequence (FCS) errors.

- etherStatsUndersizePkts is the total number of packets received that were less than 64 octets long.

- etherStatsOversizePkts is the total number of packets received that were longer than 1518 octets.

- etherStatsFragments is the total number of packets received that had an alignment error or bad FCS, and were less than 64 octets in length.

- etherStatsJabbers is the total number of packets received that had an alignment error or bad FCS and were longer than 1518 octets.

- etherStatsCollisions is the best estimate of the total number of collisions on this Ethernet segment.

- etherStatsPkts64Octets is the total number of packets received that were 64 octets in length.

- etherStatsPkts65to127Octets is the total number of packets received that were between 65 and 127 octets in length.

- etherStatsPkts128to255Octets is the total number of packets received that were between 128 and 255 octets in length.

- etherStatsPkts256to511Octets is the total number of packets received that were between 256 and 511 octets in length.

- etherStatsPkts512to1023Octets is the total number of packets received that were between 512 and 1023 octets in length.

- etherStatsPkts1024to1518Octets is the total number of packets received that were between 1024 and 1518 octets in length.

- etherStatsOwner is the entity that configured this entry and is therefore using the resources assigned to it.

- etherStatsStatus is the status of this etherStats entry.

The Ethernet RMON History group {1.3.6.1.2.1.16.2}

The History group is optional and records periodic statistical sample information from a particular network, allowing this information to be subsequently retrieved. This group contains two tables, historyControlTable and etherHistoryTable. The historyControl table is used to store configuration entries defining the interface, polling period, etc. RFC 1271 suggests two polling periods, 30 seconds for short-term polls and 30 minutes for the long-term ones. The etherHistoryTable stores Ethernet-specific statistics. Objects in this group include the following.

- historyControlTable is a list of history control entries.

  - historyControlEntry is a list of parameters that set up a periodic sampling of statistics.

    - historyControlIndex is an index that identifies an entry in the historyControl table.

    - historyControlDataSource is an identifier of the source of the data.

- historyControlBucketsRequested is the requested number of discrete time intervals over which data is to be saved.

- historyControlBucketsGranted is the number of discrete time intervals over which data shall be saved.

- historyControlInterval is the interval between 1 and 3600 seconds over which the data is sampled for each bucket.

- historyControlOwner is the entity that configured this entry and is therefore using the resources assigned to it.

- historyControlStatus is the status of this historyControl entry.

- etherHistoryTable is a list of Ethernet history entries.

  - etherHistoryEntry is a historical sample of Ethernet statistics on a particular Ethernet interface.

    - etherHistoryIndex is the history of which this entry is a part, and identified by the same value of historyControlIndex.

    - etherHistorySampleIndex is an index that uniquely identifies the particular sample this entry represents.

    - etherHistoryIntervalStart is the value of sysUpTime at the start of the interval over which this sample was measured.

    - etherHistoryDropEvents is the total number of events in which packets were dropped by the probe due to lack of resources during this interval.

    - etherHistoryOctets is the total number of octets of data received on the network.

    - etherHistoryPkts is the number of packets received during this sampling interval.

    - etherHistoryBroadcastPkts is the number of good packets received during this sampling interval that were directed to the broadcast address.

- etherHistoryMulticastPkts is the number of good packets received during this sampling interval that were directed to a multicast address.

- etherHistoryCRCAlignErrors is the number of packets received during this sampling interval that had alignment or FCS errors.

- etherHistoryUndersizePkts is the number of packets received during this interval that were less than 64 octets long.

- etherHistoryOversizePkts is the number of packets received during this sampling interval that were longer than 1518 octets.

- etherHistoryFragments is the number of packets received during this sampling interval that had an alignment error or bad FCS, and were less than 64 octets in length.

- etherHistoryJabbers is the number of packets received during this interval that were longer than 1518 octets.

- etherHistoryCollisions is the best estimate of the total number of collisions on this Ethernet segment during this interval.

- etherHistoryUtilization is the best estimate, in hundredths of a percent, of the mean Physical layer network utilization on this interface during this interval.

The Ethernet RMON Alarm group {1.3.6.1.2.1.16.3}

The Alarm group is optional, but requires the implementation of the Events group. This group compares statistical samples from variables in the probe with preconfigured thresholds. The statistical information is stored in the alarmTable, in twelve columns. When a particular sample crosses one of the preset thresholds, an event is generated. This group contains the following objects.

- alarmTable is a list of alarm entries.

- alarmEntry is a list of parameters that set up a periodic checking for alarm conditions.

  - alarmIndex is an index that uniquely identifies an entry in the alarm table.

  - alarmInterval is the interval, in seconds, over which data is sampled and compared with the rising and falling thresholds.

  - alarmVariable is the object identifier of the particular variable to be sampled.

  - alarmSampleType is the method of sampling the selected variable and calculating the value to be compared against the thresholds.

  - alarmValue is the value of the statistic during the last sampling period.

  - alarmStartupAlarm is the alarm that may be sent when this entry is first set to valid.

  - alarmRisingThreshold is a threshold that generates a single event when the current sampled value is greater than or equal to this threshold, and the value at the last sampling interval was less than this threshold.

  - alarmFallingThreshold is a threshold that generates a single event when the current sampled value is less than or equal to this threshold, and the value at the last sampling interval was greater than this threshold.

  - alarmRisingEventIndex is the index of the eventEntry that is used when a rising threshold is crossed.

  - alarmFallingEventIndex is the index of the eventEntry that is used when a falling threshold is crossed.

  - alarmOwner is the entity that configured this entry and is using the resources assigned to it.

  - alarmStatus is the status of this alarm entry.

The Ethernet RMON Host group {1.3.6.1.2.1.16.4}

The Host group is an optional group that maintains information and statistics regarding the various hosts that are discovered to be active on the network. To do so, three tables are compiled. The first, hostControlTable, six columns wide, keeps information regarding the host discovery process and the interfaces that are being used. The second, hostTable, uses ten columns to maintain statistics on each host that is discovered and indexed by MAC address. The third table, hostTimeTable, contains the same information, but is indexed by the hostTimeCreationOrder. The Host group contains the following objects.

- hostControlTable is a list of host table control entries.

  - hostControlEntry is a list of parameters that set up the discovery and collection of statistics of hosts on a particular interface.

    - hostControlIndex is an index that uniquely identifies an entry in the hostControl table, placing those statistics in the host-Table and the hostTimeTable.

    - hostControlDataSource is an identifier of the source of the data for this instance of the host function.

    - hostControlTableSize is the number of hostEntries in the host-Table and the hostTimetable.

    - hostControlLastDeleteTime is the value of sysUpTime when the last entry was deleted.

    - hostControlOwner is the entity that configured this entry and is using the resources assigned to it.

    - hostControlStatus is the status of this hostControl entry.

  - hostTable is a list of host entries.

    - hostEntry is a collection of statistics for a particular host that has been discovered on an interface of this device.

- hostAddress is the physical address of this host.

- hostCreationOrder is an index that defines the relative ordering of the creation time of hosts captured for a particular hostControlEntry.

- hostIndex is the set of collected host statistics of which this entry is a part.

- hostInPkts is the number of error-free packets transmitted to this address since it was added to the hostTable.

- hostOutPkts is the number of packets including errors transmitted by this address since it was added to the hostTable.

- hostInOctets is the number of error-free octets transmitted to this address since it was added to the hostTable.

- hostOutOctets is the number of octets transmitted by this address since it was added to the hostTable.

- hostOutErrors is the number of error packets transmitted by this address since it was added to the hostTable.

- hostOutBroadcastPkts is the number of good packets transmitted by this address to the broadcast address since this host was added to the hostTable.

- hostOutMulticastPkts is the number of good packets transmitted by this address to a multicast address since this host was added to the hostTable.

- hostTimeTable is a list of time-ordered host table entries.

  - hostTimeEntry is a collection of statistics, in relative ordering of creation time, for a particular host that has been discovered on an interface of this device.

    - hostTimeAddress is the physical address of this host.

- hostTimeCreationOrder is an index that uniquely defines an entry in the hostTime table. The ordering of the indexes is based on the order of each entry's insertion into the table.

- hostTimeIndex is the set of collected host statistics of which this entry is a part.

- hostTimeInPkts is the number of error-free packets transmitted to this address since it was added to the hostTimeTable.

- hostTimeOutPkts is the number of packets including errors transmitted by this address since it was added to the host-TimeTable.

- hostTimeInOctets is the number of error-free octets transmitted to this address since it was added to the hostTimeTable.

- hostTimeOutOctets is the number of octets transmitted by this address since it was added to the hostTimeTable.

- hostTimeOutErrors is the number of error packets transmitted by this address since it was added to the hostTimeTable.

- hostTimeOutBroadcastPkts is the number of good packets transmitted by this address to the broadcast address since this host was added to the hostTimeTable.

- hostTimeOutMulticastPkts is the number of good packets transmitted by this address to a multicast address since this host was added to the hostTimeTable.

The Ethernet RMON HostTopN group {1.3.6.1.2.1.16.5}

The HostTopN group is an optional group that requires the implementation of the host group. This group is used to prepare reports describing hosts at the top of a list that is ordered by a particular statistic. Two tables are contained in this group. The hostTopNControlTable contains ten columns and initiates the generation of a particular report. The prepared report creates four columns in the hostTopNTable. This group has the following objects.

- hostTopNControlTable is a list of top N host control entries.

  - hostTopNControlEntry is a set of parameters that control the creation of a report of the top N hosts according to several metrics. There are 10 columns in this table.

    - hostTopNControlIndex is an index that uniquely identifies an entry in the hostTopNControl table, with each entry defining one report per interface.

    - hostTopNHostIndex is the host table for which a top N report will be prepared on behalf of this entry, and associated with the host table identified by the same value of hostIndex.

    - hostTopNRateBase is the variable for each host that the hostTopNRate variable is based upon.

    - hostTopNTimeRemaining is the number of seconds left in the report currently being collected.

    - hostTopNDuration is the number of seconds that this report has collected during the last sampling interval.

    - hostTopNRequestSize is the maximum number of hosts requested for the top N table.

    - hostTopNGrantedSize is the maximum number of hosts in the top N table.

    - hostTopNStartTime is the value of sysUpTime when this top N report was last started.

    - hostTopNOwner is the entity that configured this entry and is therefore using the resources assigned to it.

    - hostTopNStatus is the status of this hostTopNControl entry.

- hostTopNTable is a list of top N host entries.

  - hostTopNEntry is a set of statistics for a host that is part of a top N report. There are four columns in this table, listed below.

- hostTopNReport identifies the top N report of which this entry is a part.

- hostTopNIndex is an index that uniquely identifies an entry in the hostTopN table among those in the same report.

- hostTopNAddress is the physical address of this host.

- hostTopNRate is the amount of change in the selected variable during this sampling interval. The selected variable is this host's instance of the object selected by hostTopNRateBase.

The Ethernet RMON Matrix group {1.3.6.1.2.1.16.6}

The Matrix group is an optional group that records statistics regarding conversations between pairs of addresses. In other words, this group compiles a traffic matrix of inter-node communication. To do so, three tables are generated, each having six columns. The matrixControlTable contains matrix parameters, the matrixSDTable is indexed by source and destination MAC addresses, and the matrixDSTable is indexed by the destination and source MAC addresses. This group contains the following objects.

- matrixControlTable is a list of information entries for the traffic matrix on each interface.

  - matrixControlEntry contains information about a traffic matrix on a particular interface.

    - matrixControlIndex is an index that uniquely identifies an entry in the matrixControl table. Each of these entries places statistical information in the matrixSDTable and matrixDSTable.

    - matrixControlDataSource identifies the source of the data from which this entry creates a traffic matrix.

    - matrixControlTableSize is the number of entries in the matrixSDTable and matrixDSTable for this interface.

- matrixControlLastDeleteTime is the value of sysUpTime when the last entry was deleted from the portion of the matrixSD-Table or matrixDSTable associated with this matrixControlEntry.

- matrixControlOwner is the entity that configured this entry and is therefore using the resources assigned to it.

- matrixControlStatus is the status of this matrixControl entry.

- matrixSDTable is a list of traffic matrix entities indexed by source and destination MAC addresses.

  - matrixSDEntry is a collection of statistics for communications between two addresses on a particular interface.

    - matrixSDSourceAddress is the source physical address.

    - matrixSDDestAddress is the destination physical address.

    - matrixSDIndex is the set of collected matrix statistics of which this entry is a part, and having the same value as matrixControlIndex.

    - matrixSDPkts is the number of packets transmitted from the source address to the destination address.

    - matrixSDOctets is the number of octets contained in all packets transmitted from the source address to the destination address.

    - matrixSDErrors is the number of error packets transmitted from the source address to the destination address.

  - matrixDSTable is a list of traffic matrix entities indexed by the destination and source MAC addresses.

    - matrixDSEntry is a collection of statistics for communications between two addresses on a particular interface.

      - matrixDSSourceAddress is the source physical address.

- matrixDSDestAddress is the destination physical address.

- matrixDSIndex is the set of collected matrix statistics of which this entry is a part, and having the same value as matrixControlIndex.

- matrixDSPkts is the number of packets transmitted from the source address to the destination address.

- matrixDSOctets is the number of octets contained in all packets transmitted from the source address to the destination address.

- matrixSDErrors is the number of error packets transmitted from the source address to the destination address.

The Ethernet RMON Filter group {1.3.6.1.2.1.16.7}

The Filter group is an optional group that allows packets to be captured based upon a filter. This is similar to a filter that can be set by a protocol analyzer, selectively capturing packets containing data of a certain protocol, bit pattern, or length. The net effect of these filters is to create logical channels that match that particular filter pattern. This group contains two tables. The filterTable, with eleven columns, stores filter parameters. The channelTable, with twelve columns, is a list of packet channel entries. The Filter group contains the following objects.

- filterTable is a list of packet filter entries.

  - filterEntry is a set of parameters for a packet filter applied on a particular interface.

    - filterIndex is an index that uniquely identifies an entry in the filter table. Each entry defines one filter that is to be applied to every packet received on an interface.

- filterChannelIndex identifies the channel of which this filter is a part, and has the same value as the value of the channelIndex object.

- filterPktDataOffset is the offset from the beginning of each packet where a match of packet data will be attempted.

- filterPktData is the data that is to be matched with the input packet.

- filterPktDataMask is the mask that is applied to the match process.

- filterPktDataNotMask is the inversion mask that is applied to the match process.

- filterPktStatus is the status that is to be matched with the input packet.

- filterPktStatusMask is the mask that is applied to the status match process.

- filterPktStatusNotMask is the inversion mask that is applied to the status match process.

- filterOwner is the entity that configured this entry and is therefore using the resources assigned to it.

- filterStatus is the status of this filter entry.

- channelTable is a list of packet channel entries.

  - channelEntry is a set of parameters for a packet channel applied on a particular interface.

    - channelIndex is an index that uniquely identifies an entry in the channel table. Each entry defines one channel, a logical data and event stream.

- channelIfIndex is the value of this object uniquely identifies the interface on this remote network monitoring device to which the associated filters are applied.

- channelAcceptType controls the action of the filters associated with this channel.

- channelDataControl controls the flow of data through this channel.

- channelTurnOnEventIndex is the value of this object identifies the event that is configured to turn the associated channelDataControl from off to on when the event is generated.

- channelTurnOffEventIndex is the value of this object identifies the event that is configured to turn the associated channelDataControl from on to off when the event is generated.

- channelEventIndex is the value of this object identifies the event that is configured to be generated when the associated channelDataControl is on and a packet is matched.

- channelEventStatus is the event status of this channel.

- channelMatches is the number of times this channel has matched a packet.

- channelDescription is a comment describing this channel.

- channelOwner is the entity that configured this entry and is using the resources assigned to it.

- channelStatus is the status of this channel entry.

The Ethernet RMON Packet Capture group {1.3.6.1.2.1.16.8}

The Packet Capture group is optional, but requires the implementation of the Filter group. This group allows packets to be captured when a particular filter is matched. Two tables are defined in this group. The bufferControlTable, with thirteen columns, controls the captured packets output from a particular channel. The captured packets are then contained in the captureBufferTable, which contains seven columns. The Packet Capture group contains the following objects

- bufferControlTable is a list of buffer control entries.

  - bufferControlEntry is a set of parameters that control the collection of a stream of packets that ave matched filters.

    - bufferControlIndex is an index that uniquely describes an entry in the bufferControl table. Each entry defines one set of packets that is captured and controlled by one or more filters.

    - bufferControlChannelIndex is an index that identifies the channel that is the source of packets for this bufferControl table, and has the same value as the channelIndex object.

    - bufferControlFullStatus shows whether the buffer has room to accept new packets or if it is full.

    - bufferControlFullAction controls the action of the buffer when it reaches the full status.

    - bufferControlCaptureSliceSize is the maximum number of octets of each packet that will be saved in this capture buffer.

    - bufferControlDownloadSliceSize is the maximum number of octets of each packet in this capture buffer that will be returned in an SNMP retrieval of that packet.

    - bufferControlDownloadOffset is the offset of the first octet of each packet in this capture buffer that will be returned in an SNMP retrieval of that packet.

    - bufferControlMaxOctetsRequested is the requested maximum number of octets to be saved in this captureBuffer, including any implementation-specific overhead.

- bufferControlMaxOctetsGranted is the maximum number of octets that can be saved in this captureBuffer, including overhead.

- bufferControlCapturedPackets is the number of packets currently in this captureBuffer.

- bufferControlTurnOnTime is the value of sysUpTime when this capture buffer was first turned on.

- bufferControlOwner is the entity that configured this entry and is using the resources assigned to it.

- bufferControlStatus is the status of this buffer Control Entry.

- captureBufferTable is a list of packets captured off or a channel.

  - captureBufferEntry is a packet captured off of an attached network.

    - captureBufferControlIndex is the index of the bufferControlEntry with which this packet is associated.

    - captureBufferIndex is an index that uniquely identifies an entry in the captureBuffer table associated with a particular bufferControlEntry.

    - captureBufferPacketID is an index that describes the order of packets that are received on a particular interface.

    - capturebufferPacketData is the data inside the packet.

    - captureBufferPacketLength is the actual length (off the wire) of the packet stored in this entry.

    - captureBufferPacketTime is the number of milliseconds that had passed since this capture buffer was first turned on when this packet was captured.

    - captureBufferPacketStatus is a value which indicates the error status of this packet.

The Ethernet RMON Event group {1.3.6.1.2.1.16.9}

The Event group is optional and controls the generation and notification of events on a particular device. A particular event may cause a log entry to be made and/or an SNMP Trap message to be sent. Two tables are included in this group, the eventTable with seven columns, and the logTable with four columns. This group contains the following objects.

- eventTable is a list of events to be generated.
  - eventEntry is a set of parameters that describe an event to be generated when certain conditions are met.
    - eventIndex is an index that uniquely identifies an entry in the event table. Each entry defines one event that is to be generated when the appropriate conditions occur.
    - eventDescription is a comment describing this event entry.
    - eventType is the type of notification that the probe will make about this event.
    - eventCommunity. If an SNMP trap is to be sent, it will be sent to the SNMP community specified by this octet string.
    - eventLastTimeSent is the value of sysUpTime at the time this event entry last generated an event.
    - eventOwner is the entity that configured this entry and is using the resources assigned to it.
    - eventStatus is the status of this event entry.
  - logtable is a list of events that have been logged.
    - logEntry is a set of data describing an event that has been logged.
      - logEventIndex is the event entry that generated this log entry and has the same value of eventIndex.

- logIndex is an index that uniquely identifies an entry in the log table amongst those generated by the same eventEntries.

- logTime is the value of sysUpTime when this log entry was created.

- logDescription is an implementation-dependent description of the event that activated this log entry.

The Token Ring RMON MIB {1.3.6.1.2.1.16}

The token ring RMON MIB was developed as an extension to the Ethernet RMON MIB discussed in the previous section. Recall that the Ethernet RMON MIB defines nine groups, statistics through events. The token ring RMON MIB extends two of these groups, statistics and history, and adds one group (see Figure 3-13) that is unique. This new group is known as tokenRing, with object identifier { rmon 10 }.

The statistics extensions allow for the collection of both token-ring MAC-Layer errors and promiscuous errors. The MAC-Layer errors are specific to the token ring protocol, while the promiscuous errors are more general in nature. In a similar manner, the history information is divided into MAC-Layer and promiscuous details. The token ring group is used to record token ring-specific statistics, such as source routing information.

Token Ring RMON MAC-Layer statistics group {1.3.6.1.2.1.16.1.2}

The token ring MAC-Layer statistics group contains one table, token-RingMLStatsTable, which records token ring network-specific errors. This group is optional and contains the following objects.

- tokenRingMLStatsTable is a list of MAC-Layer token ring statistics entries.

  - tokenRingMLStatsEntry is a collection of MAC-Layer statistics kept for a particular token ring interface.

    - tokenRingMLStatsIndex is the value of this object uniquely identifies this tokenRingMLStats entry.

- tokenRingMLStatsDataSource identifies the source of the data that this tokenRingMLStats entry is configured to analyze.

- tokenRingMLStatsDropEvents is the total number of events in which packets were dropped by the probe due to lack of resources.

- tokenRingMLStatsMacOctets is the total number of error-free octets of data in MAC packets received on the network.

- tokenRingMLStatsMacPkts is the total number of error-free MAC packets received.

- tokenRingMLStatsRingPurgeEvents is the total number of times that the ring enters the ring purge state from normal ring state.

- tokenRingMLStatsRingPurgePkts is the total number of Ring Purge MAC packets detected by the probe.

- tokenRingMLStatsBeaconEvents is the total number of times that the ring enters the beaconing state.

- tokenRingMLStatsBeaconTime is the total amount of times that the ring has been in the beaconing state.

- tokenRingMLStatsBeaconPkts is the total number of Beacon MAC packets detected by the probe.

- tokenRingMLStatsClaimTokenEvents is the total number of times the ring enters the monitor contention state.

- tokenRingMLStatsClaimTokenPkts is the total number of Claim Token MAC packets detected by the probe.

- tokenRingMLStatsNAUNChanges is the total number of NAUN changes detected by the probe.

- tokenRingMLStatsLineErrors is the total number of line errors reported in error-reporting packets detected by the probe.

- tokenRingMLStatsInternalErrors is the total number of adapter internal errors reported in error-reporting packets detected by the probe.

- tokenRingMLStatsBurstErrors is the total number of burst errors reported in error-reporting packets detected by the probe.

- tokenRingMLStatsACErrors is the total number of AC (address copied) errors reported in error-reporting packets detected by the probe.

- tokenRingMLStatsAbortErrors is the total number of abort delimiters reported in error-reporting packets detected by the probe.

- tokenRingMLStatsLostFrameErrors is the total number of lost frame errors reported in error-reporting packets detected by the probe.

- tokenRingMLStatsCongestionErrors is the total number of receive-congestion errors reported in error reporting packets detected by the probe.

- tokenRingMLStatsFrameCopiedErrors is the total number of frame-copied errors reported in error-reporting packets detected by the probe.

- tokenRingMLStatsFrequencyErrors is the total number of frequency errors reported in error-reporting packets detected by the probe.

- tokenRingMLStatsTokenErrors is the total number of token errors reported in error-reporting packets detected by the probe.

- tokenRingMLStatsSoftErrorReports is the total number of soft error-report frames detected by the probe.

- tokenRingMLStatsRingPollEvents is the total number of ring poll events detected by the probe.

- tokenRingMLStatsOwner is the entity that configured this entry and is therefore using the resources assigned to it.

- tokenRingMLStatsStatus is the status of this tokenRingML-Stats entry.

Token Ring RMON Promiscuous Statistics group {1.3.6.1.2.1.16.1.3}

The token ring promiscuous statistics group is used to collect promiscuous statistics, i.e., those that are token ring-specific but may not be collected by all management systems. The information is compiled in a single table, token-RingPStatsTable. This group is optional and contains the following objects.

- tokenRingPStatsTable is a list of promiscuous Token Ring statistics entries.

    - tokenRingPStatsEntry is a collection of promiscuous statistics kept for a particular token ring interface.

        - tokenRingPStatsIndex is the value of this object, which uniquely identifies this tokenRingPStats entry.

        - tokenRingPStatsDataSource represents the source of the data that this tokenRingPStats entry is configured to analyze.

        - tokenRingPStatsDropEvents is the total number of events in which packets were dropped due to lack of resources.

        - tokenRingPStatsDataOctets is the total number of error-free octets of data received on the network.

        - tokenRingPStatsDataPkts is the total number of error-free packets received.

        - tokenRingPStatsDataBroadcastPkts is the total number of good non-MAC packets received that were directed to an LLC broadcast address.

- tokenRingPStatsDataMulticastPkts is the total number of good non-MAC packets received that were directed to a local or global multicast or functional address.

- tokenRingPStatsDataPkts18to63Octets is the total number of error-free non-MAC packets received that were between 18 and 63 octets in length.

- tokenRingPStatsDataPkts64to127Octets is the total number of error-free non-MAC packets received that were between 64 and 127 octets in length.

- tokenRingPStatsDataPkts128to255Octets is the total number of error-free non-MAC packets received that were between 128 and 255 octets in length.

- tokenRingPStatsDataPkts256to511Octets is the total number of error-free non-MAC packets received that were between 256 and 511 octets in length.

- tokenRingPStatsDataPkts512to1023Octets is the total number of error-free non-MAC packets received that were between 512 and 1023 octets in length.

- tokenRingPStatsDataPkts1024to2047Octets is the total number of error-free non-MAC packets received that were between 1024 and 2047 octets in length.

- tokenRingPStatsDataPkts2048to4095Octets is the total number of error-free non-MAC packets received that were between 2048 and 4095 octets in length.

- tokenRingPStatsDataPkts4096to8191Octets is the total number of error-free non-MAC packets received that were between 4096 and 8191 octets in length.

- tokenRingPStatsDataPkts8192to18000Octets the total number of error-free non-MAC packets received that were between 8192 and 18,000 octets in length.

- tokenRingPStatsDataPktsGreaterThan18000Octets is the total number of error-free non-MAC packets received that were greater than 18,000 octets in length.

- tokenRingPStatsOwner is the entity that configured this entry and is therefore using the resources assigned to it.

- tokenRingPStatsStatus the status of this tokenRingPStats entry.

Token Ring RMON MAC-Layer history group {1.3.6.1.2.1.16.2.3}

The token ring nonpromiscuous history group is similar to its counterpart in the statistics group, but measured over a particular sampling interval. It contains one table, tokenRingMLHistoryTable, with 27 columns. This group is optional and contains the following objects.

- tokenRingMLHistoryTable is a list of MAC-Layer token ring statistics entries.

- tokenRingMLHistoryEntry is a collection of MAC-Layer statistics kept for a particular token ring interface.

- tokenRingMLHistoryIndex is the history of which this entry is a part, and is the same value as that of historyControlIndex.

- tokenRingMLHistorySampleIndex is an index that uniquely identifies the particular MAC-Layer sample.

- tokenRingMLHistoryIntervalStart is the value of sysUpTime at the start of the interval over which this sample was measured.

- tokenRingMLHistoryDropEvents is the total number of events in which packets were dropped by the probe due to lack of resources during this sampling interval.

- tokenRingMLHistoryMacOctets is the total number of error-free octets of data in MAC packets received on the network during this sampling interval.

- tokenRingMLHistoryMacPkts is the total number of error-free MAC packets received during this sampling interval.

- tokenRingMLHistoryRingPurgeEvents is the total number of times that the ring entered the ring purge state from the normal ring state during the sampling interval.

- tokenRingMLHistoryRingPurgePkts is the total number of Ring Purge MAC packets detected by the probe during this sampling interval.

- tokenRingMLHistoryBeaconEvents is the total number of times that the ring entered the beaconing state during this sampling interval.

- tokenRingMLHistoryBeaconTime is the amount of time that the ring has been in the beaconing state during this sampling interval.

- tokenRingMLHistoryBeaconPkts is the total number of Beacon MAC packets detected by the probe during this sampling interval.

- tokenRingMLHistoryClaimTokenEvents is the total number of times that the ring enters the monitor contention state from normal ring state or ring purge state during this sampling interval.

- tokenRingMLHistoryClaimTokenPkts is the total number of Claim Token MAC packets detected by the probe during this sampling interval.

- tokenRingMLHistoryNAUNChanges is the total number of NAUN changes detected by the probe during this sampling interval.

- tokenRingMLHistoryLineErrors is the total number of line errors reported in error-reporting packets detected by the probe during this sampling interval.

- tokenRingMLHistoryInternalErrors is the total number of adapter internal errors reported in error-reporting packets detected by the probe during this sampling interval.

- tokenRingMLHistoryBurstErrors is the total number of burst errors reported in error-reporting packets detected by the probe during this sampling interval.

- tokenRingMLHistoryACErrors is the total number of AC (address copied) errors reported in error-reporting packets detected by the probe during this sampling interval.

- tokenRingMLHistoryAbortErrors is the total number of abort delimiters reported in error-reporting packets detected by the probe during this sampling interval.

- tokenRingMLHistoryLostFrameErrors is the total number of lost-frame errors reported in error-reporting packets detected by the probe during this sampling interval.

- tokenRingMLHistoryCongestionErrors is the total number of receive congestion errors reported in error reporting packets detected by the probe during this sampling interval.

- tokenRingMLHistoryFrameCopiedErrors: the total number of frame-copied errors reported in error-reporting packets detected by the probe during this sampling interval.

- tokenRingMLHistoryFrequencyErrors is the total number of frequency errors reported in error-reporting packets detected by the probe during this sampling interval.

- tokenRingMLHistoryTokenErrors is the total number of token errors reported in error-reporting packets detected by the probe during this sampling interval.

- tokenRingMLHistorySoftErrorReports is the total number of soft error report frames detected by the probe during this sampling interval.

- tokenRingMLHistoryRingPollEvents is the total number of ring poll events detected by the probe during this sampling interval.

- tokenRingMLHistoryActiveStations is the maximum number of active stations on the ring detected by the probe during this sampling interval.

Token Ring RMON promiscuous history group {1.3.6.1.2.1.16.2.4}

The token ring promiscuous history group is similar to its counterpart in the statistics group, but measured over a particular sampling interval. It contains one table, tokenRingPHistoryTable, with 18 columns. This group is optional, and contains the following objects.

- tokenRingPHistoryTable is a list of promiscuous token ring statistics entries.

  - tokenRingPHistoryEntry is a collection of promiscuous statistics kept for a particular token ring interface.

    - tokenRingPHistoryIndex is a history of which this entry is a part and has the same value as the value of historyControlIndex.

    - tokenRingPHistorySampleIndex is an index that uniquely identifies the particular sample this entry represents.

    - tokenRingPHistoryIntervalStart is the value of sysUpTime at the start of the interval over which this sample was measured.

    - tokenRingPHistoryDropEvents is the total number of events in which packets were dropped by the probe due to lack of resources during this sampling period.

    - tokenRingPHistoryDataOctets is the total number of error-free octets of data received in non-MAC packets on the network.

    - tokenRingPHistoryDataPkts is the total number of error-free non-MAC packets received during this sampling interval.

    - tokenRingPHistoryDataBroadcastPkts is the total number of good non-MAC packets received during this sampling interval that were directed to an LLC broadcast address.

- tokenRingPHistoryDataMulticastPkts is the total number of good non-MAC packets received during this sampling interval that were directed to a local or global multicast or functional address.

- tokenRingPHistoryDataPkts18to63Octets is the total number of error-free non-MAC packets received during this sampling interval that were between 18 and 63 octets in length.

- tokenRingPHistoryDataPkts64to127Octets is the total number of error-free non-MAC packets received during this sampling interval that were between 64 and 127 octets in length.

- tokenRingPHistoryDataPkts128to255Octets is the total number of error-free non-MAC packets received during this sampling interval that were between 128 and 255 octets in length.

- tokenRingPHistoryDataPkts256to511Octets is the total number of error-free non-MAC packets received during this sampling interval that were between 256 and 511 octets in length.

- tokenRingPHistoryDataPkts512to1023Octets is the total number of error-free non-MAC packets received during this sampling interval that were between 512 and 1023 octets in length.

- tokenRingPHistoryDataPkts1024to2047Octets is the total number of error-free non-MAC packets received during this sampling interval that were between 1024 and 2047 octets in length.

- tokenRingPHistoryDataPkts2048to4095Octets is the total number of error-free non-MAC packets received during this sampling interval that were between 2048 and 4095 octets in length.

- tokenRingPHistoryDataPkts4096to8191Octets is the total number of error-free non-MAC packets received during this sampling interval that were between 4096 and 8191 octets in length.

- tokenRingPHistoryDataPkts8192to18000Octets is the total number of error-free non-MAC packets received during this sampling interval that were between 8192 and 18,000 octets in length.

- tokenRingPHistoryDataPktsGreaterThan18000Octets is the total number of error-free non-MAC packets received during this sampling interval that were greater than 18,000 octets in length.

Token Ring RMON Ring Station group {1.3.6.1.2.1.16.10}

The Ring Station group is unique to the token ring RMON MIB and is optional. It consists of tables with token ring and source routing information. The tables include the ringStationControlTable, {tokenRing 1}; the ringStationTable, {tokenRing 2}; the ringStationOrderTable, {tokenRing 3}; the ringStation-ConfigControlTable, {tokenRing 4}; the ringStationConfigTable, {tokenRing 5}; and the sourceRoutingStatsTable, {tokenRing 6}. The Ring Station group is assigned OID {rmon 10}. Following is a description of the individual tables and their objects.

The ringStationControlTable {1.3.6.1.2.1.16.10.1} contains information relating to the discovery of, and statistics regarding, the various stations on the ring:

- ringStationControlTable is a list of ringStation table control entries.

  - ringStationControlEntry is a list of parameters that set up the discovery of stations on a particular interface and the collection of statistics about these stations.

    - ringStationControlIfIndex: the value of this object uniquely identifies the interface on this remote network monitoring device from which ringStation data is collected, and has the same value as the value of ifIndex.

    - ringStationControlTableSize is the number of ringStationEntries in the ringStationTable associated with this ringStation-ControlEntry.

- ringStationControlActiveStations is the number of active ringStationEntries in the ringStationTable associated with this ringControlEntry.

- ringStationControlRingState is the current status of this ring.

- ringStationControlBeaconSender is the address of the sender of the last Beacon frame received on this ring.

- ringStationControlBeaconNAUN is the address of the NAUN in the last Beacon frame received on this ring.

- ringStationControlActiveMonitor is the address of the Active Monitor on this segment.

- ringStationControlOrderChanges is the address of add and delete events in the ringStationControlTable associated with this ringStationControlEntry.

- ringStationControlOwner is the entity that configured this entry and is therefore using the resources assigned to it.

- ringStationControlStatus is the status of this ringStationControl entry.

The ringStationTable {1.3.6.1.2.1.16.10.2} contains entries for each station that has been, or is currently on, the ring. The objects include:

- ringStationTable is a list of ring station entries.
  - ringStationEntry is a collection of statistics for a particular station that has been discovered on a ring monitored by this device.
    - ringStationIfIndex: the value of this object, which uniquely identifies the interface on this remote network monitoring device on which this station was detected, and has the same value as the value of ifIndex.
    - ringStationMacAddress is the physical address of this station.

- ringStationLastNAUN is the physical address of the last known NAUN of this station.

- ringStationStationStatus is the status of this station on the ring.

- ringStationLastEnterTime is the value of sysUpTime at the time this station last entered the ring.

- ringStationLastExitTime is the value of sysUpTime at the time this station last exited the ring.

- ringStationDuplicateAddresses is the number of times this station experienced a duplicate address error.

- ringStationInLineErrors is the total number of line errors reported by this station in error-reporting packets detected by the probe.

- ringStationOutLineErrors is the total number of line errors reported in error-reporting packets sent by the nearest active downstream neighbor of this station and detected by the probe.

- ringStationInternalErrors is the total number of adapter internal errors reported by this station in error-reporting packets detected by the probe.

- ringStationInBurstErrors is the total number of burst errors reported by this station in error-reporting packets detected by the probe.

- ringStationOutBurstErrors is the total number of burst errors reported in error-reporting packets sent by the nearest active downstream neighbor of this station and detected by the probe.

- ringStationACErrors is the total number of AC (address copied) errors pertaining to this station reported in error-reporting packets detected by the probe.

- ringStationAbortErrors is the total number of abort delimiters pertaining to this station reported in error-reporting packets detected by the probe.

- ringStationLostFrameErrors is the total number of lost-frame errors pertaining to this station reported in error-reporting packets detected by the probe.

- ringStationCongestionErrors is the total number of receive congestion errors pertaining to this station reported in error-reporting packets detected by the probe.

- ringStationFrameCopiedErrors is the total number of frame-copied errors pertaining to this station reported in error-reporting packets detected by the probe.

- ringStationFrequencyErrors is the total number of frequency errors pertaining to this station reported in error-reporting packets detected by the probe.

- ringStationTokenErrors is the total number of token errors pertaining to this station reported in error-reporting packets detected by the probe.

- ringStationInBeaconErrors is the total number of beacon frames sent by this station and detected by the probe.

- ringStationOutBeaconErrors is the total number of beacon frames detected by the probe that name this station as the NAUN.

- ringStationInsertions is the number of times the probe detected this station inserting onto the ring.

The ringStationOrder table {1.3.6.1.2.1.16.10.3} provides a list of ring station entries, in ring-order sequence:

- ringStationOrderTable is a list of ring station entries for active stations, ordered by their ring-order.

  - ringStationOrderEntry is a collection of statistics for a particular station that has been discovered on a ring monitored by this device.

- ringStationOrderIfIndex: the value of this object uniquely identifies the interface on this remote network monitoring device on which this station was detected, and has the same value as the value of ifIndex.

- ringStationOrderOrderIndex: this index denotes the location of this station with respect to other stations on the ring, and is equal to the number of hops downstream that this station is from the rmon probe.

- ringStationOrderMacAddress is the physical address of this station.

The ringStationConfig group {1.3.6.1.2.1.16.10.4} manages token ring nodes through active means, removing a station or updating that station's information as required:

- ringStationConfigControlTable is a list of token ring station configuration control entries.

  - ringStationConfigControlEntry: this entry controls active management of stations by the probe. One entry exists in this table for each entry in the ringStationOrderTable.

    - ringStationConfigControlIfIndex: the value of this object uniquely identifies the interface on this remote network monitoring device on which this station is detected, and is the same value as the value of the ifIndex object.

    - ringStationConfigControlMacAddress is the physical address of this station.

    - ringStationConfigControlRemove: setting this object to "removing" causes a Remove Station MAC frame to be sent.

- ringStationConfigControlUpdateStats: setting this object to "updating" causes the configuration information associated with this entry to be updated.

The ringStationConfig table {1.3.6.1.2.1.16.10.5} is used to record entries that are obtained with the ringStationConfigControlUpdateStats variable (listed immediately above):

- ringStationConfigTable is a list of configuration entries for stations on a ring monitored by this probe.

  - ringStationConfigEntry is a collection of statistics for a particular station that has been discovered on a ring monitored by this probe.

    - ringStationConfigIfIndex: the value of this object uniquely identifies the interface on this remote network monitoring device on which this station is detected, and has the same value as the value of the ifIndex object.

    - ringStationConfigMacAddress is the physical address of this station.

    - ringStationConfigUpdateTime is the value of sysUpTime at the time this configuration information was last updated (completely).

    - ringStationConfigLocation is the assigned physical location of this station.

    - ringStationConfigMicrocode is the microcode EC level of this station.

    - ringStationConfigGroupAddress is the low-order 4 octets of the group address recognized by this station.

    - ringStationConfigFunctionalAddress is the functional addresses recognized by this station.

The sourceRoutingStatsTable {1.3.6.1.2.1.16.10.6} collects data from the source routing information that may be contained within token ring packets:

- sourceRoutingStatsTable is a list of source routing statistics entries.

  - sourceRoutingStatsEntry is a collection of source routing statistics kept for a particular token ring interface.

    - sourceRoutingStatsIfIndex: the value of this object uniquely identifies the interface on this remote network monitoring device on which source routing statistics will be detected, and has the same value as the value of the ifIndex object.

    - sourceRoutingStatsRingNumber is the ring number of the ring monitored by this entry.

    - sourceRoutingStatsInFrames is the count of frames sent into this ring from another ring.

    - sourceRoutingStatsOutFrames is the count of frames sent from this ring to another ring.

    - sourceRoutingStatsThroughFrames is the count of frames sent, through this ring, to another ring.

    - sourceRoutingStatsAllRoutesBroadcastFrames is the total number of good frames received that were All Routes Broadcast.

    - sourceRoutingStatsSingleRouteBroadcastFrames is the total number of good frames received that were Single Route Broadcast.

    - sourceRoutingStatsInOctets is the count of octets in good frames sent into this ring from another ring.

    - sourceRoutingStatsOutOctets is the count of octets in good frames sent from this ring to another ring.

    - sourceRoutingStatsThroughOctets is the count of octets in good frames sent, through this ring, to another ring.

- sourceRoutingStatsAllRoutesBroadcastOctets is the total number of octets in good frames received that were All Routes Broadcast.

- sourceRoutingStatsSingleRoutesBroadcastOctets is the total number of octets in good frames received that were Single Route Broadcast.

- sourceRoutingStatsLocalLLCFrames is the total number of frames received that had no routing information.

- sourceRoutingStats1HopFrames is the total number of frames received whose route had 1 hop.

- sourceRoutingStats2HopsFrames is the total number of frames received whose route had 2 hops.

- sourceRoutingStats3HopsFrames is the total number of frames received whose route had 3 hops.

- sourceRoutingStats4HopsFrames is the total number of frames received whose route had 4 hops.

- sourceRoutingStats5HopsFrames is the total number of frames received whose route had 5 hops.

- sourceRoutingStats6HopsFrames is the total number of frames received whose route had 6 hops.

- sourceRoutingStats7HopsFrames is the total number of frames received whose route had 7 hops.

- sourceRoutingStatsMoreThan8HopsFrames is the total number of frames received whose route had 8 or more hops.

- sourceRoutingStatsOwner is the entity that configured this entry and is therefore using the resources assigned to it.

- sourceRoutingStatsStatus is the status of this sourceRoutingStats entry.

Bridges MIB {1.3.6.1.2.1.17}

With the trend toward larger internetworks, managing bridges becomes a requirement for many network administrators. RFC 1286 defines a bridge MIB for this purpose, which uses elements of the IEEE 802.1 bridge standard as a basis.

Included in the MIB are five groups:

- dot1dBase group — objects that are applicable to all types of bridges.

- dot1dStp group — applicable to any bridge that implements the spanning tree protocol.

- dot1dSr group — applicable to bridges that support the source routing or source routing transparent algorithms.

- dot1dTp group — applicable to bridges that support the transparent or source routing transparent algorithms.

- dot1dStatic group — applicable to any bridge that performs filtering on destination addresses.

DECnet Phase 4 MIB {1.3.6.1.2.1.18}

Digital Equipment Corporation's DECnet Phase IV is a protocol suite that frequently coexists with IP-based internetworks. RFC 1289 defines a MIB that allows these DECnet networks to be managed by IP-based management stations and SNMP. Fourteen groups are included in this MIB: the System, Network Management, Session, End, Routing, Circuit, DDCMP, DDCMP Multipoint Control, Ethernet, Counters, Adjacency, Line, Non-Broadcast, and Area groups.

Character Streams MIB {1.3.6.1.2.1.19}

The Character MIB, defined in RFC 1316, applies to interface ports that carry a character stream. This stream may be physical or virtual, serial or parallel, synchronous or asynchronous. Examples would be RS-232 or parallel printer ports. This MIB includes two tables:

- the Character Port table contains the status and parameter values for a particular port.

- the Character Session table provides details of a particular communication session for that port.

SNMP Parties {1.3.6.1.2.1.20} and SNMP Secrets {1.3.6.1.2.1.21} MIB

The SNMP Parties and Secrets MIB deals with issues of network management security and is defined in RFC 1353. Many revisions to network management security have occurred with the release of SNMPv2. Therefore, at the present time RFC 1353 is considered a "historic" document. Consult RFCs 1445, 1446, and 1447 for further details.

IEEE 802.3 Repeater MIB {1.3.6.1.2.1.22}

Repeaters are used to extend the physical transmission distance of IEEE 802.3 networks. RFC 1368 defines a MIB for these repeaters, and specifies two groups within that MIB. The Basic group contains objects that are applicable to all repeaters, such as status, parameter, and control objects. The Monitor group contains monitoring statistics for the repeater as a whole, and also for individual ports on that repeater.

Appendix H: SNMPv2 Software

At the time of this writing, two freely-available sources of SNMPv2 software have been announced. Information on this software, plus how to obtain the software, is given below.

CMU SNMP/SNMPv2 Package

The CMU SNMP/SNMPv2 package is a portable development platform for SNMP and SNMPv2 as well as a collection of network management tools. This package was developed by Carnegie Mellon University for its own use and to help spread SNMP technology into the marketplace.

This package is freely-available, but is not in the public- domain. This code may be used for any purpose, for-profit or otherwise, without fee. Derivative works may provide further restrictions or charge fees, but must leave the original copyrights intact and must give credit to the contributors in supporting documentation.

The package is available via anonymous FTP on the Internet as follows:

host:	"lancaster.andrew.cmu.edu"
area:	"pub/snmp-dist"
file:	"README"
mode:	"ascii"

The "README" file contains instructions as to the current version and file name of the latest release. Any tar file included in this directory must be retrieved in binary mode.

4BSD/ISODE SNMPv2 Package

An SNMPv2 implementation is available for the ISODE 8.0 release. The release of the 4BSD/ISODE SNMPv2 package implements version 2 of the Simple Network Management Protocol (SNMPv2).

This package is openly available but is not in the public domain. You are allowed and encouraged to take this software and use it for any lawful purpose. However, as a condition of use, you are required to hold harmless all contributors.

The software is available only via anonymous FTP. The instructions are below. If you do not have FTP-access to the Internet, you are out of luck — no exceptions.

Questions on the package may be addressed to:

ISODE-SNMPv2@ida.liu.se

All correspondence must be via electronic mail. Further, under no circumstances will any messages be answered if they relate to legal issues.

The package is available via anonymous FTP on the Internet as follows:

host:	ftp.ics.uci.edu
area:	mrose/isode-snmpV2
file:	isode-snmpV2.tar.Z

Trademarks

PostScript is a trademark of Adobe Systems

Apple, the Apple logo, AppleTalk, EtherTalk, LocalTalk, Macintosh, and TokenTalk are registered trademarks of Apple Computer, Inc.

Banyan, the Banyan logo, and VINES are registered trademarks of Banyan Systems Inc., and StreetTalk, VANGuard and NetRPC are trademarks of Banyan Systems, Inc.

DEC, DECmcc, DECnet, LAT, LAVC, Micro-VAX, MOP, POLYCENTER, ThinWire, Ultrix, VAX, and VAX Cluster are trademarks, and Ethernet is a registered trademark of Digital Equipment Corporation.

PC/TCP and LANWatch are registered trademarks of FTP Software, Inc.

HP is a trademark, and HP OpenView is a registered trademark of Hewlett-Packard Company.

Intel and Ethernet are registered trademarks of Intel Corporation.

IBM PC LAN, PC/AT, PC/XT, SNA, System/370, MicroChannel, NetBIOS, SAA, and System View are trademarks of International Business Machines Corporation; and AIX, AT, IBM, NetView, and PS/2 are registered trademarks of International Business Machines Corporation.

X and X Window System are trademarks of the Massachusetts Institute of Technology.

Microsoft, MS-DOS, LAN Manager and Windows are registered trademarks of Microsoft Corporation.

Network General and Sniffer Analyzer are trademarks of Network General Corporation.

IPX, NetWare, NetWare 386, Novell, and SPX are trademarks, and Novell is a registered trademark of Novell, Inc.

Proteon is a registered trademark of Proteon, Inc.

BSD is a trademark of the Regents of the University of California.

Network File System, NFS, Sun, Sun Microsystems Inc., Sun Microsystems, SunNet and SunOS are trademarks or registered trademarks of Sun Microsystems, Inc. SPARC is a registered trademark of SPARC International, Inc., licensed to Sun Microsystems, Inc.

OSF, OSF/1, Motif and the OSF logo are trademarks, and OSF/Motif is a registered trademark of the Open Software Foundation, Inc.

Lattisnet is a trademark of SynOptics Communications.

3COM is a registered trademark of 3Com Corporation.

UNIX is a registered trademark of UNIX System Laboratories Inc.

Xerox, and XNS are trademarks, and Ethernet and Xerox are registered trademarks of Xerox Corporation.

All other trademarks are the property of their respective owners.

Index